European Yearbook of International Economic Law

EYIEL Monographs - Studies in European and International Economic Law

Volume 38

Series Editors

Marc Bungenberg, Saarbrücken, Germany
Christoph Herrmann, Passau, Germany
Markus Krajewski, Erlangen, Germany
Jörg Philipp Terhechte, Lüneburg, Germany
Andreas R. Ziegler, Lausanne, Switzerland

EYIEL Monographs is a subseries of the European Yearbook of International Economic Law (EYIEL). It contains scholarly works in the fields of European and international economic law, in particular WTO law, international investment law, international monetary law, law of regional economic integration, external trade law of the EU and EU internal market law. The series does not include edited volumes. EYIEL Monographs are peer-reviewed by the series editors and external reviewers.

Roman Pascal Kalin

Digital Trade and Data Privacy

Cross-Border Flows of Personal Data Between Data Protection and Data Protectionism

Roman Pascal Kalin
Berlin, Berlin, Germany

ISSN 2364-8392 ISSN 2364-8406 (elctronic)
European Yearbook of International Economic Law
ISSN 2524-6658 ISSN 2524-6666 (electronic)
EYIEL Monographs - Studies in European and International Economic Law
ISBN 978-3-031-73856-2 ISBN 978-3-031-73857-9 (eBook)
https://doi.org/10.1007/978-3-031-73857-9

© The Editor(s) (if applicable) and The Author(s), under exclusive license to Springer Nature Switzerland AG 2024

This work is subject to copyright. All rights are solely and exclusively licensed by the Publisher, whether the whole or part of the material is concerned, specifically the rights of translation, reprinting, reuse of illustrations, recitation, broadcasting, reproduction on microfilms or in any other physical way, and transmission or information storage and retrieval, electronic adaptation, computer software, or by similar or dissimilar methodology now known or hereafter developed.

The use of general descriptive names, registered names, trademarks, service marks, etc. in this publication does not imply, even in the absence of a specific statement, that such names are exempt from the relevant protective laws and regulations and therefore free for general use.

The publisher, the authors and the editors are safe to assume that the advice and information in this book are believed to be true and accurate at the date of publication. Neither the publisher nor the authors or the editors give a warranty, expressed or implied, with respect to the material contained herein or for any errors or omissions that may have been made. The publisher remains neutral with regard to jurisdictional claims in published maps and institutional affiliations.

This Springer imprint is published by the registered company Springer Nature Switzerland AG
The registered company address is: Gewerbestrasse 11, 6330 Cham, Switzerland

If disposing of this product, please recycle the paper.

To my parents

Acknowledgements

This book is based on my doctoral thesis, which was developed as a research assistant at the German University of Administrative Sciences Speyer and during a research visit at the University of California, Berkeley. The thesis was finalised in Berlin and submitted in the spring of 2023.

Completing the dissertation was an enriching journey characterised by academic exploration and personal growth. It was possible only with the support and guidance of many people, only some of which are mentioned here. First and foremost, I wish to thank my doctoral supervisor, Prof Dr Wolfgang Weiß, for his dedicated academic guidance and mentorship. His expertise and advice were crucial to the progress and the finalisation of this research project. I would also like to thank Prof Dr David Roth-Isigkeit for his thorough and efficient preparation of the second opinion. Furthermore, I wish to express my gratitude to Prof Chris Jay Hoofnagle for welcoming me to Berkeley Law and for the valuable insights and perspectives I have gained through this uniquely formative experience.

This book could only be written due to the encouragement and understanding of my family. Heartfelt gratitude goes to my wife for her unfailing support, loving empathy and friendship throughout the ups and downs of this endeavour. I am grateful to my dearest friends, valued colleagues and dedicated university staff for the much-needed distraction, academic guidance, and invaluable assistance. My sincere appreciation goes to all who have supported me in my research and without whom this work would not have been possible.

Finally, I wish to thank my parents, in particular my mother. Your love, encouragement and sacrifice have been the foundation of my journey and a constant source of motivation. This book is dedicated to you.

Berlin, Germany Roman Pascal Kalin
2024

Contents

1 **Introduction to the Nexus of Digital Trade and Data Privacy** 1
   1.1 Context 1
        1.1.1 A Global Digital Revolution 1
        1.1.2 A New Frontier for International Economic Law 3
        1.1.3 Data Protection and Data Protectionism 6
        1.1.4 Mitigating the Data Privacy Collision Under
                Trade Law 9
   1.2 Research Objective 12
   1.3 Terminology 13
   1.4 Outline 15
   Jurisprudence 16
   References 16

2 **International Trade in a Global Digital Economy** 21
   2.1 Introduction 21
   2.2 Digital Transformation of the Global Economy 22
        2.2.1 Transformative Technological Innovations 23
        2.2.2 The Economics of Digital: A Contemporary
                Transformation 26
   2.3 International Trade in the Digital Economy 38
        2.3.1 Vectors of Digital Transformation of Global Trade 39
        2.3.2 On the Nexus of Cross-Border Data Flows
                and International Trade 46
   2.4 Conclusion 55
   References 57

3 **The Emergence of Digital Trade Regulation** 67
   3.1 Introduction 67
   3.2 Towards Conceptualising Digital Trade 69
        3.2.1 Reviewing Conceptual Frameworks for E-Commerce
                and Digital Trade 71

		3.2.2	From E-Commerce to Digital Trade	81
		3.2.3	A Data-Centred Concept for Trade in the Digital Economy: Towards a Definition for Digital Trade	86
	3.3	The WTO and Digital Trade		89
		3.3.1	The WTO as a Forum for Digital Trade Governance	90
		3.3.2	WTO Agreements and Digital Trade	101
		3.3.3	Evaluation	117
	3.4	Preferential Trade Agreements and Digital Trade		119
		3.4.1	Integration of Digital Trade Rules in Preferential Trade Agreements	121
		3.4.2	The Regulation of Data Flows in Preferential Trade Agreements	125
		3.4.3	Evaluation	131
	3.5	Trade Policy Implications of Digital Trade		133
		3.5.1	Developing Trade Policy for the Digital Economy	133
		3.5.2	Individual Trade Policy Considerations	135
	3.6	Conclusion		140
	Jurisprudence			142
	References			143
4	**Data Protection and Data Protectionism in International Trade**			**157**
	4.1	Introduction		157
	4.2	Fundamentals of Data Privacy Regulation in a Digital Trade Context		159
		4.2.1	Data Privacy: Conceptual Approaches and Nomenclature	160
		4.2.2	On the Multifaceted Character of Personal Data in the Digital Economy	164
		4.2.3	On the Scope of Data Privacy Laws in a Digital Economy	166
	4.3	The Regulation of Cross-Border Data Flows in a Heterogeneous Global Data Privacy Environment		170
		4.3.1	International Instruments of Data Privacy	172
		4.3.2	Regional & National Data Privacy Regulations	180
		4.3.3	Approaches to Cross-Border Data Flow Regulation	189
	4.4	The Data Privacy Collision in Digital Trade		197
		4.4.1	The Normative Discourse on Data Privacy in a Trade Context	198
		4.4.2	The Nexus of Data Privacy Regulation and Digital Trade Governance	208
	4.5	Conclusion		221
	Jurisprudence			223
	References			223

Contents

5 Mitigating the Data Privacy Collision in Digital Trade 233
   5.1   Introduction 233
   5.2   WTO Law and Domestic Data Privacy Regulations 234
         5.2.1   GATS Commitments and Domestic Data Privacy
                 Regulation 235
         5.2.2   Article XIV GATS (General Exceptions) 249
   5.3   Data Privacy Rules in Preferential Trade Agreements 268
         5.3.1   Quantitative Considerations 268
         5.3.2   Qualitative Considerations 269
         5.3.3   Evaluation 275
   5.4   Conclusion 278
   Jurisprudence 280
   References 281

6 Towards Reconciling Digital Trade and Data Privacy 287
   6.1   Introduction 287
   6.2   Fostering International Initiatives for Measuring
        and Conceptualising Digital Trade 289
   6.3   An Integrated Approach to the Digital Trade
        and Data Privacy Nexus: What Role for Trade Law? 291
   6.4   Recontextualising the Multilateral Framework for Trade
        in Services 299
   6.5   Negotiating a Digital Trade and Data Privacy Agreement 306
   Jurisprudence 311
   References 311

Abbreviations

AI	Artificial Intelligence
APEC CBPR	APEC Cross Border Privacy Rules
APEC	Asia-Pacific Economic Cooperation
BCR	Binding Corporate Rules
CCPA	California Consumer Privacy Act
CETA	Comprehensive Economic and Trade Agreement
CJEU	Court of Justice of the European Union
CoE	Council of Europe
CPTPP	Comprehensive and Progressive Agreement for Trans-Pacific Partnership
DPA	Data Protection Authority
DPD	Data Protection Directive
DPO	Data Protection Officer
EC	European Communities
ECHR	European Convention on Human Rights
ECJ	European Court of Justice
ECtHR	European Court of Human Rights
EDPB	European Data Protection Board
EEA	European Economic Area
EPA	Economic Partnership Agreement
EU Charter	Charter of Fundamental Rights of the European Union
EU	European Union
GATS	General Agreement on Trade in Services
GATT	General Agreement on Tariffs and Trade
GDP	Gross Domestic Product
GDPR	General Data Protection Regulation
ICC	International Chamber of Commerce
ICCPR	International Covenant on Civil and Political Rights
ICT	Information and Communication Technology
IMF	International Monetary Fund

IoT	Internet of Things
IP	Internet Protocol
IT	Information Technology
ITA	Information Technology Agreement
ITU	International Telecommunications Union
MFN	Most-Favoured-Nation
NAFTA	North American Free Trade Agreement
NT	National Treatment
OECD	Organisation for Economic Co-operation and Development
RCEP	Regional Comprehensive Economic Partnership
SCC	Standard Contractual Clauses
SME	Small and medium-sized enterprises
SPS Agreement	Agreement on the Application of Sanitary and Phytosanitary Measures
TBT Agreement	Agreement on Technical Barriers to Trade
TEU	Treaty on European Union
TFEU	Treaty on the Functioning of the European Union
TiSA	Trade in Services Agreement
TPP	Trans-Pacific Partnership
TRIPS	Agreement on Trade-Related Aspects of Intellectual Property Rights
TTIP	Transatlantic Trade and Investment Partnership
UDHR	Universal Declaration of Human Rights
UK	United Kingdom
UN	United Nations
UNCTAD	United Nations Conference on Trade and Development
UNESCAP	United Nations Economic and Social Commission for Asia and the Pacific
USITC	United States International Trade Commission
USMCA	United States–Mexico–Canada Agreement
USTR	Office of the United States Trade Representative
W/120	Service Sectoral Classification List
WP	Working Party
WPDR	Working Party on Domestic Regulation
WTO	World Trade Organisation

Chapter 1
Introduction to the Nexus of Digital Trade and Data Privacy

1.1 Context

1.1.1 A Global Digital Revolution

A *"digital revolution"* is sweeping all sectors of the global economy.[1] The proliferation of Information and Communication Technology (ICT) and the Internet has led to the emergence of an economic reality where added value is generated by and depended on the ubiquitous exchange of digitised information.[2] Reinforced by rapidly expanding digital connectivity and data processing capacity, the mechanisms of a knowledge-based economy have led to an increasing effect of *"combinatorial innovation"*.[3] Data has become a principal and essential driver of innovation, productivity and growth.[4] Indeed, digitised information is currency, commodity, and asset in a *"digital economy"*.[5] However, data is not the *"new oil"*, as is

---

[1] This commonly used terminology underscores the profound changes that digitalisation implies for both the economy and civil society. The notion *"revolution"* emphasizes the potential for socio-economic and political upheaval due to technological progress and is reminiscent of the period of the Industrial Revolution in the late eighteenth century. In this book, however, the term *"digital transformation"* is used to emphasize the ability to manoeuvre on the path into the digital era, see further *infra* Sect. 1.3.

[2] See for an overview of the evolution of communications technology Freeman and Louçã (2002), pp. 301–355.

[3] See further in this regard Varian (2004), pp. 1–48.

[4] Note, however, the difficulties of current methodologies and taxonomies in measuring the economic impact of ICT, data and cross-border data flows, see further *infra* Sects. 2.2.1.2 and 2.3.2.3.

[5] The concept of a *"digital economy"* is not clearly defined. The term is often employed with varying connotations and has synonyms such as *"Internet economy"* or *"Online economy"*. See further *infra* Sect. 2.2.2.2.

occasionally propagated.[6] A statement such as this, which misconstrues the economic nature of data to resemble that of a finite resource, obscures the fact that the relationship between digital data and economic value is much more nuanced. The most salient characteristic of digital data in this regard is that it is *"non-rivalrous"*—it is not finitely consumed, but can be used repeatedly and in different contexts, even simultaneously.[7] Digital data has no inherent meaning or structure and thus is perceived to constitute a *"raw material"*, the value of which can be unearthed by digital technologies.[8] The Internet enables the aggregation, analysis, and storage of digital data on a global scale, as well as the physical detachment of each of these stages.[9] Thereby, it decentralises economic activity and makes the digital economy inherently global. The Internet has been described to generate a *"borderless environment for communication"*, where *"information can flow from one location to another along a seamless web, without regard for distance and jurisdiction"*.[10] With each day, a veritable *"flow"* of data on a global scale becomes more and more essential to the viability and productivity of economic enterprises in all industries.[11] The Internet has furthermore considerably lowered entry thresholds for small businesses seeking access to digitally networked global markets.[12] The technological progress brought about by digitalisation provides a catalyst for the cross-border trade of goods and services and the exchange of information and ideas. Today, digital products that had previously been bound to physical media are increasingly being exchanged seamlessly in *"cyberspace"*. Services, which only recently were considered non-tradable economic activities, show a particular ability to be digitised and are now increasingly integrated into *"servicified"* Global Value Chains (GVCs).[13] In addition, the Internet has enabled new types of service activities, often based on digital data and driven by cross-border data flows. Some of these digital services, such as Internet search, have become indispensable to the daily operations of businesses and individuals and can arguably be considered a public good.[14] This trend has continued to accelerate during the COVID-19 pandemic and is expected to continue in a post-pandemic world.[15]

---

[6] *See* insinuated for example by The Economist (2017). *See* however Mandel (2017).

[7] *See* further Jones and Tonetti (2020).

[8] *See* further on the characteristics of digital data *infra* Sect. 2.2.2.1.3.

[9] Nguyen and Paczos (2020), p. 24.

[10] Bacchetta et al. (1998), p. 1. The notion of independence from physical boundaries and constraints, often ascribed to the Internet at the beginning of its commercial development, however, is conclusively rejected by Goldsmith and Wu (2006), pp. 49–63.

[11] *See* further Castro and McQuinn (2015).

[12] Meltzer (2014), pp. 4–8.

[13] *See* generally Miroudot and Cadestin (2017). *See* further *infra* Sect. 2.3.1.2.

[14] Yost (2021).

[15] McNamara and Newman (2020), pp. E.71–E73.

1.1.2 A New Frontier for International Economic Law

The digital economy is rigorously challenging established structures and institutions of multilateral cooperation, since digital innovation has increased the dynamics and momentum of economic and social interaction on a global scale.[16] Today, there is no multilateral framework for the governance of the global digital economy, which is characterised by a complex interplay of technological, regulatory, and economic factors. Building blocks of a transnational digital governance are being addressed primarily in existing venues of International Economic Law. From the perspective of the prevailing nation-state paradigm of industrial economic order, data flows that underlie the digital economy transcend national borders and invoke a trade rationale.[17] In trade law, as in other areas of regulation, digitalisation is unsettling established rationalities of socio-economic patterns and political equilibria. Indeed, cross-border data flows that emerge as modern *"Silk Roads"*[18] are altering pre-existing paradigms of multilateral trade governance.[19] In the same way that the pervasive and profound impact of digitalisation is considered *"disruptive"*[20] in a general economic context, the digital transformation is shaking up the institutions of multilateral trade. Shortly after the historic breakthrough of the 1994 Marrakesh Agreement which established the World Trade Organization (WTO),[21] the proliferation of ICT and digital technologies poses an unprecedented challenge to its system of rules-based economic liberalisation. The WTO, by virtue of a vast membership of 164 nations, it's tradition of successful multilateral regulation and its well-tried dispute settlement mechanism, provides a venue to address the far-reaching repercussions of the digital transformation of the global economy. As *Mira Burri* rightly points out, trade rules affect data in at least three ways: First, by regulating trade in goods and services as well as trade related aspects of intellectual property; second, by installing behind-the-border rules that demand changes in domestic regulation; and third, by limiting the policy space for domestic regulation.[22] In principle, the

---

[16] G20 (2019), p. 2, para. 11 states: *"Cross-border flow of data, information, ideas and knowledge generates higher productivity, greater innovation, and improved sustainable development, while raising challenges related to privacy, data protection, intellectual property rights, and security."*.

[17] However, there are several reasons for questioning, whether the economically relevant transfer of data can be defined as *"trade"*, *see* for example Mueller and Grindal (2018). *See* further *infra* Sect. 2.3.2.2.

[18] Chander (2013), pp. 1–17.

[19] Cf. for an assessment of the political economy of *"digital trade"*, Mitchell and Mishra (2018), pp. 1081–1088.

[20] *"Disruption"* has become a common notion describing the upheavals caused by digital transformation in more traditional industries and sectors. In this sense, the term was coined in 1997 by Christensen (2016). *See* also Manyika et al. (2013). *See* however Lepore (2014) and Krugman (2014).

[21] WTO Agreement: Marrakesh Agreement Establishing the World Trade Organization, Apr. 15, 1994, 1867 U.N.T.S. 154, 33 I.L.M. 1144 (1994).

[22] Burri (2017a), p. 68.

existing multilateral rules of WTO law are valid also for digital forms of trade due to their technology-neutral regulatory structure.[23] The cross-cutting elements of the digital paradigm affect the totality of the WTO regime, with its multilateral pillars of trade in goods, services, and trade-related aspects of intellectual property.[24] However, WTO rules stemming from the previous millennium exhibit shortcomings when it comes to addressing the data-driven economic reality of the twenty-first century. Data as a crucial economic resource as well as the rise of technological innovations such as Cloud Computing, Distributed Ledger Technologies (e.g., blockchain), Big Data, Artificial Intelligence (AI) or the Internet of Things (IoT) could not have been fully anticipated by the time of the finalisation of the Uruguay Round in 1994. In contrast to the policy issues that are addressed in the context of multilateral trade law more recently[25] as well as those that are increasingly integrated in Preferential Trade Agreements (PTAs), such as environmental regulations or labour standards, issues of digital governance represent a fundamental matter for global trade in the digital economy—a *new frontier*. The pervasive and cross-cutting features of the digital paradigm inevitably raise the question as to whether established trade disciplines and rules are sufficient to govern trade in the digital economy, or if (and how) trade governance needs to be redesigned to remain functional in the short run and relevant in the long run.[26] In this sense, it is reasonable to assume that the integration of trade governance with digital governance will be a decisive factor for the relevancy and legitimacy of WTO law in the digital economy.[27] There is growing consensus in academic literature and in government practice that WTO law needs to be reformed to meet the challenges of the digital era. In fact, some commentators even argue in favour of an International Economic Data Law.[28] In similar vein, Elizabeth Dunham, UK Information Commissioner, has underscored: *"What we need now is 21st century thinking for a 21st century problem."*, and has called for a *"Bretton Woods for data"*.[29] Yet, with regard to cross-border trade there is little consensus on the details of such a *"digital"* trade regime. This conundrum of trade governance in a digital economy is rooted in the

---

[23] However, the principle of technology neutrality does not apply horizontally to all WTO agreements, and its implications are controversial. *See infra* Sect. 3.3.2.6.2.

[24] Indeed *"e-commerce"* and *"digital trade"* ought not to be considered to be separate economic sectors, but rather cross-cutting issues relevant to global trade as a whole. *See also* Streinz (2019), p. 337. *See* further the illustration of the relation between WTO rules and digital trade López González and Ferencz (2018), p. 14.

[25] *See* for example the so-called *"Singapore Issues"* for which the 1996 Singapore Ministerial Conference set up three working groups: on trade and investment, on competition policy, and on transparency in government procurement.

[26] In this context, academic literature is increasingly addressing the implications of digital technologies for international trade, *see* for example Aaronson and Leblond (2018); Burri (2021a); Burri and Cottier (2012); Mitchell and Mishra (2021); Peng et al. (2021); Zheng (2020).

[27] *See* for example Azevêdo (2020).

[28] *See* further Streinz (2021).

[29] Denham (2021).

degree to which the reality of trade is transforming as well as in its shifting political economy against a backdrop of change in the geo-political and geo-economic environment. In the context of WTO law, the questions of how to steer the process of digitalisation have long been dominated by the discussions regarding the rise of global *"electronic commerce"* or *"e-commerce"*. A declaration adopted by the WTO Ministerial Conference in May 1998 led to the General Council launching a Work Programme on Electronic Commerce in September of that same year.[30] For the purpose of its exploratory agenda, the Work Programme defined global electronic commerce as the *„production, distribution, marketing, sale or delivery of goods and services by electronic means"*.[31] So far, however, the WTO Work Programme produced hardly any tangible results.[32] Given the gridlock in the WTO, PTAs have been and continue to be perceived as the *"second-best option"* for the development of digital trade governance.[33] Yet, the heterogeneous design and structure of the dedicated rules in current trade agreements emphasize the regulatory challenges associated with the digitalisation of trade.[34] In this context, the increasing prevalence of the term *"digital trade"* is indicative of the continuously evolving environment for trade in the digital economy.[35] Against the backdrop of rapidly evolving technological advancements, trade stakeholders throughout the world have demonstrated that they are in the process of learning how to manage trade in the digital economy.[36] In this context, academic literature increasingly contrasts the emergent templates for trade agreements developed by the major trading blocs of the US, the EU and China.[37] Finally, at the 2019 World Economic Forum in Davos, 76 WTO members, including the EU, the US and China, agreed under a Joint Statement Initiative to pursue plurilateral e-commerce negotiations in the face of *"unique opportunities and challenges"*.[38] Today, 86 participants that represent a large share of world trade have gone through several rounds of negotiations under the joint leadership of Australia, Singapore and Japan. And yet, even if there is a certain momentum in favour of updating WTO law, it remains to be seen whether these negotiations will result in meaningful reforms. However, as of this writing, the negotiation process has not been finalised.

---

[30] Cf. WTO (1998a, b)
[31] WTO (1998b), p. 1, para. 1.3.
[32] *See infra* Sect. 3.3.1.1.
[33] Burri (2017b), p. 408.
[34] *See infra* Sect. 3.4.
[35] *See infra* Sect. 3.2.2.
[36] Wolfe (2018), p. 12.
[37] *See* for example Aaronson and Leblond (2018); Willemyns (2020).
[38] WTO (2019). *See* further *infra* Sect. 3.3.1.2.

1.1.3 Data Protection and Data Protectionism

In the absence of a multilateral framework for a digital governance, the increasing socio-economic relevance of cross-border data flows and digital technologies is prompting governments to adopt unilateral regimes of data governance.[39] In a digital economy, however, unilateral data governance exhibits far-reaching spill-over effects due to the structural interdependence of global data flows on the Internet. For example, there are inherent problems in locating data in a networked environment, as it may be located almost anywhere given its intangibility, calling into question the international law of jurisdiction.[40] Indeed, a new paradigm of *"digital globalisation"* propelled by the Internet has significantly intensified the tension between international political and regulatory concertation and the sovereignty of nation states in the *"westphalian"* sense.[41] From a trade perspective, the convergence of regulatory realms under the digital paradigm results in a plethora of domestic data regulations operating as non-tariff barriers to cross-border economic activity underpinned by cross-border data flows. As a result of the *"Moratorium on Customs Duties on Electronic Transmissions"* introduced by the WTO in 1998 and repeatedly extended, barriers to trade in the digital economy are generally established not in the form of tariffs, but through regulatory measures that interfere with the flow of data across borders.[42] Such regulations include local standards for filtering and blocking Internet access, for example, as well as rules that—explicitly or implicitly—impede the cross-border flow of digitised information or render it economically unviable. Given the manifold implications of a *"borderless"* cyberspace on their sovereign territoriality and regulatory integrity, more and more jurisdictions are embracing measures of a *"localisation"* of data processing and storage within their own sphere of authority.[43] While interferences with the cross-border flow of data can serve as a protectionist instrument of a digital industrial policy in the sense of a *"data nationalism"*,[44] they may also be designed to ensure legitimate policy objectives of the digital era, such as consumer protection, cybersecurity, and notably *"data privacy"*.[45] Given the enormous economic potential at stake, the distinction between legitimate regulation of data and data flows versus trade-distorting *"data*

---

[39] *See* for a definition of data governance *infra* Sect. 1.3. In particular, this text will emphasise the emerging context as a transnational issue, cf. for example, *"Data governance is no longer a matter limited to organisational boundaries, but a multinational concern resulting from cross-border data sharing."*, OECD (2019a), p. 25. In similar vein, governments adopt policies with regard to Internet Governance, *see infra* Sect. 3.5.2.

[40] Burri (2021b), p. 41; Eichensehr (2017), p. 145. *See* also Schmitt (2017).

[41] *See* for example Kobrin (2004), pp. 128–131.

[42] *See* further *infra* Sect. 3.3.1.1.

[43] *See* further *infra* Sect. 2.3.2.4.

[44] Chander and Lê (2015).

[45] *See* for a definition of data privacy for the purpose of this book *infra* Sect. 1.3.

protectionism"[46] is naturally highly controversial. This is especially the case since legitimate public policy reasons may be used as a pretext for pursuing industrial policy objectives.[47] The issue of data privacy has hitherto not been among the conventional matters of trade law and, conversely, cross-border trade has been of little concern to the field of data privacy law.[48] Today, however, data privacy has become a critical issue for trade and trade policy.[49] This may yet be an understatement. Against the backdrop of current policy debates, they seem to be in—to borrow a dramatic metaphor from *Anupam Chander* and *Paul Schwartz*—a "*mortal contest*".[50]

The fact that digital technologies make it possible to duplicate, process, store and transmit personal data ever more effectively has long raised delicate questions with respect to the role of privacy in the digital era. Subject to the impetus of computerization and automated data processing, in the 1960s and early 1970s, the first designated "*data protection*" regulations were introduced. However, data privacy regulations have evolved differently across different jurisdictions, reflecting a wide spectrum of cultural identities and historical idiosyncrasies. These divergences have led to the fact that data privacy today assumes the status of a *sui generis* fundamental right in some jurisdictions, while in others it is more closely associated with market-based consumer protection, for example.[51] As a result, regulators have begun to include elements of transnational data governance into data privacy legislation to prevent circumvention of domestic legal protections for personal data.[52] While some consider such instruments essential to the effective safeguarding of data privacy in a networked world, others see it primarily as a detriment to innovation and economic prosperity. With the dawn of the digital age, the relevance of data privacy has reached unprecedented dimensions against the backdrop of the realities of a networked society and economy. Several high-profile controversies related to governmental mass storage and the warrantless retention of personal data or the outright surveillance of individuals have brought issues of data privacy to the forefront of public attention.[53] At the same time, the emergence of a global digital economy has dramatically exacerbated the tension between data privacy, economic prosperity and innovation. With expanding technological capabilities, the aggregation and analysis of personal data has become an important component of highly profitable business models.[54] In fact, as *Svetlana Yakovleva* and *Kristina Irion* have put it, "*Personal*

---

[46] *See* for an introduction to the notion of digital protectionism, Aaronson (2019).
[47] Mitchell and Mishra (2019), pp. 396–397.
[48] *See* with further references Burri (2021b), p. 36.
[49] Cf. generally UNCTAD (2016).
[50] Chander and Schwartz (2023), p. 50.
[51] *See* for example Schwartz and Pfeifer (2017).
[52] *See* for early European legislation in particular Kuner (2011), p. 14.
[53] Edward Snowden's disclosure of the National Security Agency's (NSA) practices in 2013 is a prominent example in this regard, *see* Aaronson and Maxim (2013); Hill (2014).
[54] *See* for example the influential work of Zuboff (2019). *See* also OECD (2013).

data is peculiar in the way it combines the dignity of a human being with economic properties valuable for commercial activity".[55] The digital economy brings into sharp relief some antagonistic elements between data privacy and trade. The changed quality and quantity of the deployment of personal data in the economy means that the previously established fragile balances between privacy and economic activity are unsettled and will have to be recalibrated.[56] Critical to this recalibration is the heterogeneity of data privacy approaches and their mechanisms, instruments, and fora at the global level. Since there are no universally recognised data privacy instruments, but rather a fragmented landscape of individual and regional regimes, the global regulatory environment of data privacy is characterised by particular complexity.[57] This complexity seems to be increasing with the continuous proliferation of data privacy regulations. The UNCTAD Global Cyberlaw Tracker, tracking cyberlaw developments throughout the world, finds that 137 out of 194 countries (71%) have adopted data protection and privacy laws, while another 9% have draft laws.[58] In addition to the heterogeneity of data privacy laws in terms of scope and structure, the ambiguity of the underlying normative rationales is of considerable significance in an economic context.[59] The positioning of a given domestic data privacy regulation on a spectrum between "*data protection*" and "*data protectionism*" is therefore highly controversial as there are is no universal understanding of either of these poles. Against this backdrop, the digital transformation of trade against a heterogenous environment of data privacy in the digital age has led to a veritable "*data privacy collision*" in trade.[60] A particularly vivid illustration of this is provided by the global debate provoked by the revised EU data protection regulation. Against the backdrop of digital transformation, the EU has updated its legal framework based on a fundamental rights appreciation of "*data protection*" in order to liberalize the flow of personal data internally between is Member States and ensure its level of protection externally with third countries.[61] The EU's General Data Protection Regulation (GDPR) operates on the basis of a general ban on transfers of personal data to third countries, from which exceptions are made under certain conditions, cf. Article 44 GDPR. Pursuant to Article 45 GDPR, this is the case for transfers based on a so-called "*adequacy*" decision by the European Commission, in which it is assessed unilaterally whether the third country in

---

[55] Yakovleva and Irion (2020), p. 202.
[56] Burri (2021b), p. 37.
[57] *See* for example Kuner (2009).
[58] Cf. UNCTAD (2024).
[59] *See* regarding the "*obscurity*" of aims of data privacy law Bygrave (2014), pp. 117–118.
[60] *See* for an account of the EU – US "*Privacy Collision*", Schwartz (2013). *See* also with regard to a "*global privacy crisis*", Chander and Schwartz (2023), p. 71; Gasser (2015), p. 339.
[61] Regulation (EU) 2016/679 of the European Parliament and of the Council of 27 April 2016 on the protection of natural persons with regard to the processing of personal data and on the free movement of such data, and repealing Directive 95/46/EC (General Data Protection Regulation). The GDPR "*protects fundamental rights and freedoms of natural persons and in particular their right to the protection of personal data*", cf. Article 1 Sec. 2 GDPR. *See* further *infra* Sect. 4.3.2.2.

question ensures an adequate level of data protection. In this context, the regulation thus features *extraterritorial effects* (cf. also Article 3 GDPR) and may be perceived in a context of a geostrategic agenda to export EU rules and standards along the lines of what *Anu Bradford* has analysed to constitute a *"Brussels Effect"*.[62] Moreover, for the EU, advancing a high level of data protection and facilitating international trade go *"hand in hand"*.[63] In this way, the GDPR is driving the global debate on the delicate balance between data protection and data protectionism, venturing its own approach to a trade-off between data privacy and *"digital"* trade. This significantly and infamously pertains to the transatlantic trade relations between the EU and the US.[64] As one legal scholar has aptly put it, the clash of attitudes and sensibilities with respect to data privacy is rooted in a systemic difference of the underlying regulatory approaches between *"dignity"* and *"liberty"*.[65] For the EU, the GDPR constitutes an exemplary gold standard of personal data protection as fundamental rights protection in an international context.[66] For the US, heightened compliance costs as well as direct interference with cross-border data flows by data privacy regulations are perceived as a crucial trade barrier for domestic data-driven industries.[67] Today, however, other governments, such as that of the People's Republic of China are taking advantage of the momentum provided by the GDPR to enact domestic data privacy regulations that are closely intertwined with their respective sociocultural imprints—thus expanding the data privacy collision.[68]

1.1.4 *Mitigating the Data Privacy Collision Under Trade Law*

Whereas the debate on the implications of *"transborder"* flows of information on the protection of individual privacy is not of a particularly recent nature, the approach to this issue in the context of regulating *"cross-border"* data flows in an economic context of trade governance is still fairly recent.[69] In addition to the traditional notion of electronic commerce, the increasingly prominent concept of digital trade represents a synthesis of trade regulation and governance elements pertaining to a data-

---

[62] Bradford (2020).
[63] European Commission (2017), p. 6, para. 3.1.
[64] *See* further Schwartz (2013). *See* for a brief account of the eventful relation Congressional Research Service (2021).
[65] Whitman (2004), pp. 1160–1164.
[66] Cf. European Commission (2020).
[67] *See* for example United States International Trade Commission (2013), pp. 5-8–5-15.
[68] This is particularly the case with China's Cybersecurity Law (CSL), which came into force in 2017, and the Personal Information Protection Law (PIPL) enacted in 2021. *See* further *infra* Sect. 4.4.
[69] Burri (2021b), p. 36; Drake (2016), p. 4. It should be noted that the notion *"cross-border"* is employed to emphasize the relevance of data flows in the context of international trade. *See* for an account of the development of the discussion in this regard Aaronson (2015), pp. 679–680.

driven economy. Recent scholarship presents the cross-border flow of digital data as a fundamental aspect of digital trade.[70] Estimates of the added value of cross-border data flows, on the one hand, and the resulting economic potential of digital trade, on the other, point to a vast economic significance.[71] To date, however, there is no universally shared definition for digital trade.[72] In fact, there are significant conceptual and statistical complexities related to digital trade in general and cross-border data flows in particular.[73] Against the backdrop of the currently applicable WTO legal framework dating from 1994, the governance of trade in an inherently global digital economy, however, is fraught with regulatory uncertainty. Especially with regard to the nexus between digital trade and data privacy, it is a matter of considerable controversy to what extent the current WTO regime regulates the cross-border flow of personal data and what room for manoeuvre there is at the domestic level for data regulation. While one element of this relates to the existence and configuration of trade commitments on data flows, other pertain to the state of equilibrium of international cooperation in the digital economy and the regulatory sovereignty of WTO members. The regulation of international trade in services under the General Agreement on Trade in Services (GATS) assumes a pivotal role in this regard.[74] Digital trade bears strong references to trade in services, as there is an intrinsic dependency between the immaterial and highly digitizable value creation through services and the seamless import and export of digital data. Indeed, the scope and conditions of multilateral economic liberalisation of trade in services has always been subject to controversy due to its intrinsic interrelation with non-tariff barriers rooted in domestic legislation and its considerable interplay with behind-the-border policymaking.[75] This results in a dual objective of the GATS enshrined in its preamble, which underscores the *"achievement of progressively higher levels of liberalization of trade in services through successive rounds of multilateral negotiations aimed at promoting the interests of all participants on a mutually advantageous basis"* while *"recognizing the right of Members to regulate, and to introduce new regulations, on the supply of services within their territories in order to meet national policy objectives"*.[76] Against this background, the GATS seeks to ensure that unintended trade-restrictive consequences resulting from divergent national regulatory standards are mitigated on the one hand and that national measures that

---

[70] *See* only Casalini and López González (2019), pp. 9–11.

[71] *See* only Manyika et al. (2016), pp. 73–85.

[72] There is also no uniform definition for electronic commerce. In fact, the terms are frequently used interchangeably. The WTO continues to employ the e-commerce concept, as it has been given a particularly broad definition under the WTO's 1998 Work Programme on Electronic Commerce. *See* further Sect. 3.2.

[73] Cf. for developments in this regard López González and Jouanjean (2017); IMF et al. (2019); IMF et al. (2023).

[74] General Agreement on Trade in Services, 15 April 1994, Marrakesh Agreement Establishing the World Trade Organization, Annex 1B, 1869 U.N.T.S. 183, 33 I.L.M. 1167 (1994).

[75] *See* for example Weiß (2020), pp. 29–31. *See* generally Lowenfeld (2009), pp. 120–125.

[76] Cf. Preamble to the GATS.

are inconsistent with multilateral trade rules are implemented in pursuit of legitimate policy objectives, on the other.[77] A particular challenge, especially with respect to data privacy, is thus to discern and address the difference between unintended trade-restrictive measures and disguised protectionism.[78] Moreover, the question arises as to whether trade law can and should be harnessed as a driver of regulatory convergence in the area of data privacy, potentially even by restricting WTO members' discretion in the design and implementation of data privacy rules.[79] It is questionable to what extent the general exception provision of Article XIV GATS can preserve the fragile balance between international trade law obligations and domestic regulatory authority in the digital era. In fact it seems that by liberalising trade in services under GATS, as *Tim Wu* has described it, *"almost by accident, the WTO has put itself in an oversight position for most of the national laws and practices that regulate the Internet"*.[80] It is evident from the general exception in Article XIV(c)(ii) GATS that the nexus of trade and data privacy has been identified by the participants during the Uruguay Round negotiations.[81] Article XIV(c)(ii) GATS provides for exemptions to trade commitments for measures of WTO members which are *"necessary to secure compliance with laws or regulations which are not inconsistent with the provisions of this Agreement including those relating to the protection of the privacy of individuals in relation to the processing and dissemination of personal data and the protection of confidentiality of individual records and accounts"*. Moreover, Article XIV(a) GATS provides for a general exception for domestic measures that are *"necessary to protect public morals or to maintain public order"*. In addition to satisfying the litigious requirements for *"necessity"* under WTO law, domestic data privacy measures must also overcome the so-called chapeau of Article XIV GATS, according to which measures must be *"[. . .] not applied in a manner which would constitute a means of arbitrary or unjustifiable discrimination between countries where like conditions prevail, or a disguised restriction on trade in services [. . .]"*. In the absence of a precedent before WTO dispute settlement bodies, there has been much speculation in academic literature about a potential challenge of domestic data privacy measures under WTO law.[82] Given that data privacy measures involve a complex mix of economic and non-economic factors, it is uncertain how WTO dispute settlement bodies would weigh in on balancing international trade commitments and domestic regulatory autonomy in relation to data privacy. In addition to the intricate technological factors affecting data privacy in a networked economy, it is no simple matter to disentangle domestic approaches and sort out the underlying normative arguments of data privacy at the international level, since the precise

---

[77] Lim and de Meester (2014), pp. 8–10.
[78] *See* generally Mattoo and Subramanian (1998).
[79] *See* regarding regulatory convergence at the WTO Weiß (2020), pp. 285–296. *See* further Ahmed (2019).
[80] Wu (2006), p. 264.
[81] *See* further Chander and Schwartz (2023), pp. 65–70.
[82] *See* for example MacDonald and Streatfeild (2014); Weber (2012). *See* further *infra* Sect. 5.2.

nature of categorising a policy measure as "*data protection*" or "*data protectionism*" is highly controversial. This is particularly the case with regard to the involvement of fundamental rights to privacy and data protection, where a potential trade-off between economic rationales of trade law and public policy interests is highly contentious.[83] In addition to the multilateral GATS, the growing number of PTAs is also worthy of note, which, as fora for the development of digital trade governance, also address the nexus between digital trade and data privacy.

1.2 Research Objective

The above observations raise a number of fundamental issues with regard to the nexus of digital trade and data privacy that warrant an in-depth analysis. What are the critical vectors of the digital transformation of trade, and how do data-driven business models and cross-border data flows shape the reality of trade in the digital economy? What is the state of conceptualisation of so-called digital trade and how do WTO law and PTAs account for the digitalisation of trade relations? What exactly are the conflicting imperatives of digital trade and data privacy, and what role can WTO law and modern PTAs play in reconciling the two realms? Against this background, the objective of this research is to comprehensively examine and synthesize the legal issues arising from the nexus of digital trade and data privacy, as well as to develop the basis for an integrated approach to digital trade and data privacy in the context of trade law. Traditionally, trade lawyers have rarely addressed data privacy, and conversely, data privacy scholars have paid little attention to the context of international trade. This book contends that this unfortunate disconnect between the two fields of law is due to a contemporary conceptual confusion of trade in the digital economy and an only gradually adapting estimation of its interaction with an emerging transnational privacy environment. Notably, the regulation of cross-border data flows involving personal data is strongly influenced by both trade and data privacy law. Against this backdrop, this research contributes to bridging a lacuna in the existing trade law literature by providing a thorough dogmatic treatment of the digital trade and data privacy nexus. This will involve, first, exploring the conceptualisation of "*digital trade*" as well as the resulting implications for trade governance and, second, analysing the ramifications of a globally diverse data privacy environment on trade in the digital economy. Third, this research assesses the question whether trade law provides suitable balancing mechanisms to reconcile the tensions between data privacy as an important element of domestic regulatory authority and international trade. Against the backdrop of an escalating friction between data privacy as a central matter of national data governance and the governance of digital trade under trade law, this book proposes an integrated approach to digital trade and data privacy and thereby advances the

---

[83] *See* for example Yakovleva (2018), pp. 482–487; Yakovleva and Irion (2020).

scholarly discourse on a *"recontextualisation"* of trade law in a global digital economy.

1.3 Terminology

This book refers to several terms and concepts which are not clearly defined or controversial in detail. In the following, these terms are defined for the purposes of this text.

1) **Cross-border data flows:** The concept of cross-border data flows is not uniformly defined.[84] The terms *"data transfer"*, *"cross-border information flows"* or *"transborder data flows"* are employed by various national and international regulatory frameworks and institutions synonymously, often without further clarification.[85] The UN consider *"transborder data flows"* to constitute a *"movement across national boundaries of machine readable data for processing, storage or retrieval"*.[86] In this text, the term cross-border data flow is employed in reference to a fluid state (*"flow"*) as opposed to the more static (*"transfer"*) to reflect the realities of an comprehensively networked global data sphere as well *"cross-border"* to specifically relate to a trade context. For the purpose of this text *"cross-border data flows"* is thus deemed to encompass all efforts of exchanging digitised information between two or more stakeholders in particular but not exclusively via the Internet.
2) **Data:** The word *"data"* is plural of „*datum*" (*"given"*) derived from the latin word *"dare"*, which translates to *"to give"*. The OECD employs a definition according to which data is the *"representation of facts stored or transmitted as qualified or quantified symbols"*.[87]
3) **Data Governance:** This text is based on a broad conception of the notion of *"data governance"*, differing considerably from the meaning given to the term in an organisational context. Data governance encompasses the rules, norms, practices and infrastructures that are established by various stakeholders such as states, international organisations, civil society and companies for the purpose of governing the collection, storage, dissemination, use and access to all types of digitised information, i.e. data.[88] *Thomas Streinz* and *Matthew Steven Erie* use the term *"transnational data governance"* to refer to the challenges resulting from the reciprocal interactions of national data governance regimes that shape

---

[84] *See* with further references Willemyns (2021), pp. 27–30.
[85] Cf. Kuner (2013), pp. 11–14.
[86] *See* with further references United States International Trade Commission (2017), p. 16.
[87] OECD (2015), p. 449.
[88] Cf. further Streinz (2019), p. 329; Erie and Streinz (2021), pp. 11–14. *See* in more detail *infra* Sect. 3.5.2.2.

cross-border data governance, including (but not limited to) the regulation of (personal) data flows.[89] This text will use this term to the same effect.

4) **Data Privacy:** The term *"data privacy"* is employed as an umbrella term for regulatory frameworks that address the protection of natural persons in the processing and dissemination of personal data. It is a hybrid of the notion of *"data protection"*, which is dominant in the European legal system, and the term *"information privacy"*, which is employed in the US. By referring to data privacy in this way, a holistic perspective is adopted in an emergent transnational data privacy environment against the background of internationally diverse regulatory cultures and approaches.

5) **Digital Transformation:** This text adopts the OECD's definition of digital transformation, according to which the term refers to the economic and societal effects of *"digitalisation"* and *"digitsation"*.[90]

6) **Digitalisation:** This text adopts the OECD's definition of digitalisation, according to which the term refers to the use of digital technologies and data as well as interconnection that results in new or changes to existing activities.[91]

7) **Digitisation**: This text adopts the OECD's definition of digitisation, according to which the term refers to the conversion of analogue data and processes into a machine-readable format.[92]

8) **Digital Products:** This text refers to digital products to designate both intangible goods and services.[93] Hence, the text does not adopt the definition provided by several trade agreements with US participation, whereas a digital product is deemed to constitute a computer program, text, video, image, sound recording, or other product that is digitally encoded, produced for commercial sale or distribution, and that can be transmitted electronically.[94] In particular, it is not intended to indicate a stance on the controversial issue of the delineation of the respective scope of GATT and GATS.

9) **Digital Service:** This text will employ the notion digital service to mean services which are digitally supplied via cross-border data flows.[95] The term can therefore refer in a given instance both to digitised *"traditional"* services as well as to newly emergent services (such as Cloud Computing, Internet Search or Online Gaming).

---

[89] Erie and Streinz (2021), pp. 11–14.

[90] OECD (2019b), p. 18.

[91] OECD (2019b), p. 18.

[92] OECD (2019b), p. 18.

[93] This definition is based on the interpretation of the WTO Dispute Settlement Bodies regarding *"products"*, *see* Appellate Body Report, *Publications and Audiovisual Products*, WT/DS363/AB/R, 21 December 2009, para. 364 with reference to Panel Report, *Publications and Audiovisual Products*, WT/DS363/R, 12 August 2009, para. 7.1188.

[94] *See* for example Comprehensive and Progressive Agreement for Trans-Pacific Partnership (CPTPP), Article 14.1. and United States-Mexico-Canada Agreement (USMCA), Article 19.1.

[95] Willemyns (2021), pp. 51–55.

10) **Digital Trade:** In the context of this book, the term digital trade refers to all forms of cross-border economic activity that depend on the flow of digital data, either in that this flow of digital data significantly facilitates or enables them. In this way, a holistic perspective is adopted on the digital transformation of trade, emphasising cross-border data flow regulation as a key component of its governance.[96]

11) **Personal Data:** The term *"personal data"* covers all information relating to an identified or identifiable natural person. The term is interpreted in a broad sense so as not to exclude a priori any legal frameworks aimed at the protection of individuals with regard to the processing of information relating to them.

1.4 Outline

This book approaches the above research objective in six chapters.

The following second chapter focuses on the digital transformation of international trade. The objective of this chapter is to illustrate the economic mechanisms of a digital economy and to outline the paradigmatic changes that data and digital technologies entail for cross-border economic activity. To this end, the chapter is divided into four sections. Following an introduction, a second section will adress the digital transformation of the global economy and the third section will outline the resulting implications for cross-border trade. A conclusion will emphasizes that data and cross-border data flows are the medium of digital transformation of trade, which in turn raises the question of the regulation of changing and emerging forms of trade in a global digital economy.

The third chapter examines the emergence of the concept of digital trade against the backdrop of the existing governance framework of international trade law. In this context, it is necessary to draw on the insights gained in the second chapter with respect to the nature of the digital transformation and to assess whether new dimensions of trade are captured by current legal frameworks under WTO law and PTAs. To this end, the chapter is divided into six sections. Following introductory remarks, the second section analyses the emergence of digital trade as a concept in International Economic Law. The following two sections focus on the current legal framework for digital trade as set forth in multilateral WTO law and PTAs. Finally, key trade policy considerations associated with digital trade are outlined and a conclusion is provided.

A fourth chapter delves deeper into the relationship between data privacy regulation and digital trade in a global digital economy. This chapter is divided into five sections. Following an introduction, the second section outlines the conception, rationale, and scope of data privacy regulation. A third section examines the regulatory mechanisms established in a global data privacy environment for

---

[96] *See* further *infra* Sect. 3.2.

regulating cross-border data flows. Against this background, the fourth section presents the collision of divergent domestic data privacy regulations in the context of international trade relations. For this purpose, approaches to data privacy regulation implemented by major trade stakeholders are outlined and contextualised against their trade profiles. A fifth section contains a conclusion.

In a fifth chapter, four sections examine the role of trade law with respect to the collision of domestic data privacy regulations in an emergent transnational data privacy environment. To this end, the first and second section will adress the impact of WTO law on domestic regulation of data privacy, focusing in particular on the scope for WTO Members to derogate from the requirements of international trade law for the sake of important policy interests involved in data privacy. Then, in a third section, the governance frameworks of modern PTAs will be outlined, incorporating individual trade-offs to the digital trade and data privacy nexus. A fourth section presents a conclusion.

The sixth and concluding chapter provides a summary of the results obtained in the previous chapters in five sections. The chapter outlines a way forward towards an integrated approach to digital trade and data privacy.

Jurisprudence

Appellate Body Report, China – Measures Affecting Trading Rights and Distribution Services for Certain Publications and Audiovisual Entertainment Products [Publications and Audiovisual Products] WT/DS363/AB/R, 21 December 2009

Panel Report, China – Measures Affecting Trading Rights and Distribution Services for Certain Publications and Audiovisual Entertainment Products [Publications and Audiovisual Products], WT/DS363/R, 12 August 2009

References

Aaronson SA (2015) Why trade agreements are not setting information free: the lost history and reinvigorated debate over cross-border data flows, human rights, and national security. World Trade Rev 14(04):671–700. https://doi.org/10.1017/S1474745615000014

Aaronson SA (2019) What are we talking about when we talk about digital protectionism? World Trade Rev 18(4):541–577. https://doi.org/10.1017/S1474745618000198

Aaronson SA, Leblond P (2018) Another digital divide: the rise of data realms and its implications for the WTO. J Int Econ Law 21(2):245–272. https://doi.org/10.1093/jiel/jgy019

Aaronson SA, Maxim R (2013) Trade and the internet: the challenge of the NSA revelations: policies in the US, EU and Canada. https://doi.org/10.2139/ssrn.2407270

Ahmed U (2019) The importance of cross-border regulatory cooperation in an era of digital trade. World Trade Rev 18(1):99–120. https://doi.org/10.1017/S1474745618000514

Azevêdo R (2020) Remarks at Joint Statement on E-commerce, Davos meeting. https://www.wto.org/english/news_e/spra_e/spra300_e.htm. Accessed 5 Apr 2024

References

Bacchetta M, Low P, Mattoo A, Schuknecht L, Wager H, Wehrens M (1998) Electronic commerce and the role of the WTO. Special studies / World Trade Organization, Geneva. https://hdl.handle.net/10419/107052. Accessed 5 Apr 2024

Bradford A (2020) The Brussels effect: how the European Union rules the world. Oxford University Press, New York

Burri M (2017a) The governance of data and data flows in trade agreements: the pitfalls of legal adaptation. UC Davis Law Rev 51:65–132

Burri M (2017b) The regulation of data flows through trade agreements. Georgetown J Int Law 48: 407–448

Burri M (ed) (2021a) Big data and global trade law. Cambridge University Press, Cambridge

Burri M (2021b) Interfacing privacy and trade. Case West Reserve J Int Law 53:35–88

Burri M, Cottier T (eds) (2012) Trade governance in the digital age. Cambridge University Press, Cambridge

Bygrave LA (2014) Data privacy law: an international perspective. Oxford University Press, Oxford

Casalini F, López González J (2019) Trade and cross-border data flows. OECD Trade Policy Papers No. 220. OECD Publishing, Paris. https://doi.org/10.1787/b2023a47-en

Castro D, McQuinn A (2015) Cross-border data flows enable growth in all industries. Information Technology & Innovation Foundation (ITIF). https://www2.itif.org/2015-cross-border-data-flows.pdf?_ga=1.8208626.1580578791.1473954628. Accessed 5 Apr 2024

Chander A (2013) The electronic silk road: how the web binds the world in commerce. Yale University Press, New Haven

Chander A, Lê UP (2015) Data nationalism. Empory Law J 64:677–739

Chander A, Schwartz PM (2023) Privacy and/or trade. Univ Chic Law Rev 90:49–135

Christensen CM (2016) The innovator's dilemma: when new technologies cause great firms to fail. The management of innovation and change series. Harvard Business Review Press, Boston, Massachusetts

Congressional Research Service (2021) U.S.-EU Privacy Shield and Transatlantic Data Flows. https://crsreports.congress.gov/product/pdf/R/R46917. Accessed 5 Apr 2024

Denham E (2021) A Bretton Woods for data: Speech at the Oxford Internet Institute. https://ico.org.uk/about-the-ico/media-centre/news-and-blogs/2021/09/a-bretton-woods-for-data/. Accessed 5 Apr 2024

Drake WJ (2016) Background Paper for the workshop on data localization and barriers to trans-border data flows. https://www3.weforum.org/docs/Background_Paper_Forum_workshop%2009.2016.pdf. Accessed 5 Apr 2024

Eichensehr KE (2017) Data extraterritoriality. Tex Law Rev 95:145–160

Erie MS, Streinz T (2021) The Beijing Effect: China's Digital Silk Road as transnational data governance. N Y Univ J Int Law Polit 54(1):1–92

European Commission (2017) Communication from the Commission to the European Parliament and the Council Exchanging and Protecting Personal Data in a Globalised World. COM(2017) 7final

European Commission (2020) Communication from the Commission to the European Parliament and the Council: Data protection as a pillar of citizens' empowerment and the EU's approach to the digital transition - two years of application of the General Data Protection Regulation. COM (2020) 264 final

Freeman C, Louçã F (2002) As time goes by: from the industrial revolutions to the information revolution. Oxford University Press, Oxford

G20 (2019) Osaka Leaders' Declaration. https://www.consilium.europa.eu/media/40124/final_g20_osaka_leaders_declaration.pdf. Accessed 5 Apr 2024

Gasser U (2015) Perspectives on the future of digital privacy. Zeitschrift für Schweizerisches Recht 134:335–448

Goldsmith JL, Wu T (2006) Who controls the Internet?: Illusions of a borderless world. Oxford University Press, New York

Hill JF (2014) The growth of data localization post-Snowden: analysis and recommendations for U.S. policymakers and business leaders. The Hague Institute for Global Justice, Conference on the Future of Cyber Governance. https://doi.org/10.2139/ssrn.2430275

IMF, WTO, OECD (2019) Handbook on measuring digital trade, First Edition. https://www.oecd.org/sdd/its/Handbook-on-Measuring-Digital-Trade-Version-1.pdf. Accessed 5 Apr 2024

IMF, WTO, UNCTAD, OECD (2023) Handbook on measuring digital trade, Second Edition, OECD Publishing, Paris/International Monetary Fund/UNCTAD, Geneva/WTO, Geneva. https://doi.org/10.1787/ac99e6d3-en

Jones CI, Tonetti C (2020) Nonrivalry and the economics of data. Am Econ Rev 110(9): 2819–2858. https://doi.org/10.1257/aer.20191330

Kobrin SJ (2004) Safe harbours are hard to find: the trans-Atlantic data privacy dispute, territorial jurisdiction and global governance. Rev Int Stud 30(1):111–131. https://doi.org/10.1017/S0260210504005856

Krugman P (2014) Creative Destruction Yada Yada. The New York Times. https://archive.nytimes.com/krugman.blogs.nytimes.com/2014/06/16/creative-destruction-yada-yada/. Accessed 5 Apr 2024

Kuner C (2009) An international legal framework for data protection: issues and prospects. Comput Law Secur Rev 25(4):307–317. https://doi.org/10.1016/j.clsr.2009.05.001

Kuner C (2011) Regulation of transborder data flows under data protection and privacy law: past, present and future. OECD Digital Economy Papers, No. 187. OECD Publishing, Paris. https://doi.org/10.1787/5kg0s2fk315f-en

Kuner C (2013) Transborder data flows and data privacy law. Oxford University Press, Oxford

Lepore J (2014) The disruption machine: what the gospel of innovation gets wrong. The New Yorker. https://www.newyorker.com/magazine/2014/06/23/the-disruption-machine. Accessed 5 Apr 2024

Lim AH, de Meester B (2014) An introduction to domestic regulation and GATS. In: Lim AH, de Meester B (eds) WTO Domestic Regulation and Services Trade: putting principles into practice. Cambridge University Press, Cambridge, pp 1–22

López González J, Ferencz J (2018) Digital trade and market openness, OECD Trade Policy Papers No. 217. OECD Publishing, Paris. https://doi.org/10.1787/1bd89c9a-en

López González J, Jouanjean M-A (2017) Digital Trade: developing a framework for analysis. OECD Trade Policy Papers, No. 205. OECD Publishing, Paris. https://doi.org/10.1787/524c8c83-en

Lowenfeld AF (2009) International economic law, Second Edition, Repr. International economic law series. Oxford University Press, Oxford

MacDonald DA, Streatfeild CM (2014) Personal data privacy and the WTO. Houston J Int Law 36(3):625–653

Mandel M (2017) The economic impact of data: why data is not like oil. https://www.progressivepolicy.org/wp-content/uploads/2017/07/PowerofData-Report_2017.pdf. Accessed 5 Apr 2024

Manyika J, Chui M, Bughin J, Dobbs R, Bisson P, Marrs A (2013) Disruptive technologies: advances that will transform life, business and the global economy. McKinsey Global Institute. https://www.mckinsey.com/capabilities/mckinsey-digital/our-insights/disruptive-technologies. Accessed 5 Apr 2024

Manyika J, Lund S, Bughin J, Woetzel L, Stamenov K, Dhingra D (2016) Digital globalization: the new era of global flows, McKinsey Global Institute. https://www.mckinsey.com/capabilities/mckinsey-digital/our-insights/digital-globalization-the-new-era-of-global-flows. Accessed 5 Apr 2024

Mattoo A, Subramanian A (1998) Regulatory autonomy and multilateral disciplines: the dilemma and a possible resolution. J Int Econ Law 1(2):303–322. https://doi.org/10.1093/jiel/1.2.303

McNamara KR, Newman AL (2020) The big reveal: COVID-19 and globalization's great transformations. Int Org 74(S1):E59–E77. https://doi.org/10.1017/S0020818320000387

References

Meltzer JP (2014) Supporting the internet as a platform for international trade: opportunities for small and medium-sized enterprises and developing countries. Brookings Global Economy & Development Working Paper 69. https://doi.org/10.2139/ssrn.2400578

Miroudot S, Cadestin C (2017) Services in global value chains: from inputs to value-creating activities. OECD Trade Policy Papers, No. 197. OECD Publishing, Paris. https://doi.org/10.1787/465f0d8b-en

Mitchell AD, Mishra N (2018) Data at the docks: modernizing international trade law for the digital economy. Vanderbilt J Entertain Technol Law 20:1073–1134

Mitchell AD, Mishra N (2019) Regulating cross-border data flows in a data-driven world: how WTO law can contribute. J Int Econ Law 22(3):389–416. https://doi.org/10.1093/jiel/jgz016

Mitchell AD, Mishra N (2021) WTO law and cross-border data flows. In: Burri M (ed) Big data and global trade law. Cambridge University Press, Cambridge, pp 83–112

Mueller M, Grindal K (2018) Is it "Trade?" Data flows and the digital economy. TPRC 46: The 46th Research Conference on Communication, Information and Internet Policy 2018. SSRN Journal. https://doi.org/10.2139/ssrn.3137819

Nguyen D, Paczos M (2020) Measuring the economic value of data and cross-border data flows: a business perspective. OECD Digital Economy Papers No. 297. OECD Publishing, Paris. https://doi.org/10.1787/6345995e-en

OECD (2013) Exploring the economics of personal data: a survey of methodologies for measuring monetary value. OECD Digital Economy Papers No. 220. OECD Publishing, Paris. https://doi.org/10.1787/5k486qtxldmq-en

OECD (2015) OECD data-driven innovation: big data and growth for well-being OECD. OECD Publishing, Paris. https://doi.org/10.1787/9789264229358-en

OECD (2019a) The path to becoming a data-driven public sector. OECD Digital Government Studies. OECD Publishing, Paris. https://doi.org/10.1787/059814a7-en

OECD (2019b) Going digital: shaping policies, improving lives. OECD Publishing, Paris. https://doi.org/10.1787/9789264312012-en

Peng S, Lin C-F, Streinz T (eds) (2021) Artificial intelligence and international economic law: disruption, regulation, and reconfiguration. Cambridge University Press, New York

Schmitt MN (2017) Tallinn manual 2.0 on the international law applicable to cyber operations, 2nd edn. Cambridge University Press, Cambridge

Schwartz PM (2013) The EU-U.S. privacy collision: a turn to institutions and procedures. Harv Law Rev 126:1966–2009

Schwartz PM, Pfeifer K-N (2017) Transatlantic data privacy law. Georgetown Law J 106(1):117–179

Streinz T (2019) Digital megaregulation uncontested? TPP's model for the global digital economy. In: Kingsbury B et al (eds) Megaregulation contested. Oxford University Press, pp 312–342

Streinz T (2021) Designing international economic data law. Proceedings of the ASIL Annual Meeting 115:73–78. https://doi.org/10.1017/amp.2021.102

The Economist (2017) The world's most valuable resource is no longer oil, but data: regulating the Internet giants. https://www.economist.com/leaders/2017/05/06/the-worlds-most-valuable-resource-is-no-longer-oil-but-data. Accessed 5 Apr 2024

UNCTAD (2016) Data protection regulations and international data flows: implications for trade and development. https://unctad.org/publication/data-protection-regulations-and-international-data-flows-implications-trade-and. Accessed 5 Apr 2024

UNCTAD (2024) Global Cyberlaw Tracker. https://unctad.org/page/data-protection-and-privacy-legislation-worldwide. Accessed 5 Apr 2024

United States International Trade Commission (2013) Digital trade in the U.S. and global economies, Part 1. https://www.usitc.gov/publications/industry_econ_analysis_332/2013/digital_trade_us_and_global_economies_part_1.htm. Accessed 5 Apr 2024

United States International Trade Commission (2017) Global Digital Trade 1: Market Opportunities and Key Foreign Trade Restrictions. Publication Number: 4716; Investigation Number:

332-561. https://www.usitc.gov/publications/industry_econ_analysis_332/2017/global_digital_trade_1_market_opportunities_and.htm. Accessed 5 Apr 2024

Varian HR (2004) Competition and market power. In: Varian HR, Farrell J, Shapiro C (eds) The economics of information: an introduction. Cambridge University Press, pp 1–48

Weber RH (2012) Regulatory autonomy and privacy standards under the GATS. Asian J WTO Int Health Law Policy 7(1):25–48

Weiß W (2020) WTO law and domestic regulation: exploring the determinants for the impact of the WTO on domestic regulatory autonomy. Beck International. Beck; Hart; Nomos, München, Oxford, Baden-Baden

Whitman JQ (2004) The two western cultures of privacy: dignity versus liberty. Yale Law J 113(6):1151–1221

Willemyns I (2020) Agreement forthcoming? A comparison of EU, US, and Chinese RTAs in times of plurilateral E-Commerce negotiations. J Int Econ Law 23(1):221–244. https://doi.org/10.1093/jiel/jgz048

Willemyns I (2021) Digital services in international trade law. Cambridge University Press, Cambridge

Wolfe R (2018) Learning about digital trade: privacy and E-Commerce in CETA and TPP. EUI Working Paper RSCAS 2018/27. https://hdl.handle.net/1814/55144. Accessed 5 Apr 2024

WTO (1998a) Ministerial Conference, Declaration on Global E-Commerce WT/MIN(98)/DEC/2, 20 May 1998

WTO (1998b) Work Programme on Electronic Commerce WT/L/274, 30 September 1998

WTO (2019) Joint Statement on Electronic Commerce WT/L/1056, 25 January 2019

Wu T (2006) The world trade law of censorship and internet filtering. Chic J Int Law 7(1):263–287

Yakovleva S (2018) Should fundamental rights to privacy and data protection be a part of the EU's International Trade 'Deals'? World Trade Rev 17(03):477–508. https://doi.org/10.1017/S1474745617000453

Yakovleva S, Irion K (2020) Pitching trade against privacy: reconciling EU governance of personal data flows with external trade. Int Data Priv Law 10(3):201–221. https://doi.org/10.1093/idpl/ipaa003

Yost D (2021) Let's Make Google a Public Good. The New York Times. https://www.nytimes.com/2021/07/07/opinion/google-utility-antitrust-technology.html. Accessed 5 Apr 2024

Zheng W (2020) The digital challenge to international trade law. NYU J Int Law Polit 52:539–592

Zuboff S (2019) The age of surveillance capitalism: the fight for a human future at the new frontier of power, 1st edn. PublicAffairs, New York

Chapter 2
International Trade in a Global Digital Economy

2.1 Introduction

In recent years, digital technologies have experienced a rapid upswing, reshaping incumbent paradigms of economic growth and socioeconomic development. On the foundation prepared by the rise of Information and Communication Technology (ICT), at the dawn of the twenty-first century, new transformative innovations are burgeoning. For decades now, progress in the field of information processing has advanced at a breakneck pace. Hence, at the beginning of the new millennium, ever more powerful digital technologies, the rapid proliferation of global networks as well as a critical mass of digitised information have ushered in the digital age. Data driven business models, fostered by an inherently global datasphere provided by the Internet are now fulfilling the promise of a veritable *digital economy*, which has been advertised since the early 1990s.[1] Indeed, the curve of technological innovation in recent years is steep.[2] At the centre of this digital transformation lies the transition from an economy of the industrial era with its prevalence of physical capital to a *new economy* in which value creation is largely determined by non-physical assets—so-called "*intangibles*".[3] Under the digital paradigm, almost all analogue information is being digitised (translated into digital bits) while the "*datafication*" of everyday circumstances is proceeding apace.[4] The resulting wealth of digital data can be easily processed, analysed and transmitted by means of an expanding set of digital

---

[1] *See* for example Tapscott (1996), p. 6. *See infra* Sect. 2.2.2.2.

[2] *See* in this context for example Brynjolfsson and McAfee (2014); Lee (2018); McAfee and Brynjolfsson (2017); Schmidt and Cohen (2013); Schwab (2016).

[3] This trend from tangible towards intangible assets is illustrated by *Fritz Machlup's* compelling analysis of an expanding "*knowledge industry*", cf. Machlup (1962), p. 37.

[4] *See* for a definition of the concept of "*digitisation*" as distinct from "*digitalisation*" *supra* Sect. 1.3. *See* for further explanation of the concept of "*datafication*" *infra* Sect. 2.2.2.1.3.

© The Author(s), under exclusive license to Springer Nature Switzerland AG 2024
R. P. Kalin, *Digital Trade and Data Privacy*, EYIEL Monographs - Studies in European and International Economic Law 38,
https://doi.org/10.1007/978-3-031-73857-9_2

innovations such as Big Data[5] and Artificial Intelligence (AI).[6] Moreover, while automated data processing has been a mainstream phenomenon for quite some time, at the beginning of the twenty-first century, the *"post-industrial"* information age[7] is raised to a new level, unfolding a data driven world of networked intelligence. Ultimately, as a result of a continuously growing data-sphere, a change in quantity has led to a change in quality: *"In the era of big data, more isn't just more. More is different."*.[8]

The following sections provide a brief overview of the key technological and economic determinants of the digital transformation of trade and place them in a historical context. This is intended to provide a deeper insight into the impact of digitalisation on global trade flows. It is this insight, in turn, that will enable a clearer appreciation of the regulatory challenges of digitalisation in the context of global trade law, which will be explored in the following chapters. To this end, this chapter begins by presenting the historical context of the transformative phases of global economic integration and discussing the technological impetus underlying the current economic transformation towards a digital economy (Sect. 2.2). Then, having established the fundamentals of the digital transformation of economic activity, the circumstances of trade in a global digital economy will be examined in more detail (Sect. 2.3).

2.2 Digital Transformation of the Global Economy

This section provides a brief introduction to the transformation of the global economy toward a data-driven digital economy. To this end, it begins by outlining the relationship between technological innovation and global economic integration as a frame of reference for the digital transformation. The second part of this section then centres on this current phase of transformation by outlining the underlying technological parameters on which the digital economy is built, as well as the resulting economic mechanisms.

---

[5]The term *"Big Data"* is usually used vaguely and without consensus on a definition. Generally, it refers to novel insights generated by the exploitation of large amounts of unstructured data, *see* Mayer-Schönberger and Cukier (2014), p. 6: *"Big Data refers to things one can do at a large scale that cannot be done at a smaller one, to extract new insights or create new forms of value, in ways that change markets, organizations, the relationship between citizens and governments, and more."*. *See* also *infra* Sect. 2.2.2.1.3.

[6]Research on the subject of artificial intelligence (AI) has been carried out with moderate success for decades. Only recently researchers succeeded in making essential progress in this area, turning the field an important building block in the advancement of the digital age. *See* further particularly with respect to the technological development of AI Peng et al. (2021), pp. 3–6.

[7]The concept of a *"post-industrial"* age was popularized by Daniel Bell, *see* Bell (2010).

[8]*See* with regard to digital data Bantjes (2008). *See* further *infra* Sect. 2.2.2.1.3.

2.2.1 Transformative Technological Innovations

Reflecting on the immense scale of socio-economic change resulting from the onset of the digital era, reference is made frequently to the Industrial Revolution, which has fundamentally altered the paradigms of the global economic sphere since the end of the eighteenth century.[9] Considering the growth of the global gross domestic product (GDP) as a crude but significant indicator of rising levels of prosperity, a remarkable statistic emerges. Since the late eighteenth century, global growth has accelerated at an unprecedented pace, driven by an avalanche of technological progress. This marked the dawn of the industrial era—a period sometimes referred to as the beginning of global growth.[10] Although these figures are only a very rudimentary indicator in a vast and highly intricate fabric of socio-economic development, they reveal a fundamental correlation between technological progress and progressive global economic integration. The last 250 years are characterised by a unique concentration of historical achievements. In this context, the concept of General-Purpose Technologies (GPT) is helpful to the analysis of the growth-accelerating role of technological innovations.[11] It is these technologies, with their flexible and versatile applications, that play a key role in driving innovation and growth. The concept of GPT suffers a definitional ambiguity, however, a GPT can be characterised as being (1) pervasive—spreading to most sectors, (2) improving over time, and (3) be able to spawn new innovations.[12] Accordingly, widespread consensus exists that, for example, the steam engine, large-scale electrification and Information and Communication Technology (ICT) exhibit GPT characteristics and thus qualify as *"engines of growth"*.[13] In this way, two phases of transformation can be identified as exemplary, illustrating the gradual evolution of global economic structures from an economy of matter to an economy of information.[14]

---

[9] WTO (2018), pp. 16–19.

[10] *See* Manyika et al. (2013), p. 24 for graphical representation of the data provided by the *"Maddison Project"* database *"Statistics on world population, GDP and per capita GDP, 1–2008 AD"*.

[11] *See* for a discussion of the merits of the GPT concept Field (2008).

[12] *See* Jovanovic and Rousseau (2005), pp. 1181–1186. *See* generally Bresnahan and Trajtenberg (1995). Cf. also Bekar et al. (2018), p. 1008. The authors employ a rather comprehensive definition of GPT that lists six key characteristics: (1) Complementarities with a cluster of technologies that define and support it, (2) Complementarities with a cluster of technologies that it enables, (3) Complementarities with a cluster of technologies that typically include those that are socially, politically and economically transformative, (4) No close substitutes, (5) Wide array of applications and (6) Initially crude but evolving in complexity.

[13] Field (2008), p. 9. *See* for a more detailed analysis of ICT development David and Wright (2003).

[14] Certainly, such immense transformations are not easily pinpointed to historical milestones. Rather, the interaction of technological innovation, socioeconomic development and economic globalization forms a historical fabric that can be dissected into different phases depending on the points of reference. For example, the relationship between technological upheaval, the concept of a self-regulating market, and the historical catastrophe of World War II has been identified within the context of a period of transformation, *see* Polanyi (2010).

2.2.1.1 First Transformation: The Economics of Matter

The to date most notable economic transformation was arguably triggered at the beginning of the eighteenth century—when the earliest rudimentary models of the steam engine as the central GPT of the Industrial Revolution have ushered in the age of mechanization. The steam engine and its associated innovations resulted in a significant restructuring not only within domestic economies, but also with regard to the patterns of cross-border trade.[15] Steam-driven technology lowered the cost of transfer of goods and commodities and significantly increased the mobility of people, labour and know-how, thus facilitating the proliferation of novel production techniques and alleviating the often-cited *"tyranny of distance"*. Although the debate about the precise beginning of globalisation will not be taken up here, a convincing argument can be made that modern globalisation was initiated largely by the technology-based transport revolution of the nineteenth century.[16] In retrospect, this phase can be identified as the onset of an accelerating spiral of technological innovation. Subsequent GPTs, driven by advancing mechanisation and the first signs of imminent globalisation, such as the dynamo and large-scale electrification have further accelerated economic integration.[17] Most importantly, the harnessing of electricity enabled communication technologies such as the electric telegraph which disseminated information at previously unimaginable speeds to distant locations. Hence, by decoupling the transmission of information from the transmission of physical records and human beings, communication technology has reduced the distances between vendors and customers like no other technological innovation before.[18] Progressive innovations in communications and transport technologies subsequently created the basis for far-reaching economic integration of the continents and soon the entire globe.

2.2.1.2 Second Transformation: The Economics of Information

Based on the technological impetus of ICT, a further transformative phase is set to begin in the second half of the twentieth century. In 1969, the Organisation for Economic Co-operation and Development (OECD) came to the conclusion: *"the computer can be considered as the key to the second industrial revolution, just as the steam engine was the centre of the first industrial revolution"*.[19] From this perspective, the extent of technological and socioeconomic upheaval in the phase of

---

[15] WTO (2018), pp. 16–19.

[16] Dreher et al. (2008), pp. 5–23; O'Rourke and Williamson (2002), p. 45.

[17] Baldwin (2019), pp. 29–30.

[18] Dreher et al. (2008), p. 8.

[19] OECD (1969), p. 27. The section goes on *"Directly or indirectly, the steam engine paved the way to the industrial society by making large quantities of cheap power available in any geographical location; computers are doing the same thing for another intangible commodity, information"*.

transition from an agrarian to a capital-centric industrial economy provides a benchmark for a new phase of economic transformation.[20] This crucial second socio-economic shift of the industrial era towards a knowledge-based economy has been reflected in a number of different academic disciplines.[21] With regard to the sociological sciences, for example, the decisive change has prompted the notion of a *"post-industrial"* society.[22] Among leading economists, the prevailing sentiment at the time was that the transition from an economy of matter to an economy of information provides the basis for a new kind of transformation in which the production of knowledge serves as the engine of economic growth.[23] It is at this point in time that concept of an *"information economy"* has been coined.[24] While the industrial economy was largely characterised by economic assets such as natural resources, means of production and other capital, in an information economy the economic value of intangibles comes to the fore.[25] Contemporary literature describes tangible and intangible assets as being *"fundamentally different"*, meaning that basic economic properties of intangibles make an intangible-rich economy behave differently from a tangible-rich one.[26] The shift towards an economy of information is deeply intertwined with the overall economic focus on intangible assets and investments in *"Knowledge Based Capital"* (KBC). According to a generally accepted methodology, overall there can be identified three types of KBC: computerised information (software and databases), innovative property (research and development) and economic competencies (brand equity, firm-specific human capital, organisational structure).[27] Investments in KBC and the overall process of value

---

[20] Richard Baldwin identifies a four-step progression of the impact of disruptive technologies: economic transformation, upheaval, backlash and resolution. The author applies this pattern to the disruptive developments of the ICT revolution and forecasts a *"globotic upheaval"*, originating from the synchronisation of automation and globalisation, Baldwin (2019).

[21] *See* for an introduction, Godin (2008), p. 8.

[22] *See* for a concise description, Bell (2010), Forword 1976, XC: *"The concept "post-industrial" is counterposed to that of "pre-industrial" and "industrial". A pre-industrial sector is primarily extractive, its economy is based on agriculture, mining, fishing, timber and other resources such as natural gas or oil. An industrial sector is primarily fabricating, using energy and machine technology, for the manufacture of goods. A post-industrial sector is one of processing in which telecommunications and computer are strategic for the exchange of information and knowledge."*.

[23] In this context, the pioneering work of *Fritz Machlup* merits attention, Machlup (1962), p. 9: *"The production of knowledge is an economic activity, an industry, if you like. Economists have analysed agriculture, mining, iron and steel production, the paper industry, transportation, retailing, the production of all sorts of goods and services, but they have neglected to analyse the production of knowledge."*.

[24] *"An economy can be separated into two domains: The first is involved in the transformation of matter and energy from one form into another. The second is involved in transforming/information from one pattern into another. The two domains are linked and inseparable.[...] The question is the relative contribution of each partner in producing economic wealth."*, Porat (1977), p. 2.

[25] Brynjolfsson and McAfee (2014), pp. 119–121.

[26] Haskel and Westlake (2017), pp. 7–15.

[27] Corrado et al. (2005), pp. 22–30.

creation from knowledge and intangibles is, however, hardly reflected in contemporary measurements such as GDP conceived under an industrial paradigm, in which such expenditures were generally considered only an intermediate expense rather than an investment.[28] A number on influential academic contributions have elaborated on how and if macroeconomic growth can be attributed to the rise of ICT technology.[29] Today, there is little doubt that investments in KBC are a key determinant of economic growth in modern economies.[30]

2.2.2 The Economics of Digital: A Contemporary Transformation

By the beginning of the twenty-first century, a third phase of technology-induced upheaval emerges. While the transition from pre-industrial (*"extractive"*) to industrial (*"fabricative"*) economy stretched over a period of more than a century, the characteristics of the post-industrial information economy combined with a continuous technological advancement have triggered a new phase of transformation. With the turn of the millennium, decades of progress in computer technology, rapidly expanding global connectivity as well as a critical mass of digital data are beginning to fundamentally reshape socio-economic patterns. The categorisation and assessment of this very recent development is inherently ambiguous, as the gradual transition to a *"post-information age"*[31] and the emergence of the digital economy remain to be clearly determined in an ex-post manner. In fact, it cannot be assumed that the broader process of digital transformation has passed its zenith and can thus be the subject of a comprehensive analysis—quite the opposite. Certainly, however, the *"rebirth"* of the computer as a means of communication, the establishment of local networks and their interconnection on a global scale via the Internet Protocol (IP) constitute important building blocks of the dawn of the digital economy.[32] Irrespective of this complexity for contemporary assessments, academic writing on technology-driven transformation identifies the impact of digital technologies on the current economic and societal circumstances as the beginning of a *"Second Machine*

---

[28] Corrado et al. (2009), p. 662.

[29] *See* only Corrado et al. (2005), pp. 11–15. As rising productivity constitutes a crucial driver of economic growth, the early debate on the relevance of intangible assets for growth is frequently associated with a so-called productivity paradox, which was described by US economist *Robert Solow* as follows: *"You can see the computer age everywhere except in the productivity statistics"*, cf. Solow (1987).

[30] OECD (2013a), pp. 26–29.

[31] Negroponte (1996), p. 163.

[32] Abbate (2000), p. 1.

Age",[33] a "*Third Industrial Revolution*"[34] or due to the interaction of physical, digital and biological innovations as the "*Fourth Industrial Revolution*".[35] Academic debate on the current transformative process is characterised by subjective assessments of current trends and is grounded in differing forecasts about the future trajectory of converging technologies, the proliferation of critical infrastructures, the development of new technologies as well as the implications of regulatory governance. However, none of these remaining uncertainties to date should obscure the fact that there exists a consensus that the advent of digital technologies is ushering in a new phase of profound technological, economic, and societal upheaval.[36] The following sections outline three key technological cornerstones of the digital paradigm—exponential technological progress, digital data and expanding networks—that underpin the emergence of a digital economy.[37] These three elements are drawn upon as part of an overview of the resulting economic mechanisms that shape the digital economy. Following this, the resulting economic mechanisms of a digital economy are outlined.

2.2.2.1 Technological Impetus for the Digital Economy

2.2.2.1.1 Exponential Progress

One of the drivers of the rapid pace of current transformation is the exponential progress being made in the development of digital technologies. In accordance with "*Moore's Law*",[38] the evolutionary curve of key components of information and computer technology does not run in a linear progression. For decades now, computer chip density and thus computing power developed exponentially, doubling approximately every 18 months. This led to an astonishing progress, given that

---

[33] Brynjolfsson and McAfee (2014).

[34] Dosi and Galambos (2013).

[35] *See* further Schwab (2016).

[36] In view of differing perceptions, a 2018 background note for the G20 Working Group on Trade and Investment, which compiles the perspectives of various international organisations such as OECD, UNCTAD and WTO, simply suggests the term "*New Industrial Revolution*", *see* OECD (2018).

[37] These three elements are frequently identified as the building blocks of the digital era, *see* for example WTO (2018), pp. 24–28.

[38] The term Moore's Law is based on the statement of the co-founder of the Intel Corporation (at the time head of research and development for Fairchild Semiconductor), Gordon Moore, who in 1965 predicted, that the number of transistors on a semiconductor would double annually, *see* Moore (1965). In the mid-1970s, Moore corrected this forecast to a period of about two years. "*Moore's Law*", however, is not the only "*law*" that shapes the digital era. "*Gilder's Law*", for example, states that bandwidth grows at least three times faster than computing power and according to "*Metcalfe's Law*" the value of a network scales as the square of the number of those connected to it, *see* Wilson (2012).

between 1986 and 2007 alone the computing capacity grew by 58% per year.[39] The characteristic feature of exponential functions consists in the fact that they first seem to progress in a very gradual way, but then, after a threshold has been reached, their progression accelerates and finally ascends almost in a right angle. This kind of seemingly sudden and explosive growth has traditionally challenged the rather linear paradigm of the human mind.[40] In recent decades, Moore's Law has driven the integration of digital technologies into the *"economy of atoms"* and has fostered digital innovation. In fact, some researchers assume that the development of digital technologies is approaching (or has already reached) the critical point of the exponential curve.[41] In the Article coining Moore's Law, Gordon Moore wrote in April of 1965: *"Integrated circuits will lead to such wonders as home computers – or at least terminals connected to a central computer - automatic controls for automobiles, and personal portable communications equipment."*[42] In fact, since these words were written, computing devices have become ever more powerful—regularly doubling in processor power, halving in cost while reducing in size. Today, the processor power of former supercomputers is integrated in millions of devices that fit in the palm of the hand, building economic potential in the hands of people in both developed and developing economies. The technological impulse of exponential progress therefore derives not only from increasing performance, but also from the fact that smaller, more effective, and less expensive devices promote digital integration on a global scale. Stakeholders often predicted the end of Moore's Law due to, for example, physical limitations to placing transistors on a semiconductor.[43] However, many experts estimate that it is unlikely that exponential innovation in computing power itself will come to end. Rather, progress will move on to a different form of computing such as quantum-, 3D-, or DNA computing.[44]

---

[39] Hilbert and López (2011), pp. 63–65.

[40] The problem of grasping the underlying mathematical implications of exponential growth is famously described by an old fable about the invention of the chessboard in which the inventor demands as reward one grain of rice on the first square of the chessboard, then two on the next, adding up to 2^{64} grains of rice. Kurzweil (2001) describes this as follows: *"By the end of the first half of the chess board, the inventor had accumulated one large field's worth (4 billion grains), and the emperor did start to take notice. It was as they progressed through the second half of the chessboard that the situation quickly deteriorated."*.

[41] Brynjolfsson and McAfee (2014), pp. 45–47. In reference to the analogy to the chessboard (*see* fn. above), *Erik Brynjolfsson* and *Andrew McAfee* point out that starting in 1958 (the first time the U.S. Bureau of Economic Analysis noted *"information technology"* as a distinct corporate investment category) exponential growth of processing power would have reached the second half of the chessboard (32 doublings) in 2006.

[42] Moore (1965), p. 114.

[43] For example, *see* Simonite (2016).

[44] *See* for example McBride (2019).

2.2.2.1.2 Connectivity

Expanding connectivity is another important technological impetus for the digital era. Connectivity is a crucial contributor to the realisation of a data-driven economy, which is highly dependent on fast and cost-effective transmission of digital data. Modern ICT, and in particular the Internet, have emerged as crucial General-Purpose Technologies (GPT) fuelling a rapidly evolving digital environment promoting development, innovation and inclusion.[45] While it is difficult to fully grasp the multifaceted impact of the Internet as a decisive driver of socio-economic development of our time, its underlying technology can roughly be described as follows: *"The Internet is the global data communication capability realized by the interconnection of public and private telecommunication networks using Internet Protocol (IP), Transmission Control Protocol (TCP), and the other protocols required to implement IP internetworking on a global scale, such as DNS and packet routing protocols."*.[46] While only 5.9% of the world's population had access to the Internet in 2000, the figure has risen to an estimated 34.3% by 2012.[47] Internet penetration in the US, for example, more than doubled from 33.8% to 78.1% between 2000 and 2012 as measured by the share of Internet users in the total population, while in China's emerging economy Internet penetration has risen from 1.8% to 40.1%.[48] Increasing global connectivity is also reflected in the numbers of fixed and mobile broadband subscriptions, which have rapidly proliferated in recent years. The number of fixed broadband subscriptions worldwide has increased from 531.8 million in 2010 to 916.7 million in 2016, while mobile broadband growth has far exceeded that, with global subscriptions rising from 824.5 million in 2010 to 3864 million in 2016.[49] Internet access via ever more affordable mobile devices has become a crucial economic factor in particular for developing countries.[50] In fact, for developing and least developed countries (LDCs) expanding digital connectivity via the Internet often provides for a level playing field and even the possibility to leapfrog developed economies in individual sectors.[51] In this context, some

---

[45] World Bank Group (2016), pp. 42–46. *See* further Clarke et al. (2015); Manyika et al. (2013), pp. 24–28; OECD (2013b), pp. 9–12.

[46] *See* Mueller et al. (2007), p. 244. There is another frequently cited definition adopted by the U.S. Federal Networking Council (FNC): *""Internet" refers to the global information system that -- (i) is logically linked together by a globally unique address space based on the Internet Protocol (IP) or its subsequent extensions/follow-ons; (ii) is able to support communications using the Transmission Control Protocol/Internet Protocol (TCP/IP) suite or its subsequent extensions/follow-ons, and/or other IP-compatible protocols; and (iii) provides, uses or makes accessible, either publicly or privately, high level services layered on the communications and related infrastructure described herein."*, FNC (1995). Internet Society (2015).

[47] United States International Trade Commission (2013), pp. 1–9.

[48] United States International Trade Commission (2013), pp. 1–9.

[49] OECD (2017b), p. 18.

[50] UNCTAD (2015a), pp. 34–43.

[51] World Bank Group (2016), pp. 42–46.

observers are even confident that *"there has never been any technology or innovation in human history that comes close in speed of adoption, significance and impact"*.[52] In addition to facilitating communication and enabling the exchange of data and information, an important feature of increasing connectivity is its role in fostering innovation. After all, innovations are rarely the result of an ingenious idea that creates a previously unknown solution to a specific problem. Such development typically arises from the creative composition of established solutions: *"the carrying out of new combinations"*.[53] The *"open source"*[54] culture of the Internet and the phenomenon of the *"crowd"*,[55] the harnessing of interconnectivity to integrate diverse abilities and skills of a global userbase, are prominent examples of this. In this sense the success of the Internet and the economy that relies on its infrastructure for some observers is based on *"permissionless innovation"*.[56]

2.2.2.1.3 Digital Data

Data, the information to be extracted from it and the knowledge thus obtained have long determined the course of human history.[57] In fact, capturing *"given circumstances"* using graphic symbols and characters for subsequent processing, analysis and transmission marks a major achievement of early cultures, reaching its prime in the eighteenth century with the flourishing of the sciences.[58] Depending on the specific reference points and subject matters, there are a variety of definitions for the concept of data. In an economic context, the OECD defines data as

---

[52] Tapscott (1996), p. 17.

[53] Schumpeter (1949), pp. 65–74. Such *"combinatorial innovation"* is not a new phenomenon of the digital era, it is a pattern that has already been observed in previous transformational phases and has recently been described in connection with the Internet as follows *"Every now and then a technology, or set of technologies, comes along that offers a rich set of components that can be combined and recombined to create new products. The arrival of these components then sets off a technology boom as innovators work through the possibilities."*, cf. Varian (2004), pp. 1–48.

[54] *"Open Source"* in this context means that the source code of a piece of software is open and freely accessible.

[55] McAfee and Brynjolfsson (2017), p. 231. The authors define the *"crowd"* as new participants and practices enabled by the net and its attendant technologies.

[56] Thierer (2014), p. 3 defines permissionless innovation as *"the tinkering and continuous exploration that takes place at multiple levels—from professional designers to amateur coders; from big content creators to dorm-room bloggers; from nationwide communications and broadband infrastructure providers to small community network-builders."*.

[57] The terms data, information and knowledge are usually put into precisely this sequence within the context of epistemology, cf. Casalini and López González (2019), p. 11.

[58] In this particular context Lord Kelvin may be quoted: *"I often say that when you can measure what you are speaking about, and express it in numbers, you know something about it; but when you cannot measure it, when you cannot express it in numbers, your knowledge is of a meagre and unsatisfactory kind[...]"*, William Thomson (1891), p. 73. From here it was only a short way to management theory's influential author *Peter Ducker's* quote: *"What you can't measure, you can't manage"*.

2.2 Digital Transformation of the Global Economy

"representation of facts stored or transmitted as qualified or quantified symbols".[59] Since the second half of the twentieth century, the collection and processing of such representation of facts has been revolutionised by the proliferation of ICT. Under the digital paradigm, once digitised, information of any kind can be represented in a universal manner and can be stored, filtered, processed, duplicated and transmitted (theoretically) in real time. The productivity gains resulting from the ICT-supported processing of extensive sets of data have popularised the conversion of analogue information into machine-readable form and the codification of pieces of information into digital *"bits"*—known as *"digitisation"*.[60] The gravitational pull of the resulting enticements of an *"economy of bits"* combined with the expanding capacity of digital technology translated into an accelerated digitisation of texts, images and media files.[61] Telecommunications have thus been dominated by digital technologies since 1990 (99.9% digital in 2007), and the majority of technological storage has been stored in digital form since the early 2000s (94% digital in 2007).[62] The observation that the amount of available information is constantly increasing has led contemporary analyses to proclaim a veritable *"explosion"* of data and information.[63] According to a study by the International Data Corporation (IDC), this trend will continue and the global data sphere will increase from 33 zettabytes in 2018 to 175 zettabytes in 2025.[64] The impact of data-driven business models and the uptake of the digital economy has given greater prominence to the economic characteristics of data.[65] Plummeting costs of data storage and the increasing technical capacity to analyse and *"mine"* these datasets for hidden value have led to a change of perspective. Instead of collecting data and discarding it after it has fulfilled its initial purpose, the *"option value"* of reusing and recombining data has gained widespread attention.[66] The economic benefit of gaining insights through correlations, revealed by the analysis of large amounts of data, has popularised the *"datafication"* of *"real world"* phenomena.[67] In this context, the developments of ICT combined with a shift in awareness concerning a hidden value of data fosters the

---

[59] OECD (2015c), p. 449.

[60] *See* only Capgemini Consulting (2012), p. 7. *See supra* Sect. 1.3 for an explanation of the scopes of *"digitisation"* used in this context, in particular in distinction to what is referred to as the process of *"digitalisation"*.

[61] Tapscott (1996), pp. 96–97.

[62] Hilbert and López (2011), p. 63.

[63] Cukier (2010); World Bank Group (2016), p. 244.

[64] Reinsel et al. (2018), p. 3. One zettabyte corresponds to 10 to the power of 21 bytes, 1000 exabytes or one billion terabytes.

[65] This is a dynamic field of research which can only be presented here in the broad outlines required for a legal assessment, *see* for example Carrière-Swallow and Haksar (2019), pp. 13–19. *See* further Jones and Tonetti (2020); MIT Technology Review (2016).

[66] Mayer-Schönberger and Cukier (2014), pp. 102–104.

[67] *Viktor Mayer-Schönberger* and *Kenneth Cukier* describe *"datafication"* as putting a phenomenon in a *"quantified format so it can be tabulated and analysed"*, Mayer-Schönberger and Cukier (2014), p. 78. This marks a clear demarcation from *"digitisation"* as the mere fact of transforming

"*unearthing [of] data from material that no one thought held any value*".[68] This way, today every circumstantial aspect is captured in digital data in order to generate value from it at a later—often yet unknown—point in time. Thus, machines are increasingly learning to "*see*", "*hear*" and "*feel*" via digital sensors.[69] Digital infrastructure such as "*smart*" devices and interfaces are integrated as independently working entities which are "*talking*" via Machine to machine (M2M) communication[70] in particular in the context of the so-called Internet of Things (IoT).[71] In similar vein, the ubiquitous digital exchange in the context of modern networking contributes to a growing wealth of data.[72] This abundance of data in the digital era is commonly referred to as Big Data.[73] In a more functional sense, Big Data has been described as the "*ability of society to harness information in novel ways to produce useful insights or goods and services of significant value*".[74] Big Data as a tool unsettles the well-established process of the constitution of knowledge.[75] The perceived reliability of causality in a "*Small Data*" world is abandoned in favour of new insights through the correlations gained by the processing of huge amounts of data in a "*Big Data*" world.[76]

2.2.2.2 The Economics of Bits and Networks: The Digital Economy

By the beginning of the twenty-first century, the exponential progress of digital technologies according to Moore's Law, the sheer quantity of data and an expanding digital connectivity enable qualitatively novel innovations that shake the foundations of the incumbent industrial economy. While there is no uniform definition for the

---

analogue information into a computer-readable format, Mayer-Schönberger and Cukier (2014), p. 83.
[68] Mayer-Schönberger and Cukier (2014), p. 76, p. 83. *See* also Lycett (2013), p. 382.
[69] Brynjolfsson and McAfee (2014), pp. 50–51.
[70] Cf. for a definition Boswarthick et al. (2012), p. 2: "*The role of M2M is to establish the conditions that allow a device to (bidirectionally) exchange information with a business application via a communication network, so that the device and/or application can act as the basis for this information exchange.*".
[71] OECD (2017b), p. 19.
[72] In this context, the term "*data exhaust*" has emerged for the digital trace that people leave and the data that is lost in the word as a by-product of people's actions and movements, Mayer-Schönberger and Cukier (2014), pp. 113–116.
[73] For an overview of Big Data techniques and technologies, cf. Manyika et al. (2011), pp. 27–36. However, some commentators emphasize that the observation of an abundance of data tends to obscure the fact that there is actually a scarcity of relevant data MIT Technology Review (2016), p. 3. *See* regarding the difference between AI and Big Data Peng et al. (2021), pp. 6–8.
[74] Mayer-Schönberger and Cukier (2014), p. 7. *See* also Boyd and Crawford (2012), p. 663.
[75] Boyd and Crawford (2012), p. 665; Cukier (2010).
[76] In view of these paradigmatic shifts, some have already declared the end of the theory, *see* Anderson (2008). This, however, probably proves to be premature, *see* Boyd and Crawford (2012), p. 666; Mayer-Schönberger and Cukier (2014), pp. 70–72.

digital economy, in 1999 the Assistant to the U.S. President for Science and Technology provided a comprehensive description: *"The digital economy is driven by a convergence of information, computing and communications, which we have come to call the Internet. This convergence is responsible for the widespread growth of electronic commerce, new competitive strategies, and changes in business processes and organizational structure. It is enabling new networked forms of activity that are neither markets nor hierarchies but based on relationships"*.[77] Against this background, it can be argued that the digital economy is characterised by the *"application of internet-based digital technologies to the production and trade of goods and services"*.[78] In the following, several key characteristics of the digital economy are outlined.

2.2.2.2.1 "Every Company Is Now a Tech Company"

While added value in the industrial economy was primarily bound to capital and tangible values—in the digital economy, it is decisively intangibles, the combination and recombination of which forms a basis for innovative products and services. This in turn means that companies no longer need the same amount of capital in the form of machines, production materials or workforce as in an industrial economy in order to be economically successful. The underlying mechanisms of an *"economy of bits"* enable the scaling of enterprises from the very beginning by concentrating on value creation through intangibles and digital data.[79] For example, modern Cloud Computing services enable small businesses to tap into computing power, software or storage capacity remotely, thus enabling them to achieve growth with little proprietary infrastructure.[80] Moreover, digital products can be duplicated *"free, perfect and instant"*, reducing the so-called marginal costs incurred in the process of reproduction to virtually zero.[81] This way, the relevance of knowledge-based capital (KBC) and the underlying progressive transition from the processing of industrial goods to the processing of data and information has been turbocharged by digital technologies. This paradigm shift of the digital era was aptly described under the

---

[77] Lane (1999), p. 317. *See* for further references and an account of the many definitions established to date OECD (2020), pp. 34–47; Willemyns (2021), pp. 47–51. Similarly, the term *"Internet Economy"* has been used by the OECD to underscore the significance of the Internet as a critical economic infrastructure of the *"new"* economy, *see* for example OECD (2013b), pp. 6–7. *See* also OECD (2008).

[78] UNCTAD (2017a), p. 156.

[79] Hofheinz and Mandel (2015), p. 4; OECD (2019b), p. 17. Economies of scale are not a unique feature of the digital economy. Rather, they have driven the industrial economy before, for example, in the case of mass production. Yet, digital business models tend to scale *"without mass"*, *see* Brynjolfsson et al. (2008), p. 23.

[80] United States International Trade Commission (2013), pp. 2–31.

[81] Brynjolfsson and McAfee (2014), pp. 61–63.

heading of *"Why Software is eating the world"*.[82] However, the *"digital"* economy cannot be clearly delineated from a *"traditional"* economy. Rather than constituting an emerging sector, the effect of the digital paradigm is a cross-cutting one that is transforming the economy as a whole. The economic principles of the digital paradigm contribute to a blurring of tangible and intangible value creation.[83] In fact, digital technologies, the expansion of interconnectivity and the increase in the accumulation of intangible assets are drivers of convergence.[84] Consequently, commentators have observed that *"every company is now tech company"*.[85]

2.2.2.2.2 The Role of Digital Data

In a digital economy, digital data is crucial for improving existing products and business processes, but also for developing new goods and services. Data is thus enhancing and enabling business models in all industries.[86] Hence, data in particular has become a decisive economic asset, creating *"data capital"*.[87] Modern ICT and in particular the Internet have a profound impact on internal and external communications and the way businesses organise and manage information flows, hence improving business processes and productivity. Yet, the link between the proliferation of data in the economy and economic growth is still controversial.[88] A 2011 McKinsey Global Institute Report estimated that the added value of networking via the Internet is mainly due to efficiency and productivity gains in traditional industries.[89] However, an intangible rich economy raises the issue that the statistical methodologies currently in use do not adequately capture its economic impact. Specifically, GDP as a measure for production does not adequately account for welfare gains from digital products.[90] This is a particular concern with regard to *"free"* products and services

---

[82] Andreessen (2011) has stated in this context: *"Six decades into the computer revolution, four decades since the invention of the microprocessor, and two decades into the rise of the modern Internet, all of the technology required to transform industries through software finally works and can be widely delivered at global scale."*.

[83] OECD (2019b), p. 17.

[84] Burri (2017a), p. 6.

[85] Mims (2018).

[86] Nguyen and Paczos (2020), pp. 10–12. On p. 5 the report explains: *"[...] data-enabled businesses are companies that have developed revenue generation strategies fully reliant on data and that would not exist without access to large amounts of data and advanced data analytics. On the other hand, data-enhanced businesses exploit data to better coordinate pre-existing business operations, facilitate decision-making and to introduce new goods and services; data does not alter or determine their core business models."*.

[87] MIT Technology Review (2016), p. 1.

[88] Carrière-Swallow and Haksar (2019), pp. 19–29 summarize the current state of research in this context.

[89] Pélissié du Rausas et al. (2011), p. 22.

[90] Brynjolfsson and McAfee (2014), pp. 107–124; IMF (2018).

2.2 Digital Transformation of the Global Economy

within a data-driven economy, which are based on the premise that consumers share their data in order to use them.[91] Against this background, the economic value of data is difficult to determine.[92] Data itself has no inherent meaning, is often unstructured and thus is frequently depicted to represent a *"raw material"*. Moreover, data both serves as a means of production akin to an economic good as well as in creating and shifting information across economic agents.[93] Data is non-fungible, in other words, it cannot be substituted like a load of gravel, for example, and it is also an experience item, the value of which only becomes apparent once it has been harnessed.[94] However, probably the most important consideration in this context is, that digital data is not depleted like material resources and assets. Instead, digital data is a non-rivalrous intangible asset that can be repeatedly used, combined and recombined.[95] In its essence, data is different.[96] In view of this amalgamation of economic characteristics, academic literature suggests that the value of data is not measured by the price others are willing to pay, but by the processing and analytical capacity of the data controller to proactively predict behaviour.[97] This evaluation implies that the quality of a dataset is a critical factor in determining its economic value. As a result, the OECD identifies several characteristics of data that make them particularly amenable to value creation. According to this, data can provide a basis for monetization if it is scarce, timely, linkable, and trustworthy.[98]

2.2.2.2.3 Data-Driven Innovation

Overall, the digital economy is characterised by the rise of data-driven innovation.[99] The macro-economic change fostered by digital innovation can be exemplified by the emergence of different facets of a digital economy. In a *"sharing economy"*, the collective use of assets such as cars and real estate changes the way in which economic benefits are derived from assets.[100] In an *"app economy"*, economic activity builds around mobile applications extending further the communication potential of the Internet, providing a source of dynamic innovation.[101] In a *"platform*

---

[91] *See* with regard to cross-border data flows *infra* Sect. 2.3.2.3.
[92] Cf. for a review of approaches to measuring the economic value of data Nguyen and Paczos (2020), pp. 32–36.
[93] Carrière-Swallow and Haksar (2019), pp. 9–19.
[94] MIT Technology Review (2016), p. 4.
[95] Carrière-Swallow and Haksar (2019), pp. 13–14; Jones and Tonetti (2020), p. 2820; Mandel (2017), p. 4; MIT Technology Review (2016), p. 4.
[96] Pistor (2020), p. 106. *See* also with regard to regulatory implications Aaronson (2021).
[97] Pistor (2020), pp. 104–111.
[98] *See* Nguyen and Paczos (2020), pp. 20–21.
[99] OECD (2015c), pp. 22–32.
[100] OECD (2019b), p. 19; The Economist (2013).
[101] OECD (2013c).

economy" new "*interactions between two or more distinct but interdependent sets of users (whether firms or individuals) who interact through the service via the Internet*" introduce new forms of collaboration.[102] As intermediaries, platforms today are characterised by a powerful pervasiveness, organising markets and industries.[103] Overall, digital technologies and the Internet shape economic activity by reducing specific costs for search, reproduction, transportation, tracking, and verification.[104] The contrast between digital and industrial business models has been described quite succinctly as follows: "*The world's largest taxi firm, Uber, owns no cars. The world's most popular media company, Facebook, creates no content. The world's most valuable retailer, Alibaba, carries no stock. And the world's largest accommodation provider, Airbnb, owns no property.*".[105] In this way, the digital economy is characterised by an extraordinary market innovation.[106] By redesigning and innovating on industries and business models, the market capitalisation of some early adopters of the digital era has quickly surpassed that of the corporate giants of the industrial age. A pioneering role in adapting to the new digital paradigm has enabled technology and information-based companies that are "*born digital*" such as Amazon, Alphabet, Meta, Alibaba and Tencent to grow at an unprecedented speed. It is worth noting, that in 2008 none of these companies were in the top 5 list of the largest companies.[107] On the back of the economic mechanisms of the digital economy, these "*superstar*"[108] companies have created an almost monopoly-like position for themselves—benefiting from the emergence of far-reaching network effects[109] underpinning the increase of winner-take-all or winner-take-most markets.[110] Moreover, the holistic impact of a digital paradigm is highlighted by the rise of corporate ecosystems, characterised by their cross-sectoral ventures that transcend industry boundaries and significantly reshape patterns of economic operation.[111] At the same time decentralised innovation via digital networks takes shape—commonly referred to as the "*crowd*".

---

[102] OECD (2019c), pp. 20–21.

[103] Kenney et al. (2021), pp. 38–40.

[104] Goldfarb and Tucker (2017), pp. 6–15.

[105] McRae (2015).

[106] Lane (1999), p. 319.

[107] Johnston (2018).

[108] *See* further Ayyagari et al. (2018).

[109] Brynjolfsson and McAfee (2014), p. 60. The term "*network effect*" describes the fact that a network has a greater value for a user with increasing participation of other users in the same network. Classic examples are social media services and AppStores or so-called platform companies such as AirBnB and Uber.

[110] McAfee and Brynjolfsson (2017), pp. 211–218.

[111] Atluri et al. (2018), pp. 8–11; United States International Trade Commission (2013), pp. 2–3.

2.2.2.2.4 Digital Globalisation

Historical evidence indicates that technological innovations have triggered distinct phases of progressive global economic integration (*see supra* Sect. 2.2.1). Economic globalisation, defined as *"the integration of economic activities across borders through markets"* is primarily driven by reduction in costs for transportation and communication as well as economic liberalisation.[112] Modern globalisation can be attributed to the technological momentum of the steam engine as the decisive GPT of the industrial era and its complementary innovations that resulted in a transport revolution in the nineteenth century (*see supra* Sect. 2.2.1.1). The impulse of ICT, in turn, significantly improved communication and coordination of global economic flows and offered possibilities of effective management of production over distance, resulting in Global Value Chains (GVCs). Both of these phases can be recognised as phases of *"unbundling"* global production.[113] Today, the digital transformation of domestic economies and economic stakeholders on the basis of Internet innovations are triggering a new phase of economic integration, which can be described as digital globalisation.[114] Propelled by the digital transformation, the current state of the global economy is both highly dynamic and highly data-driven. Digitalisation is exerting a profound and widespread impact on global economic flows.[115] Cross-border economic activity and international trade are increasingly undergirded by data. Global economic growth is organised, accompanied and accomplished by cross-border data flows. In a data-driven environment more and more industries depend on digital technologies and data flows, the economic significance of which is steadily exacerbated by new forms of competitive advantages arising from the use, the collection and the systematic analysis of business, production and customer data.[116] The rise of so-called *"born digital"* and *"born global"* companies, the increasing significance of digital services and more generally the growing reliance on intangibles in GVCs bear witness towards a nexus of digital technology, cross-border data flows and economic integration.[117] The very architecture of the Internet and its underlying infrastructure, result in a globalisation of data transfers. The Internet Protocol (IP), which serves as the backbone of the World Wide Web, is designed in such a way that information is emitted in individual *"packets"* from the sender, routed through the decentralised *"network of networks"*, and then assembled

---

[112] Wolf (2005), p. 14, p. 19.

[113] Baldwin (2011); WTO (2018), pp. 16–19.

[114] *See* for example Manyika et al. (2016), pp. 23–43; Negroponte (1996), pp. 165–167; Tapscott (1996), pp. 64–66.

[115] Lund and Manyika (2016), p. 2 identify three distinct ways digital technologies transform globalisation: (1) The proliferation of digital goods such as books and movies that can be delivered cost-effectively at a global scale; (2) *"Digital wrappers"* around traditional products such as sensors that enable other types of flows; (3) The emergence of online platforms for production, exchange and consumption. *See also* Manyika et al. (2016), pp. 33–41.

[116] Castro and McQuinn (2015), pp. 2–8; OECD (2015c), pp. 71–91.

[117] Lund et al. (2019), pp. 5–9, pp. 14–17.

at the address of the recipient according to the predetermined sequence.[118] In this way, different parts of an information, such as an e-mail sent by a sender in New York, can pass through a number of nodes in different countries before reaching a recipient in Frankfurt. In this sense, boundaries between local and global economic activity on the Internet are blurred and sometimes seemingly local activities on the net are technically cross-border in nature. Thus, as value creation in the digital economy is no longer limited by geographical distance, but increasingly takes place in the digital realm, digital added value tends to be inherently global in nature.[119] Hence, a third *"unbundling"* by means of digitally enabled flows is based on a further reduction of transport and coordination costs as well as the facilitation of the sharing of knowledge and ideas on the basis of data and information flows.[120] Following from this global character of the Internet, a clear demarcation between domestic and international economic activity tends to dissolve, as economic globalisation in the digital era could be defined as an *"inexorable integration of markets, nation-states and technologies to a degree never witnessed before"*.[121] This is a trend that has continued to gain momentum during the COVID-19 pandemic and is expected to continue in the post-pandemic phase of globalisation.[122]

2.3 International Trade in the Digital Economy

The economic characteristics of an inherently global digital economy provide the backdrop for a transforming environment for trade in the digital era. Above, it has been underscored that the Internet can be included in the catalogue of critical GPTs propelling innovation, global economic integration and fostering cross-border trade (*see supra* Sect. 2.2.2). As a matter of fact, in appreciation of its inherently global architecture, the Internet has been characterised as being "*[...] as much a trade pact as an invention*".[123] Certainly, the perception that the Internet is an important platform for all kinds of cross-border cooperation, thus also promoting economic integration and trade, is now widespread.[124] The concrete circumstances of the emergent nexus between digital technologies and international trade, however, are

---

[118] *See* also the explanation at Ashton-Hart (2016), pp. 140–142; Casalini and López González (2019), pp. 10–11.

[119] Ashton-Hart (2016), pp. 133–138. However, the Internet is not a fully global phenomenon, *see* Manyika et al. (2016), pp. 39–41.

[120] López González and Jouanjean (2017), p. 7.

[121] Friedman (2000), p. 9. Consequently, the transformation initiated by the disruptive force of technological innovation leads some to proclaim globalisation 4.0, cf. World Economic Forum (2019).

[122] McNamara and Newman (2020), pp. E71–E73.

[123] The Economist (2010).

[124] *See* with further references OECD (2015a), pp. 35–42.

inherently complex and the subject of a number of contemporary reports and studies.[125] As in other matters of foreign relations it is clear that the inherent global nature of a digital economy is by and large amplifying the ties between national economies.[126] The Internet, is introducing novel dimensions to cross-border economic activity, thus accelerating the process of global integration and shifting the patterns of global flows of goods, services, finance and information.[127] Digital innovations such as e-books, video streaming, software applications, Cloud Computing services, but also novel production processes such as 3D printing ("*additive manufacturing*") are gradually shifting cross-border economic activity from tangible routes to digital networks.[128] Hence, a wide range of products can be provided due to the increasing density of digital networking; products such as films, music, books and software are no longer imported in their physical form but made available via the Internet.[129] Goods that had to be packed, shipped, customs cleared at the border and eventually delivered to the end consumer are now digitally downloaded; services are digitally delivered to the customer upon online payment.[130] As these examples underscore, trade in the digital economy is organised, accompanied and accomplished by data transfers. Cross-border data flows via the Internet have emerged as a "*connective tissue*" that coheres communication, cooperation, and economic activity on a global scale.[131] While a detailed analysis of this transformation of trade in the digital economy would go beyond the scope of this book, in the following there will be provided a brief overview of some decisive vectors of the structural shifts in global trade. A second section then goes on to analyse the Internet and cross-border data flows as a medium of transformation towards a digitally globalised economy.

2.3.1 *Vectors of Digital Transformation of Global Trade*

Drawing on the technological foundations of the global digital economy outlined above (*see supra* Sect. 2.2.2), several vectors can be identified that contribute to the

---

[125] López González and Ferencz (2018); ICC (2016); Lund et al. (2019); Meltzer (2014a); United States International Trade Commission (2017); WTO (2018).

[126] Goldsmith and Wu (2006), pp. 147–177.

[127] Burri (2017a); Meltzer (2015); WTO (2018), pp. 19–20.

[128] 3D-printing is a prime example of emerging data-, and service-centric dimensions in international trade. While the printing instructions can be made available digitally via the Internet, a tangible product can be generated on the recipient side thus shortening or potentially entirely bypassing current value chains. See Fan and Meixner (2020); WTO (2018), pp. 93–95.

[129] In 2016 the value of imports of digitisable goods by WTO Members (not accounting for EU-intra trade), constituted around 0.8% of total imports, plummeting from 2.86% in 2000, WTO (2018), pp. 92–93.

[130] International Trade Centre (2016), pp. 43–44.

[131] Lund and Tyson (2018).

contemporary digital transformation of international trade.[132] The vectors listed below have been selected to provide a general illustration of emerging trends with regard to trade patterns in the digital economy.

2.3.1.1 Reduction of Trade Costs

A common denominator shared by technological innovations that have significantly shaped international trade is the reduction of costs for trade. Trading costs include all costs incurred in bringing a product to a final consumer, with the exception of the marginal costs of manufacturing the product itself.[133] The cost of trading goods and services can thus generally be broken down into five components: transport costs, logistic costs, cost of crossing borders, information and transaction costs as well as costs due to political barriers (tariff and non-tariff).[134] It has been shown that connectivity via the Internet is an essential factor in reducing trade costs and has a positive impact on trade overall.[135]

Firstly, digital technologies particularly reduce the cost of acquiring information and thus promote the initiation and processing of transactions. In recent years, it has become increasingly apparent that information friction is at least as important in determining trade flows as the cost of transport.[136] As global networks and the Internet permeate every aspect of the economy, the frictional losses in the coordination of cross-border trade are steadily diminishing.[137] Using various measures of information asymmetries at the product and country level, it has been established that a difference in distance effects is due to online technologies that reduce information and trust frictions associated with geographic distance.[138] The emergence of a *"platform economy"* is a prime example of the stimulating impact of digital innovation, enhanced communication and increased transparency on international trade. Online platform businesses facilitate market access for new participants, simplify cross-border communication and, most importantly, reduce search costs by

---

[132] Cf. for example Burri (2017a), pp. 9–14; López González and Ferencz (2018), pp. 9–12.

[133] Anderson and van Wincoop (2004), p. 691.

[134] Anderson and van Wincoop (2004), p. 691; WTO (2018), pp. 64–66.

[135] Freund and Weinhold (2004), p. 178. According to the econometric model of the USITC, the Internet significantly reduces trade costs of US imports and exports in digitally intensive sectors by about 26% on average, United States International Trade Commission (2014), pp. 65–66. *See* also with further information Riker (2014), pp. 3–4.

[136] Allen (2014); WTO (2018), p. 64. In trade in services, information and transaction costs are the most important trade barriers, accounting for 30% of the total trade costs variation, WTO (2018), p. 65.

[137] Terzi (2011), pp. 747–748.

[138] Lendle et al. (2012), p. 19. Using a dataset on eBay cross-border transactions and comparable offline trade flows, the authors estimated a distance effect on trade flows about 65% smaller online than offline. However, physical distance is likely to reduce trade even in online products and services that are essentially free of trade costs, *see* further Blum and Goldfarb (2006).

mediating sellers and buyers in many sectors of the economy.[139] Platforms thus either create value by reducing search frictions in multi-sided markets and consequently bringing people with matching interests together or by providing a basis for collaboration and complementary innovation.[140] Online platforms promote international trade not only by acting as multinationals themselves, but also by helping other companies to expand into foreign markets, thus improving supply and accessibility of services and goods.[141] Hence, digital platforms are creating more efficient and transparent global markets.[142]

Secondly, digitalisation significantly lowers market entry thresholds to the benefit of a variety of economic actors, allowing for a more accessible export market.[143] Hence, connectivity via the Internet opens up new markets and creates potential for previously spatially constrained businesses and stakeholders in particular with regard to developing countries.[144] As an example of innovative ICT-based value creation culture, the rise and success of the so-called *"micro-multinationals"* is particularly worth emphasising in this context.[145] These are highly innovative micro-enterprises and SMEs that are reaching a global audience in B2B and B2C businesses through the proliferation of global networks and the Internet.[146] By utilising the infrastructure of established e-commerce platforms, they are successfully positioning themselves in a highly competitive global market.[147] This way, many companies today are *"born global"*.[148]

Thirdly, digital technologies have the potential to be a decisive factor in trade facilitation, reducing the costs of crossing borders.[149] In this sense, the digitisation of customs information, electronic documentation, automatic electronic payment, and the effective use of digital technologies to facilitate cross-border processing are

---

[139] Lund and Manyika (2016), p. 5; UNCTAD (2017c), pp. 53–55.

[140] Evans and Gawer (2016), pp. 5–6.

[141] OECD (2019c), pp. 28–32.

[142] *See* further Manyika et al. (2016), p. 32.

[143] A 2011 McKinsey & Co. survey of more than 4800 SMEs in 12 countries showed that on average, companies using Internet with a high intensity grow twice as quickly as low-web-intensity companies, export twice as much as they do, and create more than twice as many jobs, cf. Lund and Manyika (2016), p. 8; Pélissié du Rausas et al. (2011), pp. 17–18.

[144] *See* for example Meltzer (2014a). The strengthening of SMEs, for example in LDCs, is, however, counterbalanced by the growing competitive advantage of the developed nations, which, due to advancing technological development, can rarely be compensated for by economically underdeveloped regions and therefore requires strategic political intervention, *see* UNCTAD (2017b), p. 17.

[145] Varian (2005); Manyika et al. (2016), pp. 43–44.

[146] Hofheinz and Mandel (2015), pp. 4–5; Meltzer (2014a), pp. 5–7.

[147] Vézina and Melin (2013).

[148] Lund and Manyika (2016), p. 8; OECD (2017a), pp. 27–28.

[149] WTO Members have refrained from formally defining the term *"trade facilitation"*, both because of the inability to agree on the delimitation and because of the desire not to exclude aspects of future work. It can be, however, broadly described as *"the simplification, modernization, and harmonization of export and import processes"*, WTO (2015), pp. 34–36.

crucial facilitators of trade. Innovations such as paperless trading[150] are significantly promoting transparency and facilitating GVCs, creating economy-wide savings.[151]

Finally, digital technologies are cutting down transportation costs and time incurred in getting goods and services from the supplier to the buyer. In goods trading, for example, AI technology improves better supply chain management as it enables autonomous transport and route planning in real time, reducing time delays and uncertainties and improving logistics through optimised freight and tracking systems.[152] Moreover, the delivery of digital products via the Internet means also that transportation costs are quasi eliminated.[153]

2.3.1.2 Increasing Significance of Service Trade

Services are increasingly at the centre of economic activity due to a continuous structural shift of the global economy.[154] This change is based on a technology- and innovation-driven reallocation of labour, which enables a shift in economic focus from manufacturing activities to the service sector.[155] It is widely recognised that the proliferation of ICT as a driver for the processing of intangible assets over distance has a crucial impact on trade in services.[156] In fact, ICT and in particular the Internet have been described as electronic *"Silk Road"*—making *"possible trade in services heretofore impossible in human history"*.[157] As a result, patterns of international trade are transforming, allowing, for example, business service suppliers in developing countries to participate in Western markets despite barriers to immigration, and permitting companies to reach a global audience—often tariff-free.[158] Hence, trade in services no longer serves merely to support the movement of goods, as with financial or logistics services, for example. The digital economy is yielding increasingly intricate service activities that can be delivered digitally over the Internet on a global scale. This has facilitated the incorporation of services in supply chain production as traded inputs and as links in the value chain along *"servicified"* GVCs.[159] GVCs today are highly agile, knowledge intensive and increasingly

---

[150] Paperless trading is defined by UNESCAP as *"taking place on the basis of electronic communications, including exchange of trade-related data and documents in electronic form"*, UNESCAP (2016), Article 3 (a).
[151] Duval and Kong (2017), p. 1.
[152] Ferencz et al. (2022), p. 12.
[153] Manyika et al. (2016), pp. 35–36; WTO (2018), pp. 84–87.
[154] OECD (2017a), pp. 11–33.
[155] WTO (2019), pp. 14–16.
[156] OECD (2017a), pp. 24–31; UNCTAD (2015b), p. 2; WTO (2019), pp. 14–16.
[157] Chander (2009), p. 281.
[158] Chander (2009), p. 282.
[159] Lanz and Maurer (2015), pp. 2–8; Low (2013), p. 63; Miroudot and Cadestin (2017), pp. 9–13; World Bank Group et al. (2017), pp. 141–152.

dependent on the integration of services.[160] Recent studies on trade in value added terms indicate that the share of services in world trade is larger than reported in traditional statistics.[161] While services trade today remains at about 20% of total cross-border trade, services in general (and digital services in particular) are considered analytically and statistically elusive.[162] In terms of value added, services account for almost 50% of global exports.[163] Since anything that can be digitised is likely to be digitised, it is reasonable to assume that any cross-border economic activity that does not necessarily involve the use of physical assets or the employment of local human resources can (and will) ultimately be delivered digitally over distance.[164] Hence, the relevance of the service sector is expected to continuously strengthen, as the Internet allows, in principle, the provision of services regardless of the physical proximity of the supplier and the consumer, thus making many economic activities tradable for the first time.[165] For the purposes of the analysis of the digital transformation of global trade, only two phenomena that contribute to an increasing relevance of trade in services for trade will be considered here.

2.3.1.2.1 The Trend Towards "Servitization"

First, in the digital economy the distinction between goods and services is increasingly blurred, resulting in ambiguities of both factual and legal nature.[166] Digital technologies promote comprehensive market transparency in which manufacturers strive to set their goods apart from the competition—which in turn results in informed customers expecting products to be individualised.[167] Increasingly, companies are approaching new opportunities of digital technologies holistically, leaving behind the focus on goods or services in favour of integrated *"bundles"*—with services in the lead role.[168] Consequently, innovative combinatorial products and *"bundles"* blur the boundaries between goods and services. This way, for example, sophisticated combinations between networked industrial goods and performance-enhancing services render machines more effective through predictive manufactur-

---

[160] Lund et al. (2019), pp. 25–41.
[161] *See* for the rationale of measuring trade in value added terms, Elms and Low (2013), pp. 83–159.
[162] Low (2013), p. 61; OECD (2017a), p. 30.
[163] WTO (2019), p. 45. Cf. in this context OECD and WTO (2024) for a TiVA (Trade in Value Added) database.
[164] *See* with regard to services, in particular, Chander (2009). *Anupam Chander* also expects further *"dematerialisation"* of the service infrastructure, *i.e.,* the systems and practices that create trust, promote social objectives and resolve disputes, cf. Chander (2009), pp. 304–308.
[165] *See* generally WTO (2019), pp. 14–16.
[166] *See* with regard to the relevant debate in WTO law *infra* Sect. 3.3.2.1.
[167] Vandermerwe and Rada (1988), p. 318.
[168] Vandermerwe and Rada (1988), p. 314.

ing and maintenance.[169] As more software and networked intelligence are integrated into physical products, machines are increasingly connected in a collaborative community, creating phenomena such as self-maintaining machines that save energy, optimize output, and reduce costs in the process.[170] These *"smart"* products, equipped with digital sensory perception and real-time data transmission capacity turn traditional manufacturers of goods and machinery into service providers. This effect of *"servitization"*[171] has been described as the *"offering of fuller market packages or 'bundles' of customer focussed combinations of goods, services, support, self-service and knowledge in order to add value to core product offerings"*.[172]

2.3.1.2.2 Digitalised Service Environment

Digital technology integration inspires the emergence of a digitalised service environment. As data proliferates within the economy, value creation revolves more around access than around ownership.[173] A prime example of this development are Cloud Computing services as *"a service model for computing services based on a set of computing resources that can be accessed in a flexible, elastic, on-demand way with low management effort."*.[174] Ownership of ICT products such as software, data servers and computers has shifted towards business models that rely on outsourcing the use of such products.[175] Furthermore, digitalisation fosters the emergence of novel combinations of service activities. In the context of a convergence of different services sectors, the question therefore arises as to whether the result is assessed as a combination of pre-existing sectors. In this case, one would have to look for predominant service aspect in order to quantify and qualify the activity. Otherwise,

---

[169] Companies increasingly provide ancillary services to their clients, in some cases transforming a simple sale into a contract for a larger package of services, often tied to a long-term lease, OECD (2019b), p. 18. *See* for example Marr (2015).

[170] This phenomena of integrating digital technologies into manufacturing is widely described as Industry 4.0, *see* Lee et al. (2014), p. 8.

[171] This term was coined by Vandermerwe and Rada (1988). Other authors reference this effect as *"servicizing"* or the *"manuservice"*, *see* Low (2013), p. 66. Cf. for an in-depth definition Miroudot and Cadestin (2017), p. 8, here it is explained that: *"the word 'servicification' was introduced later to describe a broader shift towards services not only in sales of firms but also in the way they produce"*. *See* also Lanz and Maurer (2015); Willemyns (2021), pp. 44–46.

[172] Vandermerwe and Rada (1988), p. 314.

[173] *See* with further references Carrière-Swallow and Haksar (2019), p. 13.

[174] *See* OECD (2014b), pp. 8–9. There is no standard definition for Cloud Computing. The U.-S. Institute of Standards and Technology (NIST) defines it as *"a model for enabling ubiquitous, convenient, on-demand network access to a shared pool of configurable computing resources (e.g., networks, servers, storage applications, and services) that can be rapidly provisioned and released with minimal management effort or service provider interaction"*, *see* Mell and Grance (2011), p. 2. *See* for an introduction to the legal principles governing this technology Hon (2017); Millard (2013).

[175] United States International Trade Commission (2013), pp. 2-27–2-35.

one would have to argue that the activity has in fact crossed the threshold into an entirely new category of services. Finally, a digitalised service environment is increasingly becoming data-centric. This is reflected in the economic rationale behind "*free*" services in which the service activity occurs without direct reference to monetary compensation. Digital services such as social network services or internet search engines, which use their users' data in exchange for access to their platform are a prime example.

2.3.1.3 New Barriers to Trade in the Digital Economy

The digital transformation of international trade also introduces new barriers to cross-border economic activity. In principle, this seems to correspond to a historical pattern in which the global availability of new goods and services is accompanied by a reflex to protect domestic incumbent industries.[176] Hence, all facilitations for communication, cooperation and commerce considered, the data-driven world of today is by no means "*flat*".[177] Trade barriers in the digital economy can take many forms; in particular, they can be technological or regulatory in nature. Hindrances to cross-border trade arise, for example, from the absence of effective infrastructure for the harnessing of the digital transformation as well as from the lack of appropriate regulatory frameworks for a data driven environment. Obstacles may concern restrictions to Internet access, divergent technical standards, but also a lack of interoperability of national legislation or regulatory ambiguities in the handling of new dimensions of trade.[178] A 2013 USITC report notes barriers to include so-called localisation measures, privacy and data protection measures, measures regarding IP-rights, censorship, as well as market access limitations.[179] This underscores the fact that barriers to trade in the digital economy typically are not the result of tariffs or other border measures. With regard to digitally enabled and facilitated forms of cross-border economic activity, a wide range of non-tariff barriers emerges in the form of "*behind-the-border*" rules affecting data flows and the content they convey.[180] As data flows on the Internet may cross multiple jurisdictions, digital products in theory are vulnerable to government intervention at each of these different locations.[181] In fact, contemporary research underscores a massive increase in domestic data regulations.[182] In similar vein, studies imply that recent years have

---

[176] Van der Marel (2019), p. 737.

[177] Chander (2012), p. 31; Manyika et al. (2016), p. 38.

[178] Meltzer (2014a), pp. 17–20; Nguyen and Paczos (2020), p. 28.

[179] United States International Trade Commission (2013), pp. 5-1–5-2. *See* also with further references Burri (2017a), pp. 13–14; Nguyen and Paczos (2020), p. 28; U.S. Department of Commerce (2016), pp. 4–7.

[180] Chander and Lê (2015), pp. 713–735; Pasadilla (2020).

[181] Sen (2018), pp. 325–327.

[182] Casalini and López González (2019), pp. 14–15.

seen an increase in restrictions and a corresponding decrease in openness to digitalised forms of trade.[183] As was analysed above, the services sector in particular benefits from the increasing digitalisation of economic activity, with the result that such barriers have a decisive impact on trade in services (*see supra* Sect. 2.3.1.2). In fact, recent findings underscore the negative impact of restrictive national policies on the services sector.[184] It is estimated that trade in digital services suffers particularly from such restrictions and that the abolition of digital barriers to such trade could increase the volume of global service trade significantly as service activities are often highly data intense.[185] In this manner, a number of publications argue that restrictions to the cross-border flow of data that undergirds the digital service environment have the potential to act as a protectionist instrument of a digital industrial policy in the sense of a *"data nationalism"*.[186] In this context, so-called *"data localisation"* measures are worth highlighting, which include, for example, the territoriality of data centres and other digital infrastructure within a given jurisdiction, as well as the localisation of data processing and storage for certain types of data (*see* further *infra* Sect. 2.3.2.4).

2.3.2 On the Nexus of Cross-Border Data Flows and International Trade

As underlined in the previous sections, the ubiquity of the collection, the processing and the exchange of digital data is spearheading the digital transformation. At the same time, these activities require the seamless transfer of data across the inherently global infrastructure of the Internet. Today, cross-border flows of digitised information predispose, facilitate, and synchronise almost all business processes in virtually every industry.[187] This includes notably the production of goods and development of services, the initiation of business relations, the execution of a transaction as well as the monitoring and maintenance of products or even a legal settlement of liabilities. The digitalisation of commercial processes driven by technologies such as Cloud Computing, Big Data, AI as well as the emerging IoT and production techniques such as 3D printing crucially depend on the transfer of data across borders. Indeed, it is the dissemination of data among a wide range of stakeholders—from companies, governments, and private households to automated machinery and networked

---

[183] Ferracane (2017), p. 2.

[184] WTO (2018), pp. 135–136. *See* in this context the OECD Digital Services Trade Restrictiveness Index Regulatory Database which identifies and catalogues barriers that affect trade in digitally enabled services across 50 countries OECD (2024).

[185] Ferracane and van der Marel (2018), p. 15.

[186] Chander and Lê (2015); Cory (2018), pp. 3–5. *See* with further references regarding allegations of digital protectionism Aaronson (2019), p. 546.

[187] Castro and McQuinn (2015), pp. 2–8.

equipment—which is emerging as pivotal to economic growth in the digital era.[188] This cross-border element inherent to the digital economy is closely linked to trade, resulting in the fact that: *"data is the lifeblood of international trade"*,[189] as the movement of data underpins trade both directly and indirectly.[190] However, the impact of data flows on trade is difficult to measure, as *"[they] come in different forms and they do not follow political or geographic borders but rather economic parameters that are set by changing market conditions and the regulatory / competitive environment."*.[191] This section will further explore the nexus of cross-border data flows and trade in the digital economy.

2.3.2.1 From Data Transmission to Global Data Flows

The phenomenon of global information flows, which gained momentum primarily in the nineteenth century with the technical innovations of telegraphy, has a long tradition today.[192] However, the dynamics of the digital transformation have drastically altered the patterns of global transfers of digitised information towards a globalisation of data flows.[193] With regard to cross-border data flows, prior to the all-encompassing interconnectivity achieved by modern digital networking and the Internet, cross-border data transfers were considered to be an exceptional event.[194] Data flows featured an occasional occurrence in a global economic environment in which mostly localised data sets were employed.[195] While in the 1970s, the cross-border dissemination of data was typically understood to refer to point-to-point data transfers, with the emergence of the Internet, data flows increasingly involve multiple partners communicating through networks in a distributed fashion.[196] A networked system employed in instances such as modern Cloud Computing, for example, is typically based on the total absence of a stable location of data within the provider's network, which in most cases is of global reach.[197] Data is located in the physical infrastructure that stores and transmits data, but it is very common for data storage to be distributed and automatically replicated to infrastructures in different locations, even in other countries.[198] However, data flows are not only important for

---

[188] Manyika et al. (2016), pp. 73–79; National Board of Trade (2014), pp. 9–12; Nguyen and Paczos (2020), pp. 24–25.
[189] Casalini and López González (2019), p. 8.
[190] López González and Jouanjean (2017), p. 10; Willemyns (2021), pp. 27–30.
[191] OECD (2015a), pp. 90–93.
[192] *See* for a historical perspective Drake (1995), p. 267; Tietje (2012), pp. 46–49.
[193] Manyika et al. (2016), pp. 23–42; OECD (2015b), p. 5.
[194] This is the case in particular for transfers involving personal data, *see* Kuner (2013), p. 27.
[195] Schwartz (2013), p. 1628.
[196] Kuner (2013), p. 2.
[197] Article 29 Data Protection Working Party (2012), p. 17.
[198] Hon (2017), p. 134.

business purposes, but also represent the *"lifeblood of the globalized society"*.[199] These shifts in scale and scope have altered the understanding of cross-border data sharing from a rather static notion of data transmission to a state of all-encompassing connectivity and thus a veritable flow of data.[200] This abstracted portrayal of an expanding global interconnectedness through digitised information flows is reflected in the surge of various metrics associated with connectivity, such as Internet access, Internet traffic, broadband subscriptions, or mobile data. However, there is a significant issue with these numbers, which will be addressed in the following: There are no common statistical measurement methods for gauging neither the volume nor the economic value of data flows. In the quest for such statistical data, analysts are often confronted with anecdotal evidence and estimates. Therefore, instead of listing a wide range of different performance indicators, only a few figures will be presented here to illustrate the continuously expanding environment of cross-border data flows. Global Internet traffic rose from 2000 gigabytes per second (GB/s) in 2007 to 26,600 GB/s in 2016—an increase of 33 percent annually.[201] This way, for example, as conventional trade and financial markets lost momentum during the economic crisis, global cross-border data flows grew 45-fold between 2005 and 2014.[202] In similar vein, the amount of cross-border bandwidth used between 2005 and 2017 by a factor of 148, exceeding 700 terabytes per second (Tbps) in 2017.[203]

2.3.2.2 Data Flows as Analogous to Trade Flows?

Cross-border data flows are essential to the expanding network of GVCs and a crucial by-product of it.[204] In fact, according to a frequently cited study by the McKinsey Global Institute, value added based on international data flows has already exceeded the share of trade in goods in global economic growth.[205] For instance, it has been pointed out above that data and information flows disseminated through ICT networks serve as a catalyst for the exchange of goods and services, provide a platform for new types of data-centred economic activities, and thus facilitate a new phase of digital globalisation (*see supra* Sect. 2.2.2.2). However, the character of data flows within a trade context is controversial. In particular, the attempt to draw an analogy between cross-border data flows and cross-border trade flows raises a number of concerns. Certainly, in the context of trade policy,

---

[199] OECD (2015b), p. 5. For example, Voice-over-the-Internet Protocol (VoIP) has generated a surge in global cross-border telephone calls and cross-border computer-to-computer Skype calling has similarly skyrocketed, *see* Lund and Manyika (2016), p. 2.
[200] Aaronson and Leblond (2018), p. 250.
[201] United States International Trade Commission (2017), pp. 45–49.
[202] Manyika et al. (2016), pp. 30–31.
[203] Lund et al. (2019), p. 72.
[204] Meltzer (2016), p. 8.
[205] Manyika et al. (2016), p. 73.

2.3 International Trade in the Digital Economy

international data flows are referred to as *"cross-border"* by analogy with the movements of goods and services.[206] This reflects the philosophy of the *"westphalian"* nation-state that prevails in public international law, where economic activities that transcend national borders invoke the context of International Economic Law.[207] From this perspective, *"lines of light"* are recognised as equivalent to shipping containers and air cargo, so that cyberspace is conceived as a digital analogy to the tangible trade environment.[208] However, such an equation of physical and digital trade is not necessarily practical given the technological characteristics of the Internet and the mechanisms of the digital economy.[209] Nick Ashton-Hart outlines two dimensions of the Internet in a trade context: first, the network as a platform, and second, the data that it carries and which utilize that platform.[210] Both dimensions offer important reference points for rule-based trade governance. For example, while exporters of goods, for example, prefer the direct route between two jurisdictions in order not to be exposed to unnecessary border measures, the architecture of the Internet forms a network that is in principle unaffected by national borders.[211] The Internet Protocol (IP) provides a set of shared standards, so that multiple (in most cases private) networks can be interconnected thus forming a *"network of networks"*.[212] The transmission of data under the IP takes place in small units (*"packets"*) whereby the system of interconnected networks constantly optimizes the network performance in a way that may result in a geographically complex route for each individual packet that may cross multiple jurisdictions. Hence, the logic of the Internet allows for data packets with the identical country of origin and destination to pass through a number of different third countries. This raises the question of whether it is appropriate to refer to data flows as digital trade, since trade based on data flows blurs the lines between domestic and cross-border trade.[213] Moreover, it is also difficult to fit the data flows and the value creation based on them that leverage the global platform of the Internet into the trade regime. In this sense, for example, data flows in a digital economy are often not directly reflected in monetary valuations (e.g. free services, *see supra* Sect. 2.3.1.2.2).[214] In addition, the transmission of data via the Internet, in contrast to offline trade, is

---

[206] *See* for example Casalini and López González (2019). Beyond the trade context (often in the context of addressing aspects of data privacy), the synonymous terms of *transnational* or *transborder* data flows are more frequently employed, cf. for example Drake (2016), p. 8.

[207] *See* on the relationship between political geography and the rise of digital technologies, Drake (1995); de La Chapelle and Fehlinger (2016).

[208] Gresser (2013).

[209] *See* for example Aaronson (2021), p. 344; Streinz (2019), p. 323.

[210] Ashton-Hart (2016), pp. 135–143.

[211] Ashton-Hart (2016), p. 138.

[212] Ashton-Hart (2016), pp. 136–140; Casalini and López González (2019), pp. 9–10.

[213] Streinz (2019), pp. 323–324.

[214] Aaronson (2021), p. 344; Streinz (2019), p. 323.

non-transparent in the sense that it is virtually impossible to verify the content of the individual data packets for technical and economic reasons.[215]

2.3.2.3 Measuring the Impact of Cross-Border Data Flows

While it is generally acknowledged that data and data flows have a transformative impact on international trade, the absence of significant and consistent statistical data has hindered progress in understanding the phenomenon. Overall, a proper analysis of the digital economy requires the refinement of existing statistical systems but also the development of new indicators and measurement frameworks.[216] Key aspects of digitalisation are not sufficiently reflected by conventional concepts and methodologies of economic measurement as applied in the industrial economy.[217] In terms of measuring trade in the digital economy, it is clear that new metrics are needed to capture the economic impact of digital technologies, intangibles, and data flows.[218] The proliferation of cross-border data flows is often taken as a yardstick for the increasing economic relevance of trade in the digital economy. However, this link between data flows and the statistical measurement of trade in the digital economy is fraught with difficulties, not least due to the fact that data flows are not listed as a separate category in trade statistics.[219] Assessing, on the one hand, the quantity of cross-border data flows and, on the other hand, the quality of their economic impact presents a number of significant challenges. In fact, consistent understanding of terminology, typology of data, and appropriate metrics are lacking.[220]

2.3.2.3.1 Quantitative Assessment of Cross-Border Data Flows

With regard to a quantitative assessment of cross-border data flows, a resilient dataset should include starting points and destinations of flows, key waypoints along the route, and ideally comprise information on the type of flows.[221] However, due to a general lack of common approaches and typologies, a very heterogeneous

---

[215] Ashton-Hart (2016), p. 141.
[216] *See* only OECD (2014a), pp. 18–23.
[217] *See* only OECD (2013b). *See* also *supra* Sect. 2.2.1.2.
[218] Admittedly, the challenges of measuring the wider digital economy are generally of a broader nature, *see* OECD (2013b), pp. 12–14. However, there are overlaps, for example, in the area of the typification of the relevant actors of digital transactions due to similar classification of digital transactions on a national and global level, *see* OECD (2019a), p. 238; OECD and IMF (2017), p. 4; OECD and IMF (2018), p. 5.
[219] Mandel (2014), p. 2; OECD (2015a), pp. 78–95; Nguyen and Paczos (2020), pp. 29–31; U.S. Department of Commerce (2016), p. 6; Yakovleva and Irion (2020), p. 206.
[220] Aaronson and Leblond (2018), p. 249; Mandel (2014), pp. 10–13; U.S. Department of Commerce (2016), pp. 7–10.
[221] OECD (2015a), p. 34.

range of statistics and research has emerged, based on different proxies. Recent studies have measured the volume of data flows by utilising accounts of IP-traffic,[222] infrastructural capacity,[223] used bandwidth capacity[224] or digital density.[225] However, all of these proxies are subject to significant caveats.[226] To name but a few: The analysis of IP traffic, for example, only provides a vague replication of the data that is transferred and is highly susceptible to distortion by the geographic location of specific server farms and the overall architecture of the Internet Protocol.[227] In this context, one of the most influential studies by the McKinsey Global Institute refers to the growth of the use in global cross-border bandwidth.[228] Even if this appears to be one of the more accurate methods, this form of measurement relying on capacity does not reveal actual data flows.[229]

Moreover, figures on volume alone reveal very little, as they do not allow any conclusions to be drawn about the specific function of the data that is being transferred. While important insights into the state of digital transformation of trade could be derived from a typology of data flows, there is no universal taxonomy. The multifaceted nature of data mandates distinct classifications and typologies with respect to the various policy considerations around data use. In this context, a taxonomy can differentiate between economic and social aspects (i.e. personal versus non-personal data) as well as technical dimensions (i.e. user created versus machine generated data).[230] The Swedish *Kommerskollegium* differentiates between five types of data, all of which might involve personal information: Corporate data, End-customer data (B2C), Human resources data (HR), Merchant data (B2B) and Technical data.[231] Similarly, the OECD has subdivided three main categories of data: (1) personal data or personal identifiable information, (2) sector-specific data such as business, financial or health, (3) important data as a category entailing considerable policy space.[232] In order to "*improve the availability and quality of statistics and economic analysis related to cross-border data flows and the digital economy*" the U.S. Economics and Statistics Administration and the National Telecommunications and Information Administration introduced a working

---

[222] Mandel (2014).

[223] Manyika et al. (2014), pp. 30–31.

[224] Manyika et al. (2016).

[225] Hofheinz and Mandel (2015).

[226] Alaveras and Martens (2015), pp. 6–10; Mandel (2014), pp. 9–10; OECD (2015a), p. 78; Yakovleva and Irion (2020), pp. 205–207.

[227] Alaveras and Martens (2015), pp. 6–10.

[228] Manyika et al. (2016), pp. 30–31; Lund et al. (2019), p. 72.

[229] OECD (2015a), p. 78; Yakovleva and Irion (2020), p. 206.

[230] Nguyen and Paczos (2020), p. 19.

[231] Cf. National Board of Trade (2014), p. 8. *See* also with further references, Sen (2018), pp. 343–345. The widely recognized category of "*personal data*" is further elaborated *infra* Sect. 4.2.3.

[232] Casalini and López González (2019), pp. 11–12.

categorisation of various types of cross-border data flows.[233] In this sense, it subdivides into four types of flows: (1) Purely non-commercial data traffic, including government and military communications; (2) Transaction data flows between buyers and sellers at a market price, including direct purchases, such as in online banking or advertising, and service-transactions that involve digital platforms; (3) Commercial data and services exchanged between or within businesses or other related parties at $0 market price, including supply chain, personnel, or design information; (4) Digital data and services delivered to and from end-users at $0 market price, including free email, search engine results, maps and directions, and information via social media.[234]

2.3.2.3.2 Qualitative Assessment of Cross-Border Data Flows

Adding to the considerable difficulties in determining volume, direction, and typology, there is a limited correlation between volume and economic value of cross-border data flows. Relying solely on the increase in data traffic in order to estimate economic benefits exhibits obvious shortcomings. Certainly, the quantity of data flows may be a crude indicator of an expanding datasphere. To reproduce an often-cited illustration, however, streaming a movie is economically far less relevant than transmitting an order in the financial markets, yet with the latter far less cross-border flow of data is involved.[235] Verifying the economic impact of the dissemination of data flows presents a number of issues pertaining to, for example, the nature of data flows on the Internet, the absence standard nomenclature as well as a general lack of specialised datasets.[236] Furthermore, the value of cross-border data flows is closely aligned with the thorny issue of how the value of data can be generally accounted for in the digital economy.[237] Data can assume a variety of different economic roles. For example, it can be a means of production, a traded asset, a means through which products or services are traded, and an instrument for organising trade in GVCs.[238] Hence, like the economic value of data itself, the relevance of data flows to the economy is not easily determinable. On this note, a distinctive characteristic of data flows in the context of trade is to be emphasised. Deviating from the general rationale of cross-border trade, not all economically relevant data flows on the

---

[233] U.S. Department of Commerce (2016), p. IV. In a recent trade policy review the EU has set out *"To better assess the size and value of cross-border data flows the Commission will create a European analytical framework for measuring data flows."*, European Commission (2021), p. 15, para. 3.2.3.

[234] U.S. Department of Commerce (2016), p. 3. The categorization was initially introduced by a report of the Commerce Department's Office of the Chief Economist.

[235] U.S. Department of Commerce (2016), p. 1.

[236] U.S. Department of Commerce (2016), pp. 7–16.

[237] Nguyen and Paczos (2020), p. 29. *See* also *supra* Sect. 2.2.2.1.3.

[238] López González and Jouanjean (2017), p. 10.

Internet are transactional and subject to direct monetary compensation.[239] In fact, digital services are frequently (i.e. social media or internet search engines) offered *"free of charge"*, generating *"$0 transactions"*, which nonetheless have considerable revenue associated with them.[240] Since governmental (trade) statistics largely refer to and consist of monetary transactions, it is estimated that novel forms of economic activity in a global digital economy involving non-monetarily compensated data flows is not adequately captured.[241] Data flows exchanged within multinational companies, such as in the case of research and development, for example, are commercially significant, but are largely disregarded by statistics.[242] A key problem is, for example, that current statistical classification systems do not routinely delineate digitally ordered or delivered trade flows from those that are not.[243] In the face of a general ambiguity regarding the economic value of data flows, research on trade flows in the digital economy has introduced concepts such as, *"digitally deliverable services"*,[244] *"data-intensive services"*[245] or *"ICT-enabled services"*.[246] This reflects the observation presented earlier in this chapter that data flows significantly affect the service sector. The basic idea, then, is to make data flows statistically identifiable by exploring services that are primarily delivered digitally. Yet, here too, varying definitions exacerbate a lack of common methodologies.[247] Moreover, such indirect inclusion of data flows in service statistics based on a transactional approach results in significant deficits in terms of non-monetary value added.[248] In similar vein, these concepts only vaguely reflect the impact of data dissemination as not all digitally enabled commercial activity is directly linked to the transfer of data.[249] The issues presented here are to be revisited when addressing the conceptualisation of trade in the digital economy (*see infra* Sect. 3.2).

---

[239] Mandel (2014), pp. 5–7.

[240] U.S. Department of Commerce (2016), p. 7.

[241] Mandel (2014), pp. 2–3; Meltzer (2019), pp. 27–28; U.S. Department of Commerce (2016), p. 3, p. 8.

[242] Meltzer (2014b), p. 8.

[243] *See* for further challenges in the measurement of *"digital trade"* OECD (2019a), p. 238.

[244] *See* for example Meltzer (2014a). *See* further Nicholson and Noonan (2014), p. 5. Digitally Deliverable Services are defined therein as *"services that are principally or largely enabled by information and communication technologies (ICT)"*.

[245] van der Marel (2015).

[246] Cf. UNCTAD (2015b), pp. 8–15. The report defines ICT-Enabled Services as *"services products delivered remotely over ICT networks"*.

[247] U.S. Department of Commerce (2016), pp. 11–12.

[248] Mandel (2014), p. 2. This is acknowledged by *Jessica R. Nicholson* and *Ryan Noonan*, who primarily refer to category two of the above introduced typology of data flows by the U.-S. Economics and Statistics Administration referring to *"flows of data that are traded between a seller and buyer at a market price"*, Nicholson and Noonan (2014), p. 4.

[249] *See* with further references Yakovleva and Irion (2020), p. 206.

2.3.2.4 Barriers to Data Flows Resulting from Domestic Data Governance

As a result of the rising economic relevance of data, digital industrial policies are emerging in many countries.[250] National data regulations often impose barriers to cross-border data flows in favour of the integrity of domestic policy objectives.[251] In fact, the number of national regulations with cross-border elements that can impede cross-border data transfers has skyrocketed in recent years.[252] This illustrates that, contrary to the initial expectations of the early Internet pioneers, the Internet is by no means a *"borderless"* space, but is rather threatened by fragmentation through national legal systems.[253] While it is not clear exactly what fragmentation of the Internet's complex technological and regulatory environment really means, it is clear that it is being driven by a range of forces, actors, and interests.[254]

Measures of *"data localisation"* in particular have found their way into the trade policy discourse and have recently become one of the most controversial issues in global trade.[255] Notably, there is no single definition for data localisation measures. The notion is commonly given a broad interpretation and can therefore refer, for example, to all interventions that *"specifically encumber the transfer of data across national borders"*[256] or to *"measures that raise the cost of conducting business across borders by either mandating companies to keep data within a certain border or by imposing additional requirements for data to be transferred abroad."*[257] Such measures cover all national regulatory and administrative measures that provide for a territorial element to the processing or storage of data within a given jurisdiction. However, data localisation measures can vary considerably in their stringency and design.[258] The rather general notion presented above captures both explicit (laws and

---

[250] *See* for example WTO (2017), p. 2, para. 1.9: *"There is value embedded in the control, management, and flow of data, and the way developing countries treat it will determine which development path they take in the digital age."*.

[251] Meltzer (2019), p. 35; Mitchell and Mishra (2019), pp. 396–397.

[252] Casalini and López González (2019), p. 15; Ferracane (2017), p. 2.

[253] *See* Burri (2017b), p. 70; Chander and Lê (2015), pp. 679–713; Goldsmith and Wu (2006), pp. 13–29, pp. 49–63.

[254] *See* with regard to a fragmentation of the Internet generally Hill (2012).

[255] Cory and Dascoli (2021); Willemyns (2021), pp. 64–73.

[256] Chander and Lê (2015), p. 680.

[257] Ferracane (2017), p. 2. *See* further Mishra (2019), pp. 1–2; Svantesson (2020), pp. 8–11. *See* also Article 3 (5) Regulation (EU) 2018/1807 of the European Parliament and of the Council of 14 November 2018 on a framework for the free flow of non-personal data in the EU, defining data localisation requirement as: *"any obligation, prohibition, condition, limit or other requirement provided for in the laws, regulations or administrative provisions of a Member State or resulting from general and consistent administrative practices in a Member State and in bodies governed by public law, including in the field of public procurement, without prejudice to Directive 2014/24/EU, which imposes the processing of data in the territory of a specific Member State or hinders the processing of data in any other Member State."*.

[258] Casalini and López González (2019), pp. 16–24; Svantesson (2020), pp. 8–9.

regulations prescribing a data residency in any form and prohibiting a transfer directly or indirectly) and implicit variants (through impractical regulations or unreasonable compliance costs) of data localisation.[259] In order to establish a general taxonomy of such measures, *Martina Ferracane* subdivides data localisation measures into the categories of *"strict"* and *"conditional"*.[260] According to this categorisation, localisation measures can be subdivided into those which require local processing or storage (or both) up to the forced localisation within a territory due to an outright ban on data transfers (*"strict"*) on the one hand.[261] On the other hand, regulations can also introduce a specific set of conditions which have to be met in order to allow for the transfer of data outside of a given jurisdiction (*"conditional"*).[262] *James Kaplan* and *Kayvaun Rowshankish*, in turn, differentiate between geographical restrictions on data export (forced storage and processing) and data location (additional copy) as well as between permission-based regulations and standards-based regulation.[263] The analysis of *Francesca Casalini* and *Javier López González* underscores that the focus of the respective data localisation measure will oscillate between, (and frequently be a combination of) the two poles of transfer restriction and the requirement for local storage or processing.[264] The rationale behind restricting the transfer of data in favour of a territorial connection can be traced back to a variety of national policy objectives.[265] The issue of data localisation measures is a convergence point for a wide range of domestic policy objectives with implications for trade in the digital economy, such as, Internet governance, cybersecurity, and, in particular, data privacy.[266] Consequently, the issue implicates a number of different subjects beyond trade, e.g., internet governance, national security or transparency.[267]

2.4 Conclusion

This chapter has covered the digital transformation of international trade with the brevity required while providing a robust foundation for the following analysis of the nexus between trade in the digital economy and data privacy regulation. It highlighted how the economy of *"bits"* and intangible assets has superseded the

---

[259] Mishra (2019), p. 2; Willemyns (2021), pp. 64–69.
[260] Ferracane (2017), p. 3.
[261] Ferracane (2017), p. 4.
[262] Ferracane (2017), p. 5.
[263] Kaplan and Rowshankish (2015), p. 1.
[264] Casalini and López González (2019), pp. 16–24; National Board of Trade (2014), pp. 12–16.
[265] Casalini and López González (2019), p. 13; Chander and Lê (2015), pp. 713–735; Mishra (2015), pp. 144–151. *See* with further references Nguyen and Paczos (2020), pp. 28–29.
[266] *See* with regard to data privacy *infra* Sect. 4.3.3.4.
[267] Svantesson (2020), p. 8.

economy of tangible "*atoms*" in many ways.[268] It has been illustrated, that digital technology provides tools for the harnessing of the hidden value of digital data, thereby fostering *Joseph Schumpeters'* "*creative destruction*" of incumbent economic patterns.[269] In this context, it is fitting that the "*overthrow of matter*" has been described as the central event of the twentieth century.[270] In particular, digital technology integration has massively accelerated the collection, storage, analysis, and transmission of intangible digital data. Due to its central importance for economic activity, data has become a veritable economic resource, the processing and cross-border transmission of which forms a central pillar of economic growth in the digital era. The resulting digital value creation cannot be viewed as a standalone, emerging sector, but must be understood in terms of its holistic and cross-cutting impact on the global economy.

This chapter has further underscored that cross-border trade is facing "*new frontiers*" under the impact of a comprehensive digital transformation. In this respect, digital technologies provide yet another example of the technology-driven evolution of global economic integration as they serve as a catalyst for international trade by facilitating cross-border economic activity and promoting digital globalisation. Against this background it must be reasonably assumed that the Internet will become a universal backbone infrastructure for economic activity.[271] The digital paradigm is significantly changing the patterns by which goods and services are traded across borders. Notably, the digital transformation of trade is affecting what is traded, who trades, and how trade is conducted.[272] This is particularly evident in the growing relevance of the service sector, as intangible services activities are intrinsically linked to digitalisation. Overall, cross-border data flows are firmly entrenched as a fundamental structural element of, and important medium for, the digital transformation of trade. However, it is still unclear exactly how the reciprocal nature of data flows and trade flows is materialising. While data is "*traded*" via cross-border data flows, universal structures and methodologies for measuring their impact are lacking; the economic measurement of trade is still very much adapted to the industrial paradigm. This highlights the need to re-map cross-border economic figures in a global digital economy. Moreover, cross-border data flows have been revealed to be a hinging element and the centre of a collision of economic, social, and political interests in a multipolar, digitally globalised economy. Data flows are also a focal point of convergence between inherently global digital value creation on the one hand and the pursuit of domestic policy goals of data regulation on the other. In this way, trade in the digital economy faces a convergence between domestic and international regulatory spaces. The intertwining of cross-border data flows and trade

---

[268] Negroponte (1996), p. 11.

[269] Schumpeter (1994), pp. 81–87.

[270] Dyson et al. (1996), p. 295: "*In technology, economics, and the politics of nations, wealth - in the form of physical resources - has been losing value and significance.*".

[271] OECD (2013b), p. 12.

[272] López González and Jouanjean (2017), pp. 7–12; WTO (2018), p. 9.

in the digital economy thus raises a highly complex trade policy environment that puts established forms of trade governance to the test.

References

Aaronson SA (2019) What are we talking about when we talk about digital protectionism? World Trade Rev 18(4):541–577. https://doi.org/10.1017/S1474745618000198

Aaronson SA (2021) Data is different, so policymakers should pay close attention to its governance. In: Burri M (ed) Big data and global trade law. Cambridge University Press, Cambridge, pp 340–360

Aaronson SA, Leblond P (2018) Another digital divide: the rise of data realms and its implications for the WTO. J Int Econ Law 21(2):245–272. https://doi.org/10.1093/jiel/jgy019

Abbate J (2000) Inventing the Internet, 3. print. Inside technology. MIT Press, Cambridge

Alaveras G, Martens B (2015) International trade in online services. European Commission Institute for Prospective Technological Studies. Digital Economy Working Paper. https://joint-research-centre.ec.europa.eu/system/files/2015-10/JRC97233_Workingpaper_Alaveras_Martens_InternationalTrade_Online_services_191015.pdf. Accessed 5 Apr 2024

Allen T (2014) Information frictions in trade. Econometrica 82(6):2041–2083. https://doi.org/10.3982/ECTA10984

Anderson C (2008) The end of theory: the data deluge makes the scientific method obsolete. https://www.wired.com/2008/06/pb-theory/. Accessed 5 Apr 2024

Anderson JE, van Wincoop E (2004) Trade costs. J Econ Lit 42(3):691–751

Andreessen M (2011) Why software is eating the world. https://a16z.com/2011/08/20/why-software-is-eating-the-world/. Accessed 5 Apr 2024

Article 29 Data Protection Working Party (2012) Opinion 05/2012 on Cloud Computing. 01037/12/EN WP 196

Ashton-Hart N (2016) What is the "networked economy"? In: Braga CAP, Hoekman B (eds) Future of the global trade order. First Edition. Global Governance Programme. EUI, Florence, pp 133–157. https://doi.org/10.2870/560499

Atluri V, Dietz M, Henke N (2018) The rise of ecosystems: competing in a world of sectors without borders. In: McKinsey Analytics (ed) Analytics comes of age, pp 6–17

Ayyagari M, Demirgüç-Kunt A, Maksimovic V (2018) Superstar firms, market power, and corporate inequality: the role of intangible capital. https://voxeu.org/article/role-intangible-capital-explaining-superstar-firms. Accessed 5 Apr 2024

Baldwin RE (2011) Trade and industrialisation after globalisation's 2nd unbundling: how building and joining a supply chain are different and why it matters. NBER Working Paper 17716. Cambridge, Massachusetts

Baldwin RE (2019) The globotics upheaval: globalisation, robotics, and the future of work. Weidenfeld & Nicolson, London

Bantjes M (2008) The Petabyte Age: because more isn't just more - more is different. Wired. https://www.wired.com/2008/06/pb-intro/. Accessed 5 Apr 2024

Bekar C, Carlaw K, Lipsey R (2018) General purpose technologies in theory, application and controversy: a review. J Evol Econ 28(5):1005–1033. https://doi.org/10.1007/s00191-017-0546-0

Bell D (2010) The coming of post-industrial society: a venture in social forecasting. Basic Books, New York

Blum BS, Goldfarb A (2006) Does the internet defy the law of gravity? J Int Econ 70(2):384–405. https://doi.org/10.1016/j.jinteco.2005.10.002

Boswarthick D, Elloumi O, Hersent O (2012) M2M communications: a systems approach. Wiley, Hoboken

Boyd D, Crawford K (2012) Critical questions for big data. Inform Commun Soc 15(5):662–679. https://doi.org/10.1080/1369118X.2012.678878

Bresnahan TF, Trajtenberg M (1995) General purpose technologies 'Engines of growth'? J Econom 65(1):83–108. https://doi.org/10.1016/0304-4076(94)01598-T

Brynjolfsson E, McAfee A (2014) The second machine age: work, progress, and prosperity in a time of brilliant technologies. W.W. Norton & Company, New York

Brynjolfsson E, McAfee A, Sorell M, Zhu F (2008) Scale without mass: business process replication and industry dynamics. Harvard Business School Technology & Operations Mgt. Unit Research Paper No. 07-016. https://doi.org/10.2139/ssrn.980568

Burri M (2017a) Current and emerging trends in disruptive technologies: implications for the present and future of EU's trade policy. EP/EXPO/B/INTA/2017/06. https://doi.org/10.2861/96860

Burri M (2017b) The governance of data and data flows in trade agreements: the pitfalls of legal adaptation. UC Davis Law Rev 51:65–132

Capgemini Consulting (2012) The digital advantage: how digital leaders outperform their peers in every industry. https://www.capgemini.com/wp-content/uploads/2017/07/The_Digital_Advantage__How_Digital_Leaders_Outperform_their_Peers_in_Every_Industry.pdf. Accessed 5 Apr 2024

Carrière-Swallow Y, Haksar V (2019) The economics and implications of data: an integrated perspective. International Monetary Fund, Strategy, Policy, and Review Department. No. 19/16. https://www.imf.org/en/Publications/Departmental-Papers-Policy-Papers/Issues/2019/09/20/The-Economics-and-Implications-of-Data-An-Integrated-Perspective-48596. Accessed 5 Apr 2024

Casalini F, López González J (2019) Trade and cross-border data flows. OECD Trade Policy Papers No. 220. OECD Publishing, Paris. https://doi.org/10.1787/b2023a47-en

Castro D, McQuinn A (2015) Cross-border data flows enable growth in all industries. Information Technology & Innovation Foundation (ITIF). https://www2.itif.org/2015-cross-border-data-flows.pdf?_ga=1.8208626.1580578791.1473954628. Accessed 5 Apr 2024

Chander A (2009) Trade 2.0. Yale J Int Law 34(2):281–330

Chander A (2012) Principles for trade 2.0. In: Burri M, Cottier T (eds) Trade governance in the digital age. Cambridge University Press, Cambridge, pp 17–44

Chander A, Lê UP (2015) Data nationalism. Empory Law J 64:677–739

Clarke GRG, Qiang CZ, Xu LC (2015) The internet as a general-purpose technology: firm-level evidence from around the world. http://documents.worldbank.org/curated/en/630411468338366817/pdf/WPS7192.pdf. Accessed 5 Apr 2024

Corrado C, Hulten C, Sichel D (2005) Measuring capital and technology: an expanded framework. In: Corrado C, Haltiwanger J, Sichel D (eds) Measuring capital in the new economy. NBER-Studies in Income and Wealth. University of Chicago Press, Chicago

Corrado C, Hulten C, Sichel D (2009) Intangible capital and U.S. economic growth. Rev Income Wealth 55(3):661–685. https://doi.org/10.1111/j.1475-4991.2009.00343.x

Cory N (2018) Testimony before the United States International Trade Commission on Global Digital Trade. Information Technology & Innovation Foundation. https://itif.org/publications/2018/03/29/testimony-united-states-international-trade-commission-global-digital-trade/. Accessed 5 Apr 2024

Cory N, Dascoli L (2021) How barriers to cross-border data flows are spreading globally, what they cost, and how to address them. Information Technology & Innovation Foundation. https://itif.org/publications/2021/07/19/how-barriers-cross-border-data-flows-are-spreading-globally-what-they-cost/. Accessed 5 Apr 2024

Cukier K (2010) Data, data everywhere. https://www.economist.com/special-report/2010/02/27/data-data-everywhere. Accessed 5 Apr 2024

David PA, Wright G (2003) General purpose technologies and productivity surges: historical reflections on the future of the ICT revolution. Nuffield College (University of Oxford).

References

https://ora.ox.ac.uk/objects/uuid:f7410c97-0cc6-4483-9661-38424a3bbab. Accessed 5 Apr 2024

de La Chapelle B, Fehlinger P (2016) Jurisdiction on the Internet: from legal arms race to transnational cooperation. Centre for International Governance Innovation and Chatham House. Paper Series No. 28. https://www.cigionline.org/publications/jurisdiction-internet-legal-arms-race-transnational-cooperation/. Accessed 5 Apr 2024

Dosi G, Galambos L (eds) (2013) The third industrial revolution in global business. Comparative perspectives in business history. Cambridge University Press, Cambridge

Drake WJ (1995) Territoriality and intangibility: transborder data flows and national sovereignty. In: Nordenstreng K, Schiller HI (eds) Beyond national sovereignty: international communication in the 1990s, Rev. ed., 2. printing. Communication and information science series. Ablex Publ, Norwood

Drake WJ (2016) Background Paper for the workshop on data localization and barriers to transborder data flows. https://www3.weforum.org/docs/Background_Paper_Forum_workshop%2009.2016.pdf. Accessed 5 Apr 2024

Dreher A, Gaston N, Martens P (2008) Measuring globalisation. Springer, New York

Duval Y, Kong M (2017) Digital trade facilitation: paperless trade in regional trade agreements. Asian Development Bank Institute Working Paper, No. 74. https://www.adb.org/sites/default/files/publication/321851/adbi-wp747.pdf. Accessed 5 Apr 2024

Dyson E, Gilder G, Keyworth G, Toffler A (1996) Cyberspace and the American Dream: a MagnaCarta for the knowledge age. Inf Soc 12:295–308

Elms DK, Low P (eds) (2013) Global value chains in a changing world. WTO, Geneva. https://www.wto.org/english/res_e/booksp_e/aid4tradeglobalvalue13_e.pdf. Accessed 5 Apr 2024

European Commission (2021) Communication from the European Commission: Trade Policy Review - An Open, Sustainable and Assertive Trade Policy. COM(2021) 66 final

Evans CP, Gawer A (2016) The rise of the platform enterprise: a global survey. The Center for Global Enterprise. https://www.thecge.net/app/uploads/2016/01/PDF-WEB-Platform-Survey_01_12.pdf. Accessed 5 Apr 2024

Fan Z, Meixner L (2020) 3D printing: a guide for decision-makers. World Economic Forum White Paper. https://www.weforum.org/whitepapers/3d-printing-a-guide-for-decision-makers. Accessed 5 Apr 2024

Ferencz J, González JL, García IO (2022) Artificial Intelligence and international trade: some preliminary implications. OECD Trade Policy Papers No. 260. OECD Publishing, Paris. https://doi.org/10.1787/13212d3e-en

Ferracane M (2017) Restrictions on cross-border data flows: a taxonomy. ECIPE Working Paper No. 1/2017. https://ecipe.org/publications/restrictions-to-cross-border-data-flows-a-taxonomy/. Accessed 5 Apr 2024

Ferracane M, van der Marel E (2018) Do data policy restrictions inhibit trade in services? DTE Working Paper Series No. 2. https://ecipe.org/publications/do-data-policy-restrictions-inhibit-trade-in-services/. Accessed 5 Apr 2024

Field AJ (2008) Does economic history need GPTs? SSRN Journal. https://doi.org/10.2139/ssrn.1275023

FNC (1995) FNC Resolution. Definition of "Internet". https://www.nitrd.gov/historical/fnc/internet_res.pdf. Accessed 5 Apr 2024

Freund CL, Weinhold D (2004) The effect of the Internet on international trade. J Int Econ 62(1):171–189. https://doi.org/10.1016/S0022-1996(03)00059-X

Friedman TL (2000) The Lexus and the olive tree, first edition. Anchor Books, New York

Godin B (2008) The information economy: the history of a concept through its measurement, 1949-2005. Project on History and Sociology of S&T Statistics Working Paper No. 38. https://www.csiic.ca/PDF/Godin_38.pdf. Accessed 5 Apr 2024

Goldfarb A, Tucker C (2017) Digital economics. NBER Working Paper No. 23684. https://doi.org/10.3386/w23684

Goldsmith JL, Wu T (2006) Who controls the Internet?: Illusions of a borderless world. Oxford University Press, New York

González JL, Ferencz J (2018) Digital trade and market openness. OECD Trade Policy Papers No. 217. OECD Publishing, Paris. https://doi.org/10.1787/1bd89c9a-en

Gresser E (2013) Testimony: the era of digital trade. https://usitc.gov/press_room/documents/testimony/332_531_003.pdf. Accessed 5 Apr 2024

Haskel J, Westlake S (2017) Capitalism without capital: the rise of the intangible economy. Princeton University Press, Princeton

Hilbert M, López P (2011) The world's technological capacity to store, communicate, and compute information. Science 332(6025):60–65. https://doi.org/10.1126/science.1200970

Hill JF (2012) Internet fragmentation: highlighting the major technical, governance and diplomatic challenges for U.S. Policy Makers. Berkman Center Research Paper, Harvard Belfer Center for Science and International Affairs Working Paper. Available at SSRN: https://ssrn.com/abstract=2439486

Hofheinz P, Mandel M (2015) Uncovering the hidden value of digital trade: towards a 21st century agenda of transatlantic prosperity. Progressive Policy Institute (PPI). https://www.progressivepolicy.org/wp-content/uploads/2015/07/2015.07-Mandel-Hofeinz-Uncovering-the-Value-of-Digital-Trade_Towards-a-21st-Century-Agenda-of-Transatlantic-Prosperity.pdf. Accessed 5 Apr 2024

Hon WK (ed) (2017) Data localization laws and policy: the EU data protection international transfers restriction through a cloud computing lens. Edward Elgar Publishing, Cheltenham

ICC (2016) Trade in the digital economy: a primer on global data flows for policymakers. https://iccwbo.org/news-publications/policies-reports/trade-in-the-digital-economy-a-primer-on-global-data-flows-for-policymakers/. Accessed 5 Apr 2024

IMF (2018) Measuring the digital economy. Staff Report, Washington, D.C. https://www.imf.org/en/Publications/Policy-Papers/Issues/2018/04/03/022818-measuring-the-digital-economy. Accessed 5 Apr 2024

International Trade Centre (2016) Bringing SMEs onto the E-commerce Highway, Geneva. https://intracen.org/file/bringingsmesontotheecommercehighwayfinal250516lowrespdf. Accessed 5 Apr 2024

Internet Society (2015) Internet interconnection: an internet society public policy brief. https://www.internetsociety.org/policybriefs/internetinterconnection/. Accessed 5 Apr 2024

Johnston S (2018) Largest companies 2008 vs. 2018, a lot has changed. https://milfordasset.com/insights/largest-companies-2008-vs-2018-lot-changed. Accessed 5 Apr 2024

Jones CI, Tonetti C (2020) Nonrivalry and the economics of data. Am Econ Rev 110(9): 2819–2858. https://doi.org/10.1257/aer.20191330

Jovanovic B, Rousseau PL (2005) General purpose technologies. In: Jovanovic B, Rousseau P (eds) Handbook of economic growth, Volume 1, Part B. Elsevier, pp 1181–1224

Kaplan JM, Rowshankish K (2015) Addressing the impact of data location regulation in financial services. CIGI Paper Series No. 14

Kenney M, Bearson D, Zysman J (2021) The platform economy matures: measuring pervasiveness and exploring power. Socio-Econ Rev 19(4):1451–1483. https://doi.org/10.1093/ser/mwab014

Kuner C (2013) Transborder data flows and data privacy law. Oxford University Press, Oxford

Kurzweil R (2001) The law of accelerating returns. https://www.kurzweilai.net/the-law-of-accelerating-returns. Accessed 5 Apr 2024

Lane N (1999) Advancing the digital economy into the 21st century. Inf Syst Front 1(3):317–320. https://doi.org/10.1023/A:1010010630396

Lanz R, Maurer A (2015) Services and global value chains: some evidence on servicification of manufacturing and services network. WTO Staff Working Paper, No. ERSD-2015-03. https://www.wto.org/english/res_e/reser_e/ersd201503_e.htm. Accessed 5 Apr 2024

Lee K-F (2018) AI superpowers: China, Silicon Valley and the new world order. Houghton Mifflin Harcourt, Boston

References

Lee J, Kao H-A, Yang S (2014) Service innovation and smart analytics for Industry 4.0 and big data environment. Procedia CIRP 16:3–8. https://doi.org/10.1016/j.procir.2014.02.001

Lendle A, Olarreaga M, Schropp S, Vézina P-L (2012) There goes gravity: how eBay reduces trade costs. World Bank Group Policy Research Working Paper 6253. https://doi.org/10.1596/1813-9450-6253

López González J, Jouanjean M-A (2017) Digital trade: developing a framework for analysis. OECD Trade Policy Papers, No. 205. OECD Publishing, Paris. https://doi.org/10.1787/524c8c83-en

Low P (2013) The role of services in global value chains. In: Elms DK, Low P (eds) Global value chains in a changing world. WTO, Geneva, pp 61–81. https://www.wto.org/english/res_e/booksp_e/aid4tradeglobalvalue13_e.pdf. Accessed 5 Apr 2024

Lund S, Manyika J (2016) How digital trade is transforming globalisation. E15 Expert Group on the Digital Economy - Think Piece. https://www.tralac.org/images/docs/8854/how-digital-trade-is-transforming-globalisation-e15-initiative-january-2016.pdf. Accessed 5 Apr 2024

Lund S, Tyson L (2018) Globalization is not in retreat: digital technology and the future of trade. Foreign Aff 97(3)

Lund S, Manyika J, Woetzel L, Bughin J, Krishnan M, Seong J, Muir M (2019) Globalization in transition: the future of trade and value chains. McKinsey Global Institute. https://www.mckinsey.com/featured-insights/innovation-and-growth/globalization-in-transition-the-future-of-trade-and-value-chains. Accessed 5 Apr 2024

Lycett M (2013) 'Datafication': making sense of (big) data in a complex world. Eur J Inf Syst 22(4):381–386. https://doi.org/10.1057/ejis.2013.10

Machlup F (1962) The production and distribution of knowledge in the United States. Princeton University Press, Princeton

Mandel M (2014) Data, trade and growth. Progressive Policy Institute (PPI). https://www.progressivepolicy.org/wp-content/uploads/2014/04/2014.04-Mandel_Data-Trade-and-Growth.pdf. Accessed 5 Apr 2024

Mandel M (2017) The economic impact of data: why data is not like oil. Progressive Policy Institute (PPI). https://www.progressivepolicy.org/wp-content/uploads/2017/07/PowerofData-Report_2017.pdf. Accessed 5 Apr 2024

Manyika J, Chui M, Brown B, Bughin J, Dobbs R, Roxburgh C, Hung Byers A (2011) Big data: the next frontier for innovation, competition, and productivity. McKinsey Global Institute. https://www.mckinsey.com/capabilities/mckinsey-digital/our-insights/big-data-the-next-frontier-for-innovation. Accessed 5 Apr 2024

Manyika J, Chui M, Bughin J, Dobbs R, Bisson P, Marrs A (2013) Disruptive technologies: advances that will transform life, business and the global economy. McKinsey Global Institute. https://www.mckinsey.com/capabilities/mckinsey-digital/our-insights/disruptive-technologies. Accessed 5 Apr 2024

Manyika J, Lund S, Bughin J, Nottebohm O, Poulter D, Jauch S, Ramasawamy S (2014) Global flows in a digital age. McKinsey Global Institute. https://www.mckinsey.com/capabilities/strategy-and-corporate-finance/our-insights/global-flows-in-a-digital-age. Accessed 5 Apr 2024

Manyika J, Lund S, Bughin J, Woetzel L, Stamenov K, Dhingra D (2016) Digital globalization: the new era of global flows. McKinsey Global Institute. https://www.mckinsey.com/capabilities/mckinsey-digital/our-insights/digital-globalization-the-new-era-of-global-flows. Accessed 5 Apr 2024

Marr B (2015) How big data drives success at Rolls-Royce. https://www.forbes.com/sites/bernardmarr/2015/06/01/how-big-data-drives-success-at-rolls-royce/#217a537b1d69. Accessed 5 Apr 2024

Mayer-Schönberger V, Cukier K (2014) Big data: a revolution that will transform how we live, work and think, 1. Mariner Books edition

McAfee A, Brynjolfsson E (2017) Machine, platform, crowd: harnessing our digital future, First edition. W.W. Norton & Company, New York, London

McBride S (2019) These 3 computing technologies will beat Moore's Law. https://www.forbes.com/sites/stephenmcbride1/2019/04/23/these-3-computing-technologies-will-beat-moores-law/#50a392db37b0. Accessed 5 Apr 2024

McNamara KR, Newman AL (2020) The big reveal: COVID-19 and globalization's great transformations. Int Org 74(S1):E59–E77. https://doi.org/10.1017/S0020818320000387

McRae H (2015) Facebook, Airbnb, Uber, and the unstoppable rise of the content non-generators. https://www.independent.co.uk/news/business/comment/hamish-mcrae/facebook-airbnb-uber-and-the-unstoppable-rise-of-the-content-non-generators-10227207.html. Accessed 5 Apr 2024

Mell P, Grance T (2011) The NIST definition of cloud computing. Recommendations of the National Institute of Standards and Technology U.S. Department of Commerce. https://nvlpubs.nist.gov/nistpubs/legacy/sp/nistspecialpublication800-145.pdf. Accessed 5 Apr 2024

Meltzer JP (2014a) Supporting the internet as a platform for international trade: opportunities for small and medium-sized enterprises and developing countries. Brookings Global Economy & Development Working Paper 69. https://doi.org/10.2139/ssrn.2400578

Meltzer JP (2014b) The importance of the internet and transatlantic data flows for U.S. and EU Trade and Investment. Global Economy & Development Working Paper 79

Meltzer JP (2015) The internet, cross-border data flows and international trade. Asia Pac Policy Stud 2(1):90–102. https://doi.org/10.1002/app5.60

Meltzer JP (2016) Maximizing the opportunities of the internet for international trade. Policy Options Paper. ICTSD and World Economic Forum. Available at SSRN: https://ssrn.com/abstract=2841913

Meltzer JP (2019) Governing digital trade. World Trade Rev 18(S1):23–48. https://doi.org/10.1017/S1474745618000502

Millard C (2013) Cloud computing law. Oxford University Press

Mims C (2018) Every company is now a tech company. https://www.wsj.com/articles/every-company-is-now-a-tech-company-1543901207. Accessed 5 Apr 2024

Miroudot S, Cadestin C (2017) Services in global value chains: from inputs to value-creating activities. OECD Trade Policy Papers, No. 197. OECD Publishing, Paris. https://doi.org/10.1787/465f0d8b-en

Mishra N (2015) Data localization laws in a digital world: data protection or data protectionism? NUS Centre for International Law Research Paper No. 19/05. The Public Sphere

Mishra N (2019) Privacy, cybersecurity, and GATS Article XIV: a new frontier for trade and internet regulation? World Trade Rev 19(3):1–24. https://doi.org/10.1017/S1474745619000120

MIT Technology Review (2016) The rise of data capital. https://www.technologyreview.com/2016/03/21/161487/the-rise-of-data-capital/. Accessed 5 Apr 2024

Mitchell AD, Mishra N (2019) Regulating cross-border data flows in a data-driven world: how WTO law can contribute. J Int Econ Law 22(3):389–416. https://doi.org/10.1093/jiel/jgz016

Moore GE (1965) Cramming more components onto integrated circuits. Electronics 38(8):114–117

Mueller M, Mathiason J, Klein H (2007) The internet and global governance: principles and norms for a new regime. Global Gov 13(2):237–254

National Board of Trade (2014) No transfer, no trade: the importance of cross-border data transfers for companies based in Sweden

Negroponte N (1996) Being digital. Coronet books. Hodder and Stoughton, London

Nguyen D, Paczos M (2020) Measuring the economic value of data and cross-border data flows: a business perspective. OECD Digital Economy Papers No. 297. OECD Publishing, Paris. https://doi.org/10.1787/6345995e-en

Nicholson JR, Noonan R (2014) Digital economy and cross-border trade: the value of digitally-deliverable services. U.S. Department of Commerce ESA Issue Brief #01-14. https://www.commerce.gov/sites/default/files/migrated/reports/digitaleconomyandcross-bordertrade.pdf. Accessed 5 Apr 2024

O'Rourke KH, Williamson JG (2002) When did globalisation begin? Eur Rev Econ Hist 6(1):23–50. https://doi.org/10.1017/S1361491602000023

OECD (1969) Gaps in Technology: Electronic Computers

References

OECD (2008) The Seoul Declaration for the future of the internet economy. OECD Digital Economy Papers, No. 147. OECD Publishing, Paris. https://doi.org/10.1787/230445718605

OECD (2013a) Supporting investment in knowledge capital, growth and innovation. OECD Publishing, Paris. https://doi.org/10.1787/9789264193307-en

OECD (2013b) Measuring the internet economy: a contribution to the research agenda. OECD Digital Economy Papers, No. 226. OECD Publishing, Paris. https://doi.org/10.1787/5k43gjg6r8jf-en

OECD (2013c) The App Economy. Working Party on the Information Economy DSTI/ICCP/IE (2012)1/FINAL

OECD (2014a) Measuring the digital economy: a new perspective. OECD Publishing, Paris. https://doi.org/10.1787/9789264221796-en

OECD (2014b) Cloud computing: the concept, impacts and the role of government policy. Digital Economy Papers No. 240, OECD Publishing, Paris. https://doi.org/10.1787/5jxzf4lcc7f5-en

OECD (2015a) Economic And Social Benefits of Internet Openness: 2016 Ministerial Meeting on the Digital Economy Background Report. OECD Digital Economy Papers No. 257. OECD Publishing, Paris. https://doi.org/10.1787/5jlwqf2r97g5-en

OECD (2015b) The Governance of Globalized Data Flows - Current Trends and Future Challenges: Working Party on security and Privacy in the Digital Economy. DSTI/ICCP/REG(2015)3

OECD (2015c) OECD Data-Driven Innovation: Big Data and Growth for Well-Being OECD, OECD Publishing, Paris. https://doi.org/10.1787/9789264229358-en

OECD (2017a) Services trade policies and the global economy. OECD Publishing, Paris. https://doi.org/10.1787/9789264275232-en

OECD (2017b) OECD Science, Technology and Industry Scoreboard 2017: the digital transformation. OECD Publishing, Paris. https://doi.org/10.1787/9789264268821-en

OECD (2018) Background Note for the G20 Trade and Investment Working Group Argentina Presidency 2018. https://www.oecd.org/g20/topics/trade-and-investment/Background-note-on-trade-investment-April-2018%20.pdf. Accessed 5 Apr 2024

OECD (2019a) Measuring the digital transformation. a roadmap for the future. OECD Publishing, Paris. https://doi.org/10.1787/9789264311992-en

OECD (2019b) Vectors of Digital Transformation. OECD Digital Economy Papers, No. 273. OECD Publishing, Paris. https://doi.org/10.1787/5ade2bba-en

OECD (2019c) An introduction to online platforms and their role in the digital transformation. OECD Publishing, Paris. https://doi.org/10.1787/53e5f593-en

OECD (2020) A roadmap toward a common framework for measuring the digital economy. Report for the G20 Digital Economy Task Force. https://www.itu.int/en/ITU-D/Statistics/Documents/publications/OECDRoadmapDigitalEconomy2020.pdf. Accessed 5 Apr 2024

OECD (2024) Digital Services Trade Restrictiveness Index Regulatory Database. https://qdd.oecd.org/subject.aspx?Subject=STRI_DIGITAL. Accessed 5 Apr 2024

OECD, IMF (2017) Measuring Digital Trade: Results of OECD/IMF Stocktaking Survey. BOPCOM—17/07, Paris, France. https://www.imf.org/external/pubs/ft/bop/2017/pdf/17-07.pdf. Accessed 5 Apr 2024

OECD, IMF (2018) Towards a handbook on measuring digital trade: status update. BOPCOM - 18/07, Washington D.C. https://www.imf.org/external/pubs/ft/bop/2018/pdf/18-07.pdf. Accessed 5 Apr 2024

OECD, WTO (2024) Trade in value added. TiVA database. https://www.oecd.org/sti/ind/measuring-trade-in-value-added.htm. Accessed 5 Apr 2024

Pasadilla GO (2020) Next generation non-tariff measures: emerging data policies and barriers to digital trade. ARTNeT Working Paper Series No. 187

Pélissié du Rausas M et al (2011) Internet matters: the Net's sweeping impact on growth, jobs, and prosperity. McKinsey Global Institute. https://www.mckinsey.com/industries/technology-media-and-telecommunications/our-insights/internet-matters. Accessed 5 Apr 2024

Peng S, Lin C-F, Streinz T (2021) Artificial intelligence and international economic law: a research and policy agenda. In: Peng S, Lin C-F, Streinz T (eds) Artificial intelligence and international economic law: disruption, regulation, and reconfiguration. Cambridge University Press, Cambridge, New York, Port Melbourne, New Delhi, Singapore, pp 1–26

Pistor K (2020) Rule by data: the end of markets? Law Contemp Probl 83:101–124. https://scholarship.law.duke.edu/lcp/vol83/iss2/6. Accessed 5 Apr 2024

Polanyi K (2010) The great transformation: the political and economic origins of our time, 2. Beacon paperback edition, [reprinted]. Beacon Press, Boston, Massachusetts

Porat MU (1977) The information economy: definition and measurement. Office of Telecommunications (DOC), Washington, D.C.

Reinsel D, Gantz J, Rydning J (2018) Data Age 2025: the digitization of the world from edge to core. IDC White Paper. https://www.seagate.com/files/www-content/our-story/trends/files/idc-seagate-dataage-whitepaper.pdf. Accessed 5 Apr 2024

Riker D (2014) Internet use and openness to trade. Office of Economics Working Paper, U.-S. International Trade Commission. https://www.usitc.gov/publications/332/ec201412c.pdf. Accessed 5 Apr 2024

Schmidt E, Cohen J (2013) The new digital age: reshaping the future of people, nations and business, first edition. Knopf, New York

Schumpeter JA (1949) The theory of economic development An inquiry into profits, capital, credit, interest and the business cycle. Harvard University Press, Cambridge

Schumpeter JA (1994) Capitalism, socialism, and democracy. Routledge, London, New York

Schwab K (2016) The fourth industrial revolution. World Economic Forum, Cologny/Geneva

Schwartz PM (2013) Information privacy in the cloud. Univ Pa Law Rev 161(6):1623–1662

Sen N (2018) Understanding the role of the WTO in international data flows: taking the liberalization or the regulatory autonomy path? J Int Econ Law 21(2):323–348. https://doi.org/10.1093/jiel/jgy021

Simonite T (2016) Moore's law is dead. Now what? https://www.technologyreview.com/s/601441/moores-law-is-dead-now-what/. Accessed 5 Apr 2024

Solow R (1987) We'd better watch out. New York Times Book Review, July 12, 1987

Streinz T (2019) Digital megaregulation uncontested? TPP's model for the global digital economy. In: Kingsbury B et al (eds) Megaregulation contested. Oxford University Press, pp 312–342

Svantesson DJB (2020) Data localisation trends and challenges: considerations for the review of the Privacy Guidelines. OECD Digital Economy Papers No. 301. OECD Publishing, Paris. https://doi.org/10.1787/7fbaed62-en

Tapscott D (1996) The digital economy: promise and peril in the age of networked intelligence. McGraw-Hill, New York

Terzi N (2011) The impact of e-commerce on international trade and employment. Procedia - Soc Behav Sci 24:745–753. https://doi.org/10.1016/j.sbspro.2011.09.010

The Economist (2010) The web's new walls: how the threats to the internet's openness can be averted. https://www.economist.com/leaders/2010/09/02/the-webs-new-walls. Accessed 5 Apr 2024

The Economist (2013) The rise of the sharing economy: on the internet, everything is for hire. https://www.economist.com/leaders/2013/03/09/the-rise-of-the-sharing-economy. Accessed 5 Apr 2024

Thierer AD (2014) Permissionless innovation: the continuing case for comprehensive technological freedom. Mercatus Center, George Mason University, Arlington

Thomson W (1891) Popular lectures and addresses, vol 1. Macmillan and Co., London, New York

Tietje C (2012) Global information law. In: Burri M, Cottier T (eds) Trade governance in the digital age. Cambridge University Press, Cambridge, pp 45–62

U.S. Department of Commerce (2016) Measuring the Value of Cross-Border Data Flows. Economics and Statistics Administration and the National Telecommunications and Information Administration. https://www.ntia.doc.gov/files/ntia/publications/measuring_cross_border_data_flows.pdf. Accessed 5 Apr 2024

References

UNCTAD (2015a) Unlocking the potential of e-commerce for developing countries. United Nations publication, New York. https://unctad.org/system/files/official-document/ier2015_en.pdf. Accessed 5 Apr 2024

UNCTAD (2015b) International Trade in ICT Services and ICT-enabled Services: Proposed Indicators from the Partnership on Measuring ICT for Development. Technical Notes on ICT for Development No. 3 TN/UNCTAD/ICT4D/03. https://unctad.org/system/files/official-document/tn_unctad_ict4d03_en.pdf. Accessed 5 Apr 2024

UNCTAD (2017a) World Investment Report 2017: Investment and the digital economy. United Nations publication, New York and Geneva. https://investmentpolicy.unctad.org/publications/174/world-investment-report-2017%2D%2D-investment-and-the-digital-economy. Accessed 5 Apr 2024

UNCTAD (2017b) Rising Product Digitalisation and Losing Trade Competitiveness. UNCTAD/GDS/ECIDC/2017/3. https://unctad.org/publication/rising-product-digitalisation-and-losing-trade-competitiveness. Accessed 5 Apr 2024

UNCTAD (2017c) Information Economy Report: Digitalization, Trade and Development. United Nations publication, New York, Geneva. https://unctad.org/system/files/official-document/ier2017_en.pdf. Accessed 5 Apr 2024

UNESCAP (2016) Resolution adopted by the Economic and Social Commission for Asia and the Pacific, E/ESCAP/RES/72/4, 24 May 2016

United States International Trade Commission (2013) Digital Trade in the U.S. and Global Economies, Part 1. https://www.usitc.gov/publications/industry_econ_analysis_332/2013/digital_trade_us_and_global_economies_part_1.htm. Accessed 5 Apr 2024

United States International Trade Commission (2014) Digital Trade in the U.S. and Global Economies, Part 2

United States International Trade Commission (2017) Global Digital Trade 1: Market Opportunities and Key Foreign Trade Restrictions. Publication Number: 4716; Investigation Number: 332-561

van der Marel E (2015) Disentangling the flows of data: inside or outside the multinational company? ECIPE Occasional Paper. https://ecipe.org/publications/flows-data-inside-outside-multinational-company/. Accessed 5 Apr 2024

van der Marel E (2019) Old wine in new bottles – how protectionism takes hold of digital trade. Glob Policy 10(4):737–739. https://doi.org/10.1111/1758-5899.12737

Vandermerwe S, Rada J (1988) Servitization of business: adding value by adding services. Eur Manag J 6(4):314–324

Varian HR (2004) Competition and market power. In: Varian HR, Farrell J, Shapiro C (eds) The economics of information: an introduction. Cambridge University Press, pp 1–48

Varian HR (2005) Technology levels the business playing field. https://www.nytimes.com/2005/08/25/business/technology-levels-the-business-playing-field.html. Accessed 5 Apr 2024

Vézina P-L, Melin H (2013) eBay and the rise of the micro-multinationals. OECD Observer No. 295 36-37

Willemyns I (2021) Digital services in international trade law. University Press, Cambridge

Wilson JM (2012) Computing, communication, and cognition: three laws that define the internet society: Moore's, Gilder's, and Metcalfe's. https://www.jackmwilson.net/Entrepreneurship/Cases/Moores-Meltcalfes-Gilders-Law.pdf. Accessed 5 Apr 2024

Wolf M (2005) Why globalization works, 1st edn. Yale Nota Bene, New Haven

World Bank Group (2016) World Development Report 2016: Digital Dividends. https://www.worldbank.org/en/publication/wdr2016. Accessed 5 Apr 2024

World Bank Group, OECD, WTO (2017) Measuring and analyzing the impact of GVCs on economic development: Global value chains development report 2017. World Bank Group, Washington, DC, USA

World Economic Forum (2019) Annual Meeting 2019: Globalization 4.0: Shaping a Global Architecture in the Age of the Fourth Industrial Revolution. https://www.weforum.org/

publications/globalization-4-0-shaping-a-new-global-architecture-in-the-age-of-the-fourth-industrial-revolution/. Accessed 5 Apr 2024

WTO (2015) World Trade Report 2015: speeding up trade: benefits and challenges of implementing the WTO Trade Facilitation Agreement. https://doi.org/10.30875/0949bcf3-en

WTO (2017) Communication from the African Group, Work Programme on Electronic Commerce JOB/GC/133, 20 July 2017

WTO (2018) World Trade Report 2018: the future of world trade: how digital technologies are transforming global commerce. https://doi.org/10.30875/0949bcf3-en

WTO (2019) World Trade Report 2019: the future of services trade. https://doi.org/10.30875/0949bcf3-en

Yakovleva S, Irion K (2020) Pitching trade against privacy: reconciling EU governance of personal data flows with external trade. Int Data Priv Law 10(3):201–221. https://doi.org/10.1093/idpl/ipaa003

Chapter 3
The Emergence of Digital Trade Regulation

3.1 Introduction

The emergence of a globally networked environment has led to responses on all levels of governance, with established institutions and instruments of national and international law facing challenges on fundamental issues such as regulatory design and enforcement.[1] As digital technologies have proliferated and the digital economy has expanded significantly in recent years, these new dimensions of international trade are increasingly in the focus of both the academic community[2] and international organisations.[3] Generally, there has been a debate as to whether the technological impulses resulting from digital technologies require the introduction of new rules and institutions for trade as digital globalisation renders existing regulatory frameworks inadequate.[4] This debate has been echoed in the trade community. Arguably, the implementation of a digital trade governance within the established structures, mechanisms and institutions of multilateral trade law has reached its limits—despite the fact that the WTO "*possesses intrinsic flexibility and resilience - both in the substance and in the procedure*".[5] The primary reason being that the underlying economic reality for which WTO law was initially formulated has changed significantly (*see supra* Sect. 2.3). In fact, as *Joshua Meltzer* has put it: „*WTO rules were largely designed for a world where international trade was in physical goods and services delivered in person.*".[6] Given the economic paradigm

---

[1] Burri and Cottier (2012a), p. 2.
[2] *See* for example Burri (2021a); Burri and Cottier (2012b); Peng et al. (2021a); Zheng (2020).
[3] *See* for example ICC (2016); López González and Ferencz (2018); UNCTAD (2017a), pp. 41–58; WTO (2018a).
[4] *See* only Burri (2021b), pp. 15–20; Cottier (1996), pp. 425–427.
[5] Burri (2015), pp. 38–39.
[6] Cf. Meltzer (2015), p. 97.

shift and the fact that existing trade rules were largely drafted in the pre-Internet era, the deficiencies of the WTO framework are increasingly salient. While regulatory efforts were initially aimed at facilitating cross-border *"electronic commerce"*, the current phase of regulatory intervention is confronted with issues related to a full-fledged global digital economy.[7] Yet, despite increasing awareness regarding the integration of data and data flows into cross-border economic activity, to date there is no generally accepted understanding of *"digital trade"*.[8] This ambiguity becomes particularly clear considering that the notions of *"digital trade"* and *"e-commerce"* are often used interchangeably.[9] Certainly, the relevance of the digital transformation for trade is generally acknowledged in the trade community today; and has in fact received considerable attention on an international level since the mid-1990s.[10] However, negotiating initiatives on the governance of trade in the digital economy are only recently (re-)gaining momentum.[11] The complexity of the challenges to the current legal framework for global trade is illustrated by the ongoing controversy over data governance issues and, in particular, the regulation of cross-border data flows. Although cross-border data flows are considered the *"Silk Roads"*[12] of the digital economy, there is no universal legal framework to govern them, as data flows are a statistically and regulatory elusive phenomenon that encompasses a wide range of social, political, and economic considerations (*see* also *supra* Sect. 2.3.2).[13] While some argue for data to be included in the list of trade policy issues, on a par with the movement of goods, persons, services or capital, others oppose a rationale of economic liberalisation on account of multi-faceted domestic policy considerations.[14] Differing levels of technological maturity and policy openness as well as competing strategic interests among WTO members in an emerging digital paradigm pose major obstacles to effective cooperation on digital issues. To make matters worse, the current climate of declining multilateralism favours unilateral approaches

---

[7] WTO (2018a), p. 194.

[8] *See* only López González and Ferencz (2018), p. 9; United States International Trade Commission (2013), p. XV. *See* also *infra* 3.2.

[9] *See* for example Gao (2018), p. 297, fn. 1; Weber (2015), p. 323. *See* generally Mitchell and Mishra (2018), p. 1076, fn. 2.

[10] For instance, both the WTO and the OECD Ministerial Conferences recognised the relevance of the issue of Electronic Commerce as early as in 1998. As a result, the WTO adopted the *"Declaration on Global Electronic Commerce"*, WTO (1998a). For its part, the OECD adopted the *"Action Plan for Electronic Commerce"*, OECD (1998). Similarly, the Asia-Pacific Economic Cooperation (APEC) in 1998 adopted a *"Blueprint for Action on Electronic Commerce"*, APEC (1998).

[11] Cf. in this context the ongoing plurilateral negotiations under the Joint Statement Initiative on Electronic Commerce launched in 2019, *see* further *infra* Sect. 3.3.1.2.

[12] Chander (2013), pp. 1–17.

[13] *See* only Aaronson and Leblond (2018), p. 246. However, with reference to the principles of *"free flow of information"* and *"freedom of information"*, some examples can be found where data flows have been the subject of international regulation, *see* with further references Kuner (2013), pp. 31–32.

[14] Ciuriak and Ptashkina (2018), p. 6; Mitchell and Mishra (2019), p. 390.

and fragmentation of regulatory regimes. Thus, trade law operates in a highly complex environment in which political disagreements among WTO members on the governance of the digital economy undermine its ability to function, and existing regulatory gaps are progressively being addressed through unilateral action.

Against this background, this chapter addresses some of the key issues related to the reception of the digital transformation in international trade law. In the second section of this chapter the current state of conceptualisation of trade in the digital economy is outlined (Sect. 3.2). To this end, a general overview of the current conceptual approaches to e-commerce and digital trade is provided. When examining the issue of digital trade, it is remarkable that, firstly, it is unclear what this term means and, secondly, that generally no clear distinction is made between digital trade and e-commerce. For the purposes of the present analysis, therefore, the relationship between the terms digital trade and global e-commerce will be defined. A third section will then address the governance of such digital trade under contemporary WTO law (Sect. 3.3). A fourth section provides an overview of the evolving regulation of digital trade in Preferential Trade Agreements (PTAs) (Sect. 3.4). The fifth section of this chapter presents the changing policy environment for international trade in more detail, with a focus on integrating the governance of data and data flows (Sect. 3.5).

3.2 Towards Conceptualising Digital Trade

In order to conceptualise trade in the digital economy, the notions of (global) electronic commerce and digital trade have emerged as key terminological vehicles. The widespread implementation of ICT for business purposes since the early 1990s has resulted in a significant proliferation of electronically facilitated transactions. However, the term *"e-commerce"* is ambiguous and is usually used without a specific definition. In a general business context, e-commerce arguably refers to electronically facilitated transactions involving primarily physical goods, such as in the case of online retail shopping. Against a cross-border background, conceptualisations have been drawn up in order to address policy challenges of *"global e-commerce"*. Meanwhile, the increasingly efficient integration of digital technologies and data into cross-border economic activity has recently prompted the emergence of the notion of *"digital trade"*. It is important to point out, however, that there is no universally accepted definition for either global e-commerce or digital trade.[15] Consequently, there is no foundation for measuring these concepts, nor for the establishment of a coordinated regulatory framework. In fact, the issues of measuring economic activity in the digital economy, namely the challenge of

---

[15] *See* for an account of definitions from Eurostat and Statistics Canada OECD (2019b), Chapter I, Box 1.1. *See* further for the definition of electronic commerce within the WTO Work Programme on Electronic Commerce *infra* Sect. 3.2.1.1.1.

reaching agreement on common terminology and methodology, are reflected in the field of international trade.[16] This is especially the case for measuring the impact of cross-border data flows on trade (*see supra* Sect. 2.3.2).

Against the backdrop of an unsettled context of international cooperation, international organisations, governments, and private stakeholders have pursued individual initiatives to conceptualize and measure e-commerce and digital trade. Thereby, these stakeholders have assumed various vantage points and identified diverging reference parameters to analytically map and gauge digitalised patterns of international trade. For example, some have embarked to measure concepts such as ICT-enabled services[17] while others have set out to estimate the impact of digitalisation on cross-border transactions by surveying and typologising cross-border data flows.[18] The OECD has begun to develop a framework for analysing digital trade in the form of a typology to improve understanding of issues related to trade governance and measurement.[19] The concepts developed so far are representative of the respective views of the various actors and organisations, which brings with it the difficulty that, on the one hand, there is a multitude of different approaches and, on the other hand, different terms are used for concepts that are very similar in content. Against this backdrop, a need for increased collaboration has been identified to establish functional approaches that provide the basis for an analytical framework as well as a platform for regulatory action. In this context, the joint work of the WTO, the OECD and the IMF on the development of a first edition of a handbook on measuring digital trade, that was intended to address the "*plethora of various statistical measures: e-commerce (defined in various ways), ICT-enabled services, digitally enabled services, potentially digitally enabled services, and so on*" represented an important step forward.[20]

The aim of this section is to provide a meaning to the terms e-commerce and digital trade. To this end, an overview is presented of some of the definitions that have been established by key stakeholders in global trade. Then, the notion of global electronic commerce will be contrasted with that of digital trade. Against this background, an understanding of digital trade is elaborated that will underpin the further analysis of the trade policy environment in the digital economy and, in particular, the nexus between digital trade and data privacy.

---

[16] OECD (2019b), Chapter I. Of course, the general challenges of measuring digital transformation are even more comprehensive, *see* for example OECD (2019c), p. 238. Measurement issues associated with e-commerce have been the subject of long-standing debate, *see* for example OECD (1997b), pp. 6–15.

[17] UNCTAD (2015b). The report was commissioned by UNCTAD, as a contribution to the work of the Partnership on Measuring ICT for Development and its Task Group on Measuring Trade in ICT Services and ICT-enabled Services (TGServ).

[18] Ciuriak and Ptashkina (2018), p. 22; U.S. Department of Commerce (2016). *See* with respect to measuring the economic value of data flows *supra* Sect. 2.3.2.3.

[19] López González and Jouanjean (2017), p. 12.

[20] IMF et al. (2019), p. 31. *See* also WTO (2018a), p. 52.

3.2.1 Reviewing Conceptual Frameworks for E-Commerce and Digital Trade

The following section provides an indicative overview of key stakeholders' conceptual approaches both in respect of the notion of electronic commerce as well as digital trade. This overview of individual concepts will then be complemented with regard to the state of recent collaborations aiming at conceptualising trade in the digital economy.

3.2.1.1 Individual Conceptual Frameworks

3.2.1.1.1 World Trade Organisation (WTO)

The World Trade Organisation (WTO) has been a driving force in identifying new dimensions to cross-border trade under a digital paradigm. On the basis of the Declaration on Global Electronic Commerce,[21] adopted by the WTO Ministerial Conference in May 1998, the General Council launched a *"Work Programme on Electronic Commerce"* (Work Programme) in September 1998.[22] Under the Work Programme, an indicative definition of electronic commerce in the context of cross-border trade was deemed to include the *"production, distribution, marketing, sale or delivery of goods and services by electronic means"*.[23] The Work Programme, developed at the close of the twentieth century, remained a relevant instrument by virtue of its rather comprehensive definition of e-commerce and the resulting broad nature of its mandate. To date, however, it has not yielded tangible results.[24] Currently, the WTO continues to employ the 1998 definition of global electronic commerce and has so far largely refrained from employing the notion of digital trade. This is primarily because the rather extensive definition of the Work Programme also covers wider aspects of the digitalisation of cross-border trade.[25] Against this background, the recently adopted Joint Statement Initiative on Electronic Commerce

---

[21] WTO (1998a).

[22] WTO (1998b). *See also infra* Sect. 3.3.1.1.

[23] WTO (1998b), p. 1, para. 1.3.

[24] *See* only Wunsch-Vincent and Hold (2012), p. 181. Cf. also the Progress Reports to the General Council adopted by the Council for Trade in Services, WTO (1999e), the Council for Trade in Goods WTO (1999f), the Council for TRIPs WTO (1999c) and the Committee for Trade and Development WTO (1998e). For a detailed discussion of the merits and shortcomings of the WTO Work Programme, *see infra* Sect. 3.3.3.

[25] This results in terminological ambiguities that impede a shared international approach to this issue. However, regarding joint efforts on the measurement of trade in the digital economy, the WTO participates in initiatives that subscribe to the notion of digital trade, *see infra* Sect. 3.2.1.2.

refers to the concept of electronic commerce as elaborated in the Work Programme.[26]

3.2.1.1.2 Organisation for Economic Co-Operation and Development (OECD)

The Organisation for Economic Co-operation and Development (OECD) is an international organisation with 38 members which are *"determined by consultation and co-operation to use more effectively their capacities and potentialities so as to promote the highest sustainable growth of their economies and improve the economic and social well-being of their peoples"*.[27] In 1998, the OECD adopted the *"Action Plan for Electronic Commerce"*.[28] As a result, in April 1999, a Working Party on Indicators for the Information Society (WPIIS) expert group was established and mandated to *"compile definitions of electronic commerce which are policy relevant and statistically feasible"*.[29] Consequently, in 2001, OECD member countries endorsed two definitions of electronic commerce, which were eventually revised and unified into a single comprehensive definition in 2009.[30] Hence, the OECD defines e-commerce as follows: *"An e-commerce transaction is the sale or purchase of goods or services, conducted over computer networks by methods specifically designed for the purpose of receiving or placing of orders. The goods or services are ordered by those methods, but the payment and the ultimate delivery of the goods or services do not have to be conducted online. An e-commerce transaction can be between enterprises, households, individuals, governments, and other public or private organisations."*.[31] The determination of whether a transaction falls within the scope of definition is based more on the ordering method than on the characteristics of the purchased product, the parties involved, the method of payment or the delivery channel.[32]

With regard to the context of trade in the digital economy, the OECD conducted some of the most comprehensive research on the impact of digital business models, data and data flows on cross-border transactions. To better address the policy challenges of trade in the digital economy, the organisation has introduced the

---

[26] WTO (2019a). *See* further *infra* Sect. 3.3.1.2.

[27] Cf. OECD (1960), Preamble.

[28] OECD (1998). Prior to the Ministers' meeting in Ottawa, a conference was held in Turku a year before, under the heading *"Dismantling the Barriers to Global Electronic Commerce"*, see OECD (1997a).

[29] OECD (1999), p. 4.

[30] OECD (2011), pp. 71–73.

[31] This means that included are orders made over the web, extranet or electronic data interchange (EDI). Excluded are orders made by telephone calls, facsimile or manually typed e-mail, OECD (2011), p. 72.

[32] OECD (2019b), Chapter I.

term *"digital trade"* in its research.[33] In a 2017 OECD trade policy paper *Javier López González* and *Marie-Agnes Jouanjean* define digital trade as encompassing *"digitally enabled transactions in trade in goods and services which can be either digitally or physically delivered and which involve consumers, firms, and governments."*.[34] This definition includes the above-mentioned OECD definition of electronic commerce and extends further to various types of cross-border transactions, including digitally supplied services, regardless of the method by which they are ordered.[35] The authors emphasise that at its most basic understanding, digital trade is underpinned and driven by the transfer of digital data across borders.[36] The results of the joint work of the OECD, the WTO and the IMF will be presented below (*see infra* Sect. 3.2.1.2).

3.2.1.1.3 United Nations Conference on Trade and Development (UNCTAD)

The definition of electronic commerce adopted by the United Nations Conference on Trade and Development (UNCTAD) draws on the concept adopted by the OECD. In recent studies, UNCTAD has defined: *"E-commerce will cover purchases and sales conducted over computer networks, using multiple formats and devices, including the web and electronic data interchange, using personal computers, laptops, tablets and mobile phones of varying levels of sophistication. E-commerce may involve physical goods as well as intangible (digital) products and services that can be delivered digitally."*.[37] Unlike the OECD definition, however, the UNCTAD definition explicitly includes the digital provision of goods and services. Consequently, with regard to the notion of digital trade as formulated by the OECD, UNCTAD submits that it *"may be more appropriate to talk about "trade in the digital economy", rather than "digital trade""*.[38] Yet, UNCTAD has also referred to digital trade as *"trade in purely digitized products that can be downloaded or streamed over the Internet"*.[39]

---

[33] *See* for example López González and Ferencz (2018); OECD (2017).
[34] López González and Jouanjean (2017), p. 6.
[35] OECD (2019b), Chapter I.
[36] López González and Jouanjean (2017), p. 6.
[37] *See* UNCTAD (2015a), p. 3, UNCTAD (2016), p. 1.
[38] UNCTAD (2019), p. 44.
[39] UNCTAD (2016), p. 19.

3.2.1.1.4 United Nations Economic and Social Commission for Asia and the Pacific (UNESCAP)

The United Nations Economic and Social Commission for Asia and the Pacific (UNESCAP) adopted the OECD's definition for electronic commerce.[40] With regard to digital trade, UNESCAP refers quite broadly to the *"use of digital technologies to facilitate businesses without limiting it to just online sales or purchases"*.[41] Four different categories are then identified which should provide guidance in focusing on policy issues related to digital trade. Group 1 encompasses digital-infrastructure goods, such as computers, network devices or mobile phones that are part of physical infrastructure needed to conduct digital trade. Group 2 contains digital-infrastructure services, i.e., services providing virtual infra-structure such as telecommunications services and computer services. Group 3 is about digitalised *"content"* products, such as books, music, films that are increasingly traded electronically. Group 4, finally, is about electronically enabled services that have adopted digital technologies to sell e-services.[42]

3.2.1.1.5 United Nations Commission on International Trade Law (UNCITRAL)

The United Nations Commission on International Trade Law (UNCITRAL) has adopted a Model Law on Electronic Commerce (MLES) in its basic form on 12 June 1996.[43] While there is no explicit definition of *"electronic commerce"* provided in the MLES, in Chapter I, Article 1 *"sphere of application"* it is stated that *"this Law applies to any kind of information in the form of data message used in the context of commercial activities"*. The guide to enactment confirms the intention behind the fact that no precise definition of the term is provided and emphasises regarding the technologies of electronic information transfer: *"The objectives of the Model Law are best served by the widest possible application of the Model Law."*.[44]

3.2.1.1.6 Asia-Pacific Economic Cooperation (APEC)

The Asia-Pacific Economic Cooperation (APEC) is a forum for economic cooperation in the pacific region founded in Canberra in 1989 to promote economic growth

---

[40] UNESCAP (2018), p. 3.
[41] UNESCAP (2016), p. 103.
[42] UNESCAP (2016), p. 108.
[43] *See* UNCITRAL (1999). Relevant in the context is also the Model Law on Electronic Signatures that was adopted 5 July 2001 in order to enable and facilitate the use of electronic signatures, UNCITRAL (2001).
[44] *See* UNCITRAL (1999), pp. 17–18.

3.2 Towards Conceptualising Digital Trade

through multilateral cooperation. In 1998, the Cooperation adopted a *"Blueprint for Action on Electronic Commerce"*, in which APEC Ministers agreed to a work programme building on APEC's existing work on electronic commerce.[45] Similar to that of the WTO, the definition of electronic commerce adopted by APEC is rather broad and encompasses *"all business activity conducted by using a combination of electronic communications and information processing technology"*.[46] In 2001, APEC's 13th Ministerial Meeting established the *"E-Commerce Business Alliance"* (ECBA) with a secretariat located in Beijing.

3.2.1.1.7 United States of America

In 2013, the United States International Trade Commission (USITC) in the first part of a study on digital trade defined it as: *"U.S. domestic commerce and international trade in products and services delivered via the Internet."*.[47] This definition focusses on the delivery via the Internet and notably excludes trade in physical goods and services facilitated by digital technologies. In the process of conducting the 2013 study, the Commission was confronted with comments that deemed such a rather narrow definition of digital trade to be overly restrictive. It was pointed out that the definition failed to capture the value of all the diverse activities that occur over the Internet such as intra-company activities.[48] These objections led the Commission to broaden its definition of digital trade in the second part of the study. Here, digital trade was set out to encompass *"U.S. domestic commerce and international trade in which the Internet and Internet-based technologies play a particularly significant role in ordering, producing, or delivering products and services."*.[49] However, a later report in 2017 again tended to use a similar definition to the initial report. The report's scope of investigation defines digital trade as: *"The delivery of products and services over the Internet by firms in any industry sector, and of associated products such as smartphones and Internet-connected sensors. While it includes provision of e-commerce platforms and related services, it excludes the value of sales of physical goods ordered online, as well as physical goods that have a digital counterpart (such as books, movies, music, and software sold on CDs or DVDs)."*.[50] The report provided a rather complementary definition for e-commerce: *"the sale of goods or*

---

[45] APEC (1998).

[46] *See* with further references Mitchell (2001), p. 685.

[47] United States International Trade Commission (2013), pp. 1-2–1-4.

[48] For further expert views and opinions on the definition of digital trade expressed at the public hearing and in written submissions, *see* United States International Trade Commission (2013), p. 1–3, Box 1.1.

[49] The Trade Commission refrained however from giving an exact definition, *see* United States International Trade Commission (2014), pp. 29–30.

[50] United States International Trade Commission (2017), p. 33.

services conducted over computer networks, especially networks connected by the Internet".[51]

3.2.1.1.8 European Union

In 1997, the European Commission launched an initiative to *"encourage the vigourus growth of electronic commerce"*.[52] In a communication from the Commission, the objective of achieving a coherent regulatory framework was proclaimed. The communication defines two activities as being typically covered by electronic commerce: indirect e-commerce—*"the electronic ordering of tangible goods [...] delivered using traditional channels"* and direct e-commerce—*"the online ordering, payment and delivery of intangible goods and services on a global scale"*.[53] The initiative finally resulted in the adoption of the *"E-Commerce Directive"* in 2000.[54] With regard to digital trade the European Commission has put forth a rather broad definition. In this context, the Commission refers to *"commerce enabled by electronic means – by telecommunications and/or ICT services – and covers trade in both goods and services"*[55]

3.2.1.1.9 People's Republic of China

In August 2018, the Standing Committee of the 13th National People's Congress passed the E-Commerce Law of the People's Republic of China, which took effect on 1st January 2019. For the purposes of this law, Article 2 defines electronic commerce as *"the business activities of sale of goods or provision of services through the Internet or other information networks"*.[56] China has traditionally ranked as one of the largest online retail markets in the world and therefore strongly

---

[51] United States International Trade Commission (2017), p. 148.

[52] European Commission (1997).

[53] European Commission (1997), pp. 2–3, paras. 6–11.

[54] Directive 2000/31/EC of the European Parliament and of the Council of 8 June 2000 on certain legal aspects of information society services, in particular electronic commerce, in the Internal Market (Directive on Electronic Commerce), 17 July 2000, OJ L 178. The EU's Digital Services Act (DSA) builds on the E-Commerce Directive and addresses the challenges that have emerged over the past 20 years, Regulation (EU) 2022/2065 of the European Parliament and of the Council of 19 October 2022 on a Single Market For Digital Services and amending Directive 2000/31/EC (Digital Services Act).

[55] European Commission (2024).

[56] E-Commerce Law of the People's Republic of China, adopted at the Fifth Session of the Standing Committee of the 13th National People's Congress on 31 August 2018, *see* translation by IPKey (2018).

associates the term e-commerce with the sale of physical goods over the Internet.[57] With respect to cross-border data flows, China generally reserves significant policy objections, particularly related to security concerns. China is therefore arguably sceptical towards the concept of digital trade, which places an emphasis on purely digital business models based on data flows.[58]

3.2.1.2 Joint Initiatives of Conceptualisation

Given the diversity of concepts and the overall fragmented environment of public and private stakeholders in trade governance, a universal consensus on the definition of either electronic commerce or digital trade is not (yet) apparent. Although significant progress has been made recently, adopting a common understanding of trade in the digital economy remains a considerable challenge. Indeed, the dynamic growth of the digital trading environment has prompted the emergence of number of cross-organisational cooperation projects in recent years. For example, the Universal Postal Union (UPU), the UNCTAD, the OECD as well as the WTO launched a collaborative project in 2016 to measure cross-border e-commerce flows.[59] Furthermore, in the context of the G20, the German Council Presidency in 2017 has put the issue at the top of the agenda and requested the OECD to present an issues note on the status quo, gaps and the way forward in measuring digital trade.[60] The Ministerial Declaration of the G20 Hamburg summit encouraged further work by the participating international organisations, the result of which should be presented to the G20 Trade and Investment Working Group (TIWG).[61] Meanwhile, the progress made by the OECD formed the basis for an initial stocktaking survey among OECD countries and a subsequently updated conceptual framework for digital trade.[62] This was followed by a second survey in cooperation between the OECD and the IMF, in

---

[57] In this context, a 2019 Chinese proposal for the Joint Statement Initiative on Electronic Commerce reads „*The negotiation should focus on the discussion of cross-border trade in goods enabled by the internet, together with relevant payment and logistics services while paying attention to the digitalization trend of trade in services [...]*", cf. WTO (2019b), pp. 1–2, para. 2.4.

[58] Gao (2020), pp. 15–19.

[59] *See* further OECD and IMF (2017), p. 3. This collaboration was accompanied by ongoing projects, for example, UNCTAD (2016). *See* also UNESCAP (2016), pp. 105–108.

[60] OECD (2016). The note has benefitted from inputs from UNCTAD, the World Bank Group and the WTO.

[61] In particular the G20 welcomed further work on this issue, "*for the purpose of measuring digital trade, make proposals to responsible authorities for a common understanding of digital trade that is broad enough to cover existing approaches, and flexible enough to take into account on-going technological evolution, new ways of providing goods and services, and changes in regulatory classifications; identify both biases and gaps in measuring digital trade in statistics, including related to transactions not leaving a monetary footprint; and suggest ways to address these challenges and propose any areas where early progress could be made*", G20 (2017), p. 18.

[62] González and Ferencz (2018). The OECD initiative has aimed to align with existing statistical frameworks (BPM6, SNA2008, MSITS 2010, IMTS) and has benefitted from the insights and

which a total of 74 countries participated.[63] Building on this, the Interagency Task Force on International Trade Statistics (TFITS),[64] on the basis of a specific request from the 2017 G20 ministerial meeting and with the support of an expert group of more than 20 developed and developing countries, has started work on a handbook for measuring digital trade.[65] Based on the definition of e-commerce, according to a first version of the *"Handbook on measuring digital trade"*, digital trade is to encompass *"all trade that is digitally ordered and/or digitally delivered"*, thus capitalising on existing measurement efforts, while providing a broader perspective.[66] The second edition of the handbook maintains the basic measurement framework, but provides clarifications on the concepts and definitions introduced in the first edition and guidelines for their operationalisation.[67]

3.2.1.3 Evaluation

The above review clearly shows that the circumstances of the digital transformation of international trade are by no means well-established or firmly conceptually anchored. On the contrary, the difficulties of assessing the evolutionary unfolding of digital trade are evident in the abundance of (working) definitions for both electronic commerce and digital trade. Against this background, two observations can be made. First, concerning the format of the process, a certain paradox in the definition and measurement of trade in the digital economy exists. The lack of consensus on a universal approach at the international level is characterised by a lack of available data on the state and trajectory of the digital transformation of trade. Conversely, however, without a collective approach to analytical measurement, relevant data cannot be collected in the first place. Secondly, with regard to the substantial issues, (joint) initiatives must overcome the difficulty of mapping a highly dynamic digital trade environment. Trade in the digital economy is characterised by the particular complexity of data-based value creation and inherently global business models driven by cross-border data flows (*see* also *supra* Sect.

---

concepts of existing surveys in OECD/Eurostat countries on e-commerce and ICT-use as well as UNCTAD's work on ICT-enabled services, cf. Fortanier (2017), p. 4.

[63] OECD and IMF (2017), p. 3.

[64] The Interagency Task Force on International Trade Statistics (TFITS) is the product of a merger of the Task Force on International Merchandise Trade Statistics (TFIMTS) and the Task Force on Statistics of International Trade in Services (TFSITS) in 2014. TFITS is co-chaired by WTO and OECD and meets once a year.

[65] The conceptual framework was namely basis of the 2017 and 2018 OECD Working Party on International Trade in Goods and Service (WPTGS) meetings, the Eurostat Working Groups on Balance of Payments and on Trade in Services Statistics (2017/2018), and IMF BOPCOM 2017, leading to a series of conclusions regarding several substantive issues, see OECD and IMF (2018), pp. 3–10.

[66] IMF et al. (2019), p. 11.

[67] IMF et al. (2023).

2.3.2). The cross-cutting implications of the digital paradigm are at odds with the traditional system of defining and measuring global trade based on a division between distinct trade activities to which monetary value is attributable.[68] Currently, therefore, data from a variety of proxy sources is used to capture relevant elements of digital trade. These approaches certainly illuminate some of the implications of the digital transformation of trade, but they represent only a granular perspective on cross-border trade in the digital economy.[69]

3.2.1.3.1 Digital Delivery as a Criterion for Differentiation

While creating a comprehensive taxonomy of the multitude of existing definitions for digital trade would certainly go beyond the scope of this book, in the following, a comparison of the definitions adopted by the OECD and the WTO may illustrate some the current challenges in conceptualising digital trade.[70] While the OECD has increasingly felt the necessity to adopt the notion of digital trade in order to adequately capture the broader context of digital transformation of trade, the WTO largely adheres to the notion of e-commerce.[71] The above outline of contemporary definitions has demonstrated that both e-commerce and digital trade can be generally interpreted broadly or narrowly. Indeed, the 1998 WTO definition of electronic commerce was construed very broad and is considered to have been particularly ambitious for a time, in which the impact of digital transformation was largely obscure.[72] Given its exploratory mandate, the WTO's definition goes well beyond the OECD's definition of e-commerce ("*sale or purchase of goods or services, conducted over computer networks by methods specifically designed for the purpose of receiving or placing of orders*") and notably includes "*production, distribution [and] marketing*" of goods and services by "*electronic means*".[73] In fact, the WTO's rather early definition of global e-commerce from 1998 includes aspects outside the scope of the subsequent OECD definitions.[74] The OECD's definition of e-commerce focuses on the process of electronically facilitating the ordering of digital and physical goods and services. For example, the OECD refers to "*methods specifically designed for the purpose of receiving or placing of orders*" and does not cover the purchase or sale of goods or services based on telephone, fax or manually entered

---

[68] *See* in this context IMF et al. (2019), p. 15.
[69] IMF et al. (2019), pp. 19–21.
[70] *See* for a taxonomy of electronic commerce for instance Herman (2010), pp. 7–8.
[71] *See* in particular the WTO Joint Statement Initiative on Electronic Commerce initiated in early 2019 *supra* Sect. 3.3.1.2. Cf. in this context also the para. "*3 Terminology*" of the joint communication from Canada, the EU, Singapore and other WTO Members in the run-up to the 11th WTO Ministerial Conference in 2017, WTO (2016a), para. 3.
[72] *See* for example Wunsch-Vincent and Hold (2012), p. 180.
[73] WTO (1998b), p. 1, para. 1.3.
[74] OECD (2019b), Chapter I, Box 1.1. Some authors therefore actually consider it to be synonymous with digital trade Tuthill (2017), p. 97.

e-mail orders, which could be at least partially included in the category of *"electronic means"* in the WTO definition.[75] However, the core of incongruence seems to revolve around the emphasis on fully digital business models and the digital delivery of goods and services via the Internet. In this context, the OECD's e-commerce concept seems to focus on the initiation of a transaction of goods or services. While the WTO definition includes the *"distribution"* by *"electronic means"*, the OECD definition emphasises in turn that *"the payment and the ultimate delivery of the goods or services do not have to be conducted online"*. Furthermore, the WTO Work Programme more generally includes a broader range of aspects to electronic commerce such as with regard to issues relating to the development of the infrastructure for electronic commerce.[76] By adopting the concept of digital trade, the OECD is therefore seeking to reflect a conceptual change in cross-border trade that had previously not been a priority in its definition of e-commerce, notably with regard to the digital delivery of services. This highlights an inherent difficulty in the conceptualisation of digital trade, which lies in the highly dynamic nature of the digital transformation of trade.

3.2.1.3.2 Towards a Conceptual Expansion of Cross-Border Trade

The OECD's efforts in conceptualising the broader environment of cross-border trade in the digital economy intend to capture the effects of the digital transformation of trade on the basis of data and cross-border data flows.[77] Consequently, according to OECD, there is growing consensus that digital trade *"encompasses digitally-enabled transactions of trade in goods and services that can either be digitally or physically delivered, and that involve consumers, firms, and governments"*, drawing on both the OECD's 2011 and the WTO's definition of electronic commerce.[78] It is worth noting, that both the WTO and the OECD are contributing parties to the latest efforts in establishing a handbook for measuring digital trade which addresses the challenge of devising a conceptual framework for statistical purposes.[79] In the joint initiative of the OECD, the WTO and the IMF, digital trade assumes a broader perspective entailing, for example, services that are digitally delivered while not being digitally ordered.[80] While the definition used in the handbook cannot and is not intended to capture the overall contribution of digitalisation to trade, the first and second version of the handbook specifically include a placeholder for non-monetary international transactions with respect to data, for example.[81] This underscores that a

---

[75] OECD (2011), p. 72.
[76] WTO (1998b), p. 1, para. 1.3.
[77] *See* for example López González and Jouanjean (2017), pp. 7–12.
[78] López González and Ferencz (2018), p. 9.
[79] Cf. IMF et al. (2019).
[80] IMF et al. (2019), p. 11.
[81] IMF et al. (2019), p. 15, p. 20; IMF et al. (2023), p. 29.

3.2 Towards Conceptualising Digital Trade

conceptual expansion of cross-border trade, to integrate the effects of data and data flows in particular, is under discussion.

3.2.2 From E-Commerce to Digital Trade

The subsequent elaboration is placed in the context of the effort to foster a conceptual consensus for trade governance in the digital economy. For the purpose of the analysis of the nexus of digital trade and data privacy, this section will develop building blocks of a contextual conceptualisation for digital trade. It is essentially argued here that the notion of digital trade is the articulation of a transforming environment for international trade in the digital economy underpinned by data and data flows. This environment is substantially different from that of the twentieth century and is therefore not adequately reflected by the notion of electronic commerce. This assessment is based on an aggregate of several considerations that reflect on the vectors of digital transformation of trade outlined above (*see supra* Sect. 2. 3.1) as well as on the efforts to develop a concept for digital trade for measurement purposes (*see* in particular *supra* Sect. 3.2.1.2). In order to adopt a holistic perspective on the evolutionary development from e-commerce to digital trade, two considerations in particular are raised in this context. A first consideration pertains to the chronology of the use of the respective notions over time and a second consideration refers to the substance of the terms in relation to the underlying realities of a global digital economy.

3.2.2.1 Chronological Reasoning

A first consideration is identified in the chronology of the origin and use of the notions of electronic commerce and digital trade with regard to trade governance. While the concept of e-commerce has been established for more than two decades and is therefore more clearly delineated,[82] the relative novelty of the concept of digital trade currently leaves considerable latitude in its use, both in terms of statistical measurement and regulatory governance. A first indication of a differentiation between e-commerce and digital trade can therefore be derived from the fact that the term digital trade has been generally adopted consecutively to the term e-commerce but has gained currency in recent years as the digital economy has advanced.[83]

---

[82] However, this does not mean that there is a single definition accepted universally, *see* already Mitchell (2001), p. 685. *See* also *supra* Sect. 3.2.1.

[83] It must be emphasized that the definition building process is often a gradual procedure in a multipolar and dynamic environment. In this sense, the term digital trade was used as early as the turn of the millennium, *see* for example Wunsch-Vincent (2003).

While the utilisation of electronic communication as a means of conducting cross-border commercial activities had been previously in place, the emergence of the Internet in the early 1990s propelled phenomena such as B2C online retailing or B2B supply chain management into the mainstream. Consequently, the notion of electronic commerce has gained widespread recognition. With regard to international trade, the proliferation of ICT has resulted in several initiatives during the 1990s by international organisations such as the WTO, OECD, APEC and UNCITRAL to address cross-border implications of commercial integration of the Internet and global networks.[84] The increasing integration of global e-commerce into the regime of cross-border trade is further exemplified by a review of the evolution of Preferential Trade Agreements (PTAs).[85] From 1994 and with increasing consistency from 2000 onwards, trade agreements adopted terms relating to electronic commerce in a cross-border context.[86] In this sense, the 2002 agreement between the US and Jordan contained the first dedicated provision on e-commerce.[87] Notably, the first agreement featuring a standalone chapter to promote cross-border e-commerce was concluded between Australia and Singapore in 2003 (Chapter 14).[88] From 2011 onwards, with exceptions only in 2012 and 2017, equally or more trade agreements with e-commerce provisions entered into force than without, resulting in two-thirds of the WTO Membership being party to an agreement that includes e-commerce related provisions.[89]

However, in view of the ongoing digital transformation and the emergence of a data-driven economy, more recently, the notion of digital trade has proliferated with regard to trade governance. This general trend appears to be spreading from the US to Europe, albeit with a slight delay. While in July of 2013, for example, the United States International Trade Commission (USITC) published the first part of its comprehensive study on digital trade,[90] the European Commission included a section on *"facilitating digital trade"* in its 2015 trade and investment strategy entitled *"Trade for all"*.[91] Subsequently, the EU Parliament in 2017 adopted a

---

[84] *See supra* Sect. 3.2.1.1. Some of the first trade agreements integrating provisions on electronic commerce explicitly refer to these initiatives, such as the Singapore-New Zealand Agreement of 2001 with reference to the APEC Blueprint for Action on Electronic Commerce (Part IV, Article 12) or the Australia-Singapore Agreement of 2003 with reference to the UNCITRAL Model Law on Electronic Commerce (Chapter 14, Article 6).

[85] The following remarks are complemented by a review of key elements with regard to digital trade in PTAs below, *see infra* Sect. 3.4.

[86] Willemyns (2020b), pp. 223–224. Reference is made to the Singapore - New Zealand agreement of 2001 as the first international trade agreement to explicitly address e-commerce. A closer look at this agreement reveals, however, that the parties place limited emphasis on new forms of commercial transactions involving the use of ICT.

[87] Monteiro and Teh (2017), p. 5.

[88] Wu (2017), p. 6.

[89] Willemyns (2020b), p. 224.

[90] United States International Trade Commission (2013).

[91] European Commission (2015), p. 12, para. 2.1.2.

3.2 Towards Conceptualising Digital Trade

resolution entitled *"Towards a digital trade strategy"*.[92] The recently published European trade policy review for an open, sustainable, and assertive trade policy puts forth the ambition to play a central role in creating the rules for digital trade.[93] The argument of a chronological evolution of terminology is substantiated further by the increasing prominence of rules on digital trade in PTAs.[94] Recently, digital trade chapters in agreements with US and EU participation have replaced chapters on electronic commerce, while the regulatory elements of the latter remain valid and important. It can therefore be assumed that the parties to such agreements generally assume the terminology of digital trade to be more appropriately designating the regulatory substance and general spirit of the respective chapters. One such example is provided by the chapter on digital trade (Article 19) of the USMCA Agreement between the US, Mexico and Canada, which replaced the North American Free Trade Agreement (NAFTA) when it entered into force in July of 2020. In fact, the digital trade chapter of the USMCA, which is largely based on the e-commerce chapter of the Comprehensive and Progressive Agreement for Trans-Pacific Partnership (CPTPP), marks the first chapter on digital trade globally.[95] In similar vein, the EU and the UK have now agreed on rules for digital trade in the post-Brexit trade and cooperation agreement.[96] Moreover, the EU is increasingly introducing digital trade chapters within its negotiations with potential trading partners such as Tunisia, Indonesia, Australia and also with regard to the agreement in principle on the main trade parts of a new EU-Mexico association agreement. The European Commission has developed horizontal provisions on data flows and data protection in trade agreements that explicitly address regulatory cooperation on digital trade.[97] These provisions are systematically included in bilateral negotiations such as those referred to above and are part of the EU proposal to the current plurilateral WTO Joint Statement Initiative on Electronic-Commerce.[98]

Beyond the integration of dedicated provisions and chapters in trade agreements, some stand-alone digital economy or digital trade agreements have already been signed. For instance, regarding the above-mentioned first agreement including a

---

[92] European Parliament (2017).
[93] European Commission (2021), pp. 14–15, para. 3.2.3.
[94] *See* further *infra* Sect. 3.4. Cf. also the unfolding of deliberations within the WTO Work Programme on E-Commerce and the negotiation proposals under the Joint Statement Initiative on Electronic Commerce *infra* Sect. 3.3.1.
[95] *See* Chander (2018). Although largely consistent with the e-commerce chapter of the CPTPP, the USMCA digital trade chapter contains a more advanced set of regulations specifically aimed at the data-driven economy, *see* further *infra* Sect. 3.4.2.2.1.
[96] Trade and Cooperation Agreement between the European Union and the European Atomic Community, of the one part, and the United Kingdom of Great Britain and Northern Ireland, of the Other Part, Chapter II, Heading One: Trade, Title III.
[97] European Commission (2018).
[98] WTO (2019c). It should be noted, however, that the implementation of the horizontal provisions included in the EU proposal does not explicitly refer to *"digital trade"*, but rather to *"trade in the digital economy"*, cf. p. 4, para. 2.7.

separate chapter on electronic commerce concluded between Singapore and Australia, it must be noted that the relevant chapter was replaced by a DEA signed on 6 August 2020. Similarly, the US and Japan signed a digital trade agreement in 2019, as did the UK and Singapore in February 2022. The Singapore Ministry of Trade and Industry emphasizes that these agreements are designed to establish *"digital trade rules and digital economy collaborations between two or more economies"*.[99] In this context, a Digital Economy Partnership Agreement (DEPA) between New Zealand, Chile and Singapore has been signed in an all-virtual signing ceremony in June 2020. The DEPA is the first purely digital trade agreement open to all WTO members, is intended to complement WTO negotiations on e-commerce, and builds on work in other international fora such as the APEC and the OECD.[100] The DEPA is a particularly comprehensive agreement that specifically addresses digital trade issues, such as business and trade facilitation, the treatment of digital products and related issues, data flow issues, business and consumer trust, digital identities, and emerging trends and technologies. The fact that parties increasingly negotiate these and similar matters outside of digital trade chapters of traditional trade agreements points to the critical need for regulation on digital trade, on the one hand, and the desire to establish new forms of flexible collaboration, on the other.[101] The EU has concluded digital partnerships with some of its partner countries addressing digital trade and including *"Digital Trade Principles"*. Currently the EU negotiates self-standing digital agreements with Singapore and the Republic of Korea.[102]

3.2.2.2 Conceptual Reasoning

Beyond a chronological reasoning regarding the diffusion of digital trade terminology, it can be argued that the cross-border economic activity originally addressed by referring to global electronic commerce has diversified and expanded.[103] The phenomenon of electronically facilitated business transactions precedes the existence of the Internet. Before the emergence of the world wide web, economically relevant activities were conducted cross-border, for example, via Electronic Data Interchange (EDI).[104] However, the advent of the Internet with its open and accessible communication standards has massively accelerated the integration of electronic transmissions into commercial workflows in general and into cross-border transactions in particular.[105] Since the late 1990s, the digitalisation of cross-border activity has

---

[99] Cf. Ministry of Trade and Industry Singapore (2024).
[100] World Economic Forum (2022).
[101] *See* further Peng et al. (2021b), pp. 18–20.
[102] European Commission (2024).
[103] *See* in this context OECD (2019b), Chapter 2.
[104] *See* for example Bacchetta et al. (1998), p. 9.
[105] Bacchetta et al. (1998), p. 10.

3.2 Towards Conceptualising Digital Trade

continuously raised new trade policy challenges, which at the time were associated with the concept of global electronic commerce.[106] While the integration of digital technologies and the Internet into cross-border trade was initially identified as a cross-cutting issue of key relevance to all WTO agreements, the relevant deliberations within the framework of the WTO Work Programme on e-commerce quickly stalled (*see* further *infra* Sect. 3.3.1.1). This is due in part to the fact that, because of its conceptual novelty, e-commerce was perceived by some as a complementary and sectoral phenomenon alongside traditional trade in goods and services rather than as a *"new economic frontier"*.[107] This perspective, however, could not ignore the now ubiquitous integration of digital technologies, data and cross-border data flows in almost all sectors of the global economy. As briefly summarised above, the synergies of extensive amounts of digital data, efficient global networks and continuously improving computing performance allows for previously unheard-of use-cases for digital data, entailing a transformative shift in economic paradigm (*see supra* Sect. 2.2.2). The OECD has stated: *"What is new in digital trade is the scale of transactions and the emergence of new (and disruptive) players transforming production processes and industries including many that were previously little affected by globalisation."*.[108] In particular, the role of data and its cross-border transfers via the Internet has become paramount for trade (*see supra* Sect. 2.3.2). Data has evolved from merely assisting tangible business activities of the physical world to provide a vital economic resource in its own right, underpinning an ever-expanding global digital economy. Today it is widely recognised within the international community that the ability to transfer digital data across national borders is a cornerstone of innovation, productivity and economic competitiveness in the digital economy.[109] Notwithstanding, a general scarcity of empirical evidence (*see supra* Sect. 2.3.2.3) cross-border data flows are widely regarded as key enablers of digital globalisation as well as a driving force for the transformation of international trade.[110] In essence, the change in quality resulting from a change in quantity, which characterises the impact of digital data in the context of economic activities, is reflected in international trade law and policy.[111] In other words, as economic prosperity and growth have become increasingly premised on the harnessing of the value of digital technologies and data over the past decade, trade governance is bound to reflect this shift in paradigm.

---

[106] Initial debates under the auspices of the WTO regarding the issue of electronic commerce were characterised by a broad range of topics, which included, for example, questions with regard to issues of classification of electronic transmissions within the existing multilateral trade regime, development-related issues, fiscal implications of e-commerce as well as jurisdiction and applicable law. See for example WTO (2001c). See further *infra* Sect. 3.3.1.1.

[107] *See* also Primo Braga (2010), p. 475.

[108] López González and Ferencz (2018), p. 9.

[109] *See* for example G20 (2018), p. 2, para. 9.

[110] Casalini and López González (2019), pp. 8–9; Manyika et al. (2016), pp. 30–41; Meltzer (2019a), pp. 26–28; WTO (2018a), pp. 51–59.

[111] *See* for the technological aspect with regard to digital data Bantjes (2008).

Consequently, as digital transformation has evolved, certain elements of what was considered to constitute electronic commerce (e.g., electronic facilitation of services trade) have evolved and taken on new and expanded forms (e.g., *"free"* digital services). At the same time, new dimensions to trade have emerged due to a dynamically developing digital economy. In this regard, the emergence of the notion of digital trade coincides with an increasingly data-centred economy, as evidenced by the rise of several key technologies in recent years such as Cloud Computing, Big Data, AI, Distributed Ledger Technologies (e.g., blockchain) and IoT (*see supra* Sect. 2.2.2). All of these technologies revolve around the abundance of data in a networked environment driven by cross-border data flows. Against this background, academic researchers and trade practitioners alike tend to perceive the governance of cross-border data flows as a central proxy for the governance of the policy environment of digital trade.[112] In some of these studies, digital trade is largely equated with the cross-border flow of data. This approach sometimes is combined with a framework identifying different modes of digital trade such as *"digital to real"* transactions like web-search and streaming of audio and visual content as well as different forms of *"real to real"* transactions with digital intermediation.[113] In similar vein, the OECD has embraced the notion of digital trade in order to better address digital business models underpinned by data flows as well as cross-border elements of a data driven global economy (*see supra* Sect. 3.2.1.3.2). Against this background, the notion of digital trade is assigned the role of not merely addressing *"electronically"* facilitated forms of international trade, but rather the wider challenges that arise in a *"digitally"* integrated global economic environment. In this sense, *"[t]his new era of hyperconnectivity is not just about digitally delivered trade, it is also about more physical, traditional or GVC, trade enabled by growing digital connectivity increasing access to foreign markets for firms in a way that would previously have been unimaginable"*.[114]

3.2.3 A Data-Centred Concept for Trade in the Digital Economy: Towards a Definition for Digital Trade

The previous section presented the building blocks of a contextual approach to the concept of digital trade, seeking to capture trade in the digital economy in its conceptual evolution. Against this background, with regard to an evolving digital economy and the crucial significance of data as a resource, a distinction between digital trade and e-commerce is drawn here with the objective to capture the progressive evolvement of a digital transformation of international trade. While at

---

[112] *See* only Hofheinz and Mandel (2015), p. 8; Lund and Manyika (2016), p. 3; Meltzer (2016), pp. 8–9.
[113] Ciuriak and Ptashkina (2018), pp. 5–8.
[114] Cf. López González and Jouanjean (2017), pp. 7–12.

3.2 Towards Conceptualising Digital Trade

the turn of the millennium, the notion of e-commerce was conceptualised very broadly and, for example, as a shorthand term *"that embraces a complex amalgam of technologies, infrastructures, processes, and products. It brings together whole industries and narrow applications, producers and users, information exchange and economic activity into a global marketplace called "the Internet"*",[115] the concept has subsequently been refined. It has been employed primarily to indicate specific contributions of electronic means to the transactional exchange of goods and services. Certainly, such initial considerations already reflected, that electronic transmissions disseminated through a burgeoning infrastructure of digital networks and the Internet may become of critical relevance to the future economic potential of cross-border trade. However, it seems presumptuous to claim that at the time, it was already foreseeable that digital data and its cross-border transmission would become a crucial economic factor affecting every sector of the world economy. Hence, it can be assumed that e-commerce constituted the first visible mark of a digital transformation of international trade, the full extent of which today is to be comprehensively addressed by the notion of digital trade. In this context, the notion of digital trade assumes a role as an overarching umbrella term describing the digitalisation of trade flows such as and its associated challenges for trade governance.[116] Consequently, it is argued here that the interchangeable use of the concepts of digital trade and e-commerce is due to the fact that e-commerce and associated policy issues have long been a predominant part of the wider environment of electronically facilitated and enabled cross-border flows in international trade relations.[117] Against this background, the notion of digital trade epitomises the next step in the evolutionary process of digital transformation, focusing on the role of data in the digital economy and its flow across borders in relation to economic activity.

The preceding discussion has underscored that in the current phase of the digital transformation of international trade, there is hardly common ground within the international community for assessing the paradigmatic changes brought about by digitalisation. Rather, a multitude of individual perspectives on different aspects of the digital transformation prevails.[118] Therefore, it could be argued that, given the persistent ambiguity as regards a conceptual approach for digital trade, the term does not yield an essential and clarifying insight, but merely adds another slogan—similar

---

[115] Mann (2000), p. 3.

[116] In this direction also Aaronson (2019) p. 544; Kende and Sen (2019), p. 3; Streinz (2019), p. 320; Weber (2010), p. 2; Yakovleva and Irion (2020), p. 210. *See* generally Mitchell and Mishra (2018), p. 1067, fn. 2.

[117] Gao (2017), p. 361 underscores this evolution: *"In terms of the overall regulatory philosophy, the earlier US FTAs tend to focus mostly on the "trade" aspects by trying to fit e-commerce into the existing framework of the WTO and borrowing heavily from the WTO rulebooks, while the TPP has started to recognize the unique nature of e-commerce and tried to formulate new rules befitting the "digital" nature of e-commerce. Such efforts are most evident in rules relating to issues such as transfer of source code and forced localization requirements, which are new issues created by the amorphous and border-less nature of digital trade.".*

[118] IMF et al. (2019), p. 31.

to those of *"digitalisation"* or *"digital economy"*.[119] Introducing a *"new"* term could prove to be irrelevant (or worse counterproductive) for the debate on the underlying policy issues such as with regard to the nexus of digital trade and data privacy. The debates on the definition of electronic commerce within the OECD that have been ongoing since the early 2000s can be drawn upon. There it has been established, that a clear definition must be coherent, simple, and pragmatic as well as limited to clearly defined concepts and acknowledge future forms of electronic commerce due to evolving technologies and policies.[120] Some 20 years later, however, this endeavour has proven to be an enormous effort in light of a constantly evolving economic environment shaped by the digital transformation. In this sense, regulatory mapping of the digital transformation of international trade appears to involve a continuous process of learning. In such a learning process, it is helpful to label emergent phenomena in order to render them more visible to the various disciplines, even if the underlying concept may remain somewhat vague at first, in the sense that *"the reduction of uncertainty does not require the creation of certainty"*.[121] Against this background, it must also be emphasised that the objective of this analysis is to provide a fundamental understanding of the essence of digital trade for a legal analysis and, in particular, with regard to the nexus with data privacy.

In this context and for the purpose of this research, digital trade is assigned a pragmatic definition which is based on a distinct and recurring element of the discourse on the digital transformation of trade. This widely recognised central element of digital trade centres on the role of data and cross-border data flows as the basis for essentially all economic activity in the digital economy (*see* also *supra* Sect. 2.3.2).[122] Against this backdrop, the term digital trade in the context of this analysis refers to *all forms of cross-border economic activity that depend on the flow of digital data as it significantly facilitates or enables them.* While this definition is quite broad, it is consistent with the holistic approach to the digital transformation of cross-border trade adopted above. It also reflects the cross-cutting nature of digital trade, which encompasses all pre-existing trade sectors, i.e., goods, services, and trade-related aspects of intellectual property. The concept primarily encompasses trade enabled by data flows in the first place, such as trade in digital products. However, it also encompasses trade significantly facilitated by data flows, such as trade in physical goods that involves the Internet as a platform. Hence, the term is employed to grasp a very broad idea of trade in the digital economy, extending to and including, for example, the concept of electronic commerce, which is deemed to cover primarily digitally facilitated trade in physical goods. Yet, digital trade is

---

[119] *See* in this direction *Thomas Streinz,* who deems the concepts of electronic commerce and digital trade *"misleading"* as these *"suggest the existence of separate, if ill-defined, domains and conceal a reality in which increased digitalization and interconnectedness affect all sectors of the economy"*, Streinz (2019), p. 337.

[120] OECD (2011), p. 72.

[121] Wolfe (2018), p. 12.

[122] Casalini and López González (2019); López González and Jouanjean (2017), p. 10.

construed here not as a complementary phenomenon, designating predominantly the digital delivery of goods and services, but to address a broader perspective on an emergent digital trading environment.[123] In this context, the terminology of digital trade also promises to avoid confusion with the everyday phenomenon of online shopping, popularly known as e-commerce, and to accentuate the existence of new frontiers for cross-border trade as such.[124] In this sense, it is an open concept that transcends the currently used categories of cross-border trade and is fundamentally relevant to potentially emerging categories such as *"data trade"*, for example. The concept of digital trade extends notably to include data itself as the subject of trade.[125] It encompasses areas subject to ongoing digital convergence, and thus extends to new trade policy issues in the digital economy such as data governance and Internet governance.[126] The notion of digital trade allows for a clearer focus on emerging barriers to trade in the digital economy, such as with regard to data localisation measures, Internet filtering or access restrictions as well as potentially restrictive domestic data-regulations such as with regard to cybersecurity and data privacy. For the purposes of this research on the nexus of digital trade and data privacy, this approach provides a basis for analysing the challenges of regulating a data-driven trading environment. Thus, using the term digital trade in the proposed context of an evolving technological, regulatory, and economic environment serves to provide a comprehensive understanding of the transformation of international trade resulting from data and cross-border data flows in a digitally globalised economy.

3.3 The WTO and Digital Trade

The multilateral framework of the WTO is a cornerstone of the world economic order and has been an important driving force of global integration. Its predecessor, the General Agreement on Tariffs and Trade of 1947,[127] has administered an evolving global economic sphere, advocated transparent trade rules, incrementally lowered tariff barriers and gradually relaxed protectionism while shaping

---

[123] *See* further Burri (2016a), pp. 331–332, identifies a *"broad"*definition for digital trade and contrasts this to the *„narrow"* definition of commerce in products delivered over the Internet. *See* for example, the 2013 definition by the USITC *supra* Sect. 3.2.1.1.7. *See* also Wunsch-Vincent and Hold (2012), pp. 179–180.

[124] For example, the initial US proposal for the WTO Joint Statement Initiative on Electronic Commerce argues that the use of the term digital trade, as opposed to the term e-commerce, which is widely understood to refer to trade in goods enabled by the Internet, better illustrates the broad scope of the concept, cf. WTO (2018d), fn. 1.

[125] *See* also Yakovleva and Irion (2020), p. 210.

[126] López González and Jouanjean (2017), p. 8. Indeed, it is questionable to what extent the mandate of the WTO covers standard-setting in these areas, *see* also *infra* Sect. 6.3.

[127] General Agreement on Tariffs and Trade, 30 October 1947, 61 Stat. A-11, 55 U.N.T.S. 194.

globalisation.[128] The signing of the Final Act of the Uruguay Round carried out in Marrakesh on 15 April 1994 is generally considered a milestone for global trade as it marked the official conclusion of the most comprehensive trade negotiations yet. The so-called Marrakesh Agreement created the World Trade Organisation (WTO) as an international organisation and included in its annexes important treaties such as the GATT (1994), the General Agreement in Trade in Services (GATS) and the Agreement on Trade-Related Aspects of Intellectual Property Rights (TRIPS). In addition to establishing the institutional framework of the WTO, it addressed for the first time at the multilateral level the changing reality of international trade by regulating both trade in services and trade-related aspects of intellectual property rights. The WTO framework today is the embodiment of an international trading system whose regulatory capacity extends to various types of cross-border trade flows, encompassing the movement of goods, services, people, knowledge, and ideas. Against this background, this section examines the extent to which current WTO rules cover patterns of digital trade undergirded by cross-border data flows. To this end, this section analyses initiatives taken within the WTO to address the trade-related implications of the global digital economy and evaluates the state of digital trade governance under current WTO law.

3.3.1 The WTO as a Forum for Digital Trade Governance

The WTO framework generally offers various opportunities for debate on digital trade issues as well as for the further development of the relevant legal framework. Pursuant to Article III:2 of the WTO Agreement, the WTO *"shall provide the forum for negotiations among its Members"* with regard to their trade relations in matters dealt with under WTO law. A number of WTO agreements include provisions on the monitoring and further development of the substantive provisions of the respective treaty text in the course of progressive liberalisation. As will be further illustrated below, with regard to digital trade underpinned by cross-border data flows, the framework of the GATS pertaining to the cross-border trade in digital services is of particular relevance (*see* further *infra* Sect. 3.3.2.6). Given that the GATS constituted the first multilateral agreement on trade in services, the negotiating parties agreed on a *"built-in agenda"*.[129] In fact, as a framework agreement, the GATS contains various negotiating mandates directed towards progressive liberalisation (Part IV GATS). WTO Members have pledged to *"enter into successive rounds of negotiations [...] with a view to achieving a progressively higher level of liberalization"*, Article XIX:1 GATS. Similar considerations apply to other aspects relevant to digital trade, such as with respect to domestic (data) regulations that may constitute a barrier to trade. Article VI:4 GATS entails a mandate for the

---

[128] VanGrasstek (2013), pp. 39–83; WTO (2018a), pp. 18–19.

[129] *See* in this present context Wunsch-Vincent (2004), pp. 68–69.

3.3 The WTO and Digital Trade

Council for Trade in Services (CTS) to develop necessary disciplines that ensure that measures relating to qualification requirements and procedures, technical standards and licensing requirements do not constitute unnecessary barriers to trade in services. In accordance with the obligation to start negotiations no later than 5 years after the entry into force of the WTO Agreement under Article XIX:1 GATS, negotiations were launched in 2000.[130] The *"Guidelines and Procedures for the Negotiations on Trade in Services"* adopted by the CTS on 28 March 2001 pursuant to Article XIX:3 GATS were drafted with a broad scope and in particular stated: *"There shall be no a priori exclusion of any service sector or mode of supply."*.[131] The negotiating guidelines thus extended in principle to the digital delivery of services via the Internet and to new digital services which have developed in the digital economy (*see* further *infra* Sect. 3.3.2.6). However, this *"built-in agenda"* has not yielded much progress in advancing the GATS agreement with respect to the ongoing digital transformation of trade. The Doha Round negotiations, reaffirming the aforementioned *"Guidelines and Procedures for the Negotiations on Trade in Services"* adopted by the CTS *"as the basis for continuing the negotiations"*, provided an opportunity to address controversial issues previously identified and discussed in the 1998 WTO Work Programme.[132] In this context, the 2005 Hong Kong ministerial declaration has issued specific goals in Annex C relating to services.[133] However, although a number of WTO Members engaged in negotiations and submitted proposals on a wide range of sectors, consultations on the progressive liberalisation of services trade overall suffered a similar fate as the Doha Round in general.[134] The following outline of the WTO's ability to function as a forum for the governance of digital trade focuses primarily on the WTO's 1998 Work Programme on Electronic Commerce, which was set up to examine the impact of *"global electronic commerce"* on the global trading environment.[135] This is followed by a reflection on the status of the ongoing plurilateral negotiations under the Joint Statement Initiative on Electronic Commerce.[136]

3.3.1.1 1998 WTO Work Programme on Global Electronic Commerce

As a result of the increasing awareness of the relevance of ICT, in 1996 a plurilateral initiative formed, which aimed to liberalise trade in IT goods such as computers, semiconductors and telecommunications apparatus. The resulting Information

---

[130] *See* further Adlung (2006).
[131] WTO (2001b), p. 1, para. 5.
[132] WTO (2001a), para. 15; Wunsch-Vincent (2004), p. 92.
[133] WTO (2005), Annex C.
[134] *See* Wunsch-Vincent and Hold (2012), pp. 189–190. *See* for a detailed discussion on the merits of the Doha Round Dupont and Elsig (2014).
[135] WTO (1998b).
[136] WTO (2019a).

Technology Agreement (ITA) was concluded in December 1996 at the Singapore Ministerial Conference by 29 participants.[137] Meanwhile, extended sectoral negotiations in the digitally intensive areas of telecommunications and financial services were concluded and subsequently included in the GATS framework in the form of separate protocols.[138] Against this background and in view of *"new possibilities"* arising with regard to an expanding sector for electronic commerce, the WTO Ministerial Conference in 1998 adopted a Declaration on Global E-Commerce and called for a *"comprehensive work programme"*, in order *"to examine all trade-related issues relating to global electronic commerce"*.[139] At the same time, WTO members agreed to continue their practice of not imposing tariffs on electronic transmissions (Moratorium on Customs Duties on Electronic Transmissions).[140] In accordance with its mandate, the General Council adopted a comprehensive Work Programme on electronic commerce *"to examine all trade-related issues relating to global electronic commerce, taking into account the economic, financial, and development needs of developing countries"* on 25. September 1998.[141] Without prejudice to the outcome of the programme, the term electronic commerce was defined to indicate the *"production, distribution, marketing, sale or delivery of goods and services by electronic means"*.[142] The Council's mandate to the subsidiary bodies of the Council for Trade in Services (CTS), the Council for Trade in Goods (CTG) and the Council for TRIPS (CTRIPs) included a broad range of tasks.[143] Under the Work Programme the Council itself is responsible for the task of addressing cross-sectoral issues.[144]

3.3.1.1.1 E-Commerce Debate Under Continued (Re-)Invigoration

During the subsequent time period the respective Councils met and reported back to the General Council.[145] However, from the initial *"dedicated discussion"* held under

---

[137] *See* further *infra* Sect. 3.3.2.2. The agreement was expanded in 2015, marking one of the few major achievements of the WTO subsequent to the conclusion of the Uruguay Round.

[138] Cf. regarding financial services WTO (1995); WTO (1997). Cf. regarding Basic Telecommunications, WTO (1996a).

[139] WTO (1998a).

[140] WTO (1998a).

[141] WTO (1998b).

[142] WTO (1998b), p. 1, para. 1.3.

[143] WTO (1998b), pp. 2–3, paras. 2-5.1. Cf. also the note, prepared by the WTO Secretariat to assist Members in their deliberations on trade-related issues pertaining to global electronic commerce, WTO (1998c).

[144] WTO (1998b), p. 1, para. 1.2 states: *"The General Council shall play a central role in the whole process and keep the work programme under continuous review through a standing item on its agenda. In addition, the General Council shall take up consideration of any trade-related issue of a cross-cutting nature."*.

[145] *See* for example WTO (1999a, 1999b, 1999c).

3.3 The WTO and Digital Trade   93

the auspices of the General Council in June 2001 regarding cross-cutting aspects of e-commerce, it became clear that achieving results on the issues raised by the ambitious agenda would be challenging. The debate addressed a wide range of cross-cutting issues such as the controversial classification regarding trade on the basis of electronic transmissions within the established WTO framework as well as more general issues, i.e., questions on fiscal implications of e-commerce. A summary of the dedicated discussion provided by the WTO Secretariat indicated that overall further discussions were warranted.[146] In the following years, WTO Members continued to place the issue high on the agenda of ministerial conferences and the Moratorium on Customs Duties on Electronic Transmissions was continuously extended. Nevertheless, there was hardly any progress. The overall performance of the Work Programme was hampered by continuing disagreements over substantive issues, particularly the operation of the Moratorium on Customs Duties on Electronic Transmissions or the classification of electronic transmissions as goods or services, but also by disputes over the further procedural development of the Work Programme.[147] The Work Programme hence *"oscillated"* between dialogue and gridlock.[148] In this context, the wording of the Final Declarations of the respective Ministerial Conferences shed ample light on the progress achieved under the Work Programme. The final declaration of the fourth WTO Ministerial Conference in Doha in November 2001 indicates that the work carried out so far had shown *"new challenges and opportunities"* and that the *"importance of creating and maintaining an environment which is favourable to the future development of electronic commerce"* was recognised.[149] The final declaration of the subsequent WTO Ministerial Conference in Hong Kong in December 2005 indicates that the reports of the General Council and its subsidiary bodies on the Work Programme had been noted and that the work should be *"reinvigorated"* while maintaining the existing institutional set-up.[150] The Ministerial Conference of 2009 adopted a wording according to which the work should be *"intensively reinvigorated"*.[151] In the context of the eighth WTO Ministerial Conference on 17 December 2011 the decision was taken to *"continue the reinvigoration"* of the Work Programme, whereby the importance of e-commerce was stressed both for developing countries and the least developed countries as well as for the Micro, Small and Medium Enterprises.[152] In 2013, the Ministerial Conference concluded that the *"positive*

---

[146] WTO (2001d).
[147] Ismail (2020), pp. 9–10.
[148] Venkatesh (2021).
[149] WTO (2001a), para. 34.
[150] WTO (2005), para. 46.
[151] WTO (2009a). The reports within the Work Programme in the run-up to the seventh Ministerial Conference in 2009 reflect a considerable degree of criticism regarding the development of the agenda, see WTO (2009b). During the preceding discussions, some members expressed concern that no results had been produced since the 2005 Ministerial Conference and called for a specific working agenda to be implemented according to a clear timetable.
[152] WTO (2011b).

work" should be continued since the last conference, instructed the General Council to "*substantially invigorate*" the work and identified further aspects in addition to the development-related aspects.[153] Against this background of continued invigoration, the Work Programme's Progress Report in the run-up to the 2015 Ministerial Conference in Nairobi noted that there were few common positions regarding the issues tackled by the Work Programme.[154] Consequently, the Ministerial Conference merely decided on the "*continuation*" of the Work Programme.[155]

Given the ever-growing relevance of global electronic commerce and the ever-apparent lack of multilateral governance under the Work Programme, initiatives formed to promote their respective positionings on the matter. Interest groups such as the MIKTA Group (Mexico, Indonesia, South Korea, Turkey and Australia), for example, have increased their involvement and discussed ways to raise the profile of WTO discussions on the Work Programme Moreover, the African Group and a number of Least Developed Countries (LDCs) have denounced a widening "*digital divide*". Fora such as the "*Friends of e-commerce for Development*" (FED), a non-negotiating group of WTO and UN member-states with different levels of development, explicitly stated the goal of discussing the implementation of the development goals of UNCTAD's "*eTrade for All*" initiative launched in July 2016.[156] Similarly, in 2016, the electronic World Trade Platform (eWTP) initiative—a "*private sector-led multi-stakeholder initiative*" to promote public-private collaboration for inclusive global trade—was featured in the Ministerial Declaration of the G20 Summit in Hangzhou.[157] In response, the WTO, the World Economic Forum, and the eWTP launched the Enabling E-commerce initiative in 2017, which aims to begin a "*high-level conversation about e-commerce policies and practices that can benefit small businesses*".[158] However, with regard to the decision recommendation on the status of the Work Programme in the run-up to the 2017 Ministerial Conference in Buenos Aires, the persistent disagreement within the Work Programme led to eight different text proposals being forwarded to the ministers via the General Council.[159] While one group assumed that e-commerce would largely be covered by the existing GATT and GATS rules and that the need for any clarifications to WTO law would therefore have to be evaluated,[160] another group—including the EU—argued in favour of reforming WTO law by way of a negotiating mandate.[161] Others opposed such a discussion on new multilateral rules

---

[153] WTO (2013a).

[154] WTO (2015a).

[155] WTO (2015b).

[156] *See* Friends of E-Commerce for Development UNCTAD (2024a); Ismail (2020), p. 12. *See* further on the UNCTAD's "*eTrade for All*" initiative UNCTAD (2024b).

[157] G20 (2016), p. 7, para. 30.

[158] Cf. WTO (2017b).

[159] Cf. for a summary and synopsis of these eight proposals Low (2017).

[160] WTO (2017c).

[161] WTO (2017d).

3.3 The WTO and Digital Trade

for e-commerce on the grounds that development goals were being neglected and that there were deficits in ICT infrastructure in developing countries.[162] Against this background, the latter group and other WTO members who were critical of changes to the existing rulebook for other reasons argued for greater formalisation and reorganisation of the talks or even the continuation of the Work Programme as it existed.[163] Against the backdrop of widely diverging positions,[164] the decision of the WTO ministers in Buenos Aires was limited to the smallest common denominator. In this sense, it was decided—again—to merely continue the work under the existing programme while sustaining regular reviews and maintaining the Moratorium on Customs Duties on Electronic Transmissions.[165] Against this backdrop, a group of WTO members including the EU, USA, Japan and Canada adopted a Joint Statement on Electronic Commerce initiating exploratory work toward future WTO negotiations on trade-related aspects of electronic commerce.[166] Meanwhile, at an informal meeting in November 2018, the members' differing positions on the scope, task, and further development of the Work Programme zeroed in on the Moratorium on Customs Duties on Electronic Transmissions.[167] Indeed, the Moratorium has become increasingly controversial, both in terms of the longstanding question of whether it applies to electronic transmissions as a carrier medium or also to the content transmitted, as well as the underlying problem of revenue losses, in particular among developing countries.[168]

---

[162] WTO (2016b) paras. 1.7, 1.8. *See* in particular the statement by the African Group WTO (2017e).

[163] WTO (2017f); WTO (2017g).

[164] In this context, the Chairman of the General Council noted in his report dated 1 December 2017: *"In very broad terms the positions vary from maintaining the current work program as it is; to formalising the dedicated discussion under the current work program; to establishing a new working group to consolidate all discussions on e-commerce; to establishing a working party with a mandate for future negotiations. The proposals also express varying positions on the question of the moratorium on customs duties for e-commerce."*, WTO (2017h), p. 1, para. 1.4.

[165] WTO (2017i).

[166] WTO (2017a). The statement includes the following sentences: *"We, as a group, will initiate exploratory work together toward future WTO negotiations on trade-related aspects of electronic commerce. Participation will be open to all WTO Members and will be without prejudice to participants' positions on future negotiations. A first meeting will be held in the first quarter of 2018. Welcoming the contributions since the 10th WTO Ministerial Conference in Nairobi, our work will build on WTO rules. Our initiative will be undertaken without prejudice to existing WTO agreements and mandates. We encourage all WTO Members to join us and to support and enhance the benefits of electronic commerce for businesses and consumers across the globe."*. *See* further Ismail (2020), p. 14.

[167] WTO (2018b).

[168] *See* for example WTO (2018c) claiming significantly changed realities since the introduction of the Moratorium on Custom Duties on Electronic Transmissions in 1998 as well as WTO (2020). *See* also the underlying study UNCTAD (2017b). *See* however also Makiyama and Gopalakrishnan (2019). *See* further Cheng and Brandi (2019).

3.3.1.1.2 A Forum for the Regulation of Data and Data Flows?

The Work Programme raised a number of issues relevant to the broad conception of global electronic commerce as defined by the WTO, but hardly any of them received adequate resolution. A 2017 indicative list presented by the Japanese delegation entitled *"possible way forward on electronic commerce"* has categorised the relevant aspects under the headings of improved transparency, facilitation through regulatory frameworks, open and fair trading environment, and international cooperation and development.[169] This categorisation underscores first and foremost that the Work Programme has enabled a broad discourse on trade-related issues pertaining to digital trade, encompassing a wide range of policy issues—from traditional trade concerns such as market access and liberalisation commitments for trade based on data flows to emerging issues such as with regard to Internet governance and data governance.[170] On the basis of such a categorisation, it is possible to outline the general evolution of the debate under the Work Programme. Initially, the discussions focused on rather straightforward issues of facilitating e-commerce, such as electronic authentication, contracts, payments, and the corresponding regulatory implications for consumer protection or cybersecurity. This also included a particular focus on the developmental implications of e-commerce. As trade in the digital economy gained momentum, the focus of the debate shifted to issues related to an open and fair digital trading environment. This involved questions pertaining to the underlying digital infrastructure, such as with respect to information flows, openness of networks, and non-discriminatory treatment in the formulation and application of national measures. In this way, the e-commerce debate has been extended to include digital governance issues.

Certainly, the WTO Work Programme has a logical interface with the data driven digital trade, particularly through the Moratorium on Customs Duties on Electronic Transmissions and the coverage of matters pertaining to digitally delivered services. However, the policy issues surrounding tariffs on electronic transmissions are only a very limited starting point for the complex issues of digital governance. Thus, as the digital economy has grown and matured, contributions directly related to a data-driven environment have multiplied—in particular with regard to digital services. In 2011, for example, the US and the EU circulated a jointly developed set of trade-related principles to support the development of ICT networks and services to members of the WTO Council for Trade in Services.[171] This contribution to the Work Programme can be seen as a starting point for a debate on digital trade underpinned by data flows, as it lists trade-related principles for the promotion of ICT networks and services while seeking to strengthen national regulatory

---

[169] WTO (2017j).
[170] *See* with regard to the latter *infra* Sect. 3.5.
[171] WTO (2011c).

capacities.[172] The principles that were drafted to be adopted in bilateral and multilateral trade disciplines aimed to *"support the expansion of information and communication technology (ICT) networks and services, and enhance the evolution of electronic commerce"*.[173] These trade principles for ICT services addressed inter alia the fostering of open networks (network access and use), ensuring unhindered cross-border information flows, rules on the forced use of local infrastructure or the establishment of a local presence for ICT service-suppliers within frameworks of international cooperation.[174] By referring to principles such as transparency, open networks, avoidance of data localisation measures and the prevention of restrictions on the freedom of cross-border data flows imposed by domestic regulation, the joint contribution to the Work Programme showcases an understanding of an evolving regulatory environment that increasingly depends on data flows.[175] Moreover, in the run-up to the 11th WTO Ministerial Conference in 2017, the US circulated a non-paper based on their *"digital2dozen"* initiative, which contained 16 examples of positive contributions to a flourishing digital economy.[176] Against this background, Japan and EU-led groups responded with their own proposals regarding the reinvigoration of the discussions on electronic commerce and the digital economy.[177] Finally, in a general effort to achieve tangible progress regarding the issue of electronic commerce, a number of non-papers emphasised the need for a common understanding regarding the role of data flows in a global economy. The US non-paper featured a list of *"positive contributions to a flourishing digital economy"*, underscoring issues such as *"enabling cross-border data flows"*, *"promoting free and open internet"*, and *"preventing localisation barriers"* *"preserving market-driven standardization and global interoperability"* as well as *"securing basic non-discrimination principles"*.[178] In similar vein, in order to take *"into account policy developments over the past two decades"* a communication from the EU and

---

[172] The formulation of these principles has notably informed the further development of the EU positions as evidenced in WTO (2016a) and WTO (2017k). The same is true for the US approach, cf. WTO (2016c). During the consultations following this proposal, Australia presented three additional *"ICT Principles"* in September 2012, covering online consumer protection, protection of personal data and unsolicited commercial communications, see WTO (2012b).

[173] WTO (2011c), p. 2. The communication is prefaced with a disclaimer underscoring that the principles are indeed *"without prejudice to the policy objectives and legislation of the European Union and the United States in areas such as the protection of intellectual property, the protection of privacy and of the confidentiality of personal and commercial data, and the enhancement of cultural diversity."*.

[174] WTO (2011c), p. 2, paras. 2.,3.,4. and 10. See also Ministerial Decision WTO (2013a), which promoted to *"continue to examine the trade related aspects of, inter alia, enhancing internet connectivity and access to information and telecommunications technologies and public internet sites, the growth of mobile telephony, electronically delivered software, cloud computing, the protection of confidential data, privacy and consumer protection."*.

[175] WTO (2011c), p. 2. See in this sense also Yakovleva and Irion (2020), pp. 209–210.

[176] WTO (2016c). See also Office of the United States Trade Representative (2016).

[177] WTO (2016d); WTO (2016a). See with further references Kelsey (2018), p. 282.

[178] WTO (2016c).

other co-sponsors mapped trade-related elements into four groups, namely *"regulatory frameworks"*; *"open markets"*; *"initiatives facilitating the development of e-commerce"*; and *"transparency of the multilateral trading system"*.[179] In particular within the elements of *"regulatory framework"* and *"open markets"*, the communication lists issues relating to cybersecurity, data protection, access to and use of the Internet as well as disciplines to ensure cross-border data flows, disciplines relating to the localisation of servers and disciplines addressing the transfer of and/or access to source code.[180]

These examples were chosen to illustrate two interrelated developments with respect to discussions on digital trade for which the Work Programme has provided a forum. First, aspects of digital infrastructure and, in particular, the regulation of data flows are increasingly perceived to be intertwined with cross-border trade.[181] This is particularly the case for exporters of digitally delivered services such as the US and EU. Given the increasing importance of the global digital economy, issues of digital infrastructure and data governance, including national cybersecurity and data privacy regulation, are being discussed in the WTO as a widely respected forum of cross-border economic cooperation. Second, the examples underscore that the WTO framework is considered by a significant share of its membership to provide an appropriate venue for addressing trade-related aspects of digital governance. This is especially the case for those members that wish to defend and secure their pre-existing economic influence in the digital economy.[182] In this way, the WTO has provided a broadly recognised forum for the growing convergence between issues of trade governance and digital governance. The exchange under the Work Programme ultimately informed the ongoing negotiations under the Joint Statement Initiative on Electronic Commerce on a number of topics, and in particular with regard to the regulation of cross-border data flows. Negotiations under the Joint Statement Initiative have in turn helped to reinvigorate the work of the WTO Programme recently, notably drawing on input from those members not participating in the initiative. Moreover, it will be illustrated below, that a significant part of the positions discussed in the Work Programme have gradually found their way into dedicated chapters of recent PTAs (*see infra* Sect. 3.4.1).

---

[179] WTO (2016a).

[180] WTO (2016a), para. 3.

[181] Against the background of an emerging global data economy, a *"Conference on the Use of Data in the Digital Economy"* was held at the WTO in October 2017, which dealt in detail with the evaluation of the value-added potential of data and data transfers, WTO (2017l). With regard to considerations of reconciling the *"free flow"* of data and data protection regimes, *see* for example WTO (2014), para. 4.

[182] *See* also Belli (2016); Maciel (2016).

3.3.1.2 Plurilateral Negotiations on Electronic Commerce

Given the gridlocked Work Programme and the apparent inability to resolve important aspects of digital trade governance in the context of the Doha Round, a number of WTO Members adopted a Joint Statement in 2017, stating their intention to "*initiate exploratory work together toward future WTO negotiations on trade-related aspects of electronic commerce*".[183] Subsequently, recognising "*unique opportunities and challenges*", 76 WTO members, including the EU, US and China, have agreed on plurilateral e-commerce negotiations on the side-lines of the 2019 World Economic Meeting in Davos.[184] The participants have adopted a Joint Statement confirming their consensus to commence negotiations on trade-related aspects of electronic commerce while seeking "*to achieve a high standard outcome that builds on existing WTO agreements and frameworks with the participation of as many WTO Members as possible*".[185] The initiative was flanked by the Osaka Track initiative at the G20 level which reaffirmed "*support for the necessary reform of the World Trade Organization (WTO)*" as well as "*the importance of interface between trade and digital economy*".[186] While a certain number of changes in co-sponsorship occurred, the initiative was supported primarily by developed countries but only a handful of LDCs.[187] As of 23 October 2023, 90 WTO members, accounting for over 90% of global trade, have held several negotiating rounds with Australia, Singapore and Japan spearheading the talks.

The most recent version of the negotiating text was presented in November 2023. In January 2024, the co-conveners issued a chair's text to advance the negotiations and be able to complete them in 2024.[188] Against this background, several negotiation issues have been "*parked*" and it seems that consensus can been reached on subjects pertaining to digital trade facilitation, such as with regard to electronic authentication, signatures and contracts as well as online consumer protection and unsolicited commercial messages. While originally a key objective of the initiative, however, no results are to be expected in the near future on more controversial issues, particularly with regard to domestic regulations on data and data flows. In October 2023, the US withdrew its support for a number of proposals, particularly relating to cross-border data flows and source code, in order to allow for enough

---

[183] WTO (2017a).
[184] WTO (2019a).
[185] WTO (2019a).
[186] G20 (2019), p. 2 para. 8 and para. 11. *See* in particular para. 11: "[...] *We also reaffirm the importance of interface between trade and digital economy, and note the ongoing discussion under the Joint Statement Initiative on electronic commerce, and reaffirm the importance of the Work Programme on electronic commerce at the WTO.*".
[187] Ismail (2020), p. 14.
[188] WTO (2024).

policy space for domestic policy considerations.[189] As a result, the negotiations on these issues were paused and deferred to a potential second phase of the negotiations.

The underlying controversy in the negotiations on data-related issues can be illustrated by the initial proposals published by three major trade stakeholders: the US, the EU and China.[190] In April 2019, the EU presented a rather ambitious proposal for WTO disciplines and commitments relating to electronic commerce and telecommunications services.[191] The EU proposal regarding WTO rules on e-commerce extends to a broad range of matters from provisions on electronic contracts, authentication and signatures, to consumer protection and unsolicited electronic messages, to customs duties on electronic transmissions, the transfer or access to source code, the issue of cross-border data flows, protection of personal data and privacy as well as open Internet access.[192] Additionally, the EU has submitted a proposal which aims to enhance regulatory predictability through a revision of the WTO reference paper on telecommunications services and has put forth market access requests in particular for computer and telecommunication services.[193] While the initial US proposal also deals with a wide range of topics, it is noticeable that it focuses less on the traditional aspects of e-commerce (i.e. electronic contracts, electronic signatures) and instead concentrates on data-related regulations such as the fair treatment of *"digital products"* and digital security.[194] In line with the general emphasis on this issue in US digital trade policy, the *"free flow"* of information features very prominently at the top of the proposal.[195] The proposals from the People's Republic of China, which has traditionally been reluctant to make commitments on data flows, drew critical attention. With a view to the objectives of the political regime in Beijing regarding national security in the digital age, the People's Republic tended to an exemption of the issue of cross-border data flows from the negotiations shortly after the launch of the dialogue.[196] Against this background, data-related issues have proven to be particularly thorny

---

[189] Lawder (2023).

[190] *See* further Abendin and Duan (2021); Fefer (2020), pp. 19–20; Hufbauer and Zhiyao (2019), pp. 3–4; Titievskaia (2020); Burri (2021d), pp. 24–30.

[191] WTO (2019d). By May 2019, the Council adopted negotiating directives supplementing the mandate for the Doha Round regarding the plurilateral negotiations of rules and commitments on electronic commerce, Council of the EU (2019). *See* further Titievskaia (2020).

[192] WTO (2019d), para. 2.

[193] WTO (2019d) paras. 3 and 4.

[194] WTO (2018d), pp. 2–3, paras. 3. and 5.

[195] WTO (2018d), p. 1, para. 1.

[196] WTO (2019b), p. 4, paras. 4.2 and 4.3 underscore the limits of China's initial readiness to negotiate in this matter: *"In light of their complexity and sensitivity, as well as the vastly divergent views among the Members, more exploratory discussions are needed before bringing such issues to the WTO negotiation"* and further *"It's undeniable that trade-related aspects of data flow are of great importance to trade development. However, more importantly, the data flow should be subject to the precondition of security, which concerns each and every Member's core interests. To this end, it is necessary that the data flow orderly in compliance with Members' respective laws and regulations."*.

issue for a result in the Joint Statement Initiative.[197] National peculiarities in domestic data regulations will play a major role with regard to a potential future trade rules for data flows under a second phase of the Initiative. From a European perspective, for example, rules for cross-border data flows can only be adopted alongside a robust consideration for "*data protection*", while the US is unlikely to be able to accept any overly extensive reservations regarding the free flow of data. China, on the other hand, stresses the need for reservations to data-related commitments for reasons of security. Moreover, progress in plurilateral negotiations is closely linked to the evolving national approaches to digital trade governance reflected in recent Preferential Trade Agreements (PTAs) (*see* further *infra* Sects. 3.4.2. and 5.3).[198]

3.3.2 WTO Agreements and Digital Trade

Since the landmark achievements of the Uruguay Round with respect to the Marrakesh Agreement establishing the organisation in 1994, the WTO's multilateral framework has not been significantly reformed.[199] Certainly, modifications with relevance for digital trade underpinned by data flows have been introduced by the Information Technology Agreement (ITA) in 2015 and the Trade Facilitation Agreement (TFA) in 2017. Apart from these adjustments, it proved infeasible for the 164 members to update WTO law in a timely and appropriate manner, particularly with respect to trade in the digital economy. Though legal adaptation to digital trade has not progressed, the WTO framework exhibits characteristics that legitimate its relevancy to the evolving nature of global economic integration in the face of the current digital transformation.[200] Economic liberalisation within the WTO framework is most fundamentally based on the principle of non-discrimination.[201] The most significant manifestations of this concept are the Most-Favoured-Nation (MFN) principle and the National Treatment (NT) obligation. While MFN obligations prohibit Members from favouring products, services or services suppliers from some countries over like products, services, or service suppliers from other

---

[197] Burri (2021d), p. 33.

[198] *See* also Hufbauer and Zhiyao (2019), p. 9.

[199] For detailed reviews of the current state of WTO law with regard to digital trade and e-commerce, *see* for example, Burri (2017b), pp. 71–99; Meltzer (2019a), pp. 37–43; Mitchell and Mishra (2018).

[200] *See* only Burri (2017b), pp. 93–99.

[201] The preamble of the WTO Agreement reflects on this, as it identifies: "*entering into reciprocal and mutually advantageous arrangements directed to the substantial reduction of tariffs and other barriers to trade and to the eliminations of* discriminatory treatment in international trade relations" as desirable in order to attain its goals of "*of raising standards of living, ensuring full employment and a large and steadily growing volume of real income and effective demand, and expanding the production of and trade in goods and service.*".

countries, obligations to NT refer to a country favouring itself over others.[202] In this context, the WTO Dispute Settlement Bodies provide a supervisory mechanism and, to a certain extent, the capacity to elucidate the application of multilateral law with regard to emergent forms of trade in the digital economy.[203] Furthermore, substantial parts of the WTO framework are devised to be technologically neutral, affirming their relevance also with regard to an emergent data driven trade environment.[204]

Pertinent regulations with regard to digital trade can be traced to a number of multilateral agreements such as the GATT, the GATS, TRIPS, the ITA or the TBT Agreement.[205] In fact, all areas of the WTO framework, and particularly the multilateral rules on trade in goods, services, and trade-related aspects of intellectual property that are binding on all WTO members, are affected. This underscores the general consideration, echoed in the design of the WTO Work Programme on Electronic Commerce, that regulating the emergent environment of trade in the digital economy is a multi-faceted and cross-cutting issue. This raises considerable challenges to governing digital trade under the current WTO regime, which will be addressed in more detail in the following analysis.

3.3.2.1 General Agreement on Tariffs and Trade (GATT)

The General Agreement on Tariffs and Trade (GATT) addresses cross-border trade in goods.[206] Therefore, the GATT is most relevant to digital trade in terms of the governance of trade in goods utilised to deploy the underlying physical infrastructure of the Internet and the broader data-driven environment.[207] In addition to facilitating trade in components of digital technologies, GATT rules take on particular relevance when digital technologies, such as the Internet, serve as a platform for trade in goods that are delivered in physical form.[208] Against this backdrop, it is certainly fair to say

---

[202] van den Bossche and Zdouc (2022), p. 337.

[203] Aaronson and Leblond (2018), p. 246; Burri (2017b,) pp. 95–99.

[204] With further references Burri (2017b), pp. 93–95. However, not all WTO agreements adhere to the principle of technology neutrality at all times. Moreover, the precise meaning of the concept is far from clearly defined, *see* Gagliani (2020), pp. 731–738.

[205] Wu (2017), pp. 2–6 identifies several other agreements of relevance to digital trade which are not covered in the following analysis, including Annex 1A agreements such as the Agreement on Customs Licensing, the Agreement on Import Licensing Procedure, and the Agreement on Sanitary and Phytosanitary Standards (SPS). *See* for a useful illustration of the multilateral trade agreements concerned López González and Ferencz (2018), p. 14.

[206] General Agreement on Tariffs and Trade 1994, 15 April 1994, Marrakesh Agreement Establishing the World Trade Organization, Annex 1A, 1867 U.N.T.S. 187, 33 I.L.M. 1153 (1994). On 30 October 1947 twenty-three countries signed the Final Act of the General Agreement on Tariffs and Trade. Annex 1A of the WTO Agreement contains the GATT 1994 which incorporates by references the provisions of the GATT 1947 as well as what is referred to as the "*GATT aquis*".

[207] Meltzer (2019a), p. 41.

[208] Wu (2017), p. 3.

that the ambit of the GATT in relation to the regulation of cross-border data flows may generally be limited (in particular in comparison to the GATS, *see* further *infra* Sect. 3.3.2.6). However, the role of the GATT for digital trade tends to be somewhat underestimated in relation to trade in the digital economy considering its relevance to cross-border trade in physical infrastructure goods for the Internet and digital technologies.[209]

Moreover, the advent of the digital economy has raised the question of how to deal with trade in *"digital products"*, such as books or CDs, the content of which is digitised and supplied on the basis of cross-border data flows.[210] Digital technologies and in particular the Internet, provide a vehicle for the production, storage and transmission of goods which were traditionally bound to a physical form. Overall, digital technologies tend to make the delivery of tangible goods such as software, books, music or audio-visual content intangible.[211] From the outset, the debates under the WTO Work Programme have illustrated that the issues raised by classifying trade in the digital economy in WTO law would prove to be particularly contentious.[212] It has been long debated whether trade in such *"digital products"* can be categorised as trade in goods, trade in services or must be treated as something else.[213] In fact, the determination of whether to invoke the GATT or the GATS regulatory framework is not of subordinate relevance; on the contrary, it is of crucial interest with regard to standard of protection under WTO law and domestic regulatory leeway.[214] The 1994 GATT is based on decades of regulatory evolution and constitutes a fairly comprehensive and definitive set of rules.[215] In turn, constituting the first and to date only multilateral understanding of such kind, the GATS forges a less rigid framework and allows for WTO Member States to retain a great amount of autonomy also with regard to important non-discrimination obligations. As will be illustrated below, this is the case notably for market access and NT obligations, due to the positive list approach of the GATS (*see infra* Sect. 3.3.2.6.1). While the intangibility of trade in *"digital products"* and its connection to sensitive policy areas such as audio-visual services invokes the flexible scope of the GATS, a classification of trade in *"digital products"* as goods trade seems plausible to avoid unequal treatment to their tangible counterparts with identical content.[216]

---

[209] Burri (2017b), p. 76.

[210] *See* generally Willemyns (2021), pp. 11–24.

[211] Wu (2017), p. 4.

[212] *See* further for a useful overview of key unresolved issues with respect to digital trade, including classification issues Wunsch-Vincent and Hold (2012), pp. 181–187.

[213] *See* for example Baker et al. (2001); Farrokhnia and Richards (2016).

[214] Baker et al. (2001), pp. 7–8; Mattoo and Schuknecht (2000), pp. 11–13; Willemyns (2021), pp. 17–18.

[215] Hart and Chaitoo (1999), p. 915; Wu (2017), p. 4.

[216] Baker et al. (2001), pp. 8–10; Weber (2015), pp. 325–326. Hence, with regard to the issue of delineation between the scope of GATT and GATS *Joshua Meltzer* warns about *"perverse outcomes"*, Meltzer (2019a), p. 41.

Nevertheless, with regard to a digital delivery both the GATT classification system (Harmonized System, HS Code) and the GATS Sectoral Classification List (W/120) do not provide guidance.[217] It is questionable if the physical good and its digital equivalent are *"like-products"* as defined under Article III GATT and how the like-product rules affect the application of the MFN principle with regard to *"digital products"*, for example.[218] While this issue of classification between the respective scopes of GATT and GATS with respect to *"digital products"* has long been recognised and has been the subject of considerable debate particularly in the WTO Work Programme, it has not been resolved among WTO members to date.[219] In this context, a 1998 study on the role of the WTO on e-commerce states: *"Electronic commerce could be characterized as trade in goods, trade in services, or as something different from either of these."*.[220] The prevailing opinion does not seem to want to pursue this latter approach, at least at present. Much of the academic literature dealing with cross-border data flows as an element of trade governance in the digital economy employs digital services as a proxy, given that they intrinsically rely on intangible data crossing borders.[221]

3.3.2.2 Information Technology Agreement (ITA)

The Information Technology Agreement (ITA) is of particular relevance to digital trade as it addresses trade in IT-products such as computers, semiconductors, telecommunications apparatus as well as data storage media and software. Initially agreed between 29 participants at the Singapore Ministerial Conference in December 1996 (ITA I), it was subsequently expanded at the Nairobi Ministerial Conference in December 2015 (ITA II). The underlying Ministerial Declaration on Trade in Information Technology Products of 13 December 1996 underscored the parties' belief in *"the key role of trade in information technology products in the development of information industries and in the dynamic expansion of the world economy"*.[222] It states further in paragraph 2 that: *"[...] each party shall bind and eliminate customs duties and other duties and charges of any kind, within the meaning of Article II:1(b)of the General Agreement on Tariffs and Trade 1994 [...] through equal rate reductions of customs duties beginning in 1997 and*

---

[217] Weber (2010), p. 3. *See* further regarding the GATS classification system *infra* Sect. 3.3.2.6.
[218] Hart and Chaitoo (1999), p. 916.
[219] Mitchell and Mishra (2018), pp. 1110–1111; Weber (2015), pp. 325–236. Contemporarily, a physical book crossing the border is subject to GATT rules and a given tariff, while the digital version—classified to fall into the ambit of the GATS—would not be charged any duties as a result of the Moratorium on Customs Duties on Electronic Transmissions, *see* also Sen (2018), p. 331.
[220] Bacchetta et al. (1998), p. 50.
[221] *See* for example Burri (2017b), pp. 80–84; Mitchell and Mishra (2019), pp. 397–402; Sen (2018), pp. 327–329.
[222] WTO (1996b).

concluding in 2000 [...].²²³ Hence, the ITA has a significant impact with regard to infrastructural aspects of digital trade as well as the Internet more generally since the participants to the agreement pledge to completely eliminate tariffs on IT products covered by the agreement.²²⁴ Furthermore, despite its plurilateral framework, the initiators have managed to achieve a critical mass among of 82 WTO Members currently participating in the agreement, representing around 97% of world trade in IT products.²²⁵ Trade in IT products subject to the agreement is valued at over 1.68 trillion EUR (15.4% of world trade).²²⁶ However, as IT technologies continue to converge and evolve, the ITA, too, is faced with the challenge of classifying emergent IT products.²²⁷ Therefore, liberalisation of trade in goods under the ITA is subject to controversies arising from concerns over the coverage of new technologies under the agreement.²²⁸ Nevertheless, it is rightly seen as the WTO's most important tangible success in advancing the liberalisation of digital trade.²²⁹

3.3.2.3 Agreement on Technical Barriers to Trade (TBT)

As economic liberalisation progresses, regulatory measures affecting trade in goods are increasingly coming into focus. In this context, the rules of the Agreement on Technical Barriers to Trade (TBT) address technical regulations, standards and conformity assessment procedures. The TBT rules are intended to promote the objectives of the GATT, but go beyond the GATT rules applicable to non-tariff barriers to trade, in particular by incentivising regulatory harmonisation.²³⁰ While the ITA seeks to foster trade in IT products, the TBT can ensure, in a somewhat complementary way, that technical regulations and standards in the IT sector do not constitute undue barriers to trade in the digital economy.²³¹ Notably, the issue of technical regulations and standards has implications for a wide area of domestic

---

[223] WTO (1996b).

[224] Bacchetta et al. (1998), p. 46. With regard to the coverage of the Agreement the 1996 Ministerial Declaration referred to *"all products classified (or classifiable) with Harmonized System (1996) ("HS") headings listed in Attachment A to the Annex to this Declaration; and (b) all products specified in Attachment B to the Annex to this Declaration, whether or not they are included in Attachment A"*, cf. WTO (1996b), p. 2, para. 2.

[225] WTO (2012a).

[226] European Commission (2016), p. 7, para. 3.

[227] Luff (2012), pp. 68–71; Weber (2010), pp. 6–7.

[228] Weber (2010), pp. 6–7. The scope of the ITA has been scrutinized by the WTO dispute settlement system, *see* Panel Report, *EC-IT Products*, WT/DS375/R, WT/DS376/R, WT/DS377/R, 16 August 2010. *See* further with regard to an extension of the ITA, Burri (2016a), p. 346.

[229] Mitchell and Mishra (2018), p. 1118. *See* however also the successful conclusion of negotiations aimed at reducing administrative costs and establishing a more transparent operating environment for service providers under the Joint Statement on Services Domestic Regulation WTO (2021).

[230] van den Bossche and Zdouc (2022), pp. 976–978; Weiß (2020), pp. 296–301.

[231] Luff (2012), pp. 72–74.

regulations affecting digital trade such as rules on encryption or data storage.[232] It has therefore been argued that the TBT Agreement will become ever more relevant by promoting global regulatory coherence and cooperation in the development of standards and regulations for what is called *"Industry 4.0"*.[233] Under the TBT Agreement, there is a strong incentive towards the use of relevant international standards (Article 2.4), which are presumed not to create an unnecessary obstacle to international trade (Article 2.5). New or deviating domestic technical regulations must be *"necessary"* (Article 2.2) and non-discriminatory (Article 2.1). These rules on non-discrimination as well as the transparency requirements regarding the standards and regulations adopted or proposed within a given territory of a WTO Member (Article 10) are important drivers for the lowering of barriers to digital trade. Recently, for example, WTO Members have discussed the impact of China's cyber-security regulation on trade in high-technology products, as this regulation potentially discriminates against non-domestic companies and technologies, and possibly results in the disclosure of commercially confidential and technical information.[234]

3.3.2.4 Agreement on Trade Facilitation (TFA)

The Trade Facilitation Agreement (TFA), which entered into force in February 2017 following ratification by two-thirds of WTO members, is considered one of the few achievements of the Doha Round.[235] It commits the signatories to take measures to facilitate import and export processes, including those related to digital trade.[236] In a global economy characterised by expanding GVCs, the increasing complexity requires a flexible, responsive facilitation initiatives. The agreement provides for electronic pre-arrival processing of documents (Article 7.1), electronic payment of customs duties, fees, and charges (Article 7.2) as well as the incentive to *"endeavour"* acceptance of documentation required by means of ICT in a *"single window"*[237]

---

[232] Meltzer (2019a), p. 42.

[233] Lim (2021).

[234] In this context, a meeting of the TBT Committee in 2017 addressed China's review of the cybersecurity of network products and services, *see* WTO (2017m). The Chinese regulation has also prompted intensified discussions within the Council for Trade in Services, WTO (2017n); WTO (2017o); WTO (2018e).

[235] According to some estimates, full implementation of the TFA would lower trade costs by 18% for industrial products and 10.4% for agricultural products. It has also the ability to reduce the time to import by more than one and a half days (a 47% reduction from the current average) and the time to export by almost two days (a 91% reduction from the current average), cf. WTO (2015c), p. 7.

[236] López González and Ferencz (2018), p. 13; Meltzer (2019a), p. 42; Wu (2017), p. 4.

[237] *See* generally UN Centre for Trade Facilitation and Electronic Business (2005). *See* also World Bank Group (2017), pp. 79–86. The report defines a single window *"as a system that receives trade-related information and disseminates it to all the relevant governmental authorities, thus systematically coordinating controls throughout trade processes."*.

procedure (Article 10.4). Furthermore, it obliges Members to publish important documentation on import, export, and transit procedures on the Internet (Article 1.2).

3.3.2.5 Agreement on Trade-Related Aspects of Intellectual Property Rights (TRIPS)

The Agreement on Trade-Related Aspects of Intellectual Property Rights establishes for the first time a positive obligation for WTO Members to have a minimum level of protection and enforcement of Intellectual Property Rights (IPR) in their territory.[238] IPRs—in a broad sense—concern the legal rights which result from intellectual activity in the industrial, scientific, literary and artistic fields.[239] While an in-depth examination of the relationship between digital trade and intellectual property protection within the WTO and in particular with regard to the relation with developments outside of it (e.g. in the context of the World Intellectual Property Organization, WIPO) would go beyond the scope of this text, nevertheless some fundamentals should be acknowledged.[240] TRIPS was designed as an extension to the international trade regime towards non-tangible elements within trade, yet it was essentially negotiated against an analogous background and drafted predominantly to address the IP component of trade in goods.[241] Intellectual property is involved, for example, in the selling and licensing of technology as well as in relation to infrastructural aspects of the digital economy.[242] Moreover, TRIPS significantly contributes to the interoperability of domestic regulation in the field of (digital) trade.[243] The question arises, however, as to how TRIPS addresses the fact that digital technologies have profoundly transformed the way in which protected content is created, distributed and used.[244] The WTO Work Programme, charged with the examination of IP issues arising in connection with electronic commerce explicitly referred to the matters of the protection and enforcement of copyright and related rights, of trademarks as well as to the emergence of new technologies and access to

---

[238] Agreement on Trade-Related Aspects of Intellectual Property Rights, 15 April 1994, Marrakesh Agreement Establishing the World Trade Organization, Annex 1C, 1869 U.N.T.S. 299, 33 I.L.M. 1197 (1994). Van den Bossche and Zdouc (2022), pp. 1082–1086.

[239] WIPO (2008), p. 3.

[240] See for example Taubman (2012); Wunsch-Vincent (2004), pp. 151–161.

[241] Taubman (2012), p. 304. In this context, Taubman draws upon a historical perspective of IPR in trade and among other sources refers to the WTO/GATT Ministerial Declaration on the Uruguay Round of 20 September 1986 which set a negotiating objective of developing *"a multilateral framework of principles, rules and disciplines dealing with international trade in counterfeit goods"*. See also WTO (1999d), para. 14.

[242] Bacchetta et al. (1998), pp. 59–60. See also *supra* Sect. 3.3.2.1. regarding the interface between digital trade and the GATT.

[243] Gasser and Palfrey (2012), pp. 137–141.

[244] See for example Bacchetta et al. (1998), pp. 60–61.

technology.²⁴⁵ In the context of the Work Programme, a 1999 Background Note of the WTO Secretariat indicated the opinion that the basic notions and principles of intellectual property withstood rapid technological change as well as that the language of the TRIPS Agreement was generally neutral in relation to such change and therefore would remain valid and relevant also with regard to a digitally networked environment.²⁴⁶ A frequently held view in this respect pertains to the technological neutrality of the TRIPS Agreement.²⁴⁷ While this stance did prove to be controversial and many issues concerning digital trade and IPR protection were raised, yet so far no clear consensus has been achieved.²⁴⁸ Although the TRIPS Agreement has been subject to significant modifications following the Doha Round negotiations that followed its conclusion, little progress has been made, specifically on the issues of digital trade.²⁴⁹

3.3.2.6 General Agreement on Trade in Services (GATS)

The General Agreement on Trade in Services (GATS) is arguably the most relevant WTO agreement when it comes to digital trade.²⁵⁰ This is due, on the one hand, to the comprehensive scope of the GATS. The definition of *"services"* in Article I:3 (b) GATS very broadly covers *"any service in any sector"*, except for those services *"supplied in the exercise of governmental authority"*.²⁵¹ Moreover, the supply of a service under GATS extends to *"the production, distribution, marketing, sale and delivery"* of a service, Article XXVIII:b GATS. On the other hand, as outlined above, trade in services is experiencing a particular boost in significance in the digital economy, as services due to their intangible nature are highly susceptible to digitalisation (*see supra* Sect. 2.3.1.2). In addition, digital services (*e.g.* Cloud Computing, digital payment services or Internet search) have emerged as key facilitators of a global digital economy.²⁵² Given that GATS does not presuppose

---

²⁴⁵ WTO (1998b), p. 3, para. 4.1. *See* further Wunsch-Vincent (2004), pp. 151–161.

²⁴⁶ WTO (1999d), paras. 12, 14.

²⁴⁷ *See* WTO (1999d), para. 14; Wu (2017), p. 4.

²⁴⁸ Wunsch-Vincent and Hold (2012), pp. 188–189.

²⁴⁹ Wunsch-Vincent and Hold (2012), p. 192. This concerns in particular the reference to the WIPO Internet Treaties, to which a significant share of WTO Members are signatories.

²⁵⁰ General Agreement on Trade in Services, 15 April 1994, Marrakesh Agreement Establishing the World Trade Organization, Annex 1B, 1869 U.N.T.S. 183, 33 I.L.M. 1167 (1994). *See* only Mitchell and Hepburn (2018), pp. 196–197. *See* with regard to AI in particular Chander (2021).

²⁵¹ Article I:3 c) GATS states that *"a service supplied in the exercise of governmental authority"* means any service which is supplied neither on a commercial basis, nor in competition with one or more service suppliers. *See* with further references regarding interpretation Burri (2017b), p. 82.

²⁵² Today's economic activities in the service sector are indeed much more diversified compared to when the Uruguay Round was finalised in 1994, *see* Peng (2007), pp. 294–297. *See* in particular for the case of Cloud Computing and Trade United States International Trade Commission (2017), pp. 57–85. *See* also *supra* Sect. 2.3.1.2.

a financial transaction between the service supplier and the recipient, it also extends in principle to *"free"* digital services.[253] While the scope of the GATS is particularly relevant with regard to digital trade, however, the GATS does neither explicitly refer to digital trade (or e-commerce for that matter) nor does it include a horizontal provision regarding cross-border data flows. Therefore, before looking in more detail at the regulatory complexities arising from the emergence of a digital service environment, it is important to first examine the nature of the general legal framework for cross-border trade in services under the GATS and its applicability to digital trade.

3.3.2.6.1 Regulatory Structure of the GATS

The WTO's regulatory framework for trade in services is a relatively recent concept that, unlike the regime for trade in goods, cannot build on decades of liberalisation debates and successive rounds of negotiations.[254] Indeed, the regulation of trade in services presents some peculiarities that result in the multilateral regulation of cross-border trade in services having specific characteristics that distinguish it from trade in goods.[255] As a framework agreement, the GATS differentiates between general obligations that apply to all members and service sectors on the one hand, and specific obligations that apply to members according to their national schedules on the other. The MFN principle in Article II GATS[256] as a core obligation within the WTO framework as well as the transparency obligation of Article III GATS[257] are deemed general obligations, applicable to all measures affecting trade in services under GATS, regardless of whether specific commitments have been made.[258] Yet, the general MFN obligation had been agreed to be subject to exceptions under

---

[253] Noonan and Plekhanova (2020), p. 1028. Yet, GATS includes in its Article XI a provision on *"payments and transfers"* securing the value of specific commitments undertaken by Members under the GATS, *see* in this context Panel Report, *US-Gambling*, WT/DS285/R, 10 November 2004, para. 6.441—6.442.
[254] Cf. for a detailed analysis of the genesis of the GATS, Drake and Kalypso (1992).
[255] *See* for example Adlung and Mattoo (2010), p. 49; Weiß (2020), pp. 29–31. *See* with regard specifically to digital trade and electronic commerce, Bacchetta et al. (1998), pp. 52–57.
[256] According to Article II:1 GATS "[...] *each Member shall accord immediately and unconditionally to services and service suppliers of any other Member treatment no less favourable than that it accords to like services and service suppliers of any other country.*".
[257] Article III:1 GATS requires Members to publish *"all relevant measures of general application which pertain to or affect the operation of this Agreement"*.
[258] This horizontal application of the MFN principle was controversially discussed during the Uruguay Round, *see* also with regard to singular exclusion regarding air transport Adlung (2006), pp. 868–869.

Article II:2 and the Annex on Article II Exemptions.[259] Apart from these general obligations WTO members can largely determine the degree of liberalisation of sectors and subsectors through their national schedules of specific commitments. With respect to the rules on NT (XVII GATS) and market access (Article XVI GATS) in particular, the Agreement provides Members with conditional leeway to adjust the scope of their commitments under their respective schedules of specific commitments. The GATS is based on a so-called positive list approach, according to which members' liberalisation commitments must be positively listed. Service sectors are therefore liberalised only if and to the extent that a Member so determines in its individual schedule.[260] These schedules will be attached to, and form an integral part of the GATS, Article XX:3 GATS.[261] Pursuant to Article I:2 GATS, trade in services under the GATS covers four different Modes of service supply. These types of supply are: From the territory of one Member into the territory of any other Member (Mode 1 - Cross-border Supply); in the territory of one Member to the service consumer of any other Member (Mode 2 - Consumption Abroad); by a service supplier of one Member, through commercial presence, in the territory of any other Member (Mode 3 - Commercial Presence); and by a service supplier of one Member, through the presence of natural persons of a Member in the territory of any other Member (Mode 4 - Presence of Natural Persons). Scheduled commitments may involve horizontal (cross-sectoral) or sector-specific liberalisation obligations and can be further specified for each of the four modes of supply. Furthermore, sector-specific regulations are contained in Annexes and Protocols to the GATS. The determination of WTO Members' obligations under the GATS is therefore based on three levels of regulation, namely the GATS itself and the specific national schedules, including the relevant protocols and sector-specific Annexes. Hence, GATS provides a most flexible framework in that it allows horizontal flexibility towards discrimination among WTO members, vertical flexibility towards substantial variations in market access and national treatment, and thirdly, diagonal flexibility towards extensive member-, mode- and sector-specific variations in trade conditions.[262]

3.3.2.6.2 GATS and Digital Delivery of Services

The emergence of digital trade applies considerable pressure on the regulatory structure of the GATS. A key issue related to the governance of digital trade under

---

[259] Exemptions from MFN treatment were to be submitted at the time of conclusion of the Agreement and are included in country-specific lists, cf. GATS Annex on Article II Exemptions, 2. The Annex provides in No. 6 that such exemptions *"in principle"* should not exceed a period of 10 years. However, few exemptions have been offered for termination Adlung (2006), p. 870.

[260] *See* with regard in particular to ICT services Tuthill and Roy (2012), p. 159.

[261] WTO (2001e), para. 2.

[262] Cf. Adlung (2006), pp. 867–877.

3.3 The WTO and Digital Trade

the GATS is the general applicability of the GATS to digitally delivered services. With regard to a digital delivery of services via data flows, the opinion has early on taken hold that the GATS would apply in principle to digital forms of services trade due to its regulatory framework being technology-neutral.[263] However, while some WTO documents imply a consensus on this issue, the existence of the principle of technological neutrality within the GATS is debatable.[264] There are serious arguments to reject the idea of technological neutrality of the GATS rules given the lack of an explicit and binding recognition by WTO Members.[265] Therefore, criticism of alleged judicial overreach has been voiced, against the backdrop that the principle of technology neutrality has been taken up in the jurisprudence of the WTO Dispute Settlement Body.[266]

Nevertheless, jurisprudence of the WTO Dispute Settlement Bodies has provided much-needed clarification on the applicability of multilateral trade rules to digital trade. The first WTO dispute settlement case addressing the impact of the Internet on trade in services was *US-Gambling*.[267] In this case Antigua filed a complaint with the WTO alleging that the US had breached their market access commitments under GATS regarding the supply of online gambling services.[268] In this context, both the Panel and the Appellate Body confirmed the applicability of the GATS framework to the online supply of gambling services.[269] In fact, the digital delivery of gambling

---

[263] *See* for example WTO (1998d), p. 7, para. 37; Tuthill (2017), pp. 97–98.

[264] Kelsey (2018), pp. 290–294; Willemyns (2021), pp. 103–108.

[265] Mattoo and Schuknecht (2000), pp. 15–17 point out three reasons in particular: (1) the definitions of the United Nations Central Product Classification are sometimes not technology-neutral as they may designate the means of delivery without listing electronic means; (2) during the extended negotiations on basic telecommunications the parties felt the need to adopt an explicit understanding on technological neutrality; (3) the Moratorium on Customs Duties on Electronic Transmissions in itself is contradictory to the *"likeness"* of services delivered by divergent means.

[266] Sen (2018), p. 331. *See* for the exact wording Panel Report, *US-Gambling*, WT/DS285/R, 10 November 2004, para. 6.285 *"We note that this is in line with the principle of "technological neutrality", which seems to be largely shared among WTO Members."*. This also raises the question whether new services can be regulated by litigation through the WTO dispute settlement system, respectively if and at what point this constitutes judicial activism that disregards the authorisation in the Dispute Settlement Understanding, cf. Peng (2014), pp. 1208-1220. *See* however also the more critical reference in Panel Report, *China – Publications and Audiovisual Products*, WT/DS363/R, 12 August 2009, fn. 703: *"This view was not, however, unanimous [. . .]"*. Indeed, in fn. 705 the Panel further adds that *"The reference by that panel to the principle of technological neutrality was not referred to by the Appellate Body in its report on the subsequent appeal in that case [US-Gambling]"*.

[267] *See* Panel Report, *US-Gambling*, WT/DS285/R, 10 November 2004; Appellate Body Report, *US-Gambling*, WT/DS285/AB/R, 20 April 2005.

[268] Indeed, some of the major GATS cases relate to data transmissions, *see* beside the *US-Gambling* case Panel Report, *Mexico – Telecoms*, WT/DS204/R, 2 April 2004; Panel Report, *China – Publications and Audiovisual Products*, WT/DS363/R, 12 August 2009; Appellate Body Report, *China – Publications and Audiovisual Products*, WT/DS363/AB/R, 21 December 2009; Panel Report, *China — Electronic Payment Services*, WT/DS413/R, 16 July 2012.

[269] Wunsch-Vincent (2006), p. 323.

services via the Internet was classified as a Mode 1 transaction under GATS.[270] With regard to the pertinence of the GATS regulatory framework to digital trade, this implies that the delivery of digital services via cross-border data flows is covered by Members' scheduled Mode 1 commitments under the GATS, unless otherwise specified in the schedule.[271] The GATS is therefore regarded as being neutral with regard to the means of supplying a scheduled service commitment.[272] Indeed, the WTO Panel and Appellate Body held that a GATS Mode 1 commitment applies to *"all means of delivery, whether by mail, telephone, internet, etc."*, unless otherwise specified in a Member's schedule.[273] Yet, the clarification of the applicability of GATS rules to digital trade in services gives rise to the question, which Mode of the GATS is in fact applicable to digitally supplied services. Conceptually, it is primarily Mode 1 (*"cross-border"*) as well as Mode 2 (*"consumption abroad"*) of the GATS that are conceivable with regard to the classification of online delivery.[274] This issue touches on the metaphysical question of where events occur on the Internet—in particular, if the recipient is travelling virtually to the service provider in order to receive the service or if the service is in fact provided across borders via the medium of cyberspace.[275] While many Members undertook extensive liberalisations under

---

[270] See for the latter in particular Panel Report, *US-Gambling*, WT/DS285/R, 10 November 2004, para. 6.285, which reads *"The Panel concludes that mode 1 under the GATS encompasses all possible means of supplying services from the territory of one WTO Member into the territory of another WTO Member."*. This interpretation was relied upon in Appellate Body Report, *China – Publications and Audiovisual Products*, WT/DS363/AB/R, 21 December 2009, para. 364.

[271] Meltzer (2019a), p. 25. This in turn indicates that a complete ban on cross-border data flows by means of measures of so-called data localisation effectively constitutes a *"zero quota"* and is incompatible with obligations under the GATS unless restrictions are listed, see also Tuthill (2017), pp. 101–102. *See* further in this context *infra* Sect. 3.3.2.6.4. *See* also with regard to the scheduling of *"products"* entailing tangible and intangible goods and services Appellate Body Report, *China – Publications and Audiovisual Products*, WT/DS363/AB/R, 21 December 2009, para. 364 with reference to Panel Report, *China – Publications and Audiovisual Products*, WT/DS363/R, 12 August 2009, para. 7.1188.

[272] Panel Report, *US-Gambling*, WT/DS285/R, 10 November 2004, para. 6.285: *"We note that this is in line with the principle of "technological neutrality", which seems to be largely shared among WTO"*; Sen (2018), p. 331; Tuthill (2017), pp. 97–98; Wunsch-Vincent (2006), pp. 329–334. *See* further Chander (2012), pp. 19–22, who also advocates technological neutrality with regard to regulatory standards in connection with Mode 1, which he considers appropriate, if *"the online service is required to achieve the regulatory goals at rates roughly equivalent to those achieved by online versions of the service."*.

[273] Panel Report, *US-Gambling*, WT/DS285/R, 10 November 2004, para. 6.285.

[274] *See* Wunsch-Vincent (2006), pp. 324–327. Yet, the WTO Panel in the *China-Electronic Payments* case held that the delivery of electronic payment services was subject to Mode 3 in addition to Mode 1, cf. Panel Report, *China – Electronic Payments*, WT/DS413/R, 16 July 2012, para. 7.575. *See* in this context also Tuthill and Roy (2012), pp. 159–160; Willemyns (2021), pp. 101–103.

[275] Chander (2012), p. 29.

Mode 2, there are fewer commitments under Mode 1.[276] The perception that the provision of online services via the Internet constitutes supply under Mode 1 is based on the premise that typically only data is exchanged between the service provider and the service recipient and that the service is therefore provided across borders on the basis of cross-border data flows.

3.3.2.6.3 Classification of "Digital Services"

A further challenge for the GATS framework concerns the classification of service activities which are subject to changing commercial patterns, convergence and evolving market structures in a digital economy.[277] During the negotiations of the GATS, the parties employed the Services Sectoral Classifications List (W/120) as a means of categorising the services that were to be liberalised by the multilateral agreement.[278] The GATS classification list (W/120) was initially drawn up by the GATT Secretariat in 1991 based on the UN Provisional Central Product Classification (CPC Prov.) System. The (W/120) classification list features several sectors which are relevant for trade in the digital economy such as audio-visual (2. D.), telecommunications, computer and related services (1. B.) or banking and other financial services (7. B.) as well as respective sub-sectors such as data processing and data base services (1. B. c. and d.).[279] However, since the scheduled commitments have remained largely unaltered, the currently applicable schedules generally reflect the circumstances of 1994.[280] The pre-Internet GATS classification list inevitably raises questions in the context of the modern service environment of the digital economy. Today, *"digital services"* (i.e. Cloud Computing, Internet searches) generally consist of complex combinations of sectors and subsectors of the (W/120) classification list which prompts the question of a possible overlap of different categories.[281] Against the backdrop of the somewhat antiquated status of the (W/120) classification list, the regulatory consistency of GATS schedules is challenged by the emergence of potentially novel service activities, the blurring of the demarcation between services and goods as well as the convergence of different service sectors in relation to integrated digital economy services.[282] In fact, *"digital*

---

[276] In fact, at the time of the finalisation of the Uruguay Round, Mode 1 commitments for cross-border supply were considered not feasible in many sectors and therefore rather irrelevant, see with further references Peng (2014), p. 1193.

[277] See generally Tuthill and Roy (2012); Weber and Burri (2014); Willemyns (2021), pp. 117–177.

[278] Cf. GATT Secretariat (1991).

[279] See further Burri (2017b), p. 83; Meltzer (2019a), p. 38; Sen (2018), p. 332; Tuthill and Roy (2012), pp. 160–176. See with regard to AI applications in health services Chander (2021), pp. 122–125.

[280] Adlung (2014), p. 372.

[281] Mitchell and Mishra (2018), p. 1090; Sen (2018), p. 333–334; Weber and Burri (2014), p. 91.

[282] See further Kelsey (2018), pp. 287–288; Meltzer (2019a), pp. 39–40; Mitchell and Hepburn (2018), pp. 197–198; IMF et al. (2019), p. 10.

services" may fit into multiple service categories of the GATS classification list at once or even none at all.[283] In this context, the Appellate Body Report in *US-Gambling* clearly stated that service sectors or subsectors according to (W/120) are meant to be exclusive.[284] This exclusivity of sectors under GATS, however, gives rise to confusion as to which obligations take precedence.[285] Moreover, it raises the question whether services which did not exist at the time the schedules were initially compiled—so-called *"new"* services—can be subject to the established sectors of the (W/120) list in the first place.[286]

In fact, some commentators estimate that today there are many digital services being traded across borders which may not be covered by the national schedules of the GATS.[287] In theory, the question of whether the (W/120) classification list also covers *"new"* services can be assessed according to whether it is the intrinsic nature of the service that is emphasised or the way in which it is provided.[288] This is particularly critical in conjunction with the positive list approach of the GATS, according to which only those services are liberalised for which specific commitments have been made based on the sectors set forth in the classification list (W/120).[289] In this regard, the Appellate Body in the *China - Publications and Audiovisual Products* case noted that the scheduled commitments may be interpreted differently in response to technological developments.[290] It held that: *"interpreting the terms of GATS specific commitments based on the notion that the ordinary meaning to be attributed to those terms can only be the meaning that they had at the time the Schedule was concluded would mean that very similar or identically worded commitments could be given different meanings, content, and coverage depending on the date of their adoption or the date of a Member's accession to the treaty. Such interpretation would undermine the predictability, security, and*

---

[283] *See* for an in-depth discussion Willemyns (2021), pp. 117–177.

[284] Cf. Appellate Body Report, *US-Gambling*, WT/DS285/AB/R, 20 April 2005, para. 180.

[285] Mitchell and Mishra (2018), p. 1090; Sen (2018), p. 334; Zhang (2015), pp. 11–14.

[286] Mitchell and Mishra (2018), p. 1090; Sen (2018), p. 333–334; Tuthill and Roy (2012), pp. 157–160; Zhang (2015), pp. 14–17.

[287] Tuthill (2017), p. 101.

[288] Meltzer (2019a), p. 39 ascribes to the EU and the US the opinion that it is indeed the intrinsic nature of a service that matters and that therefore the occurrence of genuinely new services is rare. In the context, he points to Annex 9.B of the Comprehensive Economic and Trade Agreement (CETA) - Understanding on new services not classified in the United Nations provisional central product classification (CPC). According to para. 1: *"The Parties agree that Chapter Twelve (Domestic Regulation) and Articles 9.3, 9.5, and 9.6 do not apply to a measure relating to a new service that cannot be classified in the CPC 1991."*. *See* also Zhang (2015), pp. 8–19, who addresses the residual category *"other"* of the (W/120) classification list and considers it to be of little use in trade negotiations, as it is widely unclear what this category encompasses.

[289] Tuthill and Roy (2012), p. 159; Weber (2010), p. 8. *See* on remedies in recent PTAs *infra* Sect. 3.4.1.

[290] *See* also Crosby (2016), p. 4; Willemyns (2021), pp. 118–126.

clarity of GATS specific commitments".[291] Nevertheless, the remaining uncertainties in the classification of digital economy services are prompting discussions related to recontextualising the GATS commitments against the backdrop of trade in the digital economy (*see infra* Sect. 6.3).

3.3.2.6.4 Regulation of Cross-Border Data Flows

The issues discussed above regarding the applicability of the GATS to the emerging services environment of the digital economy are often raised in connection with the regulation of cross-border data flows under WTO law. Since cross-border data flows are a crucial factor for digital trade (*see supra* Sect. 2.3.2), it is controversial whether and to what extent WTO rules can serve as a guarantor for unrestricted data flows. However, the 1994 WTO framework provides very few explicit provisions for the regulation of data and data flows. The GATS notably does not include a horizontal provision regarding cross-border data flows. With regard to information and data flows, merely the Understanding on Commitments in Financial Services, B. 8, obliges member to refrain from *"measures that prevent the transfer of information including transfers of data by electronic means"* while the Annex on Telecommunications, 5(c), stipulates that Members *"shall ensure that service suppliers of any other Member may use public telecommunications transport networks and services for the movement of information within and across borders"*.[292] Moreover, the GATS does not explicitly address barriers to the digital delivery of services via cross-border flows, such as data localisation measures or Internet access restrictions.[293] The fact that cross-border data regulation has been addressed only to a very limited extent in multilateral law, however, does not mean that the GATS framework is not relevant to the regulation of cross-border data flows *per se*. For example, it is clear from the GATS scheduling guidelines and the WTO case law in *Mexico-Telecoms* that a service supplier under Mode 1 does not have to be present in the

---

[291] Appellate Body Report, *China – Publications and Audiovisual Products*, WT/DS363/AB/R, 21 December 2009, paras. 396–397.
[292] These obligations, in turn, are subject to derogations for the sake of privacy and confidentiality: *"Nothing in this paragraph restricts the right of a Member to protect personal data, personal privacy and the confidentiality of individual records and accounts so long as such right is not used to circumvent the provisions of the Agreement"*, cf. WTO, Understanding on Commitments in Financial Services, B. 3 c, 8; and *"Member may take such measures as are necessary to ensure the security and confidentiality of messages, subject to the requirement that such measures are not applied in a manner which would constitute a means of arbitrary or unjustifiable discrimination or a disguised restriction on trade in services"*, cf. Annex on Telecommunications, 5(d). In this context, *see* further for the general exception of Article XIV(c)(ii) GATS for data privacy *infra* Sect. 5.2.2.2.
[293] Willemyns (2020a), pp. 121. In this respect *Ines Willemyns* demonstrates that recent PTAs address a number of such barriers Willemyns (2020a), pp. 131.

territory of the other Member.[294] This can be adapted to the regulation of data flows in the way that a WTO member cannot require the presence of a service provider in its own country, e.g., in the context of a data localisation measure, provided that Mode 1 service supply is fully liberalised.[295] Furthermore, in *US-Gambling*, the WTO Dispute Settlement Body held that a ban on online gambling services violated market access commitments.[296] The Appellate Body upheld the WTO Panel's findings that a "*[a prohibition on one, several or all means of delivery cross-border] is a "limitation on the number of service suppliers in the form of numerical quotas" within the meaning of Article XVI:2(a) because it totally prevents the use by service suppliers of one, several or all means of delivery that are included in mode 1.*" as well that that "*a measure prohibiting the supply of certain services where specific commitments have been undertaken is a limitation within the meaning of Article XVI:2(c) because it totally prevents the services operations and/or service output through one or more or all means of delivery that are included in mode 1*".[297] On this basis, it would be logical to assume that national regulations imposing a complete ban on cross-border data flows would be considered a "*zero quota*" for a particular service relying on such flows and thus may not be consistent with a Member's specific GATS commitments under Mode 1.[298] In addition, WTO jurisprudence can be interpreted to address cross-border transfers of data that occur in connection with scheduled commitments. In this sense, the WTO Panel has held in *China—Electronic Payment Services* that a: "*"sector" may include "any service activity that falls within the scope of the definition of that sector", whether or not these activities are explicitly enumerated in the definition of that sector or subsector*".[299] Opening the interpretation of schedules to changing technological conditions also requires a broad interpretation of the activities covered by the scheduled obligation, which gives important hints for dealing with sophisticated services activities in a digital economy.[300]

---

[294] Panel Report, *Mexico – Telecoms*, WT/DS204/R, 2 April 2004, para. 7.45. *See* also WTO (2001e), para. 26.

[295] Crosby (2016), p. 3.

[296] Panel Report, *US-Gambling*, WT/DS285/R, 10 November 2004, paras. 6.363, 6.367, 6.370; cf. further Appellate Body Report, *US-Gambling*, WT/DS285/AB/R, 20 April 2005, para. 265. *See* on the relationship between market access and domestic regulations in this regard Wunsch-Vincent (2006), pp. 338–339.

[297] Appellate Body Report, *US-Gambling*, WT/DS285/AB/R, 20 April 2005, paras. 241 and 251.

[298] *See* only Burri (2017b), pp. 95–96; Mitchell and Hepburn (2018), pp. 200–201.

[299] Panel Report, *China – Electronic Payment Services*, WT/DS413/R, 16 July 2012, para. 7.179.

[300] Crosby (2016), p. 4.

3.3.3 Evaluation

The assessment of the role of the WTO regulatory framework with respect to the governance of digital trade presents an ambivalent result. Indeed, WTO rules enshrine several important tenets of multilateral trade regulation that, while not originally devised in the context of a data-driven economy, nevertheless provide a substantial service to the governance of digital trade. Despite rapidly evolving economic realities, the key principles of non-discrimination embodied in the MFN principle and the NT obligation remain important pillars of the governance of cross-border economic activity. In addition, the institutional structure of the WTO, its dispute settlement mechanism, the standards of transparency of its rules, and its extensive membership are key factors guaranteeing the viability of WTO law in the digital economy.[301] In this respect, several elements of the WTO regulatory framework have contributed to the flourishing of the digital trade environment over the years. This is the case, for example, with the repeatedly extended Moratorium on Custom Duties on Electronic Transmissions, on the basis of which the digital economy has developed unhindered by customs duties on underlying cross-border data flows. In similar vein, the rules for trade in IT goods under the GATT extended by the ITA and combined with the provisions of GATS promoting competition in telecommunications markets, for example, have contributed to ever better Internet access.[302] The WTO Work Programme, notably, has provided a multilateral forum for discourse on the emergent nexus of trade regulation, international digital governance as well as economic growth and development in the digital era.[303] Given the complex challenges posed by the implications of an inherently global digital economy, scholars and practitioners argue that WTO law, as a robust and widely accepted framework of international law, can provide a forum for the governance of digital trade.[304]

At the same time, however, there is widespread concern about the disconnect between aspirations for comprehensive multilateral trade governance and the impact of multilateral trade law on the economic realities of trade in the digital economy.[305] The current state of readiness of WTO rules with regard to regulating digital trade can be illustrated by reference to the lack of results of the 1998 Work Programme on global electronic commerce. The Work Programme has long constituted a focal

---

[301] *See* also Burri (2017b), pp. 93-94; Burri (2017a), pp. 3–6. It should not be overlooked, however, that WTO law is subject to considerable challenges in view of the multipolar power relations of the twenty-first century, *see* further Weiß et al. (2022), pp. 1–7.

[302] Burri (2017b), p. 76; Meltzer (2019a), p. 42. Indeed, the GATS contains competition-related safeguards in Article VIII and IX, as well as in the Annex on Telecommunications and the Reference Paper on Regulatory Principles for Basic Telecommunications, *see* Tuthill (2017), pp. 109–113.

[303] *See* for the latter, for example, WTO (2013b); WTO (2013c). *See* also *supra* Sect. 3.3.1.1.

[304] *See* for example Aaronson and Leblond (2018), p. 251; Burri (2017b), pp. 129–132.

[305] *See* only Mitchell and Mishra (2018).

point in the efforts to provide a forum for debate on the expanding digital trade environment. The broad scope and detailed nature of the exploratory agenda of the 1998 Work Programme reflected a forward-looking outlook on the future relevance of "e-commerce".[306] This relates in particular to the rather broad definition of e-commerce and the additional consideration of infrastructural aspects. In principle, this programme design allowed for a comprehensive examination of the cross-cutting impact of the digital transformation of trade. While the theoretical aspirations were very promising, little to nothing was achieved in practice. *Sacha Wunsch-Vincent* and *Arno Hold* have done an excellent job in compiling key unresolved issues of the Work Programme. Unsolved matters of the exploratory agenda include *inter alia* issues such as agreement on a permanent Moratorium on Customs Duties on Electronic Transmissions (including a clear definition of the underlying definition of electronic transmissions); the applicability of WTO rules and specific commitments under GATS to the provision of digital services; various questions of classification of digital services and products including the scheduling of *"new"* (often fully digital) services; and the application of the general exceptions of Article XIV GATS as well as of Article VI GATS regarding domestic regulation on digital trade.[307] Against the backdrop of such an extensive list of unresolved issues, the authors concluded that the Work Programme was unable to *"convert thinking into action"*.[308] In this respect, the Work Programme reflects the impasse in the development of the multilateral trade regime under the Doha Round and is an articulation of the predicament of multilateral trade law as a whole. A serious shortfall of trade governance under contemporary WTO law can be identified, particularly with respect to the governance of cross-border data flows. The particular relevance of the 1994 GATS framework in this respect is due to the close connection between the intangible and highly digitizable service sector and the import and export of digital data. This way, the GATS approximates most closely to a framework for governance of cross-border data flows under WTO law. Although the WTO Dispute Settlement Bodies in the *US-Gambling* case clarified the general applicability of the GATS framework to digital delivery, the GATS lacks robust provisions on data flows. Services involving cross-border data flows depend on WTO Members' scheduled commitments under the GATS positive list approach, which have remained largely unchanged since 1994. In this context, *Andrew D. Mitchell* and *Neha Mishra* rightly point out that, due to the lack of a horizontal commitment regarding cross-border data flows and the complex system of service classifications, the status of legal commitments under the GATS relevant to the regulation of cross-border data flows

---

[306] Wunsch-Vincent and Hold (2012), p. 180.

[307] Furthermore, the authors have evaluated the performance of the WTO regulatory framework versus solutions in PTAs on digital trade with regard to issues raised in the WTO Work Programme on Electronic Commerce, *see* Wunsch-Vincent and Hold (2012), pp. 186–187.

[308] Wunsch-Vincent and Hold (2012), p. 181. *See* further the reports of the Council for Trade in Services WTO (1999e); the Council for Trade in Goods WTO (1999f); the Council for TRIPs WTO (1999c) and the Committee for Trade and Development WTO (1998e).

are "*uncertain*".[309] This uncertainty in WTO rules is likely to result in disputes over measures restricting cross-border data flows being decided on a case-by-case basis, which would give the WTO Dispute Settlement System a unique role in determining digital trade liberalisation (*see* with regard to data privacy *infra* Sect. 5.2).[310] Against this background, there is a general consensus among the G20 Members on the necessity of reforming the WTO to meet the challenges in relation to digital trade.[311]

3.4 Preferential Trade Agreements and Digital Trade

Preferential Trade Agreements (PTAs) have proliferated since the 1990s to the point that nearly every WTO Member is party to at least one such agreement.[312] As of 15 April 2024, 369 trade agreements are in force. The resulting, ever-expanding "*spaghetti bowl*" of PTAs reinforces the perception that the multilateral trading system has stalled and is currently incapable of meeting the challenges of a multipolar balance of power.[313] As outlined above, the realities of international trade have changed significantly with the emergence of increasingly complex GVCs that rely heavily on global networks (*see supra* Sect. 2.3).[314] Against this backdrop, major trading economies such as the US and the EU have put increased emphasis on preferential trade negotiations with allied nations.[315] In this context, territorial proximity between the parties to an agreement only matters to a very limited extent.[316] Increasingly, the contracting parties of a what are called Regional Trade Agreements (RTA) can therefore be located anywhere in the world. Moreover, these agreements frequently adopt an agenda of deep integration in order to align the regulatory regimes of the respective domestic markets and hence facilitate

---

[309] Cf. Mitchell and Mishra (2018), p. 1093.

[310] *See* also Mitchell and Hepburn (2018), pp. 206–207.

[311] *See* for example the G20 Osaka Leaders Declaration of 2019 which states: "*International trade and investment are important engines of growth, productivity, innovation, job creation and development. We reaffirm our support for the necessary reform of the World Trade Organization (WTO) to improve its functions.*", G20 (2019), p. 2 para. 8.

[312] Baldwin (2014), pp. 644–654. *See* for a historical background WTO (2011a), pp. 46–92.

[313] Bhagwati (1995). The notion is frequently associated with the portrayal of an emerging regionalism in trade whose deviations from multilateral principles of non-discrimination are at odds with the advancement of a multilateral trade order. *See* for a balanced review of the debate Baldwin (2014), pp. 639–642. and for extensive collection of further references Herrmann (2008), p. 263, fn. 2. The mutual influence of WTO law and regional trade agreements is, however, a multifaceted issue, *see* Allee et al. (2017); Cottier (2015); Panezi (2016).

[314] Kim (2015), pp. 367–368.

[315] Following the US approach of negotiating bilateral agreements, the EU in particular has begun to enter into an increasing number of trade agreements since the mid-2000s. *See* for example European Commission (2006), pp. 8–10. *See* with regard specifically to digital trade Wunsch-Vincent (2003).

[316] Weiß (2014), pp. 149–152.

cross-border commercial interaction.[317] Recent trade agreements are characterised by their tendency to transcend the WTO commitments of the contracting parties (WTO-plus). This is the case with obligations such as with regard to market access in goods and services, for example. Yet, contemporary agreements even cover areas beyond the established patterns of multilateral trade liberalisation (WTO-X) such as investment, labour market or environmental regulations.[318] Typically, the core elements of such a deep integration rationale relate to the protection of the interests of foreign companies, to the abolishment of persisting trade barriers due to domestic regulations *"behind the border"* and to the overall harmonisation of domestic trade rules.[319] Notably, an evolving trade practice has produced so-called *"mega-regional"* agreements, which generally pursue an agenda of deep integration and constitute *"set-top"* agreements to the WTO framework.[320] Recent examples of such mega-regional agreements include the Comprehensive and Progressive Agreement for Trans-Pacific Partnership (CPTPP) or the Regional Comprehensive Economic Partnership (RCEP). The combination of the number of participants and the expansion of scope beyond the traditional area of trade policy leads to the formation of clusters of *"megaregulation"*.[321]

As trade agreements have gained in substantive depth, they have been incorporating rules for e-commerce and more recently on digital trade.[322] Such rules typically consist of WTO-plus provisions (e.g., in the services sector) as well as WTO-X provisions that involve data-related dimensions of trade (e.g., rules on cross-border data flows, data localisation, or the disclosure of source code). This section provides a brief overview of the evolution of digital trade governance in the context of PTAs and what can be considered the formation of digital trade law. In the following, first, the integration of digital trade rules into trade agreements is presented.[323] In doing so, such integration of digital trade governance will first be briefly examined in terms of regulatory structure and substantive development. Given that the governance of data and cross-border data flows is a key issue of digital trade as defined above, in a second step particular attention will be placed on the regulation of cross-border data flows in PTAs.

---

[317] *See* with further references Kim (2015), pp. 361–366.

[318] *See* Horn et al. (2009), pp. 24–29.

[319] *See* for a detailed discussion Kim (2015), pp. 363–365.

[320] Bown (2017); Stoll (2017).

[321] *See* Kingsbury et al. (2019).

[322] *See* with regard to *"deep"* digital trade rules in PTAs Wunsch-Vincent and Hold (2012), pp. 204–211.

[323] In addition to the following observations, reference is made to the chronological development of the chapters on *"e-commerce"* previously addressed above, *see supra* Sect. 3.2.2.1.

3.4.1 Integration of Digital Trade Rules in Preferential Trade Agreements

With regard to the absence of substantial multilateral guidance on digital trade, PTAs are considered to be a second-best option for rule-based liberalisation of digital trade.[324] In the face of a continuously rising imperative for an effective governance of the emergent digital trade environment, PTAs have become *"experimental laboratories"* for rule-design and standard setting.[325] Given the considerable room for manoeuvre offered by the multilateral framework in the context of digital trade, heterogenous approaches have developed, creating somewhat of an *"e-spaghetti bowl"*.[326] With regard to trade in the digital economy, comprehensive modern PTAs seek to fill the regulatory vacuum that exists with respect to digital trade governance under multilateral WTO law and in particular under the GATS.[327] As of 1994 and more consistently from 2000 onwards, trade agreements adopted terms relating to digital trade in a cross-border trade context.[328] The first agreement to feature a standalone chapter on *"electronic commerce"* was concluded in 2003 between Australia and Singapore.[329] In fact, rules on e-commerce are included in more than 60% of the trade agreements that entered into force between 2014 and 2016.[330] From 2011 onwards, with exceptions only in 2012 and 2017, equally or more trade agreements with such provisions entered into force than without, resulting in two-thirds of the WTO Membership being party to an agreement that includes such provisions.[331] As a result of the increasing relevance of rules on digital trade, considerable scholarly literature exists on language and scope of contractual regimes in PTAs. Recently, scholarly projects have examined the development of digital governance in trade agreements by using computer-assisted text processing to provide a detailed analysis of the relevant chapters and provisions.[332] In a particular

---

[324] Herman (2010), p. 11; Weber (2010), p. 15. *See* also in this sense Burri (2017d), p. 408.

[325] Herman (2010), p. 6; Wunsch-Vincent and Hold (2012), pp. 192–193.

[326] Wunsch-Vincent and Hold (2012), p. 193.

[327] Burri (2021b), p. 33; Mitchell and Mishra (2018), pp. 1098–1103.

[328] Willemyns (2020b), pp. 223–224.

[329] Cf. Chapter 14 of the Free Trade Agreement between Australia and Singapore, emphasising in a preamble: *"The Parties recognise the economic growth and opportunities provided by electronic commerce, the importance of avoiding barriers to its use and development and the applicability of relevant WTO rules."*. *See* also Wu (2017), p. 6. The heterogeneous terminology found in agreements, official texts and scholarly contributions complicates the discussion of this topic. Indeed, the majority of agreements in force today employ the terminology of electronic commerce. Nevertheless, the following refers primarily to the umbrella term „*digital trade*", to identify rules that relate to various aspects of e-commerce on the one hand but also to specific data-related content on the other, *see supra* Sect. 3.2.3.

[330] Monteiro and Teh (2017), p. 6.

[331] Willemyns (2020b), p. 224.

[332] *See* for example Willemyns (2020b). Cf. in general with regard to data driven research in this particular field Alschner et al. (2017).

comprehensive approach, research by *Mira Burri* and *Rodrigo Polanco* retraces developments in digital trade governance.[333] The empirical results generated by the *"Trade Agreements Provisions on Electronic-Commerce and Data (TAPED)"* project demonstrate a number of trends and developments in the ever-growing number of PTAs, reflecting on a very dynamically evolving environment of digital trade governance. The data used in this section on digital trade provisions in PTAs are based primarily on this analysis, but also take into account research by other authors.[334]

3.4.1.1 Structural Considerations Regarding Digital Trade Rules in PTAs

With regard to structural considerations concerning digital trade provisions in trade agreements, two aspects may be considered in more detail. A first aspect concerns the external structure of such rules, i.e., the structural positioning of the regulations within the range of subjects covered by a modern trade agreement. Second, it is important to examine the extent to which the internal structure within the clusters of rules dealing specifically with digital trade has evolved.

With regard to the first question concerning external structuring, it must be emphasised that even if dedicated chapters are gradually introduced into trade agreements, trade-related issues of the digital economy are of a cross-cutting nature. As a result, preferential trade rules on digital trade relate to a wide range of issues regulated in trade agreements, such as rules on services, especially financial and telecommunications services, but also rules on trade in goods and intellectual property. Digital trade rules also pertain to trade facilitation, such as paperless trading and electronic authentication, as well as to regulatory cooperation on domestic standards of privacy, consumer protection. Consequently, provisions on digital trade are integrated into a variety of chapters other than those specifically dedicated to global electronic commerce or digital trade, thus reflecting a general lack of sectoral specificity of digital trade rules.[335]

Secondly, valuable insights can also be gained by looking at the internal structure of dedicated chapters relating to trade in the digital economy. Such a review of the internal structure of the e-commerce and digital trade chapters highlights the increasing complexity of digital trade governance in trade agreements. Research by *Mira Burri* and *Rodrigo Polanco* indicates, that as of October 2019, seven is the average number of provisions in chapters and side agreements on electronic

---

[333] *See* Burri and Polanco (2020), who claim: *"dataset includes a detailed mapping and coding of all preferential trade agreements (PTAs) that cover chapters, provisions, annexes and side documents that directly or indirectly regulate digital trade."*.

[334] *See* for example Burri (2017a), pp. 7–11; Burri (2017d), pp. 418–430; Herman (2010); Monteiro and Teh (2017); Willemyns (2020b); Wu (2017); Wunsch-Vincent and Hold (2012), pp. 192–215.

[335] Burri (2017b), pp. 99–110; Burri and Polanco (2020), p. 189; López González and Ferencz (2018), p. 16; Monteiro and Teh (2017), p. 13–14.

commerce, increasing to ten provisions on average when considering the last 5 years.[336] Furthermore, their TAPED data set demonstrates that the level of detail of PTAs with provisions on digital trade has considerably intensified over the years—as of October 2019, the average number of words in chapters and side agreements on digital trade is 835, with an average of 1476 words in the last 5 years.[337] From the increasing complexity of the rules, it can be deduced both that trade agreements appear to offer a valuable approach to shaping rules for digital trade and that an increasing number of countries are embracing this approach.

3.4.1.2 Substantive Considerations Regarding Digital Trade Rules in PTAs

With regard to substantive considerations concerning the rules on digital trade put forth by recent PTAs, the dedicated e-commerce or digital trade chapters as well as the relevant provisions in the service chapters will be addressed in the following.[338]

With regard to dedicated chapters on digital trade, first, the heterogeneity of such chapters in terms of structure, language and scope is frequently emphasised in scholarly literature.[339] However, a recurring rationale of these chapters is the response to a lack of multilateral guidance for important issues relating to a digital trading environment on the one hand and the aspiration to develop an environment conducive to digital trade on the other.[340] Hence, for clarification and guidance, some PTAs provide that WTO rules indeed apply to electronic commerce.[341] In addition, some chapters on e-commerce seek to extend the principles of non-discrimination into the digital trading environment (MFN treatment and NT obligations), often by mandating non-discriminatory treatment of *"digital products"*.[342] However, by a considerable margin, the most common rule in reference to the multilateral trade order concerns the obligation not to impose customs duties on electronic transmissions, thereby contractually stipulating the permanent application of the WTO Moratorium on Customs Duties on Electronic Transmissions.[343]

---

[336] Burri and Polanco (2020), p. 195.

[337] Burri and Polanco (2020), p. 195.

[338] Notably, chapters on the protection of IPR will not be addressed. *See* for an assessment of their role in the development of a regulatory environment for digital trade Burri (2017b), p. 105; Wunsch-Vincent and Hold (2012), pp. 211–215.

[339] *See* for example Burri and Polanco (2020), p. 193; Monteiro and Teh (2017), p. 71.

[340] Burri (2017d), pp. 419–420; Burri and Polanco (2020), pp. 197–203.

[341] Burri and Polanco (2020), pp. 197–198; Wu (2017), p. 11.

[342] Burri and Polanco (2020), pp. 200–203; Weber (2010), p. 14; Wu (2017), p. 10. This requires that the term *"digital product"* is introduced and defined, which is the case in most agreements with US participation and also with regard to several other countries that have adopted this treaty language—the EU in particular does not define digital product, *see* Willemyns (2020a), pp. 128–129.

[343] Burri and Polanco (2020), pp. 198–200; Wu (2017), pp. 11–13.

In addition to such provisions based on established WTO rules, the promotion of a trade environment that is favourable to digital trade is an important element of digital trade governance. This may include general commitments to promote and facilitate e-commerce by creating an enabling environment for digital trade, but also more specific agreements to encourage consumer trust in the online environment, foster innovation, and promote interoperability.[344] Promoting the confidence of businesses and consumers that cross-border transactions over the Internet will comply with basic legal standards with which they are familiar in the domestic market requires the integration of rules such as on consumer protection, personal data privacy or unsolicited electronic messages.[345] Moreover, enabling digital trade transactions prompts rules on administration and facilitation of electronic transactions. In this context, some agreements, for example, stipulate the adoption of the UNCITRAL Model Law on Electronic Authentication and Electronic Signatures or on paperless trading.[346] Moreover, with certain prevalence, dedicated chapters include provisions on definitional determinations. This is the case, for example regarding the terms: "*digital product*", "*electronic authentication*", "*electronic transmission*" and "*unsolicited commercial electronic message*".[347] A further distinction can be made between "*hard*" and "*soft*" rules.[348] Hard rules are those that are actually enforceable, for example, as the subject of dispute settlement proceedings. Soft rules, on the other hand, are such rules that relate to political cooperation, i.e., that depend on the further ambitions and aspirations of the parties in this matter.

Beyond the dedicated chapters, the regulation of services in trade agreements assumes a crucial role in the development of the overall digital trade environment.[349] As explained above, this applies in particular to market access restrictions under Mode 1 of the GATS. According to the WTO Dispute Settlement Bodies in *US-Gambling*, supply under Mode 1 includes the supply of services involving cross-border data flows (*see supra* Sect. 3.3.2.6.2). The development of digital trade among the parties therefore benefits from the reduction of trade restrictions on Mode 1 transactions. Yet, commitments on Modes 3 and 4 are also relevant to trade in the digital economy. This is particularly the case regarding those sectors that enable the digital trade environment, such as telecommunications services, financial services or computer-related services.[350] A number of agreements further tackle the problematic positive-list approach of the GATS, according to which only those services for which specific obligations exist are liberalised. Hence, particularly

---

[344] Burri and Polanco (2020), pp. 203–211.
[345] Wu (2017), pp. 19–22.
[346] Burri and Polanco (2020), pp. 207–211; Wu (2017), pp. 14–19.
[347] Willemyns (2020b), p. 225; Wu (2017), p. 9.
[348] Burri and Polanco (2020), p. 192; Herman (2010), p. 14.
[349] *See* only Burri (2017d), p. 419.
[350] Wu (2017), p. 13.

with regard to the NT obligation in trade in services, in some cases a negative list approach is pursued, which indirectly addresses classification issues.[351]

3.4.2 The Regulation of Data Flows in Preferential Trade Agreements

WTO-X provisions of modern PTAs that address digital trade can generally be divided into those that address the enabling of the digital trade environment (electronic authentication and combating unsolicited messages, etc.) and those that address specific data-related issues (cross-border data flows, government data, etc.).[352] In fact, empiric data has shown that parties to trade agreements are increasingly willing to address the regulatory challenges associated with international data governance, as evidenced by an increase in provisions on data flows, data localisation measures, and the forced transfer of source code, for example.[353] In the context of the conceptual approach to digital trade, reference has been made to the fact that specific data-related regulations are increasingly being incorporated into trade agreements (*see* further *supra* Sect. 3.2.2.1). Such specific data-related provisions are a fairly recent feature of PTAs and can be found in a limited number of agreements.[354] Although there is not yet a universally applicable definition of data flows, there is a clear trend towards capturing commercially relevant transfers of data as comprehensively as possible and subjecting them to contractual regulation.[355] To put this relatively new trend firmly in perspective, both quantitative and qualitative considerations regarding the regulation of data flows in recent PTAs will be addressed here.

3.4.2.1 Quantitative Considerations

First, when making a quantitative assessment of the integration of specific rules on the governance of data flows in PTAs, it is important to note that the respective policy developments are still in their early stages. In fact, the integration of rules aimed at ensuring cross-border data flows and restricting data localisation are still a rather rare appearance in trade agreements. Moreover, general provisions concerning the cross-border flow of data are rarer than data transfer-oriented provisions in

---

[351] Weber (2010), p. 14. This is particularly true for those agreements to which the US is a party, cf. Burri (2017b), p. 103.
[352] Burri (2021d), p. 7.
[353] Burri and Polanco (2020), pp. 211–220; Elsig and Klotz (2018); Willemyns (2020b), pp. 225–226.
[354] Burri (2021b), p. 25; Willemyns (2020b), p. 225.
[355] Burri (2021c), p. 68.

chapters dealing with specific services sectors, and here decisively those concerning the telecommunications sector and the financial services sector.[356] GATS-plus commitments, which deepen existing commitments or address the so-called *"new"* services, in many cases involve issues related to the governance of cross-border data flows.[357] More recently, however, a number of specific chapters on digital trade have established far-reaching horizontal agreements on cross-border data flows. Research by *Ines Willemyns* shows that rules on data flows, measures of data localisation, and source code often occur in the form of clusters.[358] This demonstrates that digital trade chapters are increasingly taking on the task of establishing data-centric rules for trade in the digital economy. There appears to be a correlation between the terminology used in PTAs and the trade policy issues addressed, as data-related rules are primarily integrated in dedicated chapters on digital trade.[359] At the same time, this trend towards data-related regulation is expected to continue against the backdrop of the stalemate in the WTO in this regard, especially in light of the recently emerging dedicated Digital Economy Agreements (*see supra* Sect. 3.2.2.1).

3.4.2.2 Qualitative Considerations

The quantitative nature of the provisions on cross-border data flows in trade agreements certainly does not say much about the quality of the commitments made. In this context, it should be emphasised that multilateral law does generally not provide for horizontal commitments on cross-border data flows (*see supra* Sect. 3.3.2.6.4). Moreover, there are no internationally recognised legal frameworks and no generally applicable standards in the area of transnational data governance. While the integration of data flow provisions into trade agreements is not an entirely new phenomenon, the recent proliferation of such provisions suggests that the parties involved increasingly recognize the imperative to regulate the nexus of cross-border data flows and digital trade. Research by *Mira Burri* and *Rodrigo Polanco* illustrates that with respect to the quality of the provisions in PTAs there has been a *"sea*

---

[356] Burri and Polanco (2020), pp. 211–212. As early as 2000, the Jordan-US Free Trade Agreement, the Joint Declaration on Electronic Commerce stated under II. Policy Issues *"Content should be transmitted freely across national borders in response to a user's request. Trade barriers to the free flow of content do not exist today and should not be created in the future."* Another example is provided by the South Korea – US FTA (KORUS) which in its financial services chapter Annex 13B Section B provides for *"Each Party shall allow a financial institution of the other Party to transfer information in electronic or other form, into and out of its territory, for data processing where such processing is required in the institution's ordinary course of business"*.

[357] Yakovleva and Irion (2020), pp. 212–214. However, a number of signatories seek to mitigate the uncertainty of the emerging services environment and exclude *"new services"* from the scope of the respective agreement, often with a view to the financial sector, *see* Zhang (2015), pp. 16–17.

[358] Willemyns (2020b), p. 225, cf. also fn. 18. In this context, the terms *"data transfer"* or *"data flow"* are currently found in ten PTAs of the dataset used; all ten of these PTAs contain rules on data localization and six contain rules on source code transfer.

[359] Burri (2021b), p. 25; Willemyns (2020b), p. 225.

change".³⁶⁰ Against the backdrop of the TAPED dataset, the authors reference PTA rules that can be characterised as either *"hard"*, i.e., enforceable, or *"soft"*, i.e., more aspirational. For example, the first non-binding provision was integrated in Article 14.05 regarding *"Cooperation"* para. (c) of the 2006 Taiwan-Nicaragua agreement and read: *"Recognizing the global nature of electronic commerce, the Parties affirm the importance of working to maintain cross-border flows of information as an essential element in fostering a vibrant environment for electronic commerce"*. In turn, the first binding rule on *"Cross-border flow of information"* was featured in Article 14.10 of the 2014 Mexico-Panama agreement: *"Each Party shall permit its persons and the persons of the other Party to transmit electronic information to and from its territory, when requested to do so by such person, in accordance with applicable data protection laws and taking into account international practices."*.³⁶¹ While non-binding provisions regarding cross-border data flows were included in trade agreements at an early stage, contemporary stipulations are more comprehensive and often formulated as binding obligations.³⁶² The proliferation of rules on cross-border data flows, on the one hand, and their increasingly binding nature, on the other, clearly demonstrate the growing relevance of digital trade. Yet, at the same time, differing sociocultural traditions, varying degrees of political openness, and divergent needs and expectations of both domestic digital industries and the general public are increasingly reflected approaches to transnational data governance, with different countries setting different priorities. Against the backdrop of a multilateral regulatory vacuum, major trading economies are increasingly utilising the political economy of trade agreements and have begun to *"export"* rules that reflect their economic and even socio-cultural approach to trade in the digital economy.³⁶³ Indeed, a number of scholarly contributions have analysed that in particular the templates of the US, the EU and China for trade in the digital economy are taking hold in current agreements.³⁶⁴

---

³⁶⁰ Burri and Polanco (2020), p. 212.

³⁶¹ Examples taken from Burri and Polanco (2020), pp. 212–213, which also illustrate an intermediate type between *"hard"* and *"soft"* provisions, exemplified by Article 15.8 on *"Cross-border Information flows"* of the 2007 South Korea–US FTA (KORUS), which reads *"Recognizing the importance of the free flow of information in facilitating trade, and acknowledging the importance of protecting personal information, the Parties shall endeavour to refrain from imposing or maintaining unnecessary barriers to electronic information flows across borders."*.

³⁶² Burri and Polanco (2020), pp. 212–213.

³⁶³ For example, the data set that *Mira Burri* and *Rodrigo Polanco* have gathered illustrates that 59% of the PTAs with digital trade provisions are negotiated between developed and developing countries and 36% between developing countries, while only 5% are negotiated between developed countries, Burri and Polanco (2020), p. 194.

³⁶⁴ Cf. for a tripartite comparison Aaronson and Leblond (2018), pp. 253–268; Willemyns (2020b), p. 227. *See* also Aaronson (2021), p. 349; Burri (2017b), pp. 99–110; Gao (2018); Wunsch-Vincent and Hold (2012), pp. 192-215.

3.4.2.2.1 United States of America

In line with its *"Digital Agenda"*, the US has included WTO-plus provisions addressing the digital trade environment in trade agreements it has concluded since 2002.[365] This approach is rooted in the fact that a number of the world's largest digital companies and pioneers of the digital economy originate from the US. As a result, the US has always championed a *"free flow of data"*—an objective that is currently actively advocated within the WTO Joint Statement Initiative on Electronic Commerce.[366] In this context, the negotiations on the Trans-Pacific Partnership (TPP) Agreement have introduced pioneering innovations towards a comprehensive template for binding provisions on data flows.[367] In fact, the e-Commerce chapter of the TPP has been claimed by the US to include *"cutting-edge obligations designed to promote the digital economy"*.[368] Although the TPP ultimately failed due to the Trump administration's withdrawal from the negotiations, the principles of this US proposal for binding rules on data flows that would bolster US strategic interests in digital trade are reflected in the provisions of the CPTPP, which was later concluded without US participation, and the subsequently negotiated USMCA between the US, Canada and Mexico.[369]

The CPTPP contains strong rules designed to ensure data flows between the parties and prohibit data localisation.[370] Article 14.11 Section 2 stipulates a binding obligation on data flows: *"Each Party shall allow the cross-border transfer of information by electronic means, including personal information, when this activity is for the conduct of the business of a covered person."* while Article 14.13 Sec. 2 provides for an explicit ban on data localisation: *"No Party shall require a covered person to use or locate computing facilities in that Party's territory as a condition for conducting business in that territory."*. Both of these clauses are designed quite broadly, in that they do not provide for any restriction on their terms *per se*. With these theoretically very comprehensive obligations, the corresponding exception clauses are of particular importance (*see infra* Sect. 5.3.2.1.). The 2020 USMCA Agreement between the US, Mexico and Canada, which replaced the North American Free Trade Agreement (NAFTA) further develops this strong stance on the issue of data and data flows. In fact, the USMCA features the first chapter on *"digital trade"* globally.[371] Although a terminological modification is certainly only a secondary indication of substantive revisions to such an agreement, the USMCA's chapter on digital trade generally represents an evolution of the CPTPP's electronic

---

[365] *See* with further references Burri (2017b), pp. 99–110; Yakovleva (2020), p. 487. *See* further with regard to the so-called *"Digital Agenda"* of the US Wunsch-Vincent (2003).

[366] Aaronson (2015), pp. 680–689. *See* further WTO (2018d), p. 2, para. 2.

[367] Burri (2021c), p. 70; Yakovleva (2020), pp. 487–490.

[368] Office of the United States Trade Representative (2016). *See* also Streinz (2019), pp. 312–314.

[369] Burri (2021c), p. 70.

[370] *See* further Burri (2017b), pp. 110–119; Burri (2021b), pp. 34–37.

[371] *See* Chander (2018).

commerce provisions.[372] While broadly consistent with the CPTPP's e-commerce chapter, the USMCA's digital trade chapter contains a number of more advanced provisions targeted toward a data-driven economy.[373] With regard to data flows, however, the provisions of Article 19.11 *"Cross-border transmission of information by electronic means"* have been kept analogous to those in the CPTPP, with a clarification regarding the applicability of public policy exemption.[374] Moreover, in the absence of a specific exemption, the USMCA in comparison to the CPTPP is based on the assumption that the requirement to use or locate computing facilities in the territory of a Party as a precondition for conducting business in that territory should be generally prohibited, cf. Article 19.12. It appears that this general US approach to the governance of data flows is continuing in recent agreements.[375] The Digital Trade Agreement (DTA) with Japan, signed in October 2019, for example, contains similarly far-reaching provisions on data flows and the location of computing facilities in Article 11 and Article 12.[376]

3.4.2.2.2 European Union

The EU has long hesitated to include explicit provisions on data flows in trade agreements.[377] However, there are indications in recent agreements that the stonewalling on the integration of data flows into EU trade agreements appears to be reaching an end, or at least being eased. For example, the Economic Partnership Agreement (EPA) with Japan, which entered into force in February 2019, contains a rendezvous clause to revisit the issue after a period of 3 years.[378] In a joint statement following the EU-Japan Summit 2022 the parties affirmed to *"consider the launch of negotiations to include data flows into the EPA taking into account inter-alia*

---

[372] Burri (2021b), pp. 37–40; Meltzer (2019b), p. 252.

[373] In contrast to the CPTPP, the USMCA further develops the approach towards digital trade governance in that it contains specific regulations on Interactive Computer Services (Article 19.17 USMCA) and Open Government Data (Article 19.18 USMCA), for example.

[374] Cf. USMCA, Article 19.11 (2) fn. 5 „*A measure does not meet the conditions of this paragraph if it accords different treatment to data transfers solely on the basis that they are cross-border in a manner that modifies the conditions of competition to the detriment of service suppliers of another Party.*".

[375] *See* further Burri (2021b), pp. 39–40.

[376] Cf. U.S.-Japan Digital Trade Agreement, Article 11 and Article 12.

[377] Burri (2021c), p. 73. *See* for example Chapter 16 of the recent EU-Canada Comprehensive Economic and Trade Agreement (CETA) *"Electronic Commerce"* which in Article 16.2 states: *"This Chapter does not impose an obligation on a Party to allow a delivery transmitted by electronic means except in accordance with the Party's obligations under another provision of this Agreement.".* *See* however for an account of other provisions in the EU's trade agreements related to data flows Naef (2023), pp. 368–373; Willemyns (2020b), p. 237.

[378] Article 8.81 of the EPA, titled „*Free flow of data*"states: „*The Parties shall reassess within three years of the date of entry into force of this Agreement the need for inclusion of provisions on the free flow of data into this Agreement.*".

exceptions for legitimate public policy objectives, based on appropriate mandates".[379] This underscores that the EU is committed to the commercial objective of ensuring data flows, but it nevertheless advocates regulatory leeway for public policy measures such as in the area of consumer protection and, in particular, data privacy. In fact, maintaining and securing strong rules on data privacy in particular is a central element to the EU's trade policy with regard to cross-border data flows. In 2018, the EU Commission drafted a negotiating proposal that aims to mitigate the tension between the digital trade policy agenda and the EU's constitutional obligation to safeguard the right to privacy and the protection of personal data as fundamental rights (*see* further *infra* Sect. 4.3.2.2). The negotiating template is intended to serve as the basis for future PTAs that balance the goal of unrestricted data flow with broad regulatory discretion to achieve policy goals (*see* further *infra* Sect. 5.3.2.2). These "*Horizontal Provisions for Cross-Border Data Flows and for the Protection of Personal Data*" contain the obligation not to restrict cross-border data flows by requiring the use of data processing facilities or network elements in the territory of the party, requiring data to be localised in the territory of a party for storage or processing, prohibiting storage or processing in the territory of the other party, making the cross-border transfer of data contingent upon use of computing facilities or network elements in the parties' territory or upon localisation requirements in the parties' territory.[380] Consequently, the 2021 EU-UK Trade and Cooperation Agreement (TCA) includes in its Title III on "*Digital Trade*" a specific chapter on "*Data Flows and Data Protection*" Article 201 Sec. 1 of which provides that "*cross-border data flows shall not be restricted*" due to various measures of localisation.[381] The only other provision of this chapter refers to the "*Protection of personal data and privacy*", Article 202 Sec. 2 TCA. In this sense, it seems that a reorganisation of the EU's domestic position on the compatibility of data flows and data protection in PTAs has been carried out.[382]

3.4.2.2.3 China

Since 2006, China has included e-commerce provisions in trade agreements to exert its influence in a bilateral forum in the face of a regulatory vacuum in an effort to facilitate the overseas expansion of Chinese e-commerce companies.[383] Although

---

[379] Cf. European Council (2022), para. 12. Moreover, in the same statement, the parties have launched the EU-Japan Digital Partnership "*in order to advance cooperation on a wide range of digital issues to foster economic growth and achieve a sustainable society through an inclusive, sustainable, human-centric digital transformation based on our common values.*" (cf. para. 10).
[380] European Commission (2018). *See* for an analysis Naef (2023), pp. 406–413.
[381] In turn, Article 201 Sec. 2 TCA stipulates that "*The Parties shall keep the implementation of this provision under review and assess its functioning within three years of the date of entry into force of this Agreement*".
[382] *See* further *infra*, Sect. 5.3.2.1. *See* also Burri (2021c), pp. 69–82.
[383] Huang (2017), pp. 316–319.

China has been sceptical of negotiations on non-traditional trade commitments, particularly with respect to digital trade, it is actively participating in the Joint Statement Initiative on Electronic Commerce to strengthen its governance authority in electronic commerce and cyberspace.[384] However, China is clearly more focused on the traditional *"trade"* aspects of digital trade, promoting the sale of physical goods over the Internet, than on the related *"digital"* governance issues.[385] China has been reluctant to include data regulation in trade agreements, as this would potentially affect the countries' censorship policies and jeopardize government control over (personal) data.[386] To be sure, recent trade agreements with Chinese participation include provisions on cross-border data flows, but apparently only where strict monitoring of data flows is possible.[387] The RCEP as the most influential agreement with Chinese participation in recent years subjects its data flow provisions to broad political reservations for *"essential security interests"* (cf. Article 12.15 Sec. 3 (b) RCEP).[388] The same exception applies to the prohibition to require a covered person to use or locate computing facilities in that Party's territory as a condition for conducting business in that Party's territory (cf. Article 12.14 Sec. 3(b) RCEP). While a measure that is inconsistent with the obligations on data flows and the location of computing facilities may also be maintained if it is *"necessary to achieve a legitimate public policy objective, provided that the measure is not applied in a manner which would constitute a means of arbitrary or unjustifiable discrimination or a disguised restriction on trade"* (cf. Article 12.14 Sec. 3(a) RCEP and 12.15 Sec. 3(a) RCEP), footnotes 12 and 14 state that *"necessity behind the implementation of such legitimate public policy shall be decided by the implementing Party"*. This is to be understood as a rejection of the WTO jurisprudence on *"necessity"* and thus increases the domestic room for data governance measures (*see* further *infra* Sect. 5.2.2.3).

3.4.3 Evaluation

The previous sections on the governance of digital trade in PTAs and the regulation of data flows have provided an outline of the ongoing regulatory evolution with respect to the digital transformation of trade in trade agreements. The continuous development of the integration of elements of digital governance in PTAs

---

[384] Gao (2020), pp. 15–16.
[385] Cf. Gao (2018), pp. 315–320. *Henry Gao*'s analysis supports the proposition that the terminology of e-commerce is used to describe aspects of electronically facilitated forms of traditional cross-border activity (particularly trade in goods), while the term digital trade instead specifically addresses the data-related dimensions of trade in the digital economy, *see* also *supra* Sect. 3.2.2.
[386] Huang (2017), pp. 323–331.
[387] Willemyns (2020b), p. 238.
[388] *See* Kelsey (2020).

underscores that the current gridlock within the WTO against the background of progressing digital transformation is manifesting in two directions. On the one hand, a plurilateral Joint Statement Initiative on Electronic Commerce has formed and negotiations are taking place towards adapting current WTO law (*see supra* Sect. 3.3.1.2). Given the uncertain outcome of a *"plurilateralization"* of digital trade governance under the WTO, the above analysis illustrates, on the other hand, that deep and comprehensive PTAs are being leveraged to make meaningful progress in creating regulatory frameworks for digital trade. Trade agreements have been found to address the shortcomings and lacunae of the current WTO framework with respect to trade in the digital economy. In addition, PTAs go beyond WTO law to include a number of provisions that address critical digital trade governance issues, such as paperless trading and e-authentication, regulatory cooperation on consumer protection, cybersecurity, and data privacy, but most notably rules on the regulation of commercially relevant data flows and the prohibition of trade-restrictive data localisation. With regard to this data governance, WTO law exercises only a very weak governance, as there are no horizontal WTO commitments on data flows and the regulation of digital services under GATS offers inadequate substantive stringency (*see supra* Sect. 3.3.2.6). This leaves remarkable leeway for PTAs to innovate in cross-border data governance. *Mira Burri* describes the current framework for digital trade regulation in PTAs as follows: *"It is neither evenly spread across different countries, nor otherwise coordinated. Indeed, it can be messy, fragmented with regard to substantive rules and the countries who endorse them, with both legal entrepreneurs and late comers; it is often power-driven and sometimes curiously not so."*.[389] Moreover, the political economy of trade agreements favours the proliferation of the digital trade templates of a small number of countries and most notably of the three largest trading powerhouses: the US, the EU, and China. Recent analyses paint a picture of divergence in the approach to integrating digital elements into trade agreements. Generally speaking, the US favours a more liberal approach to data regulations in trade agreements, the EU takes a more cautious stance and places great emphasis on data protection, while China's approach focuses primarily on the possibility of restricting data flows to protect national security.[390] This is also consistent with the parties' contributions to the Joint Statement Initative on Electronic Commerce.[391] In this context, it is certainly of particular interest to see to what extent the development of digital trade governance in PTAs can stimulate discussions at the multi- and plurilateral level and in particular under the current Joint Statement Initiative (*see supra* Sect. 3.3.1.2).[392]

---

[389] Burri and Polanco (2020), p. 189.
[390] Aaronson and Leblond (2018); Willemyns (2020b), p. 227.
[391] Willemyns (2020b), pp. 227–228.
[392] Herman (2010); Kim (2015), pp. 369–370.

3.5 Trade Policy Implications of Digital Trade

In the previous sections, the controversial conceptualisation and current regulatory governance of digital trade in WTO law and PTAs have been examined in detail. The digital transformation of trade is driving the integration of cross-border economic activity with the data-centric paradigm of the digital economy. The resulting new dimensions of trade in the digital economy introduce a new set of trade barriers, which in turn require a new set of policy responses.[393] In this respect, the digital paradigm presents a particular challenge for trade policy, as it leads to convergence between a variety of international and national policy fora and actors and implicates issues that are subject to domestic political and cultural idiosyncrasies. Certainly, transnational issues raised by cross-border flows of information are not unique to the emergent digital economy.[394] Yet, the economic and strategic relevance of networked cyberspace has exacerbated pre-existing conflicts on the extraterritorial application of domestic regulations and the role of established principles of sovereignty, jurisdictional authority and national security.[395] Moreover, trade governance in the digital economy has to account for novel *"trade and..."* pairs such as with regard to Internet governance and data governance relating to highly controversial issues such as data privacy and cybersecurity, the taxation of digital business models,[396] competition in digital markets as well as the governance of emerging digital technologies.[397,398] This section complements the above analysis of the contemporary digital trade governance with a brief examination of the emerging policy environment for digital trade, providing a context for an analysis of the particular relevance of data privacy to trade in the digital economy.

3.5.1 Developing Trade Policy for the Digital Economy

While the cross-border flow of data is a prerequisite for harnessing the economic potential of digital trade, the inherently global nature of the Internet brings with it a broad policy spectrum that encompasses both technological and socioeconomic concerns that are informed by domestic values and national particularities. It has

---

[393] *See* for example WTO (2018a), pp. 11–13; Primo Braga (2010), pp. 462–470; van der Marel (2019).

[394] *See* in particular Drake (2016), pp. 4–9, who retraces parts of this discussion to the beginning of international telegraphy. *See* also Aaronson (2015), pp. 680–685; Tietje (2012)

[395] *See* for example Goldsmith and Wu (2006), pp. 154–161; Burri (2021c), p. 40; Chander (2012), pp. 26–32.

[396] *See* for example Noonan and Plekhanova (2020).

[397] Goldfarb and Trefler (2018);Burri (2021a); Peng et al. (2021a). *See* also with regard to the EU trade discipline on source code, Irion (2021).

[398] *See* generally Burri (2017), p. 413; Mitchell and Mishra (2021), pp. 86–92.

been emphasised above that digitalisation is resulting in the dissolution of boundaries between international and national regulatory spheres, giving rise to new conflicts between national regulatory autonomy and international regulation (*see supra* Sect. 2.4). With regard to digital trade, it is be demonstrated that this leads to an increasingly active shaping of the margins and loopholes of existing trade law, so that regional approaches to the governance of digital trade emerge (*see supra* Sect. 3.4 and further *infra* Sect. 4.4.2). On the one hand, traditional areas of trade policy will have to be extended and deepened to take better account of a novel digital paradigm.[399] On the other hand, digital trade policy will have to include issues hitherto not within the ambit of trade governance such as Internet governance and data governance, for example. Certainly, a key factor for the policy environment for digital trade is the socio-economic relevance of digital technologies and data. Regulation of data as a valuable resource for digital technologies such as Big Data and AI will increasingly come into focus of International Economic Law.[400] WTO members are therefore increasingly developing specific digital trade policy strategies in an ongoing evolutionary process.[401] Generally, policies range from a more defensive position toward the socio-economic and political challenges stemming from an intrusive and ubiquitous nature of the global Internet to a more affirmative attitude spurred by the enticements of new economic frontiers and a free flow of information. *Andrew D. Mitchell* and *Neha Mishra* identify three general approaches within the complex political economy of digital trade: the *"market-based"*, the *"interventionist"* and the *"guarded"*.[402] These approaches illustrate certain points of convergence across different national governance approaches to digital trade based on distinct mentalities and socioeconomic interests related to the digital paradigm.[403] The market-based approach is characterised by a rather liberal attitude towards the regulatory governance of emergent digital industries such as illustrated by the US or Japan. In this context, the balance between consumer interests and economic considerations is often weighted in favour of what are perceived to be growth and innovation objectives.[404] The interventionist approach is characterised by a heightened focus on regulatory safeguards and guidelines, e.g., in the area of consumer protection and data privacy, as seen in the EU or Canada.[405] In this context, a generally positive attitude toward the digital paradigm is combined with the desire to set guidelines for the digital industry and to shape digital markets through regulation. The guarded approach is based on a rather defensive political

---

[399] An example in this sense is the ITA, *see supra* Sect. 3.3.2.2.

[400] Streinz (2021b).

[401] *See* for example European Parliament (2017); Office of the United States Trade Representative (2016); this is also reflected in the developments in the WTO Work Programme on Electronic Commerce, *see supra* Sect. 3.3.1.1.

[402] Mitchell and Mishra (2018), pp. 1081–1088.

[403] Mitchell and Mishra (2018), p. 1084.

[404] Mitchell and Mishra (2018), p. 1084.

[405] Mitchell and Mishra (2018), p. 1085.

stance toward digital globalisation, which includes, for example, countries with autocratic governments such as China and Russia.[406] Proponents of this approach tend toward strong control of data policies, often in combination with territorial approaches to digital regulation that secure national political influence over inherently global technologies and claim digital sovereignty and legal autonomy from the encroachments of a putatively borderless network.[407]

Such *"phenotypes"* of digital trade regulation are helpful in mapping the broader trade policy environment for digital trade. However, they are only a very rough indication of the respective approaches to digital trade policy. In fact, the transitions between these models are fluent and the approaches themselves are not clearly delimited given the multiplicity of policy interests associated with digital trade. In reality, there are bound to be overlaps due to the highly individualised focus of trade policy against the backdrop of national idiosyncrasies and preferences. In addition, it should be noted that the regulation of digital trade is a fairly new and inherently dynamic endeavour, which can lead to certain changes in the policies of individual trade actors over time. Recent examples of this are the EU and China's changing attitude toward including rules on data flows in trade agreements (*see supra* Sect. 3.4.2.2), as well as the US's increasing attention to data privacy protection in trade agreements (*see infra* Sect. 5.3.2).

3.5.2 *Individual Trade Policy Considerations*

3.5.2.1 Internet Governance

With cross-border data flows and connectivity via the Internet providing the backbone for digital trade, internet governance is a critical concern for trade in the digital economy. Hence, there is an increasing convergence and overlap between trade law and Internet governance.[408] In particular, through the hinging element of cross-border data flows, internet governance and digital trade governance face similar issues related to the balkanisation of the internet through tensions between jurisdictions, e.g. in terms of regulating cross-border data flows and ensuring trust, openness and transparency through cybersecurity, data protection and consumer protection measures.[409] In this context, trade law and, in particular, modern comprehensive trade agreements are evolving into instruments of Internet governance.[410] Today, the

---

[406] Mitchell and Mishra (2018), pp. 1085–1086.
[407] Mitchell and Mishra (2018), pp. 1085–1086.
[408] *See* for example Belli (2016); Burri (2016b); Maciel (2016); Mishra (2017), Mishra (2019a).
[409] La Chapelle and Fehlinger (2016); Mishra (2019a), pp. 477–506.
[410] Belli (2016); Watson (2018). In this context, the EU's proposal to the WTO Joint Statement Initiative on Electronic Commerce provides: *"Subject to applicable policies, laws and regulations, Members should maintain or adopt appropriate measures to ensure that end- users in their territory are able to access, distribute and use services and applications of their choice available on the*

Internet is relevant for almost all economic sectors and a key driver of economic integration on a global scale. At the same time, the Internet as a medium of cross-border cooperation and communication has tremendous socio-cultural relevance. In cyberspace, however, data and data flows cannot necessarily be assigned to a specific dimension—economic or sociocultural, medium of transmission or content by itself (*see* also *supra* Sect. 2.3.2.2). In the global data sphere, economic interests on the one hand and socio-cultural considerations on the other are therefore inextricably intertwined. This composite, resulting from the ambiguous character of the exchange of digital information on the Internet, generates a complex policy environment involving both economic as well as non-economic interests and a multitude of different stakeholders. In this context, the OECD estimates that the *"further expansion of the Internet Economy will bolster the free flow of information, freedom of expression, and protection of individual liberties, as critical components of a democratic society and cultural diversity"*.[411] As a result, Internet governance is exercised in what is known as a multi-stakeholder process, where discussions and consultations take place between a wide range of stakeholders, from the technical community to civil society and businesses, as well as governmental and non-governmental organisations. The resulting governance framework for the Internet is undergoing continuous evolution and today consists of *"complex, multifarious, and loose amalgam of policies, laws and actors"*.[412] While initially the focus has been on technical management such as, for example, maintaining the Domain Name System (DNS), the emphasis has gradually shifted to a heterogeneous set of policy processes concerning the configuration, management, and further development of the Internet.[413] In particular, the debates during the sessions of the UN's World Summit on the Information Society (WSIS) in Geneva and Tunis[414] as well as complementary initiatives within the UN[415] have contributed to expanding the scope of Internet governance and have formed its multistakeholder model (MSM).[416] Important multistakeholder institutions contributing to the platform are for instance the Internet Governance Forum (IGF), the Internet Cooperation for Assigned Names and Numbers (ICANN), the Internet Architecture Board, the Internet Society (ISOC) or the World Wide Web Consortium (W3C).

Internet, subject to reasonable and non-discriminatory network management.", WTO (2019c), p. 4, para. 2.9. In similar vein, the US proposal reads: *"A free and open Internet enables users to take advantage of a wealth of information and services anywhere in the world. Trade rules, including rules ensuring access to networks, can ensure that governments do not arbitrarily block or filter online content, nor require Internet intermediaries to do so."*, WTO (2018d), p. 2, para. 2.

[411] OECD (2008).
[412] World Bank Group (2016), p. 293.
[413] Bygrave (2015), pp. 10–18.
[414] *See* for example ITU (2005).
[415] *See* for example UN (2012) *See* further regarding the human rights context *infra* Sect. 4.4.1.2.1.
[416] World Bank Group (2016), p. 293. *See* further Hubbard and Bygrave (2009).

3.5.2.2 Data Governance

While it is apparent that the global data sphere requires regulations for an international governance of data, data governance as a concept within international law has not yet been universally defined.[417] In its most common context, the notion of data governance refers to the management of data within organisations.[418] However, against the background of a rising relevance of cross-border data flows, a broader understanding of the term extends to address a transnational governance of data.[419] In this context, *Thomas Streinz* has introduced a helpful definition for data governance, "*It describes a domain of governance in which a variety of actors (including states, international organizations, civil society, and business firms and their associations) regulate digitalized information (data) through a variety of means (including physical infrastructure, standards, and law).*" that extends (but is not limited to) cross-border data flow regulation.[420] Given the complex characteristics of data flows in today's globally connected environment, policymakers are only beginning to understand how and when to regulate data—and notably its cross-border transmission.[421] In the absence of coherent multilateral framework for data governance on the one hand, and a rising socioeconomic significance of cross-border data flows on the other, governments are increasingly resorting to unilateral measures to control the flow of digitised information.[422] There are now an increasing number of reports linking such interventions in cross-border data flows to significant negative economic effects and emphasising that they are detrimental to the potential of the digital economy as a whole.[423] In this context, the emergence of "*digital industrial*

---

[417] Recently, the EU has been addressing this subject in more detail and has formulated a strategic approach, cf. for example Regulation (EU) 2022/868 of the European Parliament and of the Council of 30 May 2022 on European data governance and amending Regulation (EU) 2018/1724 (Data Governance Act).

[418] *See* for example the EU Commission's definition of data governance in relation to the work of the Commission itself. In this context, it "*entails defining, implementing and monitoring strategies, policies and shared decision-making over the management and use of data assets. It is performed by Commission staff with established data-related roles.*", European Commission (2020).

[419] *See* in this context OECD (2019a), p. 23: "*Data governance is no longer a matter limited to organisational boundaries, but a multinational concern resulting from cross-border data sharing.*". *See* also Burri (2017b), pp. 68–69.

[420] Streinz (2019), p. 329. *See* with regard to "*transnational data governance*" further Erie and Streinz (2021), pp. 11–14.

[421] Cf. Aaronson (2021); Aaronson and Leblond (2018), p. 250. It is argued, for example, that "*data governance*" is in fact "*AI governance*" Peng et al. (2021b), p. 15.

[422] Aaronson and Maxim (2013); Cory and Dascoli (2021); WTO (2018a), p. 11.

[423] Cory and Dascoli (2021), pp. 10–17; van der Marel et al. 2014, p. 13. *See* also *supra* Sect. 2.3.1.3.

polies"[424] can be witnessed, which unilaterally regulate the cross-border flow of data. Measures such as with regard to the localisation of data within a given jurisdiction or the establishment of transfer restrictions may be adopted in the sense of a *"data nationalism"* (*see supra* Sect. 2.3.2.4).[425] However, data governance also involves a number of non-economic considerations such as cyber security, the safeguarding of personal data, national security, and the enforcement of culturally and historically evolved fundamental values on the inherently global Internet, as well as Internet access restrictions and censorship measures. In this context, interferences with the cross-border flow of data may be undertaken also in order to guarantee legitimate policy goals such as the confidentiality of personal data, measures of cybersecurity or the protection of consumer rights.[426] In an inherently global digital economy, domestic data governance regulations represent a pivotal element linking trade governance to a host of non-trade matters and public policy interest of the digital era. Given the economic potential at stake, the distinction between legitimate regulation of economically significant cross-border data flows and trade-distorting data protectionism of domestic regimes of data governance is highly controversial. In this complex policy environment, trade law is increasingly emerging as the arbiter with respect to the domestic regulation of cross-border data flows (*see infra* Chap. 5). In particular, a relatively new set of provisions proliferating in deep and comprehensive trade agreements that aim to liberalise digital trade and data flows have a crucial bearing on domestic data governance policies and vice versa.[427] The transnational data governance implemented in the context of data privacy regulations will be analysed in the following (*see infra* Sect. 4.3.3).

3.5.2.3 Interoperability

Interoperability is a key concept of the digital transformation that has gained importance in both the technological and regulatory debate on the emergence of digital trade.[428] In fact, the digital economy entails difficult interoperability challenges, particularly with regard to both the technological and regulatory requirements for the governance of digital technologies and data. With regard to an ICT context, issues of interoperability arise when IT systems are required to efficiently exchange information among each other. Interoperability refers to the ability of two or more systems or components to exchange information and to use the exchanged information.[429] While there is no fully defined concept of interoperability, due to its

---

[424] *See* for example Azmeh and Foster (2016), pp. 3–5; Mitchell and Mishra (2019), pp. 396–397.
[425] Chander and Lê (2015); Meltzer (2019b), pp. 247–250.
[426] Mishra (2019b), 347; Mitchell and Mishra (2019), pp. 392–397.
[427] Burri (2017c), p. 12; Burri (2017b), pp. 68–69; Chander (2012), p. 39; Meltzer (2016), p. 13.
[428] Cory and Dascoli (2021), pp. 18–20.
[429] IEEE Standards Board (1990), p. 42.

3.5 Trade Policy Implications of Digital Trade

many fields of application, it can be categorised into different layers in a technological context, namely technical, syntactic, semantic and organisational.[430] While technical interoperability is related to hardware and system components, syntactic interoperability is linked to data formats and semantic interoperability is associated with a common understanding of the information being exchanged—a fourth layer is identified in the organisational interoperability describing *"the ability of organizations to effectively communicate and transfer (meaningful) data (information) even though they may be using a variety of different information systems over widely different infrastructures, possibly across different geographic regions and cultures."*.[431]

Hence, interoperability in a broader sense can be defined as the *"ability of people, organizations, and systems to interact and interconnect so as to efficiently and effectively exchange and use information"*.[432] Against this backdrop, interoperability is a multi-faceted concept, which has an organisational, human, institutional and often legal dimension in addition to a technical one.[433] In view of the emergence of digital trade, regulatory systems—particularly with respect to data governance—benefit from the ability to interact effectively, both within a domestic setting as well as across borders on an international scale.[434] As divergent domestic technological and regulatory standards constitute considerable barriers to trade, interoperability is proven to foster innovation which in turn fosters trade.[435] In this context, *Urs Gasser* and *John Palfrey* define legal interoperability as one element of a interoperability framework, referring to *"the working-together among legal norms, either within a given legal system of a nation state (e.g. federal and state legislation) or across jurisdictions or nations"*.[436] In this sense, both the WTO framework as well as the rising number of comprehensive PTAs aim to advance interoperability of standards and regulation with regard to the movement of goods, services, capital and individuals.[437] Hence, interoperability can be perceived as a subset of regulatory convergence, which refers to the reduction of regulatory incompatibilities between countries in order to facilitate trade.[438]

---

[430] van der Veer and Wiles (2008), pp. 5–6. *See* for a similar yet distinct interpretation of the layers of interoperability Cory and Dascoli (2021), p. 19.
[431] van der Veer and Wiles (2008), pp. 5–6.
[432] Baird (2009), pp. 223–224.
[433] Gasser and Palfrey (2012), p. 125.
[434] Ahmed (2019), pp. 104–110.
[435] Gasser and Palfrey (2012), pp. 126–127, p. 139.
[436] Gasser and Palfrey (2012), p. 132. *See* also for regulatory interoperability Cory and Dascoli (2021), pp. 19–20.
[437] *See* for example with regard to the interoperability of data models and processes to further the cross-border exchange of trade documents and information WTO/WEF (2022), pp. 48–51.
[438] Polanco and Sauvé (2013), p. 581. *See* for further concepts in this context Weiß (2020), p. 286.

3.6 Conclusion

This chapter has addressed the emergence of digital trade and the status quo of its contemporary regulatory governance under trade law. An examination of current approaches to conceptualising the digital transformation of trade has revealed that, to date, there is no uniformly accepted definition for trade in the digital economy. Building on the results of the previous chapter's examination of the digital transformation of trade, a data-centric approach to conceptualising digital trade has been adopted here. Accordingly, digital trade refers to all forms of cross-border economic activity that depend on the flow of digital data as it significantly facilitates or enables them. This focus on the fundamental role of (cross-border) data flows as a driver of trade in the digital economy has called for an examination of the pertinence of WTO law. The analysis of the 1994 WTO framework has revealed a pattern of stagnating multilateral regulation, which provides little guidance regarding the ever-increasing relevance of data- and data-flow-centred economic activity. As digital technologies shape and transform the global economy, many of the ensuing trade issues prompted by the nexus of technology, economic growth, and global governance, are unresolved. Indeed, in the face of the digital transformation the WTO has pursued what has been referred to as a *"Kicking-the-Can-Down-the-Road Approach"*.[439] While the framework of the WTO has specific merits that predestine it to tackle issues of transnational digital governance such as the technological neutrality of WTO rules, however, there remain serious uncertainties and ambiguities with regard to the governance of digital trade. To put it differently, merely reaffirming the applicability of the 1994 WTO rules to digital trade does not do justice to either the potential or the pitfalls of trade in a data-driven digital economy. This has been described as a problem of *"technological translation"*, that is, applying legal concepts to technologies that were not foreseen at the time they were drawn up.[440] Since today's networked reality is far distant from assumptions on the relevance of cross-border data flows anticipated in 1994, even a principle of technology neutrality in WTO law (which is controversial in detail[441]) is no guarantee for the appropriateness of the given rules and runs the risk of being overstretched.[442] In fact, this hazard has arguably realised with regard to WTO law. The extent to which WTO law diverges from the economic reality of digital trade is most evident in the absence of explicit references to the governance of cross-border data flows.[443] Although WTO law can serve to regulate data flows, it does not provide sufficient tools and solutions

---

[439] Zheng (2020), pp. 553–557.

[440] Wu (2006), p. 264.

[441] *See* on the debate on technology neutrality among WTO Members in relation to GATS *supra* Sect. 3.3.2.6.2.

[442] Svantesson (2011), p. 195.

[443] Aaronson and Leblond (2018), p. 251; Sen (2018), p. 331. A limited exception are the provisions on cross-border information flows contained in the Understanding on Commitments in Financial Services and the Annex on Telecommunications, *see supra* Sect. 3.3.2.6.4.

3.6 Conclusion

for the economic liberalisation of a data-driven economy. The digital transformation represents a litmus test for the established governance structures of the WTO's "*brick and mortar*" rules.[444] This insight is not new in essence, but its full implications have only recently been truly embraced. In fact, the WTO study as early as 1998 predicted a "*dramatic growth*" of Internet based "*electronic commerce*" and stated with regard to the regulatory framework of the WTO: "*The need for regulation in some circumstances is beyond dispute — it is the design and administration of regulations that matters.*".[445] In view of the current state of the digital transformation, it is high time to conceptually update the existing rules and face the challenges of an "*International Economic Data Law*".[446]

Rule design and administration are proving to be at the core of the regulatory challenge that is the digital transformation of trade. In this respect, the lack of multilateral guidance under the WTO forms the nucleus of a regional fragmentation in the regulatory governance of trade in the digital economy. The above analysis has underscored that the regulatory vacuum presented by WTO law is increasingly being filled by preferential rules in trade agreements. With plurilateral negotiations only recently underway and given the lack of WTO governance on key areas of digital trade—notably as regards the regulation of cross-border data flows—major stakeholders such as the EU, the US and China have turned to bilateral or regional trade fora. The digital trade rules developed in PTAs therefore play a pivotal role in designing frameworks for governing digital trade in general and cross-border data flows in particular. In this sense, digital trade provisions in PTAs inform the development of national legislation on digital governance issues, such as prohibitions on data localisation or the drafting and enforcement of privacy and consumer protection regulations.[447] Arguably, some WTO Members have made concessions in bilateral and regional trade agreements that they did not want to enter into at WTO level.[448] It is certainly accurate that, with regard to digital trade, PTAs adopt elements of rule-based WTO law and do not represent a radical departure from the merits of the multilateral framework.[449] Nevertheless, due to a dynamically evolving environment of the digital transformation, it is reasonable to assume a widening gap between WTO rules and principles for digital trade rules developed in PTAs. Today, the political economy of PTAs against the backdrop of the mechanisms of a digital economy results in a critical imbalance in the liberalisation of digital trade. In fact, regional templates of the more powerful nations tend to prevail and increasingly entrench competing "*data realms*".[450] It remains to be seen to what extent these fora

---

[444] Burri (2017a), pp. 12–17.

[445] Bacchetta et al. (1998), p. 64.

[446] Streinz (2021a).

[447] *See* Mitchell and Mishra (2018), p. 1107 with regard to the TPP agreement.

[448] Herman (2010), p. 11.

[449] *See* Elsig and Klotz (2020). *See* for this influence of WTO in general Allee et al. (2017); Cottier (2015).

[450] Aaronson and Leblond (2018).

will be suitable as "*laboratories*" for the elaboration of rules that can then be adopted on a plurilateral basis.[451] The longer plurilateral governance fails to materialise, the more likely it is that individual digital governance will proliferate and that imbalances will become entrenched.[452] By the same token, the more segregated these regional regimes become, the more likely it is that the role of the WTO will be limited to a fundamental standard.[453] The necessity for a recalibration of the trade system and policy approach is particularly evident with regard to an emergent set of non-tariff barriers to international trade revolving around the access to and use of data. Resulting from the convoluted character of data flows as content and transmission medium on the one hand and as an element of considerable socio-cultural relevance on the other hand, an intricate policy environment emerges. The pervasive and ubiquitous nature of digitalisation results in a multitude of potential conflicts between, on the one hand, a national policy aimed at protecting domestic policy objectives and, on the other hand, international law trying to sustain a "*global public policy*" approach to digital technologies.[454] In this way, the issue of digital trade governance is representative of the WTO Members willingness to adapt the role of multilateral regulation to the digital and multipolar political environment of the twenty-first century. In other words, apart from the divide among WTO members on how development issues should be addressed during the Doha Round, the disagreements over digital trade are an indicator of the state of the relevance of WTO as an international organisation in the digital era.[455]

Jurisprudence

Panel Report, European Communities and its Member States – Tariff Treatment of Certain Information Technology Products [EC-IT Products], WT/DS375/R, WT/DS376/R, WT/DS377/R, adopted 16 August 2010

Panel Report, United States – Measures Affecting Cross-Border Supply of Gambling and Betting Services [US-Gambling], WT/DS285/R, adopted 10 November 2004

Panel Report, China — Measures Affecting Trading Rights and Distribution Services for Certain Publications and Audiovisual Entertainment Products [China – Publications and Audiovisual Products], WT/DS363/R, adopted 12 August 2009

Panel Report, Mexico – Measures Affecting Telecommunications Services [Mexico – Telecoms], WT/DS204/R, adopted 2 April 2004

---

[451] Generally, the provisions of the trade agreements tend stimulate multilateral discussion, *see* for example Herman (2010).

[452] Burri (2017b), pp. 126–132.

[453] Leblond (2020).

[454] Cottier (1996), p. 427.

[455] Kelsey (2018), p. 295.

Panel Report, China – Certain Measures Affecting Electronic Payment Services [China — Electronic Payment Services], WT/DS413/R, adopted 16 July 2012

Appellate Body Report, United States – Measures Affecting Cross-Border Supply of Gambling and Betting Services [US-Gambling], WT/DS285/AB/R, adopted 20 April 2005

Appellate Body Report, China — Measures Affecting Trading Rights and Distribution Services for Certain Publications and Audiovisual Entertainment Products [China – Publications and Audiovisual Products], WT/DS363/AB/R, adopted 21 December 2009

References

Aaronson SA (2015) Why trade agreements are not setting information free: the lost history and reinvigorated debate over cross-border data flows, human rights, and national security. World Trade Rev 14(04):671–700. https://doi.org/10.1017/S1474745615000014

Aaronson SA (2019) What are we talking about when we talk about digital protectionism? World Trade Rev 18(4):541–577. https://doi.org/10.1017/S1474745618000198

Aaronson SA (2021) Data is different, so policymakers should pay close attention to its governance. In: Burri M (ed) Big data and global trade law. Cambridge University Press, Cambridge, pp 340–360

Aaronson SA, Leblond P (2018) Another digital divide: the rise of data realms and its implications for the WTO. J Int Econ Law 21(2):245–272. https://doi.org/10.1093/jiel/jgy019

Aaronson SA, Maxim R (2013) Trade and the internet: the challenge of the NSA revelations: policies in the US, EU and Canada. https://doi.org/10.2139/ssrn.2407270

Abendin S, Duan P (2021) Global E-commerce talks at the WTO: positions on selected issues of the United States, European Union, China, and Japan. World Trade Rev 20(5):707–724. https://doi.org/10.1017/S1474745621000094

Adlung R (2006) Services negotiations in the Doha round: lost in flexibility? J Int Econ Law 9(4):865–893. https://doi.org/10.1093/jiel/jgl027

Adlung R (2014) Trade in services in the WTO: from Marrakesh (1994), to Doha (2001), to. . . (?). In: Narlikar A, Daunton MJ, Stern RM (eds) The Oxford handbook on the World Trade Organization. Oxford University Press, Oxford, pp 370–391

Adlung R, Mattoo A (2010) The GATS. In: Mattoo A, Stern RM, Zanini G (eds) A handbook of international trade in services. Oxford University Press, Oxford, pp 48–82

Ahmed U (2019) The importance of cross-border regulatory cooperation in an era of digital trade. World Trade Rev 18(1):99–120. https://doi.org/10.1017/S1474745618000514

Allee T, Elsig M, Lugg A (2017) The ties between the World Trade Organization and preferential trade agreements: a textual analysis. J Int Econ Law 20(2):333–363. https://doi.org/10.1093/jiel/jgx009

Alschner W, Pauwelyn J, Puig S (2017) The data-driven future of international economic law. J Int Econ Law 20(2):217–231. https://doi.org/10.1093/jiel/jgx020

APEC (1998) Blueprint for action on electronic commerce. https://www.apec.org/meeting-papers/leaders-declarations/1998/1998_aelm/apec_blueprint_for. Accessed 5 Apr 2024

Azmeh S, Foster C (2016) The TPP and the digital trade agenda: digital industrial policy and Silicon Valley's influence on new trade agreements. LSE International Development Working Paper Series 2016 No. 16-175

Bacchetta M, Low P, Mattoo A, Schuknecht L, Wager H, Wehrens M (1998) Electronic commerce and the role of the WTO. Special studies / World Trade Organization, Geneva. https://hdl.handle.net/10419/107052. Accessed 5 Apr 2024

Baird SA (2009) Government role and the interoperability ecosystem. SSRN version. J Law Policy Inf Soc 5(2):219–290

Baker SA, Lichtenbaum P, Shenk MD, Yeo MS (2001) E-products and the WTO. Int Lawyer 35:5–21

Baldwin RE (2014) Preferential trading arrangements. In: Narlikar A, Daunton MJ, Stern RM (eds) The Oxford handbook on the World Trade Organization. Oxford University Press, Oxford, pp 632–650

Bantjes M (2008) The petabyte age: because more Isn't just more - more is different. Wired. https://www.wired.com/2008/06/pb-intro/. Accessed 5 Apr Nov 2024

Belli L (2016) The Quiet Rapprochement of Internet Governance and Trade Policy. https://www.diplomacy.edu/blog/quiet-rapprochement-internet-governance-and-trade-policy. Accessed 5 Apr 2024

Bhagwati J (1995) US trade policy: the infatuation with FTAs. In: Bhagwati JN, Krueger AO (eds) The dangerous drift to preferential trade agreements. AEI special studies in policy reform. AEI Press, Washington, DC

Bown CP (2017) Mega-regional trade agreements and the future of the WTO. Global Pol 8(1):107–112. https://doi.org/10.1111/1758-5899.12391

Burri M (2015) The international economic law framework for digital trade. Zeitschrift für Schweizerisches Recht 135(2):10–72

Burri M (2016a) Designing future-oriented multilateral rules for digital trade. In: Sauvé P, Roy M (eds) Research handbook on trade in services. Research handbooks on the WTO series. Edward Elgar Publishing, Cheltenham, pp 331–356

Burri M (2016b) The World Trade Organization as an actor in global internet governance. SSRN manuscript. https://papers.ssrn.com/sol3/papers.cfm?abstract_id=2792219. Accessed 5 Apr 2024

Burri M (2017a) New legal design for digital commerce in free trade agreements. Digiworld Econ J 107:1–21

Burri M (2017b) The governance of data and data flows in trade agreements: the pitfalls of legal adaptation. UC Davis Law Rev 51:65–132

Burri M (2017c) Current and emerging trends in disruptive technologies: implications for the present and future of EU's trade policy. EP/EXPO/B/INTA/2017/06. https://doi.org/10.2861/96860

Burri M (2017d) The regulation of data flows through trade agreements. Georgetown J Int Law 48:407–448

Burri M (ed) (2021a) Big data and global trade law. Cambridge University Press, Cambridge

Burri M (2021b) Data flows and global trade law. In: Big data and global trade law. Cambridge University Press, pp 11–41

Burri M (2021c) Interfacing privacy and trade. Case Western Reserv J Int Law 53:35–88

Burri M (2021d) A WTO Agreement on Electronic Commerce: An Enquiry Into Its Legal Substance and Viability. Trade Law 4.0 Working Paper No 1, Available at SSRN: https://ssrn.com/abstract=3976133. Accessed 5 Apr 2024

Burri M, Cottier T (2012a) Introduction: digital technologies and international trade regulation. In: Burri M, Cottier T (eds) Trade governance in the digital age. Cambridge University Press, Cambridge, pp 1–14

Burri M, Cottier T (eds) (2012b) Trade governance in the digital age. Cambridge University Press, Cambridge

Burri M, Polanco R (2020) Digital trade provisions in preferential trade agreements: introducing a new dataset. J Int Econ Law 23(1):187–220. https://doi.org/10.1093/jiel/jgz044

Bygrave LA (2015) Internet governance by contract. Oxford University Press, Oxford

Casalini F, López González J (2019) Trade and Cross-Border Data Flows. OECD Trade Policy Papers No. 220. OECD Publishing, Paris. https://doi.org/10.1787/b2023a47-en

Chander A (2012) Principles for trade 2.0. In: Burri M, Cottier T (eds) Trade governance in the digital age. Cambridge University Press, Cambridge, pp 17–44

Chander A (2013) The electronic silk road: how the web binds the world in commerce. Yale University Press, New Haven

Chander A (2018) The Coming North American Digital Trade Zone. https://www.cfr.org/blog/coming-north-american-digital-trade-zone. Accessed 5 Apr 2024

Chander A (2021) Artificial intelligence and trade. In: Burri M (ed) Big data and global trade law. Cambridge University Press, Cambridge, pp 115–127

Chander A, Lê UP (2015) Data nationalism. Empory Law J 64:677–739

Cheng W, Brandi C (2019) Governing digital trade—a new role for the WTO. https://www.idos-research.de/en/briefing-paper/article/governing-digital-trade-a-new-role-for-the-wto/. Accessed 5 Apr 2024

Ciuriak D, Ptashkina M (2018) The digital transformation and the transformation of international trade. RTA exchange. International Centre for Trade and Sustainable Development (ICTSD) and the Inter-American Development Bank (IDB), Geneva, Available at SSRN: https://ssrn.com/abstract=3107811

Cory N, Dascoli L (2021) How barriers to cross-border data flows are spreading globally, what they cost, and how to address them. Information Technology & Innovation Foundation. https://itif.org/publications/2021/07/19/how-barriers-cross-border-data-flows-are-spreading-globally-what-they-cost/

Cottier T (1996) The impact of new technologies on multilateral trade regulation and governance - the new global technology regime. Chicago-Kent Law Rev 72:415–436

Cottier T (2015) The common law of international trade and the future of the World Trade Organization. J Int Econ Law 18(1):3–20. https://doi.org/10.1093/jiel/jgv005

Council of the EU (2019) Council decision supplementing the negotiating directives for the Doha Development Agenda regarding the plurilateral negotiations of rules and commitments on electronic commerce, 8993/19, 21 May 2019

Crosby D (2016) Analysis of data localization measures under WTO services trade rules and commitments. The E15 Initiative Policy Brief

Drake WJ (2016) Background paper for the workshop on data localization and barriers to transborder data flows. https://www3.weforum.org/docs/Background_Paper_Forum_workshop%2009.2016.pdf. Accessed 5 Apr 2024

Drake WJ, Kalypso N (1992) Ideas, interests, and institutionalization: "trade in services" and the Uruguay round. Int Organ 46(1):37–100

Dupont C, Elsig M (2014) Persistent deadlock in multilateral trade negotiations: the case of Doha. In: Narlikar A, Daunton MJ, Stern RM (eds) The Oxford handbook on the World Trade Organization. Oxford University Press, Oxford, pp 587–603

Elsig M, Klotz S (2018) Data flow-related provisions in preferential trade agreements. WTI Working Paper No. 03/2018

Elsig M, Klotz S (2020) Digital trade rules in preferential trade agreements: Is there a WTO impact? WTI Working Paper No. 04/2020

Erie MS, Streinz T (2021) The Beijing effect: China's digital silk road as transnational data governance. New York Univ J Int Law Polit 54(1):1–92

European Commission (1997) Communication from the Commission to the European Parliament, the economic and social committee and the committee of the regions, "A European Initiative in Electronic Commerce". COM(97) 157 final

European Commission (2006) Communication from the European Commission: Global Europe: Competing in the World. COM(2006) 567 final

European Commission (2015) Trade for all: Towards a more responsible trade and investment policy, Luxembourg. https://doi.org/10.2781/472505

European Commission (2016) The expansion of the Information Technology Agreement: an economic assessment, Luxembourg

European Commission (2018) Horizontal provisions for cross-border data flows and for personal data protection. https://ec.europa.eu/newsroom/just/items/627665 Accessed 5 Apr 2024

European Commission (2020) Data governance and data policies at the European Commission. Secretariat-General. https://commission.europa.eu/publications/data-governance-and-data-policies-european-commission_en. Accessed 5 Apr 2024 Nov 2022

European Commission (2021) Communication from the European Commission: Trade Policy Review - An Open, Sustainable and Assertive Trade Policy. COM(2021) 66 final

European Commission (2024) Digital Trade. Homepage of the EU Commission. https://policy.trade.ec.europa.eu/help-exporters-and-importers/accessing-markets/goods-and-services/digital-trade_en. Accessed 5 Apr 2024

European Council (2022) Joint Statement EU-Japan Summit 2022, https://www.consilium.europa.eu/en/press/press-releases/2022/05/12/joint-statement-eu-japan-summit-2022/. Accessed 5 Apr 2024

European Parliament (2017) Towards a digital trade strategy. 2017/2065(INI)

Farrokhnia F, Richards C (2016) E-commerce products under the World Trade Organization agreements: goods, services, both or neither? J World Trade 50(5):793–817

Fefer RF (2020) Internet Regimes and WTO E-Commerce Negotiations. Congressional Research Service R46198. https://crsreports.congress.gov/product/pdf/R/R46198/1. Accessed 5 Apr 2024

Fortanier F (2017) Measuring Digital Trade: Framework and next steps. https://unctad.org/meetings/en/Presentation/dtl_eWeek2017p22_FabienneFortanier_en.pdf. Accessed 5 Apr 2024

G20 (2016) Leaders' Communique Hangzhou Summit. https://www.consilium.europa.eu/en/press/press-releases/2016/09/05/g20-leaders-communique/. Accessed 5 Apr 2024

G20 (2017) Ministerial Declaration G20 Digital Economy Ministerial Conference. Ministerial Declaration: Shaping Digitalisation for an Interconnected World. http://www.g20.utoronto.ca/2017/g20-digital-economy-ministerial-declaration-english-version.pdf. Accessed 5 Apr 2024

G20 (2018) Leaders' declaration: Building consensus for fair and sustainable development. https://www.consilium.europa.eu/media/37247/buenos_aires_leaders_declaration.pdf. Accessed 5 Apr 2024

G20 (2019) Osaka Leaders' Declaration. https://www.consilium.europa.eu/media/40124/final_g20_osaka_leaders_declaration.pdf. Accessed 5 Apr 2024

Gagliani G (2020) Cybersecurity, technological neutrality, and international trade law. J Int Econ Law 23(3):723–745. https://doi.org/10.1093/jiel/jgaa006

Gao H (2017) The regulation of digital trade in the TPP: trade rules for the digital age. In: Chaisse J, Gao H, Lo C-F (eds) Paradigm shift in international economic law rule-making: TPP as a new model for trade agreements? Economics, law, and institutions in Asia Pacific Ser. Springer, Singapore

Gao H (2018) Digital or trade? The contrasting approaches of China and US to digital trade. J Int Econ Law 21(2):297–321. https://doi.org/10.1093/jiel/jgy015

Gao HS (2020) Across the great wall: E-commerce joint statement initiative negotiation and China. SSRN Journal. https://doi.org/10.2139/ssrn.3695382

Gasser U, Palfrey J (2012) Fostering innovation and trade in the global information society. In: Burri M, Cottier T (eds) Trade governance in the digital age. Cambridge University Press, Cambridge, pp 123–154

GATT Secretariat (1991) Services Sectoral Classification List. Doc.MTN.GNS/W/120. 10 July 1991

Goldfarb A, Trefler D (2018) AI and International Trade. NBER Working Paper Series. https://www.nber.org/system/files/working_papers/w24254/w24254.pdf. Accessed 5 Apr 2024

Goldsmith JL, Wu T (2006) Who controls the internet? Illusions of a borderless world. Oxford University Press, New York

González JL, Ferencz J (2018) Digital trade and market openness. OECD Trade Policy Papers No. 217. OECD Publishing, Paris. https://doi.org/10.1787/1bd89c9a-en

Hart M, Chaitoo R (1999) Electronic commerce and international trade rules. J World Intell Prop 2(6):911–937. https://doi.org/10.1111/j.1747-1796.1999.tb00099.x

Herman L (2010) Multilateralising regionalism: the case of E-commerce. OECD Trade Policy Papers No. 99, Paris. https://one.oecd.org/document/TAD/TC/WP(2009)42/FINAL/en/pdf. Accessed 5 Apr 2024

Herrmann C (2008) Bilateral and regional trade agreements as a challenge to the multilateral trading system. Außenwirtschaft 63(3):263–286

Hofheinz P, Mandel M (2015) Uncovering the hidden value of digital trade: towards a 21st century Agenda of transatlantic prosperity. Progressive Policy Institute (PPI). https://www.progressivepolicy.org/wp-content/uploads/2015/07/2015.07-Mandel-Hofeinz-Uncovering-the-Value-of-Digital-Trade_Towards-a-21st-Century-Agenda-of-Transatlantic-Prosperity.pdf. Accessed 5 Apr 2024

Horn H, Mavroidis PC, Sapir A (2009) Beyond the WTO?: An anatomy of EU and US preferential trade agreements. Bruegel Blueprint Series, Vol. 7. Bruegel, Brussels

Huang J (2017) Comparison of E-commerce regulations in Chinese and American FTAs: converging approaches, diverging contents, and polycentric directions? NLR 64(2):309–337. https://doi.org/10.1007/s40802-017-0094-1

Hubbard A, Bygrave LA (2009) Internet governance goes global. In: Bygrave LA, Bing J (eds) Internet governance: Infrastructure and Institutions. Oxford University Press, Oxford, pp 213–235

Hufbauer GC, Zhiyao L (2019) Global E-commerce talks stumble on data issues, privacy, and more. Peterson Institute for International Economics Policy Brief, pp 19–14. https://www.piie.com/publications/policy-briefs/global-e-commerce-talks-stumble-data-issues-privacy-and-more. Accessed 5 Apr 2024

ICC (2016) Trade in the digital economy: a primer on global data flows for policymakers. https://iccwbo.org/news-publications/policies-reports/trade-in-the-digital-economy-a-primer-on-global-data-flows-for-policymakers/. Accessed 5 Apr 2024

IEEE Standards Board (1990) IEEE standard glossary of software engineering terminology, IEEE Std 610.12-1990, New York, NY

IMF, WTO, OECD (2019) Handbook on Measuring Digital Trade, First Edition. https://www.oecd.org/sdd/its/Handbook-on-Measuring-Digital-Trade-Version-1.pdf. Accessed 5 Apr 2024

IMF, WTO, UNCTAD, OECD (2023) Handbook on Measuring Digital Trade, Second Edition, OECD Publishing, Paris/International Monetary Fund, UNCTAD, Geneva/WTO, Geneva, https://doi.org/10.1787/ac99e6d3-en

IPKey (2018) Translation of the E-Commerce Law of the People's Republic of China https://ipkey.eu/sites/default/files/documents/resources/PRC_E-Commerce_Law.pdf. Accessed 5 Apr 2024

Irion K (2021) AI Regulation in the European Union and Trade Law: How can Accountability of AI and a High Level of Consumer Protection Prevail over a Trade Discipline on Source Code. https://doi.org/10.2139/ssrn.3786567

Ismail Y (2020) E-commerce in the World Trade Organization: history and latest developments in the negotiations under the Joint Statement. https://www.iisd.org/publications/report/e-commerce-world-trade-organization-history-and-latest-developments. Accessed 5 Apr 2024

ITU (2005) Tunis Agenda for the Information Society, WSIS-05/TUNIS/DOC/6(Rev. 1)-E. https://www.itu.int/net/wsis/docs2/tunis/off/6rev1.html. Accessed 5 Apr 2024

Kelsey J (2018) How a TPP-style E-commerce outcome in the WTO would endanger the development dimension of the GATS Acquis (and potentially the WTO). J Int Econ Law 21(2):273–295. https://doi.org/10.1093/jiel/jgy024

Kelsey J (2020) Important differences between the final RCEP electronic commerce chapter and the TPPA and lessons for e-commerce in the WTO. https://www.bilaterals.org/?important-differences-between-the. Accessed 5 Apr 2024

Kende M, Sen N (2019) Cross Border E Commerce: WTO discussions and multi stakeholder roles stocktaking and practical ways forward. CTEI Working Papers. https://www.graduateinstitute.ch/library/publications-institute/cross-border-e-commerce-wto-discussions-and-multi-stakeholder-roles. Accessed 5 Apr 2024

Kim SY (2015) Deep integration and regional trade agreements. In: Martin LL (ed) The Oxford handbook of the political economy of international trade. Oxford University Press, pp 360–376

Kingsbury B, Mertenskötter P, Stewart RB, Streinz T (2019) The trans-pacific partnership as megaregulation. In: Kingsbury B et al (eds) Megaregulation contested. Oxford University Press, pp 27–60

Kuner C (2013) Transborder data flows and data privacy law. Oxford University Press, Oxford

La Chapelle B, Fehlinger P (2016) Jurisdiction on the Internet: From Legal Arms Race to Transnational Cooperation. Centre for International Governance Innovation and Chatham House. Paper Series No. 28. https://www.cigionline.org/publications/jurisdiction-internet-legal-arms-race-transnational-cooperation/. Accessed 5 Apr 2024

Lawder D (2023) US drops digital trade demands at WTO to allow room for stronger tech regulation. Reuters. https://www.reuters.com/world/us/us-drops-digital-trade-demands-wto-allow-room-stronger-tech-regulation-2023-10-25/. Accessed 5 Apr 2024

Leblond P (2020) Digital Trade: is RCEP the WTO's future? https://www.cigionline.org/articles/digital-trade-rcep-wtos-future/. Accessed 5 Apr 2024

Lim AH (2021) Trade rules for industry 4.0. In: Peng S, Lin C-F, Streinz T (eds) Artificial intelligence and international economic law: disruption, regulation, and reconfiguration. Cambridge University Press, Cambridge, pp 97–120

López González J, Ferencz J (2018) Digital trade and market openness, OECD Trade Policy Papers No. 217. OECD Publishing, Paris. https://doi.org/10.1787/1bd89c9a-en

López González J, Jouanjean M-A (2017) Digital trade: developing a framework for analysis. OECD Trade Policy Papers, No. 205. OECD Publishing, Paris, https://doi.org/10.1787/524c8c83-en

Low P. (2017) Framing future work and negotiations on e-commerce at the WTO. https://rtaexchange.org/blog/view_id_4006/. Accessed 5 Apr 2024

Luff D (2012) Convergence. In: Burri M, Cottier T (eds) Trade governance in the digital age. Cambridge University Press, Cambridge, pp 65–90

Lund S, Manyika J (2016) How digital trade is transforming globalisation. E15 Expert Group on the Digital Economy - Think Piece. https://www.tralac.org/images/docs/8854/how-digital-trade-is-transforming-globalisation-e15-initiative-january-2016.pdf. Accessed 5 Apr 2024

Maciel M (2016) E-commerce in the WTO: the next arena of Internet policy discussions? https://www.diplomacy.edu/blog/e-commerce-wto-next-arena-internet-policy-discussions#_edn3. Accessed 5 Apr 2024

Makiyama H-L, Gopalakrishnan BN (2019) The Economic Losses from Ending the WTO Moratorium on Electronic Transmissions. ECIPE Policy Brief No. 3/2019. https://ecipe.org/publications/moratorium/. Accessed 5 Apr 2024

Mann CL (2000) Electronic commerce in developing countries: issues for domestic policy and WTO negotiations. Working Paper 00-3, Washington, DC

Manyika J, Lund S, Bughin J, Woetzel L, Stamenov K, Dhingra D (2016) Digital globalization: the new era of global flows. McKinsey Global Institute. https://www.mckinsey.com/capabilities/mckinsey-digital/our-insights/digital-globalization-the-new-era-of-global-flows. Accessed 5 Apr 2024

Mattoo A, Schuknecht L (2000) Trade policies for electronic commerce. Policy Research Working Paper 2380. The World Bank

Meltzer JP (2015) The internet, cross-border data flows and international trade. Asia Pac Policy Stud 2(1):90–102. https://doi.org/10.1002/app5.60

Meltzer JP (2016) Maximizing the opportunities of the internet for international trade. Policy Options Paper. ICTSD and World Economic Forum. Available at SSRN: https://ssrn.com/abstract=2841913

Meltzer JP (2019a) Governing digital trade. World Trade Rev 18(S1):23–48. https://doi.org/10.1017/S1474745618000502

Meltzer JP (2019b) The United States-Mexico-Canada agreement: developing trade policy for digital trade. Trade Law Dev 11(2):239–268

Ministry of Trade and Industry Singapore (2024) What are Digital Economy Agreements (DEAs). https://www.mti.gov.sg/Trade/Digital-Economy-Agreements. Accessed 5 Apr 2024

Mishra N (2017) International trade, internet governance and the shaping of the digital economy. ARTNeT Working Paper Series No. 168

Mishra N (2019a) Building bridges: international trade law, internet governance, and the regulation of data flows. Vanderbilt J Transnatl Law 52(2):463–509

Mishra N (2019b) Privacy, cybersecurity, and GATS article XIV: a new frontier for trade and internet regulation? World Trade Rev 19(3):1–24. https://doi.org/10.1017/S1474745619000120

Mitchell AD (2001) Towards compatibility: the future of electronic commerce within the global trading system. J Int Econ Law 4(4):683–723. https://doi.org/10.1093/jiel/4.4.683

Mitchell AD, Hepburn J (2018) Don't fence me in: reforming trade and investment law to better facilitate cross-border data transfer. Yale J Law Technol 19(1):182–237

Mitchell AD, Mishra N (2018) Data at the docks: modernizing international trade law for the digital economy. Vanderbilt J Entertain Technol Law 20:1073–1134

Mitchell AD, Mishra N (2019) Regulating cross-border data flows in a data-driven world: how WTO law can contribute. J Int Econ Law 22(3):389–416. https://doi.org/10.1093/jiel/jgz016

Mitchell AD, Mishra N (2021) WTO law and cross-border data flows. In: Burri M (ed) Big data and global trade law. Cambridge University Press, Cambridge, pp 83–112

Monteiro J-A, Teh R (2017) Provisions on electronic commerce in regional trade agreements. WTO Staff Working Paper, No. ERSD-2017-11, Geneva. https://www.wto.org/english/res_e/reser_e/ersd201711_e.pdf. Accessed 5 Apr 2024

Naef T (2023) Data protection without data protectionism. European Yearbook of International Economic Law. Springer International Publishing, Cham

Noonan C, Plekhanova V (2020) Taxation of digital services under trade agreements. J Int Econ Law 23(4):1015–1039. https://doi.org/10.1093/jiel/jgaa031

OECD (1960) Convention on the Organisation for Economic Co-operation and Development, 14 December 1960

OECD (1997a) Dismantling the barriers to global electronic commerce, Turku (Finland): 19-21 November 1997- Conference Report. OECD Digital Economy Papers, No. 38. OECD Publishing, Paris. https://doi.org/10.1787/236647320075

OECD (1997b) Measuring electronic commerce. OECD Digital Economy Papers No. 27. OECD Publishing, Paris, https://doi.org/10.1787/237203566348

OECD (1998) A Borderless World: Realising the Potential of Global Electronic Commerce: Ottawa Ministerial Conference Conclusions. SG/EC(98)14/FINAL

OECD (1999) Defining and measuring E-Commerce: a status report: working party on indicators for the information society. DSTI/ICCP/IIS(99)4/FINAL

OECD (2008) The Seoul Declaration for the Future of the Internet Economy. OECD Digital Economy Papers, No. 147. OECD Publishing, Paris https://doi.org/10.1787/230445718605

OECD (2011) OECD guide to measuring the information society 2011. OECD Publishing, Paris. https://doi.org/10.1787/9789264113541-en

OECD (2016) Towards a G20 Initiative on Measuring Digital Trade. http://www.oecd.org/g20/summits/hamburg/Towards-a-G20-Initiative-on-Measuring-Digital-Trade.pdf. Accessed 5 Apr 2024

OECD (2017) Measuring Digital Trade: Towards a Conceptual Framework. Working Party on International Trade in Goods and Trade in Services Statistics, STD/CSSP/WPTGS(2017)3

OECD (2019a) The path to becoming a data-driven public sector. OECD Digital Government Studies. OECD Publishing, Paris. https://doi.org/10.1787/059814a7-en

OECD (2019b) Unpacking E-commerce: business models, trends and policies. OECD Publishing, Paris, https://doi.org/10.1787/23561431-en

OECD (2019c) Measuring the digital transformation. A roadmap for the future. OECD Publishing, Paris, https://doi.org/10.1787/9789264311992-en

OECD, IMF (2017) Measuring digital trade: results of OECD/IMF stocktaking survey. BOPCOM - 17/07, Paris, France. https://www.imf.org/external/pubs/ft/bop/2017/pdf/17-07.pdf. Accessed 5 Apr 2024

OECD, IMF (2018) Towards a handbook on measuring digital trade: status update. BOPCOM - 18/07, Washington D.C. https://www.imf.org/external/pubs/ft/bop/2018/pdf/18-07.pdf. Accessed 5 Apr 2024

Office of the United States Trade Representative (2016) The Digital 2 Dozen. https://ustr.gov/sites/default/files/Digital-2-Dozen-Final.pdf. Accessed 5 Apr 2024

Panezi M (2016) The WTO and the Spaghetti Bowl of Free Trade Agreements. Four Proposals for moving forward. CIGI Policy Brief, No. 87, 2016

Peng S (2007) Trade in telecommunications services: Doha and beyond. J World Trade 41(2): 293–317. https://doi.org/10.54648/trad2007012

Peng S (2014) Regulating new services through litigation? Electronic commerce as a case study on the evaluation of "judicial activism" in the WTO. J World Trade 48(6):1189–1222

Peng S, Lin C-F, Streinz T (eds) (2021a) Artificial intelligence and international economic law: disruption, regulation, and reconfiguration. Cambridge University Press, New York, NY

Peng S, Lin C-F, Streinz T (2021b) Artificial intelligence and international economic law: a research and policy agenda. In: Peng S, Lin C-F, Streinz T (eds) Artificial intelligence and international economic law: disruption, regulation, and reconfiguration. Cambridge University Press, Cambridge, pp 1–26

Polanco R, Sauvé P (2018) The treatment of regulatory convergence in preferential trade agreements. World Trade Rev 17(4):575–607. https://doi.org/10.1017/S1474745617000519

Primo Braga CA (2010) E-commerce regulation: new game, new rules? In: Mattoo A, Stern RM, Zanini G (eds) A handbook of international trade in services. Oxford University Press, Oxford, pp 459–479

Sen N (2018) Understanding the role of the WTO in international data flows: taking the liberalization or the regulatory autonomy path? J Int Econ Law 21(2):323–348. doi:https://doi.org/10.1093/jiel/jgy021

Stoll P-T (2017) Mega-regionals: challenges, opportunities and research questions. In: Rensmann T (ed) Mega-regional trade agreements. Springer, Cham, pp 3–24

Streinz T (2019) Digital megaregulation uncontested? TPP's model for the global digital economy. In: Kingsbury B et al (eds) Megaregulation contested. Oxford University Press, pp 312–342

Streinz T (2021a) Designing international economic data law. Proc ASIL Annual Meeting 115:73–78. https://doi.org/10.1017/amp.2021.102

Streinz T (2021b) International economic law's regulation of data as a resource for the artificial intelligence economy. In: Peng S, Lin C-F, Streinz T (eds) Artificial intelligence and international economic law: disruption, regulation, and reconfiguration. Cambridge University Press, Cambridge, pp 175–192

Svantesson DJB (2011) The regulation of cross-border data flows. Int Data Priv Law 1(3):180–198. https://doi.org/10.1093/idpl/ipr012

Taubman A (2012) TRIPS encounters the internet. In: Burri M, Cottier T (eds) Trade governance in the digital age. Cambridge University Press, Cambridge, pp 299–322

Tietje C (2012) Global information law. In: Burri M, Cottier T (eds) Trade governance in the digital age. Cambridge University Press, Cambridge, pp 45–62

Titievskaia J (2020) WTO e-commerce negotiations: European Parliament Think Tank. At a glance. https://www.europarl.europa.eu/RegData/etudes/ATAG/2020/659263/EPRS_ATA(2020) 659263_EN.pdf. Accessed 5 Apr 2024

Tuthill L, Roy M (2012) GATS classification issues for information and communication technology services. In: Burri M, Cottier T (eds) Trade governance in the digital age. Cambridge University Press, Cambridge, pp 157–178

Tuthill LL (2017) Implications of the GATS for digital trade and digital trade barriers in services. Digiworld Econ J 107:95–115

U.S. Department of Commerce (2016) Measuring the value of cross-border data flows. Economics and Statistics Administration and the National Telecommunications and Information Administration. https://www.ntia.doc.gov/files/ntia/publications/measuring_cross_border_data_flows.pdf. Accessed 5 Apr 2024

UN (2012) Resolution adopted by the Human Rights Council 20/ 8, The promotion, protection and enjoyment of human rights on the Internet, A/HRC/RES/20/8

UN Centre for Trade Facilitation and Electronic Business (2005) Recommendation and guidelines on establishing a single window to enhance the efficient exchange of information between trade and agreement. Recommendation No. 33. https://unece.org/DAM/cefact/recommendations/rec33/rec33_trd352e.pdf. Accessed 5 Apr 2024

UNCITRAL (1999) UNCITRAL Model Law on Electronic Commerce with Guide to Enactment 1996: With additional Article 5 bis as adopted in 1998. United Nations, New York

UNCITRAL (2001) Model law on electronic signatures, 5 July 2001. United Nations, New York

UNCTAD (2015a) Unlocking the potential of e-commerce for developing countries. United Nations Publication, New York. https://unctad.org/system/files/official-document/ier2015_en.pdf. Accessed 5 Apr 2024

UNCTAD (2015b) International Trade in ICT Services and ICT-enabled Services: Proposed Indicators from the Partnership on Measuring ICT for Development. Technical Notes on ICT for Development No. 3 TN/UNCTAD/ICT4D/03. https://unctad.org/system/files/official-document/tn_unctad_ict4d03_en.pdf. Accessed 5 Apr 2024

UNCTAD (2016) In Search of Cross-border E-commerce Trade Data. UNCTAD Technical Notes on ICT for Development No. 6. TN/UNCTAD/ICT4D/06. https://unctad.org/system/files/official-document/tn_unctad_ict4d06_en.pdf. Accessed 5 Apr 2024

UNCTAD (2017a) Information economy report: digitalization, trade and development. United Nations Publication, New York. https://unctad.org/system/files/official-document/ier2017_en.pdf. Accessed 5 Apr 2024

UNCTAD (2017b) Rising Product Digitalisation and Losing Trade Competitiveness. UNCTAD/GDS/ECIDC/2017/3. https://unctad.org/publication/rising-product-digitalisation-and-losing-trade-competitiveness. Accessed 5 Apr 2024

UNCTAD (2019) Digital economy report 2019: Value creation and capture: implications for developing countries, Geneva. https://unctad.org/publication/digital-economy-report-2019. Accessed 5 Apr 2024

UNCTAD (2024a) Friends for E-Commerce for Development, Mapping e-Trade for All Development Objectives into a WTO Framework for E-Commerce. https://unctad.org/system/files/non-official-document/eweek2018c01FED_en.pdf. Accessed 5 Apr 2024

UNCTAD (2024b) eTrade for all initiative. https://etradeforall.org/. Accessed 5 Apr 2024

UNESCAP (2016) Asia-Pacific Trade and Investment Report: Recent Trends and Developments, Bangkok. https://www.unescap.org/publications/asia-pacific-trade-and-investment-report-2016-recent-trends-and-developments. Accessed 5 Apr 2024

UNESCAP (2018) Embracing the E-commerce Revolution in Asia and the Pacific. https://www.unescap.org/resources/embracing-e-commerce-revolution-asia-and-pacific.   Accessed 5 Apr 2024

United States International Trade Commission (2013) Digital Trade in the U.S. and Global Economies, Part 1. https://www.usitc.gov/publications/industry_econ_analysis_332/2013/digital_trade_us_and_global_economies_part_1.htm. Accessed 5 Apr 2024

United States International Trade Commission (2014) Digital Trade in the U.S. and Global Economies, Part 2. https://www.usitc.gov/publications/industry_econ_analysis_332/2014/us_international_trade_commission_announces.htm. Accessed 5 Apr 2024

United States International Trade Commission (2017) Global Digital Trade 1: Market Opportunities and Key Foreign Trade Restrictions. Publication Number: 4716; Investigation Number: 332-561. https://www.usitc.gov/publications/industry_econ_analysis_332/2017/global_digital_trade_1_market_opportunities_and.htm. Accessed 5 Apr 2024 van den Bossche P, Zdouc W (2022) The law and policy of the World Trade Organization: text, cases, and materials, 5th edn. Cambridge University Press, Cambridge

van der Marel E (2019) Old wine in new bottles—how protectionism takes Hold of digital trade. Glob Policy 10(4):737–739. https://doi.org/10.1111/1758-5899.12737

van der Marel E, Bauer M, Lee-Makiyama H (2014) A friendly fire on economic recovery: A methodology to estimate the costs of data regulations. ECIPE Working Paper, No. 02/2014, Brussels. https://ecipe.org/publications/dataloc-methodology/. Accessed 5 Apr 2024

van der Veer H, Wiles A (2008) Achieving Technical Interoperability - the ETSI Approach. European Telecommunications Standards Institute ETSI White Paper No. 3

VanGrasstek C (2013) The history and future of the World Trade Organization. World Trade Organization, Geneva

Venkatesh K (2021) E-commerce Related Discourse At The WTO: Brief History And Subsequent Developments. https://www.mondaq.com/india/international-trade-investment/958702/e-commerce-related-discourse-at-the-wto-brief-history-and-subsequent-developments. Accessed 5 Apr 2024

Watson B (2018) A role for trade rules in Internet governance. https://www.rstreet.org/2018/01/11/a-role-for-trade-rules-in-internet-governance/. Accessed 5 Apr 2024

Weber RH (2010) Digital trade in WTO-law - taking stock and looking ahead. Asian J WTO Int Health Law Policy 5(1):1–24

Weber RH (2015) Digital trade and E-commerce: challenges and opportunities of the Asia-Pacific regionalism. Asian J WTO Int Health Law Policy 10(2):321–348

Weber RH, Burri M (2014) Classification of services in the digital economy. Springer, Berlin

Weiß W (2014) Wirtschaftsräume: Freihandelszonen, Zollunionen und Gemeinsame Märkte. In: von der Decken K, Giegerich T (eds) Räume im Völker- und Europarecht. Veröffentlichungen des Walther-Schücking-Instituts für Internationales Recht an der Universität Kiel, vol 189. Duncker & Humblot, Berlin, pp 145–178

Weiß W (2020) WTO law and domestic regulation: exploring the determinants for the impact of the WTO on domestic regulatory autonomy. Beck International. Beck; Hart; Nomos, München, Oxford, Baden-Baden

Weiß W, Ohler C, Bungenberg M (2022) Welthandelsrecht, 3. Auflage. Studium und Praxis. C.H. Beck, München

Willemyns I (2020a) Addressing digital services in PTAs: only convergence in the 11th hour? In: Hoffmann RT, Krajewski M (eds) Coherence and divergence in services trade law. European yearbook of international economic law. Springer International Publishing, Cham, pp 117–138. https://doi.org/10.1007/978-3-030-46955-9_6

Willemyns I (2020b) Agreement forthcoming? A comparison of EU, US, and Chinese RTAs in times of Plurilateral E-commerce negotiations. J Int Econ Law 23(1):221–244. https://doi.org/10.1093/jiel/jgz048

Willemyns I (2021) Digital services in international trade law. Cambridge University Press, Cambridge

WIPO (2008) Intellectual property handbook. World Intellectual Property Organization (WIPO), Geneva

Wolfe R (2018) Learning about digital trade: privacy and E-Commerce in CETA and TPP. EUI Working Paper RSCAS 2018/27. https://hdl.handle.net/1814/55144. Accessed 5 Apr 2024

World Bank Group (2016) World Development Report 2016: Digital Dividends. https://www.worldbank.org/en/publication/wdr2016. Accessed 5 Apr 2024

World Bank Group (2017) Doing Business 2017: Equal Opportunity for All. https://archive.doingbusiness.org/en/reports/global-reports/doing-business-2017. Accessed 5 Apr 2024

World Economic Forum (2022) Digital economy agreements are a new frontier for trade—here's why. https://www.weforum.org/agenda/2022/08/digital-economy-agreements-trade/. Accessed 5 Apr 2024

WTO (1995) Second Protocol to the GATS, S/L/11, 24 July 1995

WTO (1996a). Fourth Protocol to the GATS, S/L/20, 30 April 1996

References

WTO (1996b) Ministerial Declaration on Trade in Information Technology Products, WT/MIN (96)/16, 13 December 1996
WTO (1997) Fifth Protocol to the GATS, S/L/45, 3 December 1997
WTO (1998a) Ministerial Conference, Declaration on Global E-Commerce WT/MIN(98)/DEC/2, 20 May 1998
WTO (1998b) General Council, Work Programme on Electronic Commerce WT/L/274, 30 September 1998
WTO (1998c) WTO Agreements and Electronic Commerce, WT/GC/W/90, 14 July 1998
WTO (1998d) Council for Trade in Services, Note by the Secretariat, S/C/W/68, 16 November 1998
WTO (1998e) Committee for Trade and Development, Development Implications of Electronic Commerce, WT/COMTD/W/51, 23 November 1998
WTO (1999a) Interim Report to the General Council, Council for Trade in Services, S/C/8, 31 March 1999
WTO (1999b) Communication from the Chairman of the Council for Trade in Goods, WT/GC/24, 12 April 1999
WTO (1999c) Council for Trade-Related Aspects of Intellectual Property Rights, Progress Report to the General Council, IP/C/18, 30 July 1999
WTO (1999d) Council for Trade-Related Aspects of Intellectual Property Rights, Background Note, IP/C/W/128, 19 February 1999
WTO (1999e) Council for Trade in Services, Progress Report, S/L/74, 19 July 1999
WTO (1999f) Council for Trade in Goods, Information provided to the General Council, G/C/W/158, 26 July 1999
WTO (2001a) Ministerial Declaration Doha WT/MIN(01)/DEC/1, 20 November 2001
WTO (2001b) Council for Trade in Services, Guidelines and Procedures for the Negotiations on Trade in Services, S/L/93, 29 March 2001
WTO (2001c) Dedicated Discussion on Electronic Commerce Under the Auspices of the General Council on 15th June 2001, WT/GC/W/436, 6 July 2001
WTO (2001d) Dedicated Discussion on Electronic Commerce - Summary by the Secretariat, WT/GC/W/436, 6. July 2001
WTO (2001e) Guidelines for the scheduling of specific commitments, S/l/92, 28 March 2001
WTO (2005) Ministerial Declaration Hong Kong, WT/MIN(05)/DEC, 22 December 2005
WTO (2009a) Ministerial Decision, Work Programme in Electronic Commerce, WT/L/782, 11 December 2009
WTO (2009b) Work Programme in Electronic Commerce, Dedicated Discussions under the auspices of the General Council, 9 November 2009, WT/GC/W/613
WTO (2011a) World Trade Report 2011: The WTO and preferential trade agreements: From co-existence to coherence. https://doi.org/10.30875/0949bcf3-en
WTO (2011b) Ministerial Decision, Work Programme in Electronic Commerce, WT/L/843, 17 December 2011
WTO (2011c) Communication from the EU and the USA, Contribution to the Work Programme on Electronic Commerce, S/C/W/338, 13 July 2011
WTO (2012a) 15 Years of the Information Technology Agreement: Trade, innovation, and global production networks. https://www.wto.org/english/res_e/publications_e/ita15years_2012full_e.pdf. Accessed 5 Apr 2024
WTO (2012b) Council for Trade in Services, Communication from Australia, S/C/W349, 26 September 2012
WTO (2013a) Ministerial Decision, Work Programme in Electronic Commerce, WT/L/907, 11 December 2013
WTO (2013b) Committee on Trade and Development, Electronic Commerce, Development and Small, Medium-Sized Enterprises, Background Note by the Secretariat, 14 February 2013
WTO (2013c), Committee on Trade and Development, Report from the Workshop on Electronic Commerce, WT/COMTD/W/198, 27 June 2013

WTO (2014) Work Programme on Electronic Commerce, Communication by the United States, S/C/W/359, 27 November 2014
WTO (2015a) Work Programme on Electronic Commerce, Review of Progress, WT/GC/W/701, 24 July 2015
WTO (2015b) Ministerial Decision, Work Programme in Electronic Commerce, WT/L/977, 19 December 2015
WTO (2015c) World Trade Report 2015: Speeding up trade: benefits and challenges of implementing the WTO Trade Facilitation Agreement. https://doi.org/10.30875/0949bcf3-en
WTO (2016a) Work Programme on Electronic Commerce. Trade Policy, the WTO and the Digital Economy, JOB/GC/97/Rev.1, 22 July 2016
WTO (2016b) Work Programme on Electronic Commerce, Review of Progress, WT/GC/W/728, 8 December 2016
WTO (2016c) Work Programme on Electronic Commerce. Non-Paper from the USA, JOB/GC/94, 16 July 2016
WTO (2016d) General Council, Work Programme on Electronic Commerce, Reinvigorating Discussions on Electronic Commerce, JOB/GC/96/Rev 1., 14 July 2016
WTO (2017a) Joint Statement on electronic commerce, WT/MIN(17)/60, 13 December 2017
WTO (2017b) Press Release, World Economic Forum and eWTP launch joint public-private dialogue to open up e-commerce for small business, 11 December 2017
WTO (2017c) Communication from China, Japan et. al., WT/MIN(17)/26, 8 December 2017
WTO (2017d) Communication from EU, Canada et. al., WT/MIN(17)/15/Rev.1, 8 December 2017
WTO (2017e) Statement by the African Group, 20. October 2017, JOB/GC/144
WTO (2017f) Communication from Lao PDR, Panama, Qatar and Singapore, WT/MIN(17)/30, 8 December 2017
WTO (2017g) Communication from the African Group, JOB/GC/155, 21 November 2017
WTO (2017h) Work Programme on Electronic Commerce, Report by the Chairman, WT/GC/W/739, 1 December 2017
WTO (2017i) Ministerial Decision, Work Programme on Electronic Commerce, WT/MIN(17)65, 18 December 2017
WTO (2017j) General Council, Communication from Japan, Possible Way Forward on Electronic Commerce, JOB/GC/130, 14 July 2017
WTO (2017k) Communication from the European Union, An Enabling Environment To Facilitate Online Transactions, TN/S/W/64, 23 May 2017
WTO (2017l) Conference on the Use of Data in the Digital Economy. https://www.wto.org/english/res_e/reser_e/datadigitaleco17_e.htm. Accessed 5 Apr 2024
WTO (2017m) Press Release, Members debate cyber security and chemicals at technical barriers to trade committee. https://www.wto.org/english/news_e/news17_e/tbt_20jun17_e.htm. Accessed 5 Apr 2024
WTO(2017n) Council for Trade in Services, Communication from the U.S., Measures Adopted and Under Development by China Relating to Its Cybersecurity Law, S/C/W/374, 26 September 2017
WTO(2017o) Council for Trade in Services, Communication from the US, Measures Adopted and Under Development by China Relating to Its Cybersecurity Law, S/C/W/376, 23 February 2018
WTO (2018a) World Trade Report 2018: The future of world trade: How digital technologies are transforming global commerce. https://doi.org/10.30875/0949bcf3-en
WTO (2018b) Work Programme on Electronic Commerce, Review of Progress, WT/GC/W/756, 17 December 2018
WTO (2018c) Work Programme on Electronic Commerce, Communication from India and South Africa, WT/GC/W/747, 13 July 2018
WTO (2018d) Joint Statement on Electronic Commerce Initiative, Communication from the United States, JOB/GC/178, 12 April 2018

WTO (2018e) Council for Trade in Services, Communication from the US, Measures Adopted and Under Development by China Relating to Its Cybersecurity Law—Questions to China, S/C/W/378, 3 October 2018

WTO (2019a) Joint Statement on Electronic Commerce, WT/L/1056, 25 January 2019

WTO (2019b) Joint Statement on Electronic Commerce, Communication from China, INF/ECOM/19, 24 April 2019

WTO (2019c) Joint Statement on Electronic Commerce Initiative, Communication from the EU, INF/ECOM/22, 26 April 2019

WTO (2019d) Joint Statement on Electronic Commerce Initiative, Communication from the EU, 26 April 2019, INF/ECOM/22

WTO (2020) Work Programme on Electronic Commerce, Communication from India and South Africa, WT/GC/W/798, 10 March 2020

WTO (2021) Press Release, Negotiations on services domestic regulation conclude successfully in Geneva, 2 December 2021. https://www.wto.org/english/news_e/news21_e/jssdr_02dec21_e.htm. Accessed 5 Apr 2024

WTO (2024) 13th Ministerial Conference Briefing Note E-commerce. https://www.wto.org/english/thewto_e/minist_e/mc13_e/briefing_notes_e/ecommerce_e.htm. Accessed 5 Apr 2024

WTO/WEF (2022) The Promise of Trade Tech: Policy approaches to harness trade digitalization

Wu M (2017) Digital Trade-Related Provisions in Regional Trade Agreements: Existing Models and Lessons for the Multilateral Trade System. RTA Exchange https://rtaexchange.org/pdf/Digital%20Trade%20Related%20Provisions%20in%20RTA_%20WU.pdf. Accessed 5 Apr 2024

Wu T (2006) The world trade law of censorship and internet filtering. Chic J Int Law 7(1):263–287

Wunsch-Vincent S (2003) The digital trade agenda of the U.S.: parallel tracks of bilateral. Reg Multilat Liberal Außenwirtschaft 58:7–46. https://doi.org/10.2139/ssrn.393961

Wunsch-Vincent S (2004) WTO, E-commerce, and Information Technologies. From the Uruguay Round through the Doha Development Agenda. UN ICT Task Force

Wunsch-Vincent S (2006) The internet, cross-border trade in services, and the GATS: lessons from US–gambling. World Trade Rev 5(3):319–355. https://doi.org/10.1017/S1474745606002965

Wunsch-Vincent S, Hold A (2012) Towards coherent rules for digital trade. In: Burri M, Cottier T (eds) Trade governance in the digital age. Cambridge University Press, Cambridge, pp 179–221

Yakovleva S (2020) Privacy protection(ism): the latest wave of trade constraints on regulatory autonomy. Univ Miami Law Rev 74:416–519

Yakovleva S, Irion K (2020) Pitching trade against privacy: reconciling EU governance of personal data flows with external trade. Int Data Priv Law 10(3):201–221. https://doi.org/10.1093/idpl/ipaa003

Zhang R (2015) Covered or not covered: that is the question: Services Classification and Its Implications for Specific Commitments under the GATS. WTO Working Paper ERSD-2015-11

Zheng W (2020) The digital challenge to international trade law. NYU J Int Law Polit 52:539–592

Chapter 4
Data Protection and Data Protectionism in International Trade

4.1 Introduction

With respect to digital trade, much of the controversy generated by the proliferation of national data privacy laws stems from the fact that the underlying regulation is frequently seeking to govern the cross-border flow of personal data. The emerging field of data privacy law in the 1960s and 1970s actively sought remedies to block personal data from being transferred outside a given jurisdiction in order to circumvent domestic legal protections for that data. In the face of a global environment for the processing of personal data, a variety of national data privacy frameworks have thus adopted domestic data flow regulations of transnational relevance that affect the transfer of personal data across borders.[1] Such regulation of data flows that arose in the context of safeguarding individual approaches to data privacy in a nascent information society has more and more evolved to contain fundamental implications for a highly networked global digital economy.[2] Although international discourse on data flows and data privacy has always been driven in roughly equal measure by considerations of human rights protection and cross-border economic activity, underlying policy tensions are heightening against the backdrop of the economic relevance of digital trade.[3] As much of social and economic activity has shifted to the digital realm, issues of data privacy, data security, and data confidentiality have become more important at virtually all levels of human activity in the digital era. In

---

[1] Kuner (2011), p. 14; Svantesson (2011).
[2] Bygrave (2014), p. 123. *See* for a brief review of the evolution of the debate on cross-border data flows Drake (2016).
[3] *See* further for an EU-US perspective Schwartz (2013), p. 1971. The confluence of safeguarding fundamental human rights to privacy and facilitating the free flow of data across borders for reasons of economic activity is reflected in a number of data privacy frameworks, for example in the OECD Privacy Guidelines and the EU's data protection framework, *see infra* Sect. 4.3. *See* also Drake (2016).

recent years, a number of incidents have highlighted the vulnerability of individuals with regard to their personal data in a digitally networked environment, prompting governments to act.[4] The UNCTAD Global Cyberlaw Tracker, which maps the emergence of cyber laws globally, notes that 137 out of 194 countries (71%) have adopted legislation to secure the protection of data and privacy, while another 9% have a draft legislation.[5] As a result, data privacy requirements have tightened their grip on (cross-border) economic activity in recent years. In fact, data privacy law today has far-reaching significance, as it aims to regulate the exploitation of personal data, potentially interfering with a number of processes that are commonplace in a digital economy.[6] In a trade policy discourse, therefore, data privacy laws as a key instrument of domestic data governance are often addressed against the backdrop raising non-tariff barriers to trade in the digital economy.[7]

The nexus of digital trade and data privacy in a digital economy has stimulated a controversial debate over the delicate balance between "*data protection*" and "*data protectionism*". Indeed, it is reasonable to assume that a broad range of digital trade will regularly involve the exchange of personal data.[8] As an example, digital business models such as social network or search engine services are generally supplied "*for free*"—without direct monetary compensation—relying on the consumers "*paying*" with their personal data. In the context of trade law, academic literature has proposed a high-level distinction between services that require "*systematic, structural and continuous*" cross-border flow of personal data and those that do not.[9] While these digital services are certainly affected by data privacy regulations, the same is true for goods trade, as e-commerce relies on cross-border data flows and modern consumer products are typically digitally integrated. The processing of personal data such as names, addresses or credit card data will be regularly incurred as part of the process of ordering, paying for and fulfilling a cross-border transaction.[10] A multifaceted character of personal data in a digital economy binds together the underlying governance regimes of digital trade and data privacy and creates the potential for conflict between (some) of the underlying normative values. Today, the fault lines are so profound that a consideration of the recent policy debate suggests that trade and privacy are engaged in a kind of "*mortal contest*".[11]

---

[4] As an example, published by Edward Snowden in 2013, NSA surveillance practices have recently disrupted the political landscape, Aaronson and Maxim (2013); Hill (2014). *See* further OECD (2015a), pp. 210–215.

[5] Cf. UNCTAD (2024).

[6] Bygrave (2014), p. 5.

[7] *See* only Aaronson (2019); Burri (2021), pp. 35–43; Mishra (2015); Pasadilla (2020); Yakovleva (2020b); Yakovleva and Irion (2020), pp. 202–203.

[8] Attention may be drawn here again to the inherent complexities of measuring cross-border data flows, *see supra* Sect. 2.3.2.3. *See* on the weak link between the measurement of data flows and personal data Yakovleva and Irion (2020), p. 205.

[9] *See* in particular Naef (2023), pp. 237–242.

[10] *See* for further examples Casalini and López González (2019), pp. 28–34.

[11] Cf. Chander and Schwartz (2023).

Against this backdrop, this chapter analyses the nature of the relationship between data privacy and digital trade. Initially, data privacy will be contextualised with respect to cross-border trade in the digital economy (Sect. 4.2). To this end, the fundamentals of data privacy regulation are explored in more detail, explaining the nomenclature and scope of application of data privacy laws. Then the regulation of cross-border data flows under data privacy law is examined as a key element that influences the relationship with digital trade (Sect. 4.3). Next, what is referred to here as the *"data privacy collision"* in the field of digital trade between data protection and data protectionism is subjected to further analysis (Sect. 4.4).

4.2 Fundamentals of Data Privacy Regulation in a Digital Trade Context

The emergence of digital trade and the development of data privacy law share a common fundamental impetus.[12] Both phenomena are linked to the evolutionary development of an ever-expanding global data sphere, in which the transmission of personal data in particular has evolved from a discrete event to a ubiquitous and pervasive flow (*see supra* Sect. 2.2.2.1).[13] Indeed, the field of data privacy regulation is intricately intertwined with innovation in the ICT sector and the advancement of digital technologies.[14] The evolving technological capabilities to duplicate, process, store, and transmit data relating to natural persons ever more effectively have raised the question of how to ensure the protection of privacy rights in a globalising data sphere.[15] In particular, the automated processing of personal data, facilitated by databases and turbocharged by digital technologies such as Big Data and AI, combined with the expanding body of data that can be linked to individuals, has altered the quality of threats to individual privacy. As a result, the right to privacy, which is widely regarded as a human right, has been found to be under threat. Therefore, in response to rising concerns about the nascent information economy of the 1960s and early 1970s, regulatory frameworks were adopted to address the status of individual rights in a computerised environment. *Lee Bygrave* sums up the catalysts for the field of data privacy law as follows: *"data privacy law results from an attempt to secure the privacy, autonomy and integrity of individuals and thereby the bases for democratic, pluralist society in the face of massive growth in the amount of personal data gathered and shared by organizations"*.[16]

---

[12] *See* further with regard to an argument that modern regimes of data privacy law and trade law were built in full contemplation of each other Chander and Schwartz (2023), pp. 56–70.

[13] *See* with further references Kuner (2013), pp. 26–27; OECD (2006), p. 6.

[14] Bygrave (2014), pp. 9–10; Gasser (2016).

[15] *See* generally Gasser (2016), p. 63; OECD (2006), p. 8.

[16] Bygrave (2014), p. 8.

This first section will outline the fundamentals of data privacy regulation in the context of digital trade. As with digital trade, there is no clear conceptual definition for data privacy. Privacy is a concept that is highly susceptible to interpretation and fraught with sociocultural idiosyncrasies. The underlying normative complexity of data privacy is apparent even in the diversity of the terminology used on an international level, such as *"informational privacy"*, *"data protection"*, or simply *"privacy"*—notions that have been introduced to the trade policy debate. Therefore, a brief introduction to the nomenclature of *"data privacy"* will be given first. With a view to a normative conflict between trade liberalisation and data privacy regulation, the underlying issue of the multifaceted character of personal data in a digital economy will then be addressed. Finally, the scope of data privacy legislation in a data-driven economy will be delineated by presenting some of the most common conceptualisations for *"personal data"*.

4.2.1 Data Privacy: Conceptual Approaches and Nomenclature

With regard to data privacy regulations in the context of cross-border trade, it should first be addressed that the relevant terminology such as with regard to *"data privacy"*, *"information privacy"* or *"data protection"* is often employed without clear conceptual attribution or in an interchangeable manner.

This terminological ambiguity reflects a general lack of conceptual consensus within the emergent field of transnational data privacy law. By and large, the aforementioned notions can be ascribed to different jurisdictional backgrounds and contexts. As the present analysis is not dedicated to a dogmatic framing of the field of data privacy in a global context, this section will not trace the nuances of the aforementioned (or additional) concepts in detail.[17] In the context of trade in the digital economy, the aim here is rather to disentangle the terms most commonly used in trade policy discourse, *"information privacy"* (or simply *"privacy"*) and *"data protection"* and their respective conceptual underpinnings in order to prevent terminological confusion. In addition, this section specifies the use of the term *"data privacy"* for the purposes of this work.

Addressing data privacy in a transnational context is inherently challenging because the underlying notion of *"privacy"*, both as a social and legal construct, is essentially a complex conglomeration of various socio-cultural implications and connotations. In this context, legal scholars and practitioners have long lamented the lack of a firm and reliable definition and meaning of *"privacy"*.[18] Although the

---

[17] *See* in this regard Bygrave (2014), pp. 23–29; Kuner (2009a), pp. 308–309.

[18] *See* for example Solove (2002), pp. 1088–1089: *"All up, the field shows bewildering conceptual and terminological diversity. [...] The most famous case in point is 'privacy'"*. *See* also Bygrave (2014), p. 27 with further references to the debate. *See* further Solove (2006), pp. 479–483.

right to privacy is conceptually ambiguous, it has been recognised as a fundamental human right in a number of international legal instruments, including Article 12 of the 1948 Universal Declaration of Human Rights (UDHR), Article 8 of the 1950 European Convention on Human Rights (ECHR), and Article 17 of the 1966 International Covenant on Civil and Political Rights (ICCPR).[19] To be sure, privacy pertains to an element of social behaviour that has long shaped the human experience in the form of written rules and customs, however, the origins of the modern legal concept of privacy can be attributed to the US.[20] In the US, privacy as a legal concept has initially been conceived as referring to the protection of one's individual sphere from interference. The influential 1890 essay by *Samuel Warren* and *Louis Brandeis* on "*The Right to Privacy*" certainly points to this approach.[21] Further scholarly work suggests that privacy has (at least) two dimensions, relational and informational, both of which involve control over the personal sphere, the body, and information about oneself.[22] Indeed, in the context of the discourse on data privacy law and policy, the definition of privacy in terms of information control is a widely popular concept.[23]

With the dawn of the information age, the nature of the interaction between information and the individual in society and economy has changed dramatically (*see supra* Sect. 2.2.1.2). The proliferation of ICT has promoted the collection, storage, and processing of personal information, which has provided the impetus for an evolutionary development of the scope of the concept of "*privacy*" in light of technologically driven transformation.[24] It is particularly in the context of automated data processing and the emergence of large databases that a general understanding of the right to privacy has developed with respect to information that makes an individual identifiable, as "*[...] certain uses of databases foster a state of powerlessness and vulnerability created by people's lack of any meaningful form of participation in the collection and use of their personal information*".[25] Since the 1970s, concerns about automated processing of personal data, particularly in Western democracies, have led to the enactment of legislation, both nationally and internationally, based on the concept of privacy.[26] In this context, the concept of

---

[19] Bygrave (2014), pp. 82–98. *See* for a critical appraisal of the genesis of privacy as a human right Diggelmann and Cleis (2014). *See* further *infra* Sect. 4.4.1.2.1.

[20] Holvast (2009), pp. 15–16.

[21] Cf. Warren and Brandeis (1890) manifesting privacy as a "*right to be let alone*". For a discussion of the article and its perception in common law, *see* Solove and Schwartz (2018), p. 10.

[22] Holvast (2009), p. 16. *See* with further references to the debate on the remit of privacy Bygrave (2014), p. 27.

[23] With further references Bygrave (2014), p. 28.

[24] *See* with further references Bygrave (2014), pp. 24–25; Gasser (2016) *See* in general with regard to the evolutionary conceptualisation of privacy Solove (2002), who notes at p. 1142: "*A conception of privacy must be responsive to social reality since privacy is an aspect of social practices. Since practices are dynamic, we must understand their historical development*".

[25] Solove (2001), p. 1423. *See also* Schwartz and Solove (2011), pp. 1819–1828.

[26] *See* with regard to introduction of data privacy legislation and the regulation of cross-border data flows further *infra* Sect. 4.3.

"*information privacy*" has gained significant ground in US law.[27] By contrast, the term "*data protection*" has gained popularity in the European legal system.[28] The Hessian Data Protection Act of 1970 is widely regarded as the first data protection law, followed by a number of national laws in Europe such as, for example, in Germany (1977), France (1978), Austria (1978) and Sweden (1973).[29] The concept of data protection today is clearly tied to European law and the European legal tradition. Arguably, data protection addresses a specific sub-segment of privacy brought about by technological change.[30] The evolutionary development of the concept of privacy is evident, for example, with regard to the deliberations of the Council of Europe, whose "*Convention for the Protection of Individuals with Regard to Automatic Processing of Personal Data*" (Convention 108) of 1981 aimed to address the previously identified gaps with respect to an "*adequate protection to the right of personal privacy vis-à-vis modern science and technology*".[31] Consequently, Article 1 of Convention 108 in its original version provided for a definition of data protection as "*to secure in the territory of each Party for every individual, whatever his nationality or residence, respect for his rights and fundamental freedoms, and in particular his right to privacy, with regard to automatic processing of personal data relating to him ('data protection')*". This fundamental rights-based approach to data protection has laid the foundation for the EU's influential Directive 95/46/EC of the European Parliament and of the Council of 24 October 1995 on the protection of individuals with regard to the processing of personal data and on the free movement of such data (Data Protection Directive-DPD)[32] and its successor the Regulation (EU) 2016/679 of the European Parliament and of the Council of 27 April 2016 on the protection of natural persons with regard to the processing of personal data and on the free movement of such data, and repealing Directive 95/46/EC (General Data Protection Regulation—GDPR). The EU has accorded "*data protection*" the status of a separate fundamental right alongside the right to privacy as reflected in the European Charter of Fundamental Rights (EU Charter).[33] The EU Charter entered into force in December 2009 in

---

[27] *See* for an introduction Schwartz (2009), pp. 906–907; Solove and Schwartz (2018), p. 1. *See* also Gasser (2016), p. 62.

[28] Bygrave (2014), pp. 25–26.

[29] *See* with further examples and references Kuner (2011), p. 14; Schwartz (2013), pp. 1969–1970.

[30] *See* with further references Kuner (2009a), p. 308: "*The concepts 'data protection' and 'privacy' are 'twins but not identical'.*".

[31] Council of Europe (1981), p. 2. *See* also further *infra* Sect. 4.3.1.2.

[32] Recital 11 of the EU's DPD states: "*Whereas the principles of the protection of the rights and freedoms of individuals, notably the right to privacy, which are contained in this Directive, give substance to and amplify those contained in the Council of Europe Convention of 28 January 1981*".

[33] The EU's dual approach to a normative foundation of the fundamental rights character of data privacy has led to difficulties in delineating the respective scope of protection. Although there is much overlap between the right to privacy on the one hand and a right to data protection on the other, an evaluation of the case law of the European Court of Justice and the European Court of

conjunction with the Treaty of Lisbon and notably features two separate provisions in Article 7 ("*Respect for private and family life*") and Article 8 ("*Protection of personal data*"). As regards Article 8 of the Charter, para. 1 of which provides for a "*right to the protection of personal data concerning him or her*", the Explanatory Notes to the EU Charter point out that this provision is based, inter alia, on Article 8 ("*Respect for private life*") of the Council of Europe's European Convention of Human Rights (ECHR) and Convention 108.[34] In fact, data privacy was even somewhat retroactively introduced to the interpretation of Article 8 ECHR, which at the time of its entry into force in 1953 could not yet take into account this development.[35]

Overall, the difference in nomenclature between the notions "*information privacy*" (or simply "*privacy*") and "*data protection*" can be broadly considered a bifurcated development in an emerging field of law, one that runs primarily along a transatlantic divide. With regard to terminology, *Lee Bygrave* demonstrates that both concepts suffer their respective share of inadequacies—to note just one for each concept: While data protection is misleading in relation to the field of "*data security*" (as it is not the data that is protected but rather the individual), the concept of privacy suffers a well-established definitional instability.[36] In light of this, more recently, the notion of "*data privacy*" has become increasingly prominent in scholarly literature, as it provides a somewhat neutral approach to transnational data privacy issues in between the regionally sourced concepts of data protection and (information) privacy.[37] Therefore, against the background of the perspective of trade law, this text employs this terminology in order to steer clear of privileging one terminology over the other, but rather to bridge the (transatlantic) terminological gap in the emergent field of transnational law relating to the protection of natural persons with regard to the processing of their personal data. The term "*data privacy*" thus refers here to the emerging transnational field of law that is subject to the jurisdictional traditions of many countries.[38]

Human Rights reveals differences in their scope, *see* Kokott and Sobotta (2013). *See* also Naef (2023), pp. 42–47.

[34] Cf. European Union (2007).

[35] *See* with further references to the jurisprudence of the European Court of Human Rights Kokott and Sobotta (2013), p. 223. *See* also Bygrave (2014), pp. 82–98.

[36] *See* further Bygrave (2014), p. 28.

[37] Bygrave (2014), p. 29. *See* for example Schwartz (2019), p. 775.

[38] *See* also Chander and Schwartz (2023), p. 55; Schwartz (2019), p. 775. In this text, reference is also made in part to "*information privacy*" or "*data protection*" when specifically addressing the respective legal context.

4.2.2 On the Multifaceted Character of Personal Data in the Digital Economy

It has been emphasised throughout this book that the digital economy is based on the economic patterns that result from collecting, transmitting, and compiling data by means of digital technology. Data can serve a variety of different functions in an economic context and is notably a non-rivalrous asset, meaning it can be reused and re-contextualised with great flexibility. The economic value of data, as outlined above, lies primarily in the potential to gain valuable insights and, more broadly, to derive predictions from its computational analysis (*see supra* Sect. 2.2.2.1.3). In view of the constantly growing global data sphere, the emergence of a Big Data world has gained considerable attention in society and academia.[39] In this present context, it is important to understand that Big Data analytics are effective regardless of the reference object of the underlying dataset. Indeed, the technology can be applied to data on technical aspects such as the maintenance of an engine, on environmental conditions such as the weather, but also on the intimate circumstances of an individual's personal life. Digital technologies not only allow for comprehensive datafication of almost all aspects of daily life, but subsequently also for the extrapolation and prediction of a wide range of circumstances related to human agency and behaviour both as participants in markets but also in social relations.[40] The accessibility of personal data as a precious resource, the ease with which it can be processed on a global scale via ICT, and the proliferation of new forms of computing technologies have led to the increasing integration of personal data into economic activity. In fact, within a few years of the advent of the digital economy, personal data is undergoing extensive marketisation—data relating to the individual is "*commodified*" and is considered a tradable asset.[41] *Shoshana Zuboff* has convincingly analysed that a number of digital economy companies take advantage of computerised collection and processing of personal data for commercial purposes, thus establishing a form of "*surveillance capitalism*".[42] Indeed, the World Economic Forum (WEF) has referred to personal data as a "*new asset class*".[43] The proliferation of data-driven technologies and the "*commodification*" of personal data poses the very real risk that personal data will be misused for fraud, discriminatory practices, infringement of basic civil liberties, or for intrusive surveillance by either government or commercial entities, with both economic and non-economic costs.[44] In particular, elements that are quintessential to human personality and social interaction interwoven in the concept of personal data are being subjected to the

---

[39] *See* only Cukier (2010); Mayer-Schönberger and Cukier (2014); Manyika et al. (2011).

[40] Roessler (2015), pp. 141–142.

[41] Roessler (2015), pp. 146–150; Schwartz (2004), pp. 2069–2076.

[42] Zuboff (2019).

[43] World Economic Forum (2011).

[44] Schwartz (2004), pp. 2072–2073; Yakovleva and Irion (2020), pp. 7–8.

4.2 Fundamentals of Data Privacy Regulation in a Digital Trade Context

market forces of the digital economy, potentially distorting personal autonomy and identity.[45] In this sense, privacy is widely recognised a fundamental human right, involving a societal dimension that is intimately intertwined with the political and structural integrity of democratic societies.[46]

Against this background, personal data possess an inherently ambiguous character from the vantage point of trade law. Notably, personal data can both be an economic asset and an element relevant to fundamental human rights such as the right to privacy.[47] In fact, as *Svetlana Yakovleva* and *Kristina Irion* have put it: "*Personal data is peculiar in the way it combines the dignity of a human being with economic properties valuable for commercial activity.*".[48] On the one hand, personal data assume paramount significance for individual rights and societal cohesion in the digital age, on the other hand, personal data is an important economic asset in a digital economy, the cross-border transfer of which is a viable part of digital trade. It follows that data privacy regulations governing the use of personal data are a focal point for both economic and non-economic considerations, including issues such as economic welfare, human rights protection, but also digital sovereignty and national security in the digital age. Orchestrating the trade-off between the free circulation of personal data in a digital economy and the control of its processing and dissemination through data privacy legislation is hence a thorny endeavour, as it involves economic, social, and individual factors.[49] As a consequence, the multifaceted nature of personal data as a reference object for a number of policy considerations results in a wide variation in the underlying normative rationales for data privacy laws, and thus in a fragmentation of data privacy regulations and the standards of protection on a global scale as such.[50] Against the backdrop of an absence of a global standard for the protection of individuals in the processing of personal data this fragmentation of data privacy rules gives rise to a "*data privacy collision*" in the context of digital trade, which will be addressed in a subsequent section (*see infra* Sect. 4.4).

---

[45] Roessler (2015), pp. 146–150.
[46] Yakovleva (2018), pp. 481–487. *See* with regard to "*constitutive privacy*" Solove (2006), p. 487 and for a EU perspective on the foundational values of data protection Naef (2023), pp. 31–37. *See* also *infra* Sect. 4.4.1.2.
[47] Roessler (2015), pp. 144–145; Yakovleva (2018), pp. 481–487.
[48] Yakovleva and Irion (2020), p. 202.
[49] Acquisti et al. (2016), p. 445.
[50] *See* also Yakovleva (2018), p. 487.

4.2.3 On the Scope of Data Privacy Laws in a Digital Economy

When addressing the nexus of data privacy and digital trade it is important to understand and define the regulatory scope of data privacy laws in terms of the data affected. Data privacy law regulates all or the majority of phases of the processing of certain types of data, i.e. it deals with the way in which data are collected, registered, stored, used and disseminated.[51] Indeed, the issue of data typology is critical to both the statistical measurement of trade in the digital economy and the regulation of data and data flows under data privacy law.[52] Domestic data regulations will regularly designate specific types and grades of data. In fact, the current global environment of data regulations offers a myriad of categories in this regard, as data itself is a very elusive asset. However, given the threat to privacy, significant for both individual freedom and societal cohesion, a substantial number of currently existing data governance frameworks distinguish between data that render an individual identifiable and those that do not. Although no uniform data typology is available at the international level, it is striking that a distinction that is made quite uniformly by a variety of international and domestic frameworks refers to "*personal data*".[53] The underlying notion of personal data is mostly conceptualised rather broadly and can relate, for example, to external aspects of the individual, such as activity, their whereabouts at a given time or physical characteristics, but also to highly sensitive matters such as health status, sexual orientation, or political affiliation.[54] This indicates that the regulation of the processing of personal data in a digital economy has a rather broad scope and, in particular, encompasses the processing of data in an economic context. In the following, some of the definitions used at the international level will be illustrated in order to provide an idea of the overall consistency of the data categories implied.

4.2.3.1 Identification of Common Conceptualisations

In view of the increasing number of data privacy regulations on a global level, some of the most influential conceptions concerning the types of data that fall within the scope of the respective legislations will be outlined in the following. Arguably the most relevant concepts in this regard are "*personally identifiable information*", which is employed predominantly in the US, and "*personal data*", which is generally used in the European legal tradition.[55] Additionally, a certain number of

---

[51] Bygrave (2014), p. 1.

[52] Some of the challenges in developing a robust typology for data and data flows have already been addressed above, *see supra* Sect. 2.3.2.3.

[53] Sen (2018), p. 343.

[54] OECD (2013a), pp. 7–9.

[55] OECD (2013a), pp. 7–9.

diverging conceptualisations can be found in practice or in academic literature.[56] One of these approaches is that of *"personal information"*. It is these three categories that are exemplified here in order to illustrate some of the differences in the design of data typology under data privacy law.

4.2.3.1.1 Personally Identifiable Information

The concept of personally identifiable information (PII) is one of the most central to privacy regulation in the US, as it defines the scope of a substantial body of privacy laws and regulations.[57] Although the term is a key element to US privacy law, there is no single definition, but rather a number of competing definitions, each with its own set of challenges.[58] Moreover, PII is sometimes even used interchangeably with the term personal information in scholarly literature.[59] The US Department of Commerce defines PII as designating *"any information about an individual maintained by an agency, including (1) any information that can be used to distinguish or trace an individual's identity, such as name, social security number, date and place of birth, mother's maiden name, or biometric records; and (2) any other information that is linked or linkable to an individual, such as medical, educational, financial, and employment information"*.[60] Therefore, the difference between PII and non-PII is generally considered to be that PII can directly identify a person while non-PII is not identifying in and of itself.[61]

4.2.3.1.2 Personal Data

In the European legal sphere, the term personal data has been used consistently for some time now.[62] Article 2 of Convention 108 of the European Council which opened for signature in January 1981 stipulates: *"'personal data' means any information relating to an identified or identifiable individual ("data subject")"*. Consequently, Article 2 (a) of the 1995 DPD states: *"'personal data' shall mean any information relating to an identified or identifiable natural person ('data subject'); an identifiable person is one who can be identified, directly or indirectly, in particular by reference to an identification number or to one or more factors specific to his physical, physiological, mental, economic, cultural or social identity;"*. The

---

[56] *See* for example OECD (2013a), p. 8.
[57] Solove and Schwartz (2018), p. 794.
[58] Solove and Schwartz (2018), p. 794.
[59] With further references Schwartz and Solove (2011), p. 1828.
[60] U.S. Department of Commerce (2010), p. 2-1. *See* for an account of the current typology and a plaidoyer for a PII 2.0 Schwartz and Solove (2011), pp. 1865–1892.
[61] OECD (2013a), p. 8.
[62] Kuner et al. (2020), Art. 4, pp. 105–108.

GDPR, directly applicable in the EU since 2018, continues this European tradition. Article 4 Sec. 1 GDPR defines: *"'personal data' means any information relating to an identified or identifiable natural person ('data subject'); an identifiable natural person is one who can be identified, directly or indirectly, in particular by reference to an identifier such as a name, an identification number, location data, an online identifier or to one or more factors specific to the physical, physiological, genetic, mental, economic, cultural or social identity of that natural person;"*. In the context of Regulation (EU) 2018/1807 on a framework for the free flow of non-personal data in the European Union, non-personal data are consequently defined as follows: *"'data' means data other than personal data as defined in point (1) of Article 4 of Regulation (EU) 2016/679"*.[63]

In addition to the EU's legal system, other data privacy regimes use this concept of *"personal data"*. The 1980 OECD Privacy Guidelines (as well as the updated version of 2013), for example, define *"personal data"* as *"any information relating to an identified or identifiable individual (data subject)"*.[64] Furthermore, Article 2 a) of the Madrid Resolution, a joint proposal for international standards on the protection of privacy with regard to the processing of personal data, adopted by the International Conference of Data Protection and Privacy Commissioners in 2009, defines *"personal data"* as *"any information relating to an identified natural person or a person who may be identified by means reasonably likely to be used"*.[65]

4.2.3.1.3 Personal Information

In addition to the concepts of personal data and PII, the concept of personal information is relatively common. The Chinese Cybersecurity Law (CLS) of 2017 refers to personal information as: *"all kinds of information, recorded electronically or through other means, that taken alone or together with other information, is sufficient to identify a natural person's identity, including but not limited to natural persons' full names, birth dates, national identification numbers, personal biometric information, addresses, telephone numbers, and so forth"*.[66] Against this background, Article 4 of the 2021 Personal Information Protection Law (PIPL) defines personal information as *"all kinds of information, recorded by electronic or other means, related to identified or identifiable natural persons, not including information after anonymization handling"*.[67]

---

[63] Cf. Article 3 Sec. 1 Regulation (EU) 2018/1807 of the European Parliament and of the Council of 14 November 2018 on a framework for the free flow of non-personal data in the European Union.
[64] OECD (2013b), p. 13, para. 1. b).
[65] Cf. Madrid Resolution (2009), Article 2 a).
[66] Cf. Chinese Cybersecurity Law, Article 76 Sec. 5, *see* for a translation DigiChina (2018).
[67] Personal Information Protection Law of the People's Republic of China, passed at the 30th meeting of the Standing Committee of the 13th National People's Congress on 20 August 2021, *see* for a translation DigiChina (2021c).

Similarly, the 2015 APEC Privacy framework designates personal information to mean *"any information about an identified or identifiable individual"*.[68] Moreover, the California Consumer Privacy Act (CCPA) identifies personal information as *"information that identifies, relates to, describes, is reasonably capable of being associated with, or could reasonably be linked, directly or indirectly, with a particular consumer or household"*.[69]

4.2.3.2 Evaluation

Against the background of the conceptualisations presented in this section, it can first be stated that there is no unified concept on a global level and further that the existing conceptualisations are fraught with definitional inconsistencies. For example, the exact definitions of both personal data and PII are not commonly agreed upon.[70] Certainly, it is generally the case that the relevant data specifically relates to a natural person in one way or another by making that person identifiable. In this sense, it can be stated that data privacy law overall is relevant to *"certain kinds of information which can be linked to persons"*.[71] However, since the concept of personal data, for example, can be construed both very broad or very narrow and very abstract or concrete, it can be arguable what data is actually covered by the underlying data privacy instrument.[72] In fact, it is necessary to take into account jurisdictional particularities as well as domestic interpretations and case law when evaluating compliance with a given data privacy law. Moreover, divergences in the data typology employed by data privacy laws can be exacerbated by the additional designation of specific categories of data relating to an individual. In fact, some data privacy laws specify subcategories of such data that require special treatment. This pertains notably to particularly *"sensitive"* personal data such as with regard to race or ethnicity, religious or philosophical beliefs, genetic information or sexual orientation.[73] Moreover, the difficulty in determining whether or not data actually fall within the scope of a given concept is multidimensional. In fact, it is becoming

---

[68] APEC (2005), p. 9. *See* further *infra* Sect. 4.3.1.4.
[69] California Consumer Privacy Act, Title 1.81.5 of the California Civil Code added by Stats. 2018, Chapter 55, Sec. 3., Sec. 1798.140.
[70] *See* for example Casalini and López González (2019), p. 12; Schwartz and Solove (2011), p. 1835. Generally, the scope of personally identifiable information is considered to be narrower than the scope of personal data.
[71] Bygrave (2014), p. 126.
[72] National Board of Trade (2014), p. 6.
[73] *See* for example Article 9 of the GDPR stating in Sec. 1 *"Processing of personal data revealing racial or ethnic origin, political opinions, religious or philosophical beliefs, or trade union membership, and the processing of genetic data, biometric data for the purpose of uniquely identifying a natural person, data concerning health or data concerning a natural person's sex life or sexual orientation shall be prohibited"*. Article 9 Sec. 2 GDPR contains several exceptions to the prohibition of Sec. 1.

increasingly difficult to distinguish between sets of data that do or do not contain personal data as technology makes it possible to link a variety of data to an identifiable individual, such as search terms, GPS locations, or IP addresses.[74] To add to this, instruments like the de-personalisation of data used to be considered a useful data management tool, the anonymisation of data sets, however, is increasingly being challenged by digital technologies such as Big Data and AI.[75] Digital technologies may enable data processors to transform anonymised data into data that makes an individual identifiable, thereby challenging the very distinction between personal and non-personal data.[76] Notably, recital 26 of the EU's GDPR pursues a risk-based approach in referring to the *"means reasonably likely to be used"* to identify a natural person taking into account *"objective factors, such as the costs of and the amount of time required for identification, taking into consideration the available technology at the time of the processing and technological developments"*.[77] While such rules are generally not oriented towards absolutes in light of continuous technological development, it is reasonable to expect that the range of data that cannot be *"re-identified"* will continue to decrease considerably. In turn, with regard to a broadening scope of the conceptualisation of personal data, data privacy law could indeed advance to become a *"law of everything"*.[78] Against this backdrop, it is evident that trade law and policy, as well as the underlying methodologies for measuring cross-border economic activity, need to develop a robust understanding of the categorisation of personal data, given the importance of the scope of data privacy rules for trade in the digital economy. This concerns not least the interpretation of *"personal data"* within the meaning of Article XIV(c)(ii) GATS.[79] At the same time, the evaluation of the data typologies underlying data privacy laws has illustrated one of the diverse challenges that trade law faces against the backdrop of an evolving set of domestic data governance (*see supra* Sect. 3.5.2.2).

4.3 The Regulation of Cross-Border Data Flows in a Heterogeneous Global Data Privacy Environment

Today, there is no generally accepted legal framework for the regulation of cross-border data flows. As explained above, this can be attributed, among other things, to a lack of typology for cross-border data flows, an incomplete understanding of their relevance for society and the economy, and the multitude of (at times conflicting)

---

[74] OECD (2013a), p. 8.

[75] Ohm (2010); Rubinstein (2013).

[76] Burri (2021), p. 39. *See* also European Commission (2020b), pp. 11–12.

[77] *See* further Finck and Pallas (2020), pp. 13–20.

[78] Purtova (2018).

[79] *See* further *infra* Sect. 5.2.2.2.

policy interests involved in a digitally globalised world (*see supra* Sect. 2.3.2). The above analysis has further illustrated that there is an overlap between trade law and the regulation of cross-border data flows, in particular with regard to trade in (digital) services. However, it has been argued that current WTO law under the 1994 GATS, does not provide a sufficiently robust legal framework to govern the data-driven economy of trade in the twenty-first century (*see supra* Sect. 3.3.2). Although the GATS is applicable to digital trade, its dynamic interpretation against the backdrop of evolving technologies is not sufficient to provide clear guidelines for data and cross-border data flows.[80] While the approach to the governance of a *"cross-border"* flow of data under trade law is of relatively recent origin, the debate on the regulatory implications of the *"transborder"* flow of personal data is by no means particularly novel.[81] Advances in ICT and the resulting development of a global environment for data flows have put the regulation of cross-border transfers of personal data high on the political agenda since the second half of the twentieth century.[82] In response to the dawn of the information age, the 1970s saw the introduction of regulations for cross-border data flows predominantly within the context of data privacy law.[83] In fact, it is this element of data privacy regulation that is most often addressed in the context of digital trade governance.

Such elements of a transnational data governance by means of national data privacy legislation are deeply intertwined with the heterogeneity of data privacy standards at the global level. As has been outlined above, the divergence in data privacy standards is caused among other things by the significant influence of socio-cultural idiosyncrasies and the multifaceted character of personal data in a digital economy (*see supra* Sect. 4.2). While there is increasing convergence of data privacy principles at the highest level, at a more detailed level, and particularly in the implementation of these principles, there are significant differences between international, regional, and national data privacy instruments.[84] *Anupam Chander* and *Paul Schwartz* have illustrated this *"regulatory thicket"* of data privacy rules using the example of standards for consent as a basis for lawful processing of data, noting that there is no single approach that meets all global privacy rules for consent.[85] Against this backdrop, the regulation of data flows is generally not perceived to constitute a core substantive element of a data privacy framework, but rather serves as a conflict-of-laws rule between different legal regimes.[86] In fact, the regulation of

---

[80] Therefore, trade agreements increasingly take on the task of regulating data and data flows, *see supra* Sect. 3.4.2.

[81] Aaronson (2015), pp. 679–685.

[82] Drake (2016). *See* with regard to a changing environment for international data flows *supra* Sect. 2.3.2.1.

[83] Drake (2016), p. 5; Svantesson (2011), pp. 180–181.

[84] Gunasekara (2007), p. 153; OECD (2015b), p. 15. *See* for a discussion of the basic principles of data privacy law, Bygrave (2014), pp. 145–167. *See* further with regard to possibilities for interoperability of data privacy data transfer regimes *infra* Sect. 6.3.

[85] *See* Chander and Schwartz (2023), pp. 76–80.

[86] Cf. Kuner (2013), p. 63, pp. 133–138; Weber (2013), p. 119.

cross-border flows of personal data has been instrumental in preventing the outsourcing of data processing operations to jurisdictions with more lax data privacy rules.[87] In this context, *Christopher Kuner* has traced in detail the beginnings of the regulations of *"transborder"* data flows through different data privacy frameworks.[88] Four main reasons are generally identified to justify a restriction on cross-border data flows under data privacy law: (1) preventing circumvention of national data privacy laws; (2) protecting against data processing risks in other countries; (3) difficulties in enforcing data protection and privacy rights abroad; and (4) enhancing consumer and individual confidence.[89] In addition, there is a fifth policy concern identified in the academic literature, which is the preservation of a country's ability to access the personal data of its citizens.[90] Against this background, and in view of the focus of this chapter, which is to examine the nexus between digital trade and data privacy, the following considers in more detail the regulation of cross-border flows of personal data under a number of data privacy laws. Consequently, some of the most relevant data privacy frameworks both at the international and national level will be analysed with regard to their impact on cross-border flows of personal data.[91] From this outline, regulatory patterns will be derived which are relevant for the analysis of general approaches to data flow regulations under data privacy law.

4.3.1 *International Instruments of Data Privacy*

Against the backdrop of regulatory fragmentation of transnational data privacy resulting in domestic barriers to the cross-border flow of personal data, international initiatives have aimed to harmonize a globally diverse set of rules. That said, there is considerable heterogeneity in data privacy frameworks at the international level as well in relation to a number of factors such as their nature as binding regulatory instruments and their ability to yield a direct effect on individuals.[92] This section introduces some of the key data privacy instruments on the international level

---

[87] Hon (2017), pp. 24–25; Svantesson (2011), p. 180.
[88] *See* for example Kuner (2011, 2013, 2015).
[89] Cf. in detail Kuner (2013), pp. 107–120. *See* also Naef (2023), pp. 129–135.
[90] Hon (2017), p. 26.
[91] The following sections outline key international frameworks and selected national regulations. The section does not address private sector and technological approaches or regulations related to security or law enforcement, *see* for example Kuner (2013), pp. 81–99.
[92] Kuner (2013), pp. 25–26. In this respect, a number of international instruments are intended to serve as the basis for national legislation. *See* for example with regard to the Convention 108 drafted by the Council of Europe *infra* Sect. 4.3.1.2.

4.3 The Regulation of Cross-Border Data Flows in a Heterogeneous Global... 173

highlighting the respective rules they provide for the cross-border transfer of personal data.[93]

4.3.1.1 United Nations

The UN's efforts to address the issue of data regulation are rooted in a human rights perspective. Both the 1948 UDHR and the 1966 ICCPR recognize the ability to "*seek, receive and impart information and ideas*"—"*regardless of frontiers*"—as essential to freedom of expression.[94] Further, the right to privacy as a human right is recognised in Article 12 UDHR and Article 17 of the ICCPR. In response to the rise of automated data processing on a global level, the UN tackled the issue of data flow regulation and adopted resolution 45/95 on 14 December 1990, which provides for Guidelines for the Regulation of Computerised Personal Data Files.[95] However, the guidelines only provide for rather loose stipulations with regard to cross-border data flows.[96] Reference is made to comparable standards of protection that are intended to facilitate the free circulation of information relating to personal data.[97] Point 9 of the Guidelines on transborder flows provides in this respect: "*When the legislation of two or more countries concerned by a transborder data flow offers comparable safeguards for the protection of privacy, information should be able to circulate as freely as inside each of the territories concerned. If there are no reciprocal safeguards, limitations on such circulation may not be imposed unduly and only in so far as the protection of privacy demands.*". In addition to the unspecified requirements for comparability of protective measures, the non-binding nature of the guidelines in particular is an impediment to their effective implementation.

4.3.1.2 Council of Europe Convention 108 and Additional Protocols

The aim of the Council of Europe (CoE), founded in London in 1949, is to achieve a greater unity between its members through "*common action in economic, social, cultural, scientific, legal and administrative matters and in the maintenance and further realisation of human rights and fundamental freedoms*".[98] Within the scope of its central competence for human rights protection, the CoE opened for signature

---

[93] Technically, international instruments encompass data privacy legislation within the European Union consisting of 27 member states. However, the EU is considered here as a single jurisdiction; a discussion of EU data privacy legislation and its impact on cross-border flows of personal data is therefore provided *infra* Sect. 4.3.2.1.
[94] Cf. Article 19 UDHR and Article 19 Sec. 2 ICCPR. *See* with further references Kuner (2013), p. 32.
[95] UN (1990).
[96] Bygrave (2014), p. 53.
[97] Weber (2013), p. 119.
[98] Council of Europe (1949), Chapter I, Article 1, a, b.

the "*Convention for the Protection of Human Rights and Fundamental Freedoms*" in 1950, which provides for a binding catalogue of human rights, the compliance with which is adjudicated by the European Court of Human Rights in Strasbourg (ECtHR). In this context, Article 8 of the Convention addresses the "*Right to respect for private and family life*". As a result of two resolutions in the early 1970s on the protection of personal data in the public and private spheres with regard to automated data processing and technological change, the Committee of Ministers commissioned a panel of experts in 1976 to draft a treaty, which was opened for signature in January 1981 under the title "*Convention for the Protection of Individuals with Regard to Automatic Processing of Personal Data*".[99] Article 1 of this Convention 108 provided for a legal definition of data protection while emphasising fundamental rights protection as the primary goal: "*The purpose of this Convention is to secure in the territory of each Party for every individual, whatever his nationality or residence, respect for his rights and fundamental freedoms, and in particular his right to privacy, with regard to automatic processing of personal data relating to him ("data protection")*".[100] The CoE is committed to the broad impact of Convention 108 beyond European states, as its signature is not limited to its members, creating a common platform.[101] In this sense, Convention 108 is not self-executing and thus not directly applicable to individuals, but obliges signatory states to implement the protective safeguards it contains in their respective national laws.[102] However, Convention 108 is the first binding international instrument designed to protect individuals from abuses that may arise from the collection and processing of personal data, while also regulating the cross-border flow of personal data.[103] Indeed, Article 12 of Convention 108 in its original version provided that parties to the Convention are banned from prohibiting the transfer of personal data among each other or from subjecting it to a special authorisation solely for the purpose of protecting privacy (Article 12 Sec. 2). While legislation of a party could provide for transfer restrictions for certain categories of personal data, it could not do so if "*equivalent*" protection existed in the recipient Party (Article 12 Sec. 3a).

---

[99] The Convention for the Protection of Individuals with regard to Automatic Processing of Personal Data, ETS 108, 28 January 1981 entered into force 1 December 1985.

[100] This version of Convention 108 explicitly refers to the territories of the contracting parties. For the later versions of Convention 108, which conceptually permit extraterritorial application, cf. de Hert and Czerniawski (2016), p. 232.

[101] Bygrave (2014), pp. 31–36. In 2013, Uruguay became the first non-European country to accede to the convention. Currently, 55 countries have ratified Convention 108.

[102] Cf. Council of Europe (1981), p. 8 para. 38. Para. 39 explains: "*The "measures within its domestic law" can take different forms, depending on the legal and constitutional system of the State concerned: apart from laws they may be regulations, administrative guidelines, etc. [...]*".

[103] However, *Christopher Kuner* points out that there is no direct judicial enforcement as the jurisdiction of the ECtHR does not extend to Convention 108. In this respect, the author references the possibility of an extensive interpretation of Article 8 ECHR, *see* Kuner (2013), p. 37.

4.3 The Regulation of Cross-Border Data Flows in a Heterogeneous Global...   175

In 2001 the CoE adopted an Additional Protocol regarding the aspects of supervisory authorities and transborder data flows.[104] Article 2 of the Additional Protocol specifically encompassed transfers of personal data to a recipient which is not subject to the jurisdiction of a party to the Convention. In such cases, personal data may be transferred only if the recipient state or organisation is able to ensure an *"adequate"* level of protection (Article 2 Sec. 1). Derogations are provided for in cases where domestic law allows transfers on the basis of the specific interests of the data subject, other legitimate prevailing interests, or contractual safeguards which are found to be adequate by the competent local authorities (Article 2 Sec. 2a and b). In light of efforts to achieve greater harmonisation of European data protection regimes, the requirements for cross-border transfers under the Additional Protocol are reminiscent of the requirements of the EU's DPD, which had entered into force a few years earlier.[105]

Considering *"new challenges to the protection of individuals with regard to the processing of personal data"* the CoE in 2010 initiated a process of modernisation which resulted in the adoption of a further protocol amending Convention 108.[106] This amendment to Convention 108 reorganised the original title on transborder flows of personal data and, in particular, integrated the provisions of Article 2 of the 2001 Additional Protocol. Accordingly, based on the underlying objective of protecting fundamental rights and freedoms with respect to the processing of personal data, the purpose of regulating cross-border data flows is to ensure that information originally processed in the territory of a Party remains protected by *"appropriate"* data protection principles.[107] The most relevant provisions in Article 14 of the *"Convention 108+"* regarding transborder flows of personal data reads:

> 1. A Party shall not, for the sole purpose of the protection of personal data, prohibit or subject to special authorisation the transfer of such data to a recipient who is subject to the jurisdiction of another Party to the Convention. Such a Party may, however, do so if there is a real and serious risk that the transfer to another Party, or from that other Party to a non-Party, would lead to circumventing the provisions of the Convention. A Party may also do so, if bound by harmonised rules of protection shared by States belonging to a regional international organisation.
>
> 2. When the recipient is subject to the jurisdiction of a State or international organisation which is not Party to this Convention, the transfer of personal data may only take place where an appropriate level of protection based on the provisions of this Convention is secured.
>
> 3. An appropriate level of protection can be secured by:
>
> a. the law of that State or international organisation, including the applicable international treaties or agreements; or

---

[104] Cf. Article 2 of the Additional Protocol to the Convention for the Protection of Individuals with regard to Automatic Processing of Personal Data regarding supervisory authorities and transborder data flows, ETS 181, 8 November 2001.

[105] Wagner (2018), p. 327.

[106] Cf. for details Council of Europe (2018). *See* also Kuner (2013), pp. 39–40.

[107] Council of Europe (2018), p. 4.

b. ad hoc or approved standardised safeguards provided by legally-binding and enforceable instruments adopted and implemented by the persons involved in the transfer and further processing.

4. Notwithstanding the provisions of the previous paragraphs, each Party may provide that the transfer of personal data may take place if:

a. the data subject has given explicit, specific and free consent, after being informed of risks arising in the absence of appropriate safeguards; or

b. the specific interests of the data subject require it in the particular case; or

c. prevailing legitimate interests, in particular important public interests, are provided for by law and such transfer constitutes a necessary and proportionate measure in a democratic society; or

d. it constitutes a necessary and proportionate measure in a democratic society for freedom of expression.

4.3.1.3 OECD Privacy Guidelines

Since 1961, the OECD has advised governments on developing policies that promote resilient, inclusive, and sustainable growth through evidence-based policy analysis, recommendations, and standards. The OECD has adopted Guidelines on the Protection of Privacy and Transborder Flows of Personal Data (OECD Privacy Guidelines) in 1980 in order to support the harmonisation of national privacy legislation and, while upholding human rights at the same time prevent interruptions in international flows of data.[108] Following an OECD expert group coining the term "*transborder data flows*" in 1974,[109] the 1980 Privacy Guidelines established a set of non-binding principles in order to standardize the transnational governance of such flows. The Guidelines were intended to establish a consensus on basic principles that could be incorporated into or serve as the basis for national legislation. In this context, the 1980 OECD Guidelines served as an influential model for regulating the cross-border flow of personal data worldwide.[110] In fact, the norms created in the context of the OECD have had considerable influence on other international frameworks such as the APEC Privacy Framework (*see infra* Sect. 4.3.1.4).[111] A review process initiated by the Seoul Declaration for the Future of the Internet Economy in 2008 led to the conclusion that the Guidelines needed to be updated.[112]

---

[108] OECD (2002).

[109] *See* with further references Drake (2016), p. 5.

[110] Bygrave (2014), p. 50; Solove and Schwartz (2018), p. 1098.

[111] APEC (2005), p. 5: "*The previous version of the Framework (2005) was modelled upon the OECD Guidelines (1980) which at that time represented the international consensus on what constitutes fair and trustworthy treatment of personal information. The updated Framework (2015) draws upon concepts introduced into the OECD Guidelines (2013) with due consideration for the different legal features and context of the APEC region.*"

[112] OECD (2013b), pp. 19–23.

4.3 The Regulation of Cross-Border Data Flows in a Heterogeneous Global...

Consequently, the OECD Guidelines were revised in 2013 due to *"significant changes"* in the environment of the implementation of traditional privacy principles.[113] In this context, the rules regarding restrictions on cross-border data flows were consolidated, taking into account that a number of OECD member states had already enacted mechanisms to protect personal data.[114] Both the 1980 as well as the 2013 version of the OECD Privacy Guidelines define transborder flows of personal data as *"movements of personal data across national borders"*.[115] The 2013 OECD Privacy Guidelines provide for a system of *"accountability"*, with Part IV para. 16 of the Guidelines emphasising that:

> A data controller remains accountable for personal data under its control without regard to the location of the data.

With a view to restricting the movement of personal data, Part IV para. 17 the OECD Guidelines provide for the following:

> A Member country should refrain from restricting transborder flows of personal data between itself and another country where
>
> (a) the other country substantially observes these Guidelines or
>
> (b) sufficient safeguards exist, including effective enforcement mechanisms and appropriate measures put in place by the data controller, to ensure a continuing level of protection consistent with these Guidelines.[116]

Moreover, Part IV para. 18 implements a proportionality approach to cross-border data flow regulation:

> Any restrictions to transborder flows of personal data should be proportionate to the risks presented, taking into account the sensitivity of the data, and the purpose and context of the processing.[117]

The original explanatory Memorandum to the 1980 Guidelines emphasizes that the level of data privacy in the destination country must not be identical, but rather foresee *"equivalent protection"* meaning *"substantially similar in effect"*, thus referring to the principles set forth in para. 7 et seq. of the Guidelines.[118] These provisions regarding the regulation of data flows, however, do not take precedence over the application of para. 6 of the OECD Privacy Guidelines, which provides that the *"Guidelines should be regarded as minimum standards which can be supplemented by additional measures for the protection of privacy and individual liberties, which*

---

[113] The Foreword to the 2013 OECD Privacy Guidelines governing the protection of privacy and transborder data flows of personal data lists a number of such changes, such as for example, the volume of personal data being collected, used and stored and the extent of threats to privacy, OECD (2013b), pp. 3–4.

[114] OECD (2013b), pp. 29–31. *See* further Bygrave (2014), pp. 48–49.

[115] *See* OECD (2002), p. 13, Part I, para. 1(c); OECD (2013b), p. 13, Part I, para. 1 e).

[116] OECD (2013b), p. 16, Part IV para. 17 [emphasis added by the author].

[117] OECD (2013b), p. 16, Part IV para. 18 [emphasis added by the author].

[118] OECD (2013b), p. 61; Wagner (2018), p. 329.

may impact transborder flows of personal data.". Nevertheless, it must be recognised that the OECD Privacy Guidelines' data flow regulation regime can be understood in terms of preventing the restrictive impact of divergent domestic data privacy regulation against a background of economic imperatives. This is underscored by the proportionality-based assessment of data flow restriction in Part IV para. 18 of the Guidelines, which implies a balancing of interests of data privacy and economic cooperation.

4.3.1.4 APEC Privacy Framework

In 2005, Members of the APEC adopted the APEC Privacy Framework, *"recognizing the importance of the development of effective privacy protections that avoid barriers to information flows, ensure continued trade, and economic growth in the APEC region"*.[119] Based on the OECD Guidelines, the APEC Privacy Framework is non-binding and designed to take into account the different social, cultural, economic and legal backgrounds of individual member economies, requiring flexibility in the implementation of its principles.[120] The framework has been updated in 2015.[121] With regard to the regulation of data flows, the APEC Privacy Framework, like the OECD Privacy Guidelines, relies on the principle of *"accountability"*. Principle 9 of the APEC Framework therefore states:

> A personal information controller should be accountable for complying with measures that give effect to the Principles stated above. When personal information is to be transferred to another person or organization, whether domestically or internationally, the personal information controller should obtain the consent of the individual or exercise due diligence and take reasonable steps to ensure that the recipient person or organization will protect the information consistently with these Principles.[122]

With regard to possible restrictions on data flows, the APEC Framework leaves considerable room for manoeuvre. While member economies *"should take all reasonable and appropriate steps to identify and remove unnecessary barriers to information flows and avoid the creation of any such barriers"*,[123] the framework opens up a wide range of possible exceptions as it *"is not intended to impede governmental activities authorized by law when taken to protect national security, public safety, national sovereignty or other public policy"*.[124] In addition to these

---

[119] APEC (2005), Foreword.
[120] APEC (2005), p. 7. *See* further on the APEC Framework Greenleaf (2009).
[121] APEC (2015).
[122] APEC (2015), Part III, Principle 9.
[123] APEC (2015), p. 23.
[124] APEC (2015), p. 9. Even the qualification that exceptions should be *"limited and proportional to meeting the objectives to which the exceptions relate"* cannot outweigh the broad and open nature of the exceptions. On the contrary, there are uncertainties as to what *"limited"* and *"proportional"* are in reference to.

substantial limitations, the implementation of the principles of the framework is intended to be very flexible including legislative, administrative, industry self-regulatory or a combination of these instruments.[125] Moreover, the APEC Privacy Framework has initiated the development of the 2011 APEC system of cross-border privacy rules (CBPR), which is a voluntary, accountability-based system.[126] The CBPR System implements the APEC Privacy Framework as it provides a privacy certification that stakeholders can join to facilitate privacy-respecting data flows among APEC economies.[127] Such data processing standards are set by private actors based on the principles of the APEC Privacy Framework and must be assessed as compliant with the minimum requirements of the CBPR system. The CBPR system comprises four elements (1) self-assessment; (2) compliance review; (3) recognition/acceptance; (4) dispute resolution and enforcement.[128] In this context, the CBPR System has been compared to the Binding Corporate Rules (BCRs) used under the European data protection framework[129] and to the EU-US Privacy Shield as they both provide instruments for self-assessment and compliance review.[130] Against this backdrop, the APEC Privacy Framework exhibits some structural weaknesses, particularly when compared to the OECD Guidelines.[131] However, the APEC Privacy Framework, often criticised for its rather low standard of protection, has in particular made an important contribution to the further development of the concept of accountability in an emergent field of transnational data privacy law.[132]

4.3.1.5 Madrid Resolution

In view of the heterogeneity of data privacy regulations on an international level, the International Conference of Data Protection and Privacy Commissioners addressed the task of establishing universal standards by adopting a resolution on *"International Standards on the Protection of Personal Data and Privacy"* in 2009 (Madrid Resolution).[133] The purpose of the Madrid Resolution is, among other things, *"the facilitation of the international flows of personal data needed in a globalized world."*

---

[125] APEC (2005), p. 31.

[126] Bygrave (2014), p. 78.

[127] Currently there are nine participating economies: the US, Mexico, Japan, Canada, Singapore, Republic of Korea, Australia, Chinese Taipei, Philippines.

[128] *See* further Solove and Schwartz (2018), p. 1204.

[129] Voskamp et al. (2013). *See* further Article 29 Data Protection Working Party (2014). *See* further *infra* Sect. 4.3.2.2.

[130] Wall (2017).

[131] Greenleaf (2009), pp. 29–33.

[132] Kuner (2013), p. 51.

[133] Kuner (2013), pp. 58–59.

(Article 1b)).¹³⁴ For this reason, the Madrid Resolution stipulates in Article 15 lit. 1 that:

> as a general rule, international transfers of personal data may be carried out when the State to which such data are transmitted affords, as a minimum, the level of protection provided for in this Document.

In cases in which this standard of protection for personal data does not exist in the territory to which data is exported, it is necessary to *"guarantee that recipient will afford such level of protection."* Article 15 lit. 2. In accordance with Article 15 lit. 2 of the Madrid Resolution, contractual clauses or, in the case of multinational companies, internal data privacy rules may be relied upon to ensure the level of protection at the recipient's end.

4.3.2 Regional & National Data Privacy Regulations

Given the absence of regulatory harmonisation on an international level, data privacy is typically governed by national regulations or private-sector instruments.¹³⁵ The differences between the various regulations resulting from the absence of regulatory coherence on a global scale ultimately prompt normative mechanisms to prevent the circumvention of a given level of protection. Therefore, from early on, a number of data privacy laws have established *"data export controls"* to interfere with or outright prohibit the cross-border transfer of personal data from one jurisdiction to another.¹³⁶ While the first global data privacy law, adopted in 1970 in the German state of Hesse, did not yet contain such rules, mechanisms for data flow regulation were introduced shortly thereafter in the laws of other European countries such as France (1978), Finland (1987), Austria (1978) and Sweden (1973).¹³⁷ As one of the world's first national data privacy laws, Article 11 of the Swedish Data Protection Act (Datalag), adopted in 1973, reflects the conceptualisation of such provisions: *"Personal data contained in personal registers may not be disclosed if there is reason to believe that the data will be used for automatic processing in breach of this Act. If there is reason to believe that personal data will be used for automatic processing abroad, the data may only be disclosed with the consent of the Swedish Data Protection Authority. Such consent may only be given if it can be assumed that the disclosure of the data will not result in an unlawful invasion of privacy. [...]".*¹³⁸ Christopher Kuner has analysed the state of regulation in relation to cross-border data flows of these early European laws. His research shows that

---

[134] Madrid Resolution (2009), Article 1, b).
[135] Bygrave (2014), pp. 99–116; Kuner (2013), p. 26.
[136] Hon (2017), pp. 28–29; UNCTAD (2016), p. 3.
[137] *See* with further references Kuner (2011), p. 14.
[138] Cf. Swedish Data Protection Act, Datalag (1973:289), 11 May 1973. *See* also originally Svantesson (2011), p. 180.

early data privacy laws in Europe ranged in its requirements for data transfers from explicit authorisation from a Data Protection Authority (DPA), to implementing the relevant provisions of Convention 108 in its initial drafting from 1981, to the consent of the individual or respectively a similar level of protection in the country to which the personal data is exported.[139] In fact, *Kuner* underscores that with regard to the regulation of data flows, *"even within the same geographic region and among laws that demonstrate a number of similarities, there were important differences in the approaches taken"*.[140] These differences related to parameters such as the enforcement, the administration of exceptions, but also the scope of the regulation in terms of whether only imports or also exports of personal data were covered.[141] Certainly, since the first national data privacy laws in Europe, there has been considerable regulatory harmonisation with regard to the regulation of data flows in the European single market (*see* further *infra* Sect. 4.3.2.2). Nevertheless, given the proliferation and diversification of data privacy policies outside of the EU, the different configurations and implementations of these rules have considerable relevance to the regulation of data flows. A comprehensive representation of the plethora of national data privacy laws and the analysis of the corresponding mechanisms of cross-border data flow regulation goes beyond the scope of this book.[142] Instead, against the backdrop of trade law and the emergence of digital trade in particular, this section will focus on the regulation of cross-border data flows under the data privacy regimes adopted by some of the major stakeholders in global trade, notably the EU, the US, and China. This particular perspective is pertinent in that the national approach to data privacy regulation will also inform the design of the respective digital trade templates, on the one hand, and elucidate the fundamentals of what is referred to here as a *"data privacy collision"*, on the other (*see* further *infra* Sect. 4.4).

4.3.2.1 United States of America

In the absence of comprehensive federal privacy legislation, the legal framework in the US is influenced by both a variety of statutes and case law with individual rules for the public and private sector that rely strongly on self-regulation.[143] Notably, there is no omnibus legislation for data privacy in the US, as the Federal Privacy Act of 1974 applies only to US citizen data processed by the federal government.[144]

---

[139] *See* with further references Kuner (2011), p. 14; Kuner (2013), p. 27.
[140] Kuner (2013), p. 27.
[141] Kuner (2013), p. 27.
[142] *See* for example Chander and Lê (2015); Kuner (2013), pp. 83–91.
[143] Schwartz (2013), p. 1974. *See* for a helpful overview of the sources of the current *"patchwork"* of privacy protection in the US as well as the debate regarding a federal privacy law in the US Fischer (2021).
[144] *See* further Schwartz (2009), pp. 922–931; Solove and Schwartz (2018), pp. 665–684.

Privacy practices of private organisations in particular are subject to a variety of ad hoc and sector-specific regulations, such as for financial information or health data, which are often enacted in response to serious privacy violations.[145] The resulting highly fragmented and even inconsistent body of data privacy law consists of a *"bewildering assortment of numerous federal and state laws that differ significantly from each other"*.[146] Current legislation is based on different concepts of data relating to an individual, such as Personally Identifiable Information (PII), for example, which in themselves often lack a clear typology.[147] While there is no explicit reference to (information) privacy in the US federal constitution, a number of states provide for a constitutional right to privacy. However, a number of federal states are driving the development of a US data privacy framework through the adoption of state-level data privacy laws. This is particularly the case for the California Consumer Privacy Act (CCPA), which is perceived to serve as a catalyst for US data privacy law.[148] Against this backdrop, a initiatives for a federal privacy statute have been gaining bipartisan support recently.[149] In a recent development, the American Privacy Rights Act (APRA), a bipartisan, bicameral bill on data privacy at federal level, was tabled in April 2024.[150] The draft legislation has been put forth by U.S. House Committee on Energy and Commerce Chair Cathy McMorris Rodgers and Sen. Maria Cantwell, chair of the Senate Committee on Commerce, Science and Transportation, which emphasises the crucial link between data privacy and digital trade.

Notably, in the US, data privacy does not enjoy the status of a fundamental right. In fact, the US legal system primarily adopts a harm-based approach to data privacy and—contrary to the EU—does not a assume a preventive but rather a reactive stance on privacy infringements.[151] In an exercise of *"regulatory parsimony"* the US privacy framework generally permits the collection and processing of personal data, unless there has been compelling circumstances that prompt the legislature to act in favour of the need for legal authorisation.[152] Information privacy is perceived as a matter of consumer interest and the objective of legal instruments in this regard is primarily to monitor and police market failures.[153] This is reflected in the fact that oversight of privacy legislation in the US is part of the responsibility of the Federal Trade Commission (FTC)—a federal agency originally not created to function as a

---

[145] Gunasekara (2007), p. 153; Humerick (2018), pp. 83–99.

[146] Solove and Schwartz (2019), p. 2.

[147] *See* with regard to PII Schwartz and Solove (2011), pp. 1828–1836.

[148] *See* further Chander et al. (2021).

[149] *See* with regard to the American Data Privacy and Protection Act (ADPPA) Edelman (2022).

[150] Bracy (2024).

[151] Humerick (2018), p. 83, pp. 88–99.

[152] Schwartz (2013), p. 1967.

[153] Schwartz and Pfeifer (2017), pp. 132–138.

privacy protection agency but to *"protect consumers and promote competition"*.[154] Moreover, it can be argued that data privacy considerations are often given less emphasis when competing with interests of national security and law enforcement, freedom of expression, or economic efficiency.[155] Finally, the US approach to data privacy is reflected in a fierce opposition to the stringent and fundamental rights based European data protection standards and stems from what was analysed to be a systemic difference in the role of privacy between *"dignity"* and *"liberty"*.[156]

Against this backdrop, it seems plausible that, given a fragmented data privacy system that relies largely on self-regulation, it is no objective of contemporary US data privacy laws to particularly scrutinize transfers of personal data abroad to foreign jurisdictions. Overall, there is little reason in the US regulatory tradition to determine whether the processing of personal data abroad would undermine the domestic level of data privacy protection, given the difficulty of establishing a definitive internal standard of protection in a given case. Consequently, with regard to the regulation of cross-border flows of personal data, US law generally does not provide for transfer restrictions.[157]

4.3.2.2 European Union

The European approach to *"data protection"* is characterised by a fundamental rights-based appreciation rooted in human dignity, individual privacy, and informational self-determination.[158] In this sense, the EU's data protection regime draws heavily on a European legal tradition under the CoE's regulatory instruments of the ECHR and Convention 108 with regard to both the right to privacy as well as the protection of individual rights and freedoms in relation to the processing of personal data (*see supra* Sect. 4.3.1). In this sense, the CoE has played a decisive role in the development of data protection as a fundamental right in Europe.[159] Data protection is considered a fundamental right *sui generis*, the respect for which is part of the European constitutional order under EU primary law.[160] Similar to Article 8 ECHR, Article 7 of the EU Charter stipulates that everyone has the right to respect for his or her private and family life, home and communications. Moreover, pursuant to Article 8 (*"Protection of personal data"*) of the EU Charter, everyone has a right

---

[154] *See* for the FTC's role with regard to data privacy, Hoofnagle (2016); Humerick (2018), pp. 84–93.
[155] Sedgewick (2017), p. 1522.
[156] Whitman (2004), pp. 1160–1164. *See* also Petkova (2019).
[157] Schwartz (2013), p. 1973. *Schwartz* further refers to a failed Congressional initiative aimed at introducing an export limit in the 1970s.
[158] Naef (2023), pp. 31–37; Schwartz and Pfeifer (2017), pp. 122–132.
[159] *See* Kuner (2013), p. 36.
[160] Kokott and Sobotta (2013), pp. 222–223. Cf. also Article 16 Sec.1 TFEU.

to the protection of his or her personal data.¹⁶¹ In contrast to the sectoral approach to data privacy law pursued in the US, the EU has adopted an omnibus approach, in which a single law regulates the processing of personal data in both private and public spheres.¹⁶² The 1995 DPD—a *"patchwork"* between the different national legislations of EU members—aimed to reduce barriers to trade within the European single market while establishing common rules for data protection and retaining a high level of protection for transfers abroad.¹⁶³ Indeed, the regulation of the transfer of personal data outbound of a harmonised European market for personal data was a central element of the regime, regulated in Article 25 et seq. DPD.¹⁶⁴ Based on the EU's competence under Article 16 TFEU, formalised by the Treaty of Lisbon, a reform of the DPD was part of the efforts to further harmonize European data protection law in the European Commission's strategy for a digital single market.¹⁶⁵ In the meantime, the case law of the Court of Justice of the European Union had also provided substantial impetus for an overhaul of the EU's secondary law on data protection. Indeed, ECJ rulings, for example in *Google-Spain*¹⁶⁶ and *Schrems I*,¹⁶⁷ provided important cornerstones for the reform, while circumstances such as the NSA scandal, revealed by Edward Snowden in 2013 provided political momentum.¹⁶⁸ The result of this reform is the GDPR, which aims to further unify, clarify and strengthen the European approach to data protection against the background of the digital transformation.¹⁶⁹ In fact, the GDPR is widely considered to constitute a *"gold standard"* of data protection regulation.¹⁷⁰ Article 5 Sec. 1 GDPR lays out clear principles relating to the processing of personal data such as with regard to lawfulness, fairness and transparency, purpose limitation, data minimisation, data accuracy, storage limitation, integrity and confidentiality. In addition, the GDPR features comprehensive legal safeguards such as, for example, the *"right to erasure (right to be forgotten)"* in Article 17 GDPR, the *"right to restriction of processing"*

---

[161] *See* on the relationship between the Charter, the Convention and the general principles developed by the case law of the ECJ in the field of privacy Kokott and Sobotta (2013). *See* also Naef (2023), pp. 19–31.

[162] Solove and Schwartz (2018), p. 1094.

[163] *See* Schwartz (2013), p. 1972 citing *Spiros Simitis*. The European Commission started to conduct studies on diverging levels of data protection between member states and the resulting trade barriers already in 1973, cf. with further references Kuner et al. (2020), Article 44, pp. 758–759.

[164] Gunasekara (2007), p. 164; Kuner et al. (2020), Article 44, pp. 775–777.

[165] Burri and Schär (2016), p. 480.

[166] ECJ, C-131/12, *Google Spain*, 13 May 2014, ECLI:EU:C:2014:317.

[167] ECJ, C-362/14, *Schrems I*, 6 October 2015, ECLI:EU:C:2015:650.

[168] Burri (2021), pp. 49–50; Burri and Schär (2016), pp. 480–488.

[169] *See* Burri and Schär (2016), p. 489. Cf. in detail European Commission (2010).

[170] Buttarelli (2016).

4.3 The Regulation of Cross-Border Data Flows in a Heterogeneous Global...

in Article 18 GDPR as well as *"the right to data portability"* in Article 20 GDPR, thus considerably strengthening individual rights.[171]

The fact that the EU accords data protection the status of a fundamental right has furthermore resulted in a particular stringent regulation of cross-border data flows in order to prevent circumvention of the GDPR's high level of data protection. The EU's approach to data protection promotes an outlook on the processing of personal data that is geared less to economic considerations and instead adopts a proactive stance on legal safeguards for individuals in relation to their personal data.[172] Recent ECJ case law in *Opinion 1/15*,[173] *Schrems I* and *Schrems II*[174] indicates that European data protection law contains, in an extraterritorial dimension, a right to continuous protection of personal data.[175] In this context, the provisions of the GDPR on cross-border transfers of personal data in Chapter V of the GDPR represent a systematic evolution of the EU's regime for regulating data flows, building largely on the corresponding provisions of Chapter IV of the DPD in that it adopts a system of unilateral *"border control"*.[176] Pursuant to Article 44 GDPR the cross-border flow of personal data is regulated under the GDPR in the form of a general ban of transfers with the possibility of a legal permission to transfer data according to requirements laid down in Article 45 et seq. GDPR. In this respect, the GDPR provides for a *"three-tiered system"* of legal bases for cross-border transfers, with the adequacy decision first, appropriate safeguards in the middle, and derogations at the end.[177]

At the heart of the European regulation on cross-border data transfers is the adequacy finding under Article 45 GDPR as the first tier, which certifies that a third country provides an *"adequate level of protection"*.[178] Since Article 45 Sec. 1 sentence 2 GDPR emphasises that in the cases of a positive evaluation of the third country's data protection framework a specific authorisation for a transfer of personal data is not needed, the adequacy finding which is taken by the Commission according to Article 45 Sec. 2 and 3 GDPR is indeed the best way to enable transfers of personal data under the EU's data protection law.[179] This unilateral assessment of third country law proves to be highly controversial in a trade context, especially given the economic relevance of the cross-border flow of personal data and with

---

[171] Burri (2021), pp. 49–50; Burri and Schär (2016), pp. 488–497; Schwartz (2013), pp. 1994–2001.
[172] Humerick (2018), pp. 99–108; Schwartz and Pfeifer (2017), pp. 129–132.
[173] ECJ, *Opinion 1/15*, 26 July 2017, ECLI:EU:C:2016:656.
[174] ECJ, C-311/18, *Schrems II*, 16 July 2020, ECLI:EU:C:2020:55.
[175] Naef (2023), pp. 55–64.
[176] Svantesson (2011), pp. 191–193. See further on the development of Article 44 et seq. GDPR Kuner et al. (2020), Article 44, pp. 756–761.
[177] *See* further Kuner et al. (2020), Article 45, pp. 774–775.
[178] According to Article 45 Sec. 1 first sentence GDPR: *"[a] transfer of personal data to a third country or an international organisation may take place where the Commission has decided that the third country, a territory or one or more specified sectors within that third country, or the international organisation in question ensures an adequate level of protection."*.
[179] Wagner (2018), pp. 320–323.

regard to an extraterritorial application of the GDPR's data protection standard (*see infra* Sect. 4.4.2.2.1). Indeed, the way in which the Commission assesses the adequacy of the level of protection, is addressed somewhat vaguely in Article 45 Sec. 2 (a)–(c) GDPR.[180] The determination of an adequate level of data protection in a third country has been subject of several rulings of the ECJ, notably *Schrems I* and *Schrems II*.[181] In the *Schrems I* case, in which the Commission's adequacy decision for the Safe Harbour agreement covering transatlantic data flows between the EU and the US was declared invalid, the ECJ ruled that in order to have a standard adequate under Article 25 DPD, a foreign jurisdiction has to "*ensure, by reason of its domestic law or its international commitments, a level of protection of fundamental rights and freedoms that is essentially equivalent to that guaranteed within the European Union by virtue of Directive 95/46 read in the light of the Charter*".[182] The Court has further emphasised that a foreign data privacy regime has not to be identical in terms of the level of protection but rather is needs to prove effective in practice.[183] These high requirements for a level of data protection were affirmed in the ECJ's *Schrems II* decision, which invalidated the Privacy Shield that had been introduced as a successor to Safe Harbour between the EU and the US.[184] Evidence of the stringent level of data protection in the EU is also provided by the relatively low number of adequacy decisions in recent years. In fact, an adequacy decision by the Commission has only been issued to a handful of jurisdictions. In fact, so far only Andorra, Argentina, Canada, Faroe Islands, Guernsey, Isle of Man, Israel, Japan, Jersey, New Zealand, Republic of Korea, Switzerland, the UK and Uruguay have been certified by the Commission. The adequacy decision for the US extends to commercial organisations participating in the EU-US Data Privacy Framework.

The second tier of the EU's system for cross-border flows of personal data concerns such cases where an adequacy decision is not in place. In this regard, Article 46 GDPR in conjunction with Article 47 GDPR provide for additional requirements that compensate for the lack of an adequate level of data protection in a third country thus rendering data flows permissible. Article 46 GDPR holds for the provision of "*appropriate safeguards*", the two most common of which are Standard Contractual Clauses (SCCs) (Article 46 Sec. 2 (c) GDPR) and Binding Corporate Rules (BCRs) (Article 46 Sec.2 (b) GDPR).[185] SCCs are model contract

---

[180] Wagner (2018), pp. 321–322.

[181] Chander and Schwartz (2023), pp. 71–73; Kuner et al. (2020), Article 45, pp. 779–782.

[182] ECJ, C-362/14, *Schrems I*, 6 October 2015, ECLI:EU:C:2015:650, para. 73.

[183] ECJ, C-362/14, *Schrems I*, 6 October 2015, ECLI:EU:C:2015:650, para. 74.

[184] ECJ, C-311/18, *Schrems II*, 16 July 2020, ECLI:EU:C:2020:55.

[185] Cf. recital 108 to the GDPR stating: "*Such appropriate safeguards may consist of making use of binding corporate rules, standard data protection clauses adopted by the Commission, standard data protection clauses adopted by a supervisory authority or contractual clauses authorised by a supervisory authority. Those safeguards should ensure compliance with data protection requirements and the rights of the data subjects appropriate to processing within the Union, including the availability of enforceable data subject rights and of effective legal remedies, including to obtain*

clauses that have been pre-approved by the European Commission and need to be integrated into contractual relations between the exporter and importer of personal data.[186] BCRs are policies of conduct that are typically applied in the context of multinational organisations transferring data within a corporate framework that crosses multiple jurisdictions.[187]

Finally, the third tier of the EU system for cross-border data flows foresees derogations for data transfers where there is neither an adequacy decision nor appropriate safeguards in place.[188] Article 49 Sec. 1 (a)–(g) GDPR lists requirements such as, for example, explicit consent to the proposed transfer, the necessity of the transfer for the performance of a contract or the implementation of pre-contractual measures as well as the necessity for important reasons of public interest that allow for an exemption of the ban on data transfers. However, as in general, these exceptions must be interpreted narrowly, so as not undermine the relevance of the first and second tier of the EU's system of cross-border data flow regulation.

4.3.2.3 People's Republic of China

The People's Republic of China's regulatory activity in the area of data governance has expanded considerably in recent years.[189] In China, the regulation of cross-border data flows is generally governed by an interplay of various procedural, substantive, and subsidiary norms.[190] A first milestone was achieved with the 2017 Cybersecurity Law (CSL).[191] Article 37 CSL holds that Critical Information Infrastructure Operators need to pass a security assessment by government agencies before transmitting personal data.[192] The interpretation of the relevant Article 37 CSL, however, which deals with outgoing data traffic of "*personal information*" and "*important data*", was rather unclear from the written text, as it is China's usual practice to publish practical details outside the relevant legislation.[193] With the enactment of two further regulations concerning data security and data privacy in the fall of 2021, crucial further building blocks for China's data governance regime

---

effective administrative or judicial redress and to claim compensation, in the Union or in a third country". *See* further Naef (2023), pp. 148–155.

[186] The Commission released the latest version of the SCCs under the GDPR on 4 June 2021, replacing the three sets of SCCs adopted under the DPD.

[187] Article 4 Sec. 20 GDPR defines BCRs as: "*personal data protection policies which are adhered to by a controller or processor established on the territory of a Member State for transfers or a set of transfers of personal data to a controller or processor in one or more third countries within a group of undertakings, or group of enterprises engaged in a joint economic activity.*".

[188] *See* further Kuner et al. (2020), Article 49, pp. 843–846.

[189] *See* generally Gao (2021).

[190] *See* for a helpful overview Davis Polk (2021).

[191] Casalini and López González (2019), p. 22.

[192] *See* Hufbauer and Zhiyao (2019), pp. 3–7.

[193] Sacks et al. (2021).

have been put in place. The Data Security Law (DSL) and the Personal Information Protection Law (PIPL) develop and specify the data localisation, data privacy and data security requirements of the CSL.[194] The DSL refers to *"core national"* and *"important"* data that notably relate to safeguarding *"national sovereignty, security, and development interests"* (cf. Article 1 DSL).[195] For *"outbound security management"* of *"important"* data, Article 31 DSL provides that the provisions of the CSL shall apply. The PIPL, in turn, contains a more elaborate regime for cross-border transfers of *"personal information"*. Article 38 PIPL specifies four alternative requirements for Personal Information Handlers which all involve the oversight of Chinese *"State Cybersecurity and Informatization Department"*. Accordingly, data handlers must either pass a security assessment organised by the department according to Article 40 PIPL; undergo personal information protection certification conducted by a specialised body according to provisions by the department; conclude a contract with the foreign receiving side in accordance with a standard contract formulated by the department, agreeing upon the rights and responsibilities of both sides; or fulfil other conditions provided in laws or administrative regulations or by the department.[196] Whichever alternative is selected, Article 38 PIPL clearly states that necessary measures must be taken to ensure that the activities of foreign recipients in handling personal data meet the standard of protection of personal information under the PIPL. Article 40 PIPL stipulates that Critical Information Infrastructure Operators as well as Personal Information Handlers handling personal information reaching quantities provided by the State cybersecurity and informatization department shall store personal information collected and produced within the borders of China domestically or must in principle pass a security assessment organised by the State cybersecurity and informatization department when they need to provide it abroad.[197] The practical application and configuration of data governance regulations that regulate the cross-border transfer of personal data, however, are complex and still evolving. In February 2023, the Cyberspace Administration of China (CAC) has issued the long-awaited final version of the Measures on the Standard Contract for Cross-Border Transfer of Personal Information followed by a release of guidelines for the filing of standard contracts in May 2023.[198] After businesses and industry stakeholders voiced criticism regarding the onerous regulatory conditions for cross-border data flows, the CAC released in March 2024 the final version of the *"Provisions on Promoting and Standardizing Cross-Border Data Flows"* which aim to clarify and alleviate some of the rigorous requirements.[199]

---

[194] Skadden, Arps, Slate, Meagher & Flom LLP (2021).

[195] While *"important"* data are not defined, *"core national"* data are defined in Article 21 of the DSL as data *"related to national security, the lifelines of the national economy, important aspects of people's livelihoods, major public interests, etc."*, see for a translation DigiChina (2021d).

[196] See for a translation DigiChina (2021c).

[197] See for a translation DigiChina (2021c).

[198] Li et al. (2023).

[199] Luo and Dan (2024).

4.3.3 Approaches to Cross-Border Data Flow Regulation

In this section, the patterns of data flow regulation identified by reviewing various data privacy frameworks will be organised and mapped. Consequently, this section presents some of the most salient approaches to regulating the cross-border flow of personal data under data privacy law, followed by an evaluation and an assessment of their mutual interaction. The exercise of developing a taxonomy of approaches to cross-border data flow regulation, however, inevitably encounters the conundrum of the heterogeneity of the various international and national data privacy frameworks. In general, with regard to the global landscape of data privacy law, there are precedents for a broad range of approaches to cross-border data flow regulation that seek to accommodate the underlying political, cultural, and historical preferences of a particular jurisdiction with regard to data privacy. Depending on their design and implementation, data privacy laws may affect cross-border flows of personal data very differently. Beside *de jure* obligations relating to the cross-border transfer of personal data, data privacy laws frequently feature a number of *de facto* implications, which have to be taken into account. Accordingly, there are a variety of angles from which to consider data flow regulation under privacy laws, which is conducive to the emergence of a number of different approaches to taxonomies.[200]

Certainly, a distinction can be made at the highest level between those data privacy regimes that permit the cross-border transfer of personal data without restrictions—either explicit or implicit (or due to their non-existence)—and those that stipulate specific conditions for the cross-border transfer of personal data including rules on data privacy that foresee a localisation of data within a given jurisdiction. In such a general context, features of data privacy law such as the recognition of data privacy as a human right or the default position of rules that are either favourable or unfavourable to the flow of personal data are discussed.[201] Furthermore, *Christopher Kuner* has introduced a taxonomy of data flow regulation which differentiates between data privacy regulations that asses the status of a third country's data privacy law (*"geographically-based approach"*) and those approaches that emphasize the accountability of the data-exporting organisation (*"organizationally-based approach"*).[202] A similar taxonomy has been used in scholarly literature differentiating between self-regulation, regimes of border control and those that rely on exporter liability.[203] In a more granular approach, *Francesca Casalini* and *Javier López González* have drawn up a useful indicative taxonomy of approaches to cross-border data flow regulation against the backdrop of data privacy

---

[200] *See* Casalini and López González (2019), pp. 16–24; Kuner (2013), pp. 61–79; Rotenberg (2020), pp. 94–97. *See* also for data localisation measures in particular *supra* Sect. 2.3.2.4.
[201] Kuner (2013), p. 61.
[202] Kuner (2013), pp. 64–76.
[203] Svantesson (2011), pp. 190–194.

laws.[204] The taxonomy distinguishes three general levels of restrictiveness to the movement of data: free flow, flow conditional on safeguards and flow conditional including on ad-hoc authorisation. The first category encompasses the absence of regulations and those regulations that permit the transfer of data freely under private sector accountability. Secondly, the taxonomy lists data privacy regulations that make the transfer subject to various conditional safeguards such as adequacy findings or contractual instruments such as BCRs as well as consent of the data subject. A final category encompasses a strict application of the adequacy principle as well as the ad hoc authorisation of transfers of personal data. The authors have illustrated the approaches along a continuum ranging from no-regulation to ad-hoc approval and emphasize that the respective distinction of approaches can be blurry and that the rules will furthermore impact economic activity with regard to their transparency, their efficiency as well as the non-discriminatory nature of their implementation.[205] In addition to the *"hard"* requirements of a given approach under a data privacy law, it is these *"soft"* criteria that determine whether and how an obstruction of economically relevant data flows materializes. Against the background of the analysis of the nexus of digital trade and data privacy, this text will adopt *Christopher Kuners'* taxonomy and integrate further approaches to cross-border data flow regulation that specifically relate to the perspective of trade in the digital economy.

4.3.3.1 Self-regulatory Approach

The self-regulatory approach to regulating the cross-border flow of personal data is tantamount to the absence of legal restrictions on the transfer of personal data abroad in the form of data privacy laws. Against this background, the applicable data privacy instruments (provided they exist) do not prescribe or impose any conditions that apply to the cross-border flow of personal data. Instead, the relevant jurisdiction relies on data exporters to independently ensure compliance with basic data privacy standards. The transferring organizations are entrusted with regulating their own behaviour with regard to the cross-border flow of personal data. Therefore, this approach is most consistent with the economic ideal of a *"free flow"* of personal data, as there are *de jure* no limitations on the cross-border transfer of data by regulatory authorities. As a result, this approach is particularly popular in economies with thriving digital industries, most notably the US, which adopts and promotes this self-regulatory approach to cross-border transfers of personal data (*see supra* Sect. 4.3.2.1). Nevertheless, self-regulation of cross-border transfers of personal data comes with the challenge of taking into account potentially divergent rules in the country of destination of the transfer. The fact that standards for data transfers voluntarily adopted through self-regulation must first be developed and then

---

[204] Casalini and López González (2019), p. 16.
[205] Casalini and López González (2019), p. 16.

enforced by a number of different organisations based on different legal systems is a serious hurdle to this approach.[206]

4.3.3.2 Accountability Approach ("Organizationally-Based")

The concept of accountability is recognised as a prominent approach in data privacy law.[207] The accountability (or *"organizationally-based"*) approach holds data controllers responsible to adhere to a particular set of privacy standards regardless of the location of the processing of personal data.[208] Rather than legislatively requiring a certain level of protection for personal data abroad and subjecting the cross-border flow of personal data to a prior assessment of such level, this approach requires private organisations to take measures to *"that align with external criteria found in law – generally accepted principles or industry best practices – and foster a level of data protection commensurate with the risks to individuals raised by loss or inappropriate use of data"*.[209] In the context of cross-border data flow regulation, this means that the original collector of the information remains accountable under the original standard, regardless of the circumstances that apply in the organisations or jurisdictions to which the data is made available.[210] This reliance on organisations to establish a certain level of protection allows for a more flexible approach to cross-border data transfers, effectively providing that cross-border data flows are not *per se* restricted under the accountability approach.[211] The fact that the responsibility for securing a given level of protection for personal data transmitted internationally is placed in the hands of private enterprises requires the installation of a number of safeguards and measures on the part of the organisations. Common accountability measures may include: Binding in-house privacy and information management programs, application of industry codes of conduct, third-party certifications or international standards, as well as the establishment of procedures and the appointment of a Data Protection Officer.[212] As has been illustrated above, the accountability approach has been incorporated into the APEC Privacy Framework,[213] the OECD Privacy Guidelines[214] as well as the Madrid Resolution.[215] Moreover,

---

[206] Weber (2013), p. 121. *See* further *infra* Sect. 4.3.3.5.
[207] *See* generally Alhadeff et al. (2012).
[208] Kuner (2013), p. 71; Weber (2013), p. 122.
[209] Centre for Information Policy Leadership (2009), p. 10.
[210] Crompton et al. (2009), p. 5.
[211] Kuner (2013), p. 72.
[212] *See* for a sample of measures Article 29 Data Protection Working Party (2010), p. 11; Centre for Information Policy Leadership (2018), pp. 4–10.
[213] *See supra* Sect. 4.3.1.4.
[214] *See* OECD (2013b), p. 16, Part IV, para. 16: *"A data controller remains accountable for personal data under its control without regard to the location of the data."*.
[215] Cf. Madrid Resolution (2009), Article 11: *"The responsible person shall: Take all the necessary measures to observe the principles and obligations set out in this Document and in the applicable national legislation, and have the necessary internal mechanisms in place for demonstrating such*

jurisdictions that follow the accountability approach are, for example, Canada, Australia or New Zealand.[216]

4.3.3.3 Adequacy Approach ("Geographically-Based")

Under the adequacy approach to regulating data flows, approval for the transfer of personal data abroad generally depends on whether the geographic destination of the data export ensures a certain level of data privacy. Data privacy laws that follow the adequacy approach typically consider the level of data privacy in the third country in a holistic manner in order to determine whether a transfer of personal data is permissible, which is why it is also referred to as the geographically based approach.[217] In this sense, this concept functions as a sort of *"border control"* for personal data.[218] Jurisdictions that take this approach to regulating data flows typically unilaterally set requirements for the level of data protection required by the receiving jurisdiction by benchmarking the foreign standards against their domestic system. In doing so, the terminology that is employed is often similar, as these systems generally require a *"similar"*, *"equivalent"*, *"appropriate"* or *"acceptable"* standard of data privacy in the country to which personal data is exported.[219] Nevertheless, the typical example of this approach is the determination of the level of protection of the third country through the concept of *"adequacy"*.[220] The conditions for the flow of personal data under the adequacy approach may be chosen and prioritised differently in each data privacy framework, which has been described as a *"splintering of adequacy"*.[221] Nevertheless, if the adequacy of the level of protection of personal data is established, transfers of personal data are generally permitted without further requirements. If no adequacy decision is issued or if it is declined, typically additional safeguards for the transfer of personal data must be complied with. Moreover, one-off derogations for a transfer may include for instance that the data subject has explicitly consented to the transfer in question or that the transfer is necessary for the performance of a contract between the individual and the exporter or, moreover, that the transfer is necessary for important reasons of public interest.[222] The most prominent example of this regulatory approach is the EU's

---

observance both to data subjects and to the supervisory authorities in the exercise of their powers, as established in section 23.".

[216] Rotenberg (2020), pp. 106–107.

[217] Kuner (2013), pp. 64–66; Weber (2013), p. 122.

[218] Kuner (2013), pp. 64–66; Svantesson (2011), p. 191.

[219] Weber (2013), p. 122.

[220] Kuner (2013), pp. 66–71.

[221] Chander and Schwartz (2023), pp. 71–76.

[222] UNCTAD (2016), p. 13. Examples of the regulation of the latter exceptions are provided by Article 49 GDPR, or Article 15 lit. 3 of the Madrid Resolution (2009).

4.3 The Regulation of Cross-Border Data Flows in a Heterogeneous Global...

GDPR but other jurisdictions have also adopted this approach in principle or in part such as Japan, Argentina or Switzerland.[223]

4.3.3.4 Data Localisation Approach

Data privacy considerations are among the most frequent reasons for governmental control over data flows and data localisation requirements.[224] Depending on the individual design and the practical implementation of a data privacy framework, data privacy rules may completely block the outbound transfer of personal data and thus entail measures of data localisation (*see* generally *supra* Sect. 2.3.2.4). A wide variety of localisation rules exist, which may apply generally to all data of national origin or more narrowly to specific types of data, for example.[225] To be sure, the most significant impact on international data flows results from data privacy laws that outright prohibit the transfer of personal data or prescribe the processing and storage of personal data to be performed only within the boundaries of the respective jurisdiction. For example, the 2014 Russian Law No. 242-FZ "*On Amendments to Certain Laws of the Russian Federation Clarifying the Procedure for Processing Personal Data in Information and Telecommunications Networks*" provides for a rather broad mandate for data localisation, since it requires personal data of Russian citizens to be processed in databases located in Russia.[226] However, data localisation measures provided for in data privacy laws may also target specific categories of personal data concerning health status, financial information, ethnicity, or the like. In these cases, the relevant data privacy framework will typically incorporate *de jure* requirements that provide for "*strict*" data localisation to ensure national control over such data.[227] For example, the Australian regulation under the "*My Health Records Act 2012*" in relation to the "*My Health Record*" system provides as a general rule that records must not be held or taken outside Australia and that information associated with records must not be processed or handled outside Australia.[228] A third example for data privacy related data localisation involves data privacy rules that rely on the "*adequacy*" of third country levels of protection in order for a transfer to be legal. In cases where the adequacy decision is not achieved, outbound data transfers of personal data are typically prohibited. Certainly, most of these frameworks will provide for the possibility of additional safeguards or derogations with regard to personal data transfers (*see* for example Sect. 4.3.2.2). And yet, even if the

---

[223] *See* with further examples Chander and Schwartz (2023), pp. 126–134, Appendix A; Rotenberg (2020), pp. 103–105.
[224] *See* with examples Chander and Lê (2015), pp. 718–721; Mishra (2019), p. 8.
[225] *See* also Casalini and López González (2019), p. 16.
[226] Poskauer (2015).
[227] *See* for a distinction between "*conditional*" and "*strict*" forms of data localization *supra* Sect. 2.3.2.4.
[228] Cf. Article 77 of the My Health Records Act 2012. No. 63, 2012.

barriers to data flows thus appear to be *de jure "conditional"*, as they may rely on additional safeguards or derogations the resulting compliance circumstances may exert sufficient economic pressure to transform a *de jure "conditional"* transfer restriction into a *de facto "strict"* data localisation measure. This is usually the case if a domestic data privacy regulation imposes such high requirements for the lawfulness of the cross-border flow of personal data that the transfer as such becomes economically non-viable. The particular standard for a level of *"adequate"* protection which influences the requirements for additional safeguards is therefore directly correlated to the scope of data flow restrictions. If the data privacy requirements relevant for outbound transfers of personal data is set at such a high threshold that companies cannot reasonably comply with it in a cost-effective manner, in practice, a similar scenario arises as with the localisation of data under binding regulation.[229] This is the case, for example, when there is no adequacy decision in place and conditional safeguards are unable to shield against a third country's surveillance, as has been analysed, for example, with respect to the EU's GDPR.[230] In this context, data localisation, in fact, may be a *"practical response"* to the implementation of the GDPR, particularly in response to the ECJ's findings in *Schrems II*.[231]

Similarly, rules on ad hoc authorisations for transfers that involve the oversight of a particular authority can become *de facto "strict"* data localisation measures as a result of the respective implementation practice by national authorities or have a chilling effect on data exporters activities in general. Pursuant to Article 36 of the Chinese PIPL, for example, personal information handled by state organs shall be stored within the mainland territory of the People's Republic of China and *"truly necessary"* transfers are subject to a security assessment. Moreover, so-called Critical Information Infrastructure Operators and Personal Information Handlers that handle certain quantities provided by the State cybersecurity and informatisation department must store personal information collected and produced within the borders of China domestically (cf. Article 40 PIPL). Transfers requests must pass a security assessment organised by the State Cybersecurity and Informatisation Department.

4.3.3.5 Evaluation

The above approaches will now be weighed and put in relation to each other. First of all, it should be noted that the approach of self-regulation of data privacy practices proves to be the one that entails the least degree of intervention in cross-border data flows. However, the *"free flow"* of data comes at the price of a rather precarious level of protection for individuals with respect to the cross-border processing of their personal data. A common argument suggests that this flexible approach meets the

---

[229] Casalini and López González (2019), p. 22; Svantesson (2020), p. 25.

[230] *See* further Naef (2023), pp. 77–100.

[231] Chander (2020), pp. 777–778; Christakis (2020).

4.3 The Regulation of Cross-Border Data Flows in a Heterogeneous Global...

needs of businesses and ensures diligent compliance through the associated reputational risk to companies.[232] However, the self-regulatory approach has been heavily criticised as being based on a more or less unchecked sense of responsibility on the part of organisations, generally weak enforcement, and a lack of democratic basis.[233] The numerous critics therefore denounce the ineffective compliance and enforcement mechanisms as well as the lack of transparency.[234] In particular, scholarly literature that considers data privacy to be deeply intertwined with fundamental rights protection has criticised that governments should not evade their international obligations by attempting to outsource the protection of human rights by means of self-regulation.[235]

Against this backdrop, both the accountability approach and the adequacy approach to regulatory requirements affecting cross-border transfers are more stringent. Yet, there are clear differences between the two approaches. The adequacy approach focuses primarily on the assertion of a specific level of data privacy regulation, as it evaluates the data privacy standard of the third-party jurisdiction against the domestic standards. In turn, as *Christopher Kuner* points out, "*the accountability approach is less a standard of data protection than a process for structuring compliance and responsibility*".[236] Arguably, there are inherent upsides to holding data exporters accountable once a data transfer has occurred. However, accountability of private organisations alone will typically not be sufficient to compensate for an individuals' loss of control over their personal data.[237] This is notably the case if transfers occur even though mandatory legal provisions on the storage or processing of personal data in a third country conflict with the data privacy rights of the individual at home. Critics therefore consider proposals to prioritize accountability over adequacy to be "*misguided*" and emphasize that accountability can be an "*additional layer of protection*", rather than a substitute.[238] Thus, in weighing the two approaches, there is in essence a rather rigid and ex ante enforceable adequacy approach and the supposedly more flexible accountability approach, which relies primarily on ex post enforcement. The success of both models, however, depends on the concrete design of the framework and resources of the enforcement mechanism.[239] The adequacy approach is contingent on the determination, selection and individual adaption of the criteria for establishing an adequacy decision.[240] The governance of the "*border control*" approach requires a delicate balance between the protection of individuals' personal data and the necessity of

---

[232] Svantesson (2011), pp. 190–191; Weber (2013), p. 121.
[233] Weber (2013), pp. 120–121.
[234] *See* with further references Svantesson (2011), p. 190.
[235] Svantesson (2011), p. 191.
[236] Kuner (2013), p. 76.
[237] *See* further Svantesson (2011), p. 193.
[238] Svantesson (2011), p. 194.
[239] Crompton et al. (2009), p. 5.
[240] *See* for example Wagner (2018); Weber (2013), pp. 123–127.

cross-border data transfers in a digitally globalised economy and society.[241] Naturally, the unilateral definition of a standard, necessary to facilitate the unimpeded transfer of data in a digital economy, provides footholds for political considerations and strategic planning.[242]

In view of the above, it could be assumed that data localisation measures are the best possible way to protect individuals with regard to their personal data, since the domestic level of data protection cannot be undermined in these cases by transferring the data to other jurisdictions. However, it is debatable whether data localisation measures actually provide more privacy and security. In fact, a common argument against data localisation is that data can be stored much more securely in a modern cloud solution than in a single location, which could provide a "*jackpot scenario*" for hackers.[243] In general, the effectiveness of data localisation as a form of data regulation is reasonably doubtful, as it contradicts the decentralised architecture of the Internet and creates considerable economic inefficiencies.[244] The Internet allows for systems to be accessed remotely, making logical security just as important as physical security, perhaps even more so.[245]

Finally, it is important to emphasize that the adequacy, accountability, self-regulation or data localisation approaches are not mutually exclusive. In fact, in reality they do rarely exist in their pure form.[246] Rather, they form part of the international data privacy landscape in various combinations and emphases. For instance, elements of accountability have also been incorporated into the EU data protection framework under the GDPR, which is widely regarded as the most influential example of the adequacy approach. Two widely recognised accountability instruments within the GDPR are, in particular, Standard Contractual Clauses (SCCs) and Binding Corporate Rules (BCRs) pursuant to Article 46 Sec. 2 GDPR.[247] Moreover, the OECD Privacy Guidelines, which rely largely on the concept of adequacy, also explicitly advise member countries to encourage and support self-regulation in the form of codes of conduct or other means.[248] Also, it is not unheard of, for data localisation measures relating to certain types of data to be integrated into a data privacy framework that is otherwise based on adequacy or accountability. The difficulties of delineation between the approaches become particularly apparent in cases in which the practical implementation of data privacy rules produces the effect of *de facto* data localisation. Given the many challenges of an increasingly complex data environment, it is reasonable to assume that the

---

[241] Svantesson (2011), p. 191.

[242] *See infra* Sect. 4.4.2.2.1 with regard to the conflation of political and economic considerations under the EU's GDPR against the backdrop of the role of data protection in the digital economy.

[243] With further references Chander and Lê (2015), pp. 718–721.

[244] Mishra (2019), pp. 4–7.

[245] Hon (2017), p. 316.

[246] Weber (2013), pp. 122–123.

[247] *See supra* Sect. 4.3.2.2. *See* also Kuner (2013), p. 72.

[248] OECD (2013b), p. 17, Part V, para. 19 d).

approaches will continue to converge as complementary elements under the policy rationale of data privacy.[249]

4.4 The Data Privacy Collision in Digital Trade

The regulatory dissonance in data privacy law on a global level resulting from the lack of an international framework is reflected in the governance of digital trade. It has been demonstrated that international efforts to establish universal data privacy rules have not been effective to date and that, as a result, unilateral domestic data privacy regimes regulate the transfer of personal data in a wide variety of ways, from self-regulation through to data localisation (*see supra* Sects. 4.3.2 and 4.3.3) Against this backdrop, this section takes a closer look at the underlying trade policy discourse and the normative rationales implicated in the nexus of digital trade and data privacy. The multifaceted nature of personal data binds data privacy laws to a variety of interests in a digitalised economy and society, both economic and non-economic in nature (*see supra* Sect. 4.2.2). To complicate matters further, the goals and purposes of data privacy law are inherently ambiguous and often not clearly defined or delineated.[250] While many data privacy instruments relate to privacy protection, data privacy laws provide a foothold for a wide range of policy considerations, notably due to their extensive implications for data processing and cross-border data flows.[251] This ambiguity of the normative rationales associated with data privacy may be explained by the lack of a clear definition of privacy, which leaves room for interpretation and individual emphasis (*see supra* Sect. 4.2.1). Most notably, both economic considerations and the protection of human rights have always been and continue to be inextricably intertwined with respect to data privacy, and the underlying normative trade-off determines the design and implementation of data privacy laws at the global level.[252] This interweaving of economic and fundamental rights dimensions in data privacy has been referred to as a "*Gordian Knot*".[253] Consequently, the specific design and implementation of a data privacy regime (including associated elements of transnational data regulation) is based on a delicate balancing

---

[249] *See* also Kuner (2013), p. 76.
[250] *See* with further references regarding the "*obscurity*" of aims of data privacy law Bygrave (2014), pp. 117–118.
[251] Bygrave (2014), pp. 118–125.
[252] Chander and Schwartz (2023), pp. 105–113; Yakovleva (2020b), pp. 500–507. This applies in particular to the EU data protection framework, in the design of which the economic rationale of the internal market clearly figured prominently, but in which the preservation of data protection as a fundamental right, especially vis-à-vis third countries, also plays an important role, *see supra* Sect. 4.3.2.2. Similarly, the OECD privacy guidelines aim to protect fundamental rights while minimizing the economic distortions caused by different data privacy regimes, *see supra* Sect. 3.2.1.1.2.
[253] With further references to the work of Professors *Radim Polčák* and *Dan Jerker B. Svantesson*, *see* Yakovleva (2020b), p. 503.

of a range of considerations, including notably both human rights protection and economic welfare, as well as notions of regulatory sovereignty and national security in a digital world. With regard to the nexus of digital trade and data privacy, however, the economic rationale of international trade provides a relatively well-defined benchmark against which the individual design of national data privacy regulations can be measured. The trade policy discourse provides an international venue for weighing, evaluating, and elaborating the normative underpinnings of data privacy in a digital economy. In this context, however, scholarly literature identifies a normative divide between the two fields, particularly with respect to the ideal of economic liberalisation and the safeguarding of the national right to regulate, notably with respect to the protection of fundamental rights involved in data privacy.[254]

This section examines the ensuing normative discourse on data privacy in the context of digital trade. It goes on to analyse what is referred to here as the "*data privacy collision*" of data privacy frameworks in cross-border trade. To this end, an analysis of case studies will provide further insight in the individual role that data privacy can assume in digital trade governance.

4.4.1 The Normative Discourse on Data Privacy in a Trade Context

The trade policy discourse on the nexus between data privacy and digital trade is often perceived in terms of a dichotomy between economic (trade) and non-economic (privacy) arguments.[255] It has been emphasised before, that digital trade enabled and facilitated by cross-border data flows is facing novel barriers, many of which are rooted in domestic data regulations (*see supra* Sect. 2.3.1.3). There is in fact quite substantial potential for digital trade to be seriously impeded by regulatory obstacles rooted in national data privacy laws. These and similar reservations about the proliferation of data privacy laws on a global scale, however, largely reflect an economic discourse on data privacy.[256] This contrasts with the perception that data privacy, as an expression of human dignity, should not be subjugated to the commercial pursuit of wealth maximisation.[257] This section further explores the underlying normative rationales involved in the data privacy collision in that it identifies a number of aspects involved in a trade-off that is forming in relation to privacy in a digital trade context.

---

[254] *See* further Burri (2021), pp. 35–43; Chander and Schwartz (2023), pp. 105–113; Yakovleva (2020a); Yakovleva (2020b), pp. 499–515.

[255] *See* Chander and Schwartz (2023), pp. 105–113.

[256] *See* further Yakovleva (2020b), pp. 464–499.

[257] *See* further regarding this "*moral value approach*" Yakovleva (2020b), pp. 500–506.

4.4.1.1 Economic Discourse

In an economic discourse, two main lines of argument are regularly raised in relation to the nexus of digital trade and data privacy. On the one hand, data privacy laws are perceived as a source of economic inefficiencies, particularly because they impose substantial compliance costs, up to and including imposing data localisation requirements that restrict the cross-border flow of personal data and potentially render trade non-viable. With respect to cross-border trade in particular, data privacy is often met with the accusation that it involves a form of data protectionism. On the other hand, it is argued that there are economic benefits to be gained from robust data privacy standards in terms of the trust that can be generated for the digital environment. In this sense, data privacy may contribute significantly to the growth of cross-border online transactions.

4.4.1.1.1 Data Privacy as a Protectionist Compliance Burden

A common argument levelled against data privacy regulations in economic theory relates to economic inefficiencies, as data privacy rules prevent "*complete information*" and thus cut off potentially relevant information from economic actors.[258] Moreover, in a trade context, the inconsistencies between data privacy laws on a global scale, in particular, can result in significant compliance costs for companies that operate in multiple jurisdictions. Given that trade in the digital economy, driven by cross-border data flows and the Internet, is inherently global, it is apparent that a multiplicity of data privacy rules individually regulating the usage, collection, storage, and cross-border transfer of personal data has the potential to raise barriers to digital trade. As has already been emphasised, socio-cultural differences in the design and implementation of data privacy laws have resulted in a heterogeneous global regulatory environment (*see supra* Sect. 4.3). In the absence of harmonised data privacy rules, organisations must adapt to a wide range of different regulations, standards, and policies, creating a significant bureaucratic burden both time-consuming and financially burdensome.[259] UNCTAD, for example, identifies three compliance burdens: Registration requirements, requirements to appoint Data Protection Officers (DPO) as well as the requirement to establish local offices or data centres.[260] All of these measures are fraught with considerable costs, which may render digital trade economically unviable. For local activities in a third country, data privacy requirements concerning the security of processing of personal data, conceptualisation of retention and deletion including the corresponding interaction

---

[258] *See* for a brief introduction to the economic theory of privacy put forth by the Chicago School Acquisti (2010), pp. 5–10.
[259] Manyika et al. (2016), pp. 101–102.
[260] UNCTAD (2016), p. 20.

with data subjects as well as with the local Data Protection Authorities (DPA) have to be taken into account. Against the background of considerable pecuniary risks under local rules, this requires not only legal counselling and expertise but also the deployment of trained personnel and adequate funding. Regulatory uncertainty associated with new, ambiguous or overly complex legislations can cause delays in developing or launching products and stalling of the commercial decision-making process against the background of a highly dynamic digital trade environment, thus "*dampening*" innovation.[261] At the same time, the complexity of data privacy laws on a global scale favours a "*managerialization*" of compliance and thus favours larger companies with established customer base.[262] One example in this context is certainly the compliance with requirements for the authorisation of cross-border data flows under different privacy laws. In the absence of a global authorisation for the cross-border flow of data, contractual safeguards for data transfers must be certified and managed on a case-by-case basis, such as with regard to the APEC system for cross-border data protection rules (CBPR)[263] or the Binding Corporate Rules (BCR) and Standard Contractual Clauses (SCC) under the EU's GDPR.[264] Moreover, at times, data privacy regulations may force a complete relocation of economic activity, as data privacy frameworks may provide for "*strict*" data localisation either *de jure* or *de facto* (*see supra* Sect. 4.3.3.4). Adapting economic activity to data localisation is not only associated with higher costs and greater inefficiencies in digital trade transactions, but also with significant compliance expenses for businesses.[265] In particular, local data centres and digital infrastructures need to be established and maintained, while regulatory developments need to be closely monitored, as national data localisation regulations often carry heavy fines. A further compliance issue stems from the difficulty of identifying the data privacy law applicable to the processing of personal data in a given case. In this context, it is not solely a matter of where data processing operations are carried out by companies geographically. In an effort to ensure effective operation in a digitally globalised environment, some data privacy rules are likely to have extraterritorial effect, either explicitly or in their concrete implementation, so that they may also have to be complied with by data processors located in third countries.[266]

An economic approach, particularly relating to cross-border trade in data privacy, considers data privacy regulations as a pretext for pursuing a digital industrial policy.[267] The allegation is that in a complex political environment, there is a serious

---

[261] Swire and Litan (2010), pp. 77–78.

[262] Chander and Schwartz (2023), pp. 81–82.

[263] *See* further *supra* Sect. 4.3.1.4.

[264] *See* further *supra* Sect. 4.3.2.2.

[265] Mishra (2019), p. 5.

[266] This is the case for example with the European data protection regime under the GDPR, *see* Fabbrini and Celeste (2021); Kuner (2015). *See* further *infra* Sect. 4.4.2.2.1.

[267] Yakovleva (2020b), pp. 473–481. *See* generally on digital industrial policies through data restrictions, Mitchell and Mishra (2019), pp. 396–397.

hazard that the data privacy rationale will be used as a fig leaf for discriminatory practices. This criticism levelled at domestic data privacy rules is part of an effort to gear the ambiguous notion of *"protectionism"* towards trade in the digital economy. In fact, with regard to the digitalisation of trade, the notion of protectionism has been transposed into the environment of a data-driven economy and has been actively used to shape the underlying policy debate, notably around the issue of cross-border data flows.[268] To be sure, scholars of international data privacy law do not perceive a general association between economically protectionist measures and national data privacy laws.[269] Nevertheless, this policy framing is particularly in line with the US's strategy towards the digital economy dating back to the Clinton administration;[270] it is addressed primarily towards the EU's data protection regime.[271] Generally, though, topical discussions in the trade community revolve around barriers to digital trade and particularly hindrances towards the *"free flow"* of data by means of data localisation (*see* generally *supra* Sect. 2.3.2.4).[272] While there is no uniform definition of digital protectionism among the different stakeholders in a multipolar digital economy, a consensus has emerged that it is threatening to the economic potential of digital trade.[273] In fact, much of the international trade community now embraces the notions of *"digital protectionism"*, *"data protectionism"* or *"data nationalism"*, yet, not only does the definition seem to vary significantly in substance, but the concept itself appears to be in constant evolution.[274]

4.4.1.1.2 Data Privacy as an Enabling Factor for Trade

When considering the relationship between digital trade and data privacy, it is important to be aware that a robust framework of data privacy goes hand in hand with consumer confidence and trust in the networked economy.[275] Studies have consistently shown that data privacy and data security are key concerns in deter-

---

[268] *See* for a comprehensive review of the concept of protectionism with regard to digital trade Aaronson (2019), pp. 545–550; Yakovleva (2020b), pp. 429–463.

[269] Bygrave (2014), pp. 123–126. *See* further with regard to the interplay with sovereignty considerations *infra* Sect. 4.4.1.2.2.

[270] *See* Aaronson (2015), p. 683; Yakovleva (2020b), pp. 475–476. However, the US approach towards digital protectionism seems to evolve, *see* Aaronson (2017), p. 232. *See* also *supra* Sect. 4.3.2.1.

[271] *See* further Naef (2023), pp. 133–135.

[272] Cory and Dascoli (2021); Mitchell and Mishra (2019), pp. 111–112. *See* also with regard to the discussions in the WTO Work Programme on Electronic Commerce *supra* Sect. 3.3.1.1.

[273] van der Marel et al. (2014), p. 13.

[274] Aaronson (2019), pp. 548–549. *See* in particular the extensive research of *Svetlana Yakovleva* on this matter who questions among other things, whether the digital protectionism label is a trigger to redefine barriers to trade in the digital era, Yakovleva (2020b), pp. 473–481; pp. 496–499.

[275] OECD (2015a), pp. 209–234; UNCTAD (2016), pp. 3–4.

mining whether consumers order online or not.[276] Confidence in the treatment of personal information has long been recognised as a key value for a networked society.[277] Therefore, data privacy is a crucial aspect of establishing trust in the digital environment which, in turn, is a building block to foster innovation and promote growing prosperity in a digital economy.[278] As this trust depends on the legal protection of individuals against abuse of their rights in relation to their personal data, data privacy becomes an important business concern. In fact, a widely used rationale for enacting data privacy regulation involves considerations of consumer protection (*see* for example *supra* Sect. 4.3.2.1).[279] In this context, a statement of the Computer & Communications Industry Association underscores: "*With the growth of digital flows and e-commerce have come concerns about the protection of personal data, and the security of digital transactions and content. These concerns are not just shared by consumers. Protection of data is at the core of the Internet's sustained growth as a platform for expression and trade in goods and services. In fact, the lifeblood of Internet-based industry—which today has grown to include a substantial component of all industries— is the trust that global Internet users have in online platforms.*".[280] Given the direct link between trust in the digital environment and the economic potential of digital trade, building trust in cross-border online transactions is crucial for contractual trade relations between countries as well. Indeed, in the absence of global digital governance, contractual trade arrangements may serve as coordinating elements between domestic privacy instruments (*see infra* Sect. 5.3). Given these positive effects of data privacy rules on cross-border economic activity, the notion that data privacy rules as non-tariff barriers primarily hinder digital trade can be challenged.[281] In this sense, the argument of economic inefficiency is countered by an alternative position which assumes that robust data privacy regulations support digital trade.[282] In fact, the emergence of global ICT networks and the Internet has led scholars of economic theory to consider more closely the trade-offs involved in privacy and information sharing, often embracing a nuanced perspective.[283] The key consideration behind this is that strong data privacy protection standards substantially improve consumer confidence in the digital environment and thus result in greater participation in online transactions. It follows from this logic that ensuring a minimum level of data protection is essential for digital

---

[276] *See* with further references Casalini and López González (2019), p. 29; OECD (2015a), p. 211. *See* in particular for the EU with further references, Yakovleva and Irion (2020), p. 207.

[277] Reidenberg (1995).

[278] *See* regarding a potential role for the WTO in fostering consumer trust, Mitchell and Mishra (2019), p. 403.

[279] This is notably the case for the data privacy framework of the US, *see* for example Schwartz and Pfeifer (2017), pp. 132–138.

[280] *See* with further references UNCTAD (2016), p. 103.

[281] *See* for example Yakovleva and Irion (2020), pp. 207–208.

[282] Swire and Litan (2010), pp. 79–85.

[283] *See* with further references Acquisti (2010), pp. 4–5; Swire and Litan (2010), p. 86.

4.4 The Data Privacy Collision in Digital Trade

trade, as the absence of or too low a privacy standard in itself entails the hazard of creating a barrier to trade.[284] In this sense, the introduction of robust data privacy standards may actually contribute to the reduction of trade barriers.[285]

4.4.1.2 Societal and Moral Discourse

The economic discourse relating to the nexus between data privacy and digital trade is countered by the notion that the moral values and societal benefits associated with data privacy protection, particularly relating to fundamental rights, outweigh potential economic disadvantages.[286] Moreover, in a trade context, the purely economic approach to data privacy is considered an attempt to displace a moral value approach by labelling data privacy as protectionism.[287]

4.4.1.2.1 Safeguarding of Human Rights

While international human rights instruments were originally considered to lack sufficient detail to function as data privacy instruments, and consequently had only a limited significance as a normative basis for data privacy issues, this has changed today.[288] In fact, a key normative basis for data privacy is found in international human rights instruments, particularly with regard to the right to privacy or private life.[289] The right to privacy is enshrined in several international treaties, most notably in Article 12 UDHR, Article 17 ICCPR[290] as well as in Article 8 ECHR, and Article 7 EU Charter.[291] As a result of the recognition of privacy as a human right, the protection of individuals in the processing and storage of their personal data is accorded a high priority in many countries, which has led to an increase in

---

[284] Burri (2017), pp. 13–14; Yakovleva and Irion (2020), pp. 207–208. *See* also Mitchell and Mishra (2019), p. 403.

[285] In this context, the wording of some provisions on data protection in recent EU trade agreements reveals the underlying notion that data privacy rules are actually eliminating barriers to data flows, cf. Willemyns (2020), p. 237 referring to Article 45 of the EU–Algeria agreement.

[286] *See* further Yakovleva and Irion (2020), p. 208.

[287] Cf. Yakovleva (2020b), pp. 500–515.

[288] Bygrave (2014), p. 82.

[289] Bygrave (2014), pp. 82–99; Kuner (2013), p. 33.

[290] Article 12 UDHR reads: *"No one shall be subjected to arbitrary interference with his privacy, family, home or correspondence, nor to attacks upon his honour and reputation. Everyone has the right to the protection of the law against such interference or attacks."* Similarly, the ICCPR stipulates in Article 17 that *"no one shall be subjected to arbitrary or unlawful interference with his or her privacy, family, home or correspondence, nor to unlawful attacks on his or her honour and reputation."*.

[291] In retrospect, however, it is obscure why the concept of privacy gained such broad recognition so quickly, given its relative novelty and the lack of a settled constitutional tradition in many countries, *see* Diggelmann and Cleis (2014).

data privacy laws as the digital realm has expanded. Most notably, the EU has granted *"data protection"* the status of a fundamental right *sui generis* and has geared its regulation under the GDPR to this effect (*see supra* Sect. 4.3.2.2). Consequently, Article 8 Sec. 1 of the EU Charter provides that *"everyone has the right to the protection of personal data concerning him or her"*, while Article 1 Sec. 2 GDPR reads *"This regulation protects fundamental rights and freedoms of natural persons and in particular their right to the protection of personal data."*.

Overall, the human rights discourse is advancing rapidly in relation to the digital paradigm. Moving social, political, and economic activities to the digital realm affects a range of human rights, including the right to privacy, the freedom of expression, and the freedom of information.[292] In this context, the UN Human Rights Council emphasised early on that the *"same rights that people have offline must also be protected online"*.[293] International attention to privacy in the digital sphere has increased, particularly as a result of the post-9/11 counterterrorism measures and in the wake of the NSA scandal prompted by Edward Snowden's revelations.[294] Against the background of the threat to privacy by means of mass surveillance and largescale retention of personal data, the first UN resolution on this matter has been adopted on 18 December 2013, emphasising that *"unlawful or arbitrary surveillance and/or interception of communications, as well as unlawful or arbitrary collection of personal data, as highly intrusive acts, violate the rights to privacy and to freedom of expression and may contradict the tenets of a democratic society"*.[295] A report by the UN High Commissioner for Human Rights based on this resolution, which is still influential today, traces down further the link between the right to privacy and the collection and analysis of personal data using digital technologies.[296] In 2015, the UN appointed the first Special Rapporteur on the Right to Privacy, the purpose of the mandate of which includes reviewing government policies and laws on the interception of digital communications and collection of personal data.[297]

This intrinsic link between data privacy and the respect for a human right to privacy adds a moral dimension to the debate on the nexus between digital and data privacy (*see* also *supra* Sect. 4.2.2). For advocates of a *"moral value approach"*, data privacy bears an intrinsic link to human dignity.[298] In addition, proponents point out that data privacy is not only closely linked to individual self-determination, but also to social coexistence in a democratic civil society.[299] In fact, privacy protection is

---

[292] Bygrave (2014), p. 83.

[293] UN General Assembly, Human Rights Council, The promotion, protection and enjoyment of human rights on the Internet, 29 June 2012, A/HRC/20/L.13.

[294] Nyst and Falchetta (2017), pp. 105–107. *See* also Hill (2014).

[295] UN (2013). *See* further UN (2014a).

[296] UN (2014b), para. 1. *See* also Nyst and Falchetta (2017), pp. 105–110.

[297] UN (2015).

[298] Yakovleva (2018), pp. 481–482.

[299] *See* with further references Yakovleva and Irion (2020), p. 208.

assigned a societal dimension, according to which it is a constitutive element of civil societies.[300] As *Paul Schwartz* describes it: *"Constitutive privacy is a matter of line-drawing along different coordinates to shape permitted levels of scrutiny. Its limits on access to information will, in turn, have an impact on the extent to which certain actions or expressions of identity are encouraged or discouraged."*.[301] In this sense, *Shoshana Zuboff*, for example, has argued that *"the assault on behavioral data is so sweeping that it can no longer be circumscribed by the concept of privacy and its contests"* and further that what is at stake relates to *"the sanctity of the individual and the ideals of social equality, the development of identity, autonomy, and moral reasoning; the integrity of contract, the freedom that accrues to the making and fulfilling of promises; norms and rules of collective agreement; the functions of market democracy; the political integrity of societies; and the future of democratic sovereignty."*.[302] In this context, *Urs Gasser* has identified a *"modern moment in technology"*, the seismic shifts of which make it necessary to rethink data privacy.[303] In a trade context, however, this approach inevitably faces the difficulty of quantifying such societal and moral benefits of data privacy and thereby effectively counterweighing the economic discourse.[304]

4.4.1.2.2 Data Sovereignty

Recently, a debate has unfolded around the notion of *"sovereignty"* in the digital realm predicated on the premise of a comprehensive data-driven economic and societal reality. A lively political and academic debate is based on a number of related terms for which there is often no specific definition.[305] For example, *"internet or cyber-sovereignty"* can be understood as implying control over data flows in a domestic cyber space and determining the modalities of the use of data for socio-cultural and economic purposes.[306] Another branch of this debate revolves around the concept of *"digital sovereignty"*.[307] In similar vein, the notion of *"data sovereignty"*, is not precisely defined and is often referred to as an umbrella term.[308] In his context, *Urs Gasser* describes data sovereignty to be *"an immune system response triggered by the power shifts associated with the unprecedented surveillance capabilities of foreign governments and technology companies."*.[309] The Fraunhofer

---

[300] *See* with further references Chander and Schwartz (2023), pp. 108–110; Solove (2006).
[301] *See* with further references Schwartz (1999), p. 1665.
[302] Cf. Zuboff (2016). *See* also Yakovleva (2018), p. 482; Yakovleva and Irion (2020), p. 208.
[303] Gasser (2021), p. 199.
[304] Yakovleva (2020b), pp. 507–508.
[305] Svantesson (2020), p. 17.
[306] Mitchell and Mishra (2019), pp. 395–396. *See* also Cory and Dascoli (2021), p. 6.
[307] *See* for example Mitchell and Samlidis (2022); Fleming (2021).
[308] With further references Hon (2017), pp. 26–27.
[309] *See* with further references Gasser (2021), p. 200.

Institute understands data sovereignty to refer to the "*ability to formulate self-defined data-usage rules, influence and trace the data/information flows while being free in the decision of (not) sharing data and migrating data whenever and wherever it is desirable.*".[310] The Asia Cloud Computing Association (ACCA) has put forth a rather comprehensive definition, underscoring that "*Traditionally, data sovereignty is the respect for the rights associated with data – based on where the entity that has control of the data resides. [. . .]*" and emphasising that "*[. . .] with the globalization of data flows, the picture is less clear.*".[311] In this sense, principles of data sovereignty intrinsically relate to subjects dealt with under data privacy law.[312] Indeed, there is considerable overlap between the implementation of data privacy laws and the assertion of national sovereignty in the digital realm.[313] Under the impact of the digital transformation foreign relations have witnessed the emergence of a form of "*data geopolitics*".[314] A number of commentators have described the complex political economy of digital trade as well as the rise of different "*data realms*".[315] Given that the relevance of personal data has manifold implications for both economic and societal realities, the question of how to govern personal data in a transnational context and what influence is to be reserved for domestic policies is a sensitive one. In an economic context in particular, personal data is a valuable resource that is vital for the development of strategic use-cases of digital technologies such as Big Data and AI as well as digital business models. In this sense, there is evidence for a link between "*informational sovereignty*" in the adoption of data privacy laws, as there are several examples of debates in which data privacy laws were attributed an economic element by seeking to discourage the processing of data abroad.[316] In a related context, data sovereignty is often linked to data localisation measures.[317]

4.4.1.3 Evaluation

An evaluation of the trade policy discourse on the nexus of trade and data privacy underscores that the ambiguous normative background of data privacy, rooted in the multifaceted nature of personal data and sociocultural variations of national regulations, is echoed in the context of digital trade. This analysis has underscored that it is

---

[310] Lauf (2021), p. 11.

[311] Cited according to Hon (2017), pp. 27–28.

[312] Hon (2017), p. 27; Mitchell and Samlidis (2022), p. 375; Fleming (2021).

[313] Kuner (2013), pp. 28–31.

[314] The Economist (2012).

[315] *See* for example Aaronson and Leblond (2018); Mitchell and Mishra (2018), pp. 1081–1088.

[316] Bygrave (2014), pp. 124–125; Kuner (2013), pp. 28–31. *See* with regard to the extraterritorial application of data privacy laws *infra* Sect. 4.4.2.2.1.

[317] Svantesson (2020), pp. 17–19. *See* with regard to China's data governance approach Erie and Streinz (2021), pp. 24–35.

primarily a balance between an economic rationale implicated in cross-border trade and a non-economic human rights rationale that are at odds with each other. With regard to the fundamental rights dimension of personal data in relation to trade, *Spiros Simitis* is famously quoted: *"This is not bananas we are talking about!"*.[318] Indeed, there is a widespread perception that a neoliberal rationale of digital trade and the moral value of data privacy are fundamentally incompatible, as an economic approach fails to take into account the intrinsic value of privacy as a fundamental right, which thus invariably leads to divergent perspectives on what constitutes an optimal level of protection.[319] Different levels of protection, in turn, require a reconciliation mechanism that is often found in the unilateral regulation of cross-border flows of personal data. In this context, data privacy has a direct impact on the governance of digital trade, as the extent to which economic and non-economic factors are reconciled in a given framework directly influences the regulation of cross-border data processing (*see infra* Sect. 4.4.2.1). It should be noted, however, that even if economic criteria are considered exclusively, no unanimous consensus exists that data privacy regulations as such produce (only) economic inefficiencies. Indeed, when considering the effects of data privacy on digital trade there are number of nuances to consider, for example the stringency and effectiveness of the legislation, the underlying typology for personal data, and the specific circumstances regulated.[320] In this sense, there can be no *"'final,' definitive, and all-encompassing economic assessment of whether we need more, or less, privacy protection"* as *"privacy means too many things, its associated trade-offs are too diverse, and consumers valuations of personal data are too nuanced"*.[321] Arguably, the exploitation of the commercial value of personal data is usually accompanied by a reduction in private benefits and sometimes even social welfare, while both disclosure of personal data and control of its dissemination through data privacy laws can have both positive and negative consequences.[322] However, given that both economic and societal considerations, as well as individual idiosyncrasies and preferences, factor into this trade-off, *"valuing any such trade-off will be extremely difficult and will vary with the beholder"*.[323]

---

[318] Andrews (1999). *See* further Chander and Schwartz (2023), pp. 110–113.

[319] *See* further Yakovleva (2018), pp. 482–487; Yakovleva (2020b), pp. 508–513. In this context the author analyses the limits of the economic approach to data privacy and calls for a *"broader multidisciplinary discourse"*.

[320] Swire and Litan (2010), pp. 85–88.

[321] Acquisti (2010), p. 19.

[322] Acquisti et al. (2016), pp. 483–484.

[323] Swire and Litan (2010), p. 89.

4.4.2 The Nexus of Data Privacy Regulation and Digital Trade Governance

The previous sections have outlined some of the building blocks of the trade policy conflict around the fundamental nexus between the regulation of data privacy and the governance of digital trade in an inherently global digital economy. The nexus of digital trade and data privacy is most clearly demonstrated through the lens of the regulation of cross-border data flows. In this sense, given that the governance of digital trade necessarily involves a governance of cross-border data flows, and that domestic data privacy legislation tends to include transnational elements of data flow regulation due to the heterogeneity of protection standards on a global level, the two fields are inextricably intertwined. This section will first take a closer look at the central relevance of data privacy regulation for digital trade governance. Then, evidence from case studies is used to substantiate the specific role of data privacy in the governance of digital trade.

4.4.2.1 Data Privacy as a Cornerstone of Digital Trade Governance

In a digital economy, data privacy legislation has a particularly broad scope of application, since by its nature it relates to the processing of data, which is omnipresent in virtually all processes on the Internet (*see supra* Sect. 4.2).[324] In fact, given the ubiquitous nature of personal data processing in a digital economy, data privacy law emerges as a critical arbiter of the terms and conditions of a given (cross-border) economic transaction. Against the backdrop of the decentralised architecture of the Internet, domestic data privacy rules are confronted with the challenge of effectively regulating the elusive resource of personal data in an inherently global environment (*see supra* Sect. 4.3). Consequently, a national regulator can hardly limit the intent and application of a data privacy regulation to its territorial sphere of influence, but must consider, one way or another, how to deal with cross-border elements in the processing of personal data and how the principles pursued by the regulation can be effectively implemented and enforced in a networked world. Thus, the broad scope of application of data privacy laws in a digitally globalised world as well as their inherent relevance to cross-border economic activity put the regulation of data privacy at the centre of digital trade governance. Yet, at the same time, the different approaches, instruments, and normative values behind national data privacy regimes create a complex terrain for digital trade. The central importance of data privacy for digital trade is most clearly reflected in the regulation of cross-border data flows through data privacy instruments. In this sense, the individually balanced trade-offs between the data privacy discourses shape the underlying national data privacy standards, the heterogeneity of which is reflected in the various

---

[324] Kuner (2010), p. 178.

4.4 The Data Privacy Collision in Digital Trade

standards of cross-border data flow regulation.[325] As *Svetlana Yakovleva* has analysed, a "*bottom-up*" economic regulation of privacy, which starts from a theoretical level without data privacy protections and provides only as much protection as is necessary to achieve the instrumental goal of establishing a level of trust sufficient to enable the online environment, tends to be less trade-restrictive than a "*top-down*" public policy approach in which generally high protection may be curtailed in response to competing interests.[326] The author therefore argues that if data privacy is granted for its own sake as an independent normative value outside of an economic rationale, such as in the case of the recognition of fundamental rights to privacy (and data protection), the level of protection tends to be higher than the level necessary to promote social welfare under an approach that is purely geared towards economic efficiency.[327] The above analysis of data privacy frameworks has illustrated that the tolerance of unchecked outbound flow of personal data typically increases in proportion to the emphasis placed on economic considerations in the implementation of a data privacy regime. The prevailing view among regulators seems to be that higher standards for data privacy—that is, data privacy standards that incorporate and emphasise other normative discourses (notably human rights protection) in addition to the economic discourse—can be most effectively implemented and enforced within the scope of a national data privacy law, thus warranting a rigorous system for monitoring data flows and even prompting extraterritorial effect of domestic data privacy principles.

It is important to reiterate that the trade-off between data privacy and digital trade is not (only) a two-dimensional endeavour involving a dichotomy between economic interests and human rights. As data flows are a hinging element in a digital economy, the nexus of digital trade and data privacy involves an intricate web of economic and non-economic considerations including considerations of trade, socio-cultural progress, national security and regulatory sovereignty. Beyond the consideration of data privacy as a fundamental right, a strong regulation of cross-border data flows can be also observed, for example, where governments adopt a strict data privacy regime on the grounds of considerations of data sovereignty and national security. This is particularly the case since the national prerogative to determine what is necessary to safeguard data privacy is very broad, given the sociocultural particularities of privacy protection in a heterogeneous data privacy environment. In particular, there is no global consensus on the necessity, effectiveness, or adequacy of data privacy measures. Thus, at the international level, it is difficult to scrutinize the legitimacy of data privacy, which makes it susceptible to all kinds of reasoning, up to and including its misuse in a protectionist manner.[328] In the absence of a globally binding data privacy standard with exemplary character, data privacy regulation is largely free to encompass various instruments of data regulation which

---

[325] *See* generally Casalini and López González (2019), p. 16.
[326] Cf. Yakovleva (2018), pp. 482–484.
[327] Cf. Yakovleva (2020b), p. 511.
[328] *See infra* Sect. 5.2 for more details on the review of data privacy laws in the context of WTO law.

accommodates unilateral approaches to digital trade governance. This forms the basis for a contemporary data privacy collision in the context of digital trade.

4.4.2.2 The Role of Data Privacy in Digital Trade: Case Studies

The following remarks provide a closer examination of the concrete positions of the EU, the US and China with regard to what is referred to as a contemporary data privacy collision in trade. These observations are closely intertwined with the respective approaches to an individual trade-off between economic and non-economic rationales in general and between digital trade and data privacy more specifically.

4.4.2.2.1 European Union

The EU's approach to the regulation of data privacy is characterised by a human rights-based appreciation of privacy and data protection (*see supra* Sect. 4.3.2.2). Indeed, this normative foundation of the European framework of data protection is also of key relevance to the EU's international relations, given its commitment to the universality and indivisibility of human rights and fundamental freedoms and respect for human dignity, as set out under the Lisbon Treaty in Article 3 Sec. 5 and Article 21 TEU. Scholars have highlighted that this constitutional set-up puts the EU in a unique position with regard to the global governance of data privacy.[329] In addition to the protection of fundamental rights, however, EU data protection law has always embraced an economic logic in which regulatory harmonisation was intended to counteract the obstacles to intra-EU trade resulting from the differing protection regimes of the individual EU member states. For instance, the 1995 DPD was explicitly designed both to protect fundamental rights as well as to create a harmonised set of rules for data protection in order to foster trade and cooperation.[330] In fact, EU data protection law has long recognised the nexus between trade and data

---

[329] Schwartz (2019); Yakovleva and Irion (2020), p. 215.

[330] Article 1 Sec. 1 DPD states: *"In accordance with this Directive, Member States shall protect the fundamental rights and freedoms of natural persons, and in particular their right to privacy with respect to the processing of personal data."* Sec. 2 reads: *"Member States shall neither restrict nor prohibit the free flow of personal data between Member States for reasons connected with the protection afforded under paragraph 1"*. Moreover, Recital 8 to the DPD reads: *"Whereas, in order to remove the obstacles to flows of personal data, the level of protection of the rights and freedoms of individuals with regard to the processing of such data must be equivalent in all Member States; whereas this objective is vital to the internal market but cannot be achieved by the Member States alone, especially in view of the scale of the divergences which currently exist between the relevant laws in the Member States and the need to coordinate the laws of the Member States so as to ensure that the cross-border flow of personal data is regulated in a consistent manner that is in keeping with the objective of the internal market as provided for in Article 7a of the Treaty; whereas Community action to approximate those laws is therefore needed"*.

4.4 The Data Privacy Collision in Digital Trade

privacy that arises from the multifaceted nature of personal data in a global digital economy and the ambiguous normative discourses underlying data privacy (*see supra* Sects. 4.2.2 and 4.4.1). For example, Recital 56 to the DPD emphasised: *"Whereas cross-border flows of personal data are necessary to the expansion of international trade"*. Similarly, the 2018 GDPR attempts to strike a balance between a *"free flow"* of personal data as a driver for digital trade liberalisation and the fundamental right to the protection of personal data as a constitutional principle of the EU.[331] In this sense, the EU strives to reconcile the two aforementioned normative discourses on the protection of fundamental rights to privacy and data protection and the pursuit of economic prosperity.[332] Indeed, for the EU, promoting a high level of data protection and facilitating international trade go *"hand in hand"*.[333] A European Strategy for Data was outlined in 2020 to *"enable the EU to become the most attractive, most secure and most dynamic data-agile economy in the world"*.[334] Yet, as Recital 101 to the GDPR makes abundantly clear, the EU allows for a cross-border flow of personal data towards third countries—*"necessary"* for the *"expansion of international trade and international cooperation"*—only when in *"full compliance"* with the GDPR. In this context, the GDPR has been described to accord a *"data embargo power"*.[335]

In view of the GDPR's rather stringent three tiered framework for cross-border data flows (*see supra* Sect. 4.3.2.2), its substantive expansion of data privacy rights for individuals, the central role of the European Commission within the GDPR framework, as well as a strict liability regime with hefty pecuniary penalties, data privacy scholars anticipated a threat to the tenuous understanding that the EU had reached on international flows of personal data—particularly with regard to the US.[336] The criticism that the GDPR features a strategic stance with regard to trade cannot simply be brushed aside. Given the multifaceted nature of personal data and its processing in a global digital economy, the transnational implications of the EU's rigorous pursuit of a high level of data protection are arguably also of political, economic, and strategic relevance. In this respect, the GDPR is a particularly relevant example of a unilateral regulatory approach to addressing the nexus of digital trade and data privacy. Indeed, it represents one of the most influential models for data privacy regulation as a building block of a strategic framework for transnational data governance. In this sense, scholarly literature on trade law is increasingly addressing the link between data privacy and digital trade under the EU data protection framework.[337] In the following, two essential components of this discussion will be addressed in the required brevity.

---

[331] Kokott and Sobotta (2013), p. 223; Wagner (2018), p. 320.
[332] Yakovleva (2020b), p. 502.
[333] European Commission (2017), p. 6, para. 3.1.
[334] European Commission (2020a), p. 25.
[335] Schwartz (2019), p. 774.
[336] Humerick (2018), pp. 103–107; Schwartz (2013), pp. 1994–2001.
[337] *See* with further references Chander and Schwartz (2023), pp. 90–94; Yakovleva and Irion (2020).

First, the European data protection framework under the GDPR is adopting an explicit extraterritorial approach in pursuit of the highest possible effectivity of its rules.[338] Confronted with an inherently global digital economy and against the backdrop of its ambition to serve as a guarantor of fundamental rights, European data protection law extends beyond EU territory thus incorporating aspects of transnational data governance.[339] Already under the DPD the ECJ has underscored a *"particularly broad territorial scope"* for teleological reasons, for example, in the *Google-Spain* case, which has only been strengthened in subsequent judgements.[340] The GDPR has bolstered this extraterritorial scope of the EU data protection law in Article 3 Sec. 1 GDPR which reads: *"This Regulation applies to the processing of personal data in the context of the activities of an establishment of a controller or a processor in the Union, regardless of whether the processing takes place in the Union or not."*. In particular, Article 3 Sec. 2 GDPR stipulates that the regulation applies to the processing of personal data of data subjects who are in the Union by a controller or processor not established in the Union, where the processing activities are related to commercially targeting or profiling data subjects in the Union.[341] The extension of jurisdiction beyond the EU's territorial borders has provoked criticism due to its creation of legal uncertainty.[342] Critics warn that it is a matter of ensuring that the scale of extraterritoriality of a given regulation remains proportionate to the protective purpose, since the effects of unrestricted extraterritoriality on both state and individual interests are not to be disregarded.[343] Lack of certainty about jurisdiction can have a significant impact on individuals and businesses, which may refrain from participating in e-commerce, but it can also create confusion about the duties and responsibilities of public authorities.[344] In this context, *Dan Svantesson* warns against extending the EU regulation too far as this *"undermines [...] legitimacy"* and *"[...] makes a Regulation that has the potential to inspire positive*

---

[338] *See* generally with regard to the concept of extraterritoriality as it relates to regulation of international data transfers under the EU's DPD Kuner (2015).

[339] Schwartz (2013), p. 1973. *Schwartz* cites *Spiros Simitis*: *"Data protection does not stop at national borders. Transfers of information must be bound to conditions that attempt in a targeted fashion to protect the affected parties."* Consequently, Recital 2 of the GDPR states: *"The principles of, and rules on the protection of natural persons with regard to the processing of their personal data should, whatever their nationality or residence, respect their fundamental rights and freedoms, in particular their right to the protection of personal data".*

[340] Cf. ECJ, C-131/12, *Google Spain*, 13 May 2014, ECLI:EU:C:2014:317, para. 54. *See* further Fabbrini and Celeste (2021), pp. 18–19.

[341] *See* further Recitals 23 and 24 to the GDPR. Recital 23 first sentence reads: *"In order to ensure that natural persons are not deprived of the protection to which they are entitled under this Regulation, the processing of personal data of data subjects who are in the Union by a controller or a processor not established in the Union should be subject to this Regulation where the processing activities are related to offering goods or services to such data subjects irrespective of whether connected to a payment.".*

[342] *See* with further references de Hert and Czerniawski (2016), pp. 239–240.

[343] de Hert and Czerniawski (2016), pp. 239–240.

[344] Kuner (2010), p. 178.

4.4 The Data Privacy Collision in Digital Trade   213

developments in data protection around the globe come across as little more than data protection imperialism".[345] In addition to the explicit provision in Article 3 GDPR, there are other extraterritorial elements in the EU data protection rules as well. *Christopher Kuner* has argued that the GDPR's adequacy approach under EU law "*requires that personal data be accompanied by the protections of EU law wherever they are transferred*", thus emphasising a variation of the "*personality principle*" due to the significant pressure on the traditional territoriality principle in the Internet era.[346] Certainly, as the underlying root cause for this conundrum lies in the inherently global nature of the Internet and cross-border data flows, the extraterritorial extension of jurisdiction of domestic laws is not unique to the EU.[347] Rather, the discrepancy between territorially oriented trade rationale and data privacy law as an enunciation of regulation in a global data sphere "*without borders*" is somewhat inherent. However, the adequacy requirement of the GDPR raises a number of complex trade policy issues, as it implies a unilateral assessment of a third country's data protection standards and requires an individual weighing of both economic and non-economic factors. For example, the European Commission takes "*actual and potential commercial relations*" and the "*third country's pioneering role in the field of data protection, which could serve as a model for other countries in its region*", as strategic criteria for the initiative to assess the adequacy of the level of protection under GDPR.[348] Indeed, given the pre-eminent position of "*adequacy*" for the flow of personal data, the criteria for an adequate level of data protection, as well as the procedure by which an adequacy decision is adopted, are of paramount significance. Summarising the various critiques towards the EU's procedure of adequacy determination, *Christopher Kuner* has evaluated it to be a "*triumph of bureaucracy and formalism over substance*" and the slow pace of adopting adequacy decisions to "*be caused, at least in part, by the opacity and poorly defined nature of the process*".[349] In fact, some commentators argue it is primarily this unilateral evaluation of a third countries data privacy law that renders EU data protection law into a trade issue.[350] In any case, the political resolve to enforce data privacy standards by restricting cross-border data flows and extending jurisdiction, on the one hand, as well as the practical design and administration of the normative process of this enforcement, on the other hand, are highly relevant to digital trade. However, this extension of jurisdiction is closely related to the widespread perception that the EU is deliberately exercising its regulatory power to

---

[345] Svantesson (2015), p. 234.

[346] Kuner (2009b), pp. 4–8. *See* for an explanation of jurisdictional bases most relevant for data privacy law Kuner (2010), pp. 188–189.

[347] Fabbrini and Celeste (2021), pp. 21–23; Kuner (2010), p. 191.

[348] European Commission (2017), p. 8, para. 3.1.

[349] Kuner (2017), p. 911. *See* further with regard to an assessment of the adequacy mechanism under WTO law *infra* Sect. 5.2.2.2.

[350] "*Admitting the legitimacy of such an approach invites trade war upon trade war as nations take turns standing in judgment of one another's internal regulatory regimes.*" *See* Singelton (2002).

unilaterally impose its rules in a global environment. The unilateral imposition of European regulations and standards through the regulatory competence of the EU by means of its extraordinary economic market power, has been described by *Anu Bradford* with the notion of the *"Brussels effect"*.[351] In fact, the EU approach to *"border control"* for personal data under the GDPR has acted as a catalyst for the international proliferation of the adequacy approach, as a number of countries seek the EU's seal of adequacy.[352] This is notably the case, since a European adequacy decision is contingent on the lawfulness of onward transfers of personal data from the foreign jurisdiction.[353] This tends to perpetuate the establishment of data flow restrictions, as foreign legislation itself will require a data flow regulation in order to guarantee an *"adequate"* level of protection.[354] The European regulatory framework for data protection has served and continues to serve as a blueprint for privacy and data protection legislation worldwide, notably prompting the adoption of omnibus legislation on data privacy.[355] While a number of countries have adopted European style data protection frameworks, the *"outliers"* have long been the US and China.[356] Indeed, agreement on European standards at the global level certainly seems illusory.[357] Moreover, recent research underscores a *"splintering"* of the adequacy standard, as a common substantive definition of adequacy and a uniform process are lacking on a global level.[358]

Secondly, although the EU consistently emphasizes the protection of fundamental rights as a primary impetus for the GDPR, its activities with regard to transnational data privacy are also significantly influenced by trade policy considerations.[359] Today, though technically possible, the European Commission refrains from legalising cross-border data flows in the trade context by way of an international agreement and rather employs adequacy decisions.[360] In this respect, the European Commission clearly states that the dialogues on data protection and the trade negotiations with third countries *"have to follow separate tracks"* and stresses that an adequacy finding is the *"the best avenue to build mutual trust, guaranteeing uninhibited flow of personal data, and thus facilitate commercial exchanges*

---

[351] Bradford (2020). *See* with regard to the EU's data protection law Schwartz (2019), pp. 778–783.

[352] Svantesson (2011), p. 184.

[353] Cf. Article 45 Sec. 2 (a) GDPR *"When assessing the adequacy of the level of protection, the Commission shall, in particular, take account [. . .] rules for the onward transfer of personal data to another third country or international organisation which are complied with in that country or international organisation"*.

[354] Bygrave (2014), p. 123.

[355] Gunasekara (2007), p. 164; Schwartz (2013), pp. 1973–1979. *See* further Greenleaf (2012), pp. 72–79.

[356] Greenleaf (2012), p. 70.

[357] Kuner (2017), pp. 917–918.

[358] Chander and Schwartz (2023), pp. 70–76.

[359] Chander and Schwartz (2023), p. 111.

[360] Cf. also with further references to the legal relationship between international agreements and adequacy decisions Kuner et al. (2020), Article 45, pp. 777–778.

involving transfers of personal data to the third country in question. Such decisions can therefore ease trade negotiations or may complement existing trade agreements, thus allowing them to amplify their benefits.".[361] And indeed, a significant number of trade agreements concluded by the EU recently have been backed by an adequacy decision under Article 45 Sec. 3 GDPR. While Canada, a party to the CETA agreement, holds an adequacy decision dating back to 2001, more recent adequacy decisions for Japan,[362] South Korea[363] and the United Kingdom[364] have been issued in close temporal connection to the conclusion or negotiation of trade agreements. In fact, circumstantial evidence demonstrates an intricate interweaving of the adequacy decision under the GDPR and commercial ties under trade agreements.[365] For example, in the transatlantic relationship with the US, the European data protection framework forms not a rigid and unilateral set of rules, but rather is subject to a certain degree of *"collaborative lawmaking"*.[366] This pertains most notably to the Safe Harbor agreement between the EU and the US and the subsequent Privacy Shield arrangement, both of which were declared invalid by the ECJ following a lawsuit filed by Austrian data privacy activist *Maximilian Schrems*. Data flows between the EU and the US form one of the most extensive connections in the world and certainly the most critical for the EU in terms of digital trade, as the US is arguably its primary trade partner. However, between the economic partners the issue of data privacy has long been a source of friction.[367] Negotiations on adequacy of data privacy between the US and the EU in the aftermath of the enactment of the DPD ended in dispute, and the US never requested a formal adequacy decision.[368] Although the transatlantic data privacy dispute has long divided the two trading partners, it appeared to have been tentatively settled under the Safe Harbor agreement, acting as a *"shared escape valve"*.[369] The Safe Harbor agreement operated between 2000 and 2015 and was designed as a system of self-certification.

---

[361] European Commission (2017), p. 9, para. 3.1.

[362] Commission Implementing Decision (EU) 2019/419 of 23 January 2019 pursuant to Regulation (EU) 2016/679 of the European Parliament and of the Council on the adequate protection of personal data by Japan under the Act on the Protection of Personal Information, C/2019/304/, OJ L 76, 19 March 2019.

[363] Commission Implementing Decision of 17 December 2021 pursuant to Regulation (EU) 2016/679 of the European Parliament and of the Council on the adequate protection of personal data by the Republic of Korea under the Personal Information Protection Act, C(2021) 9316 final.

[364] Commission Implementing Decision of 28 June 2021 pursuant to Regulation (EU) 2016/679 of the European Parliament and of the Council on the adequate protection of personal data by the United Kingdom, C(2021) 4800 final.

[365] *See* for example Chander and Schwartz (2023), pp. 92–94; Schwartz (2019), pp. 786–803.

[366] Schwartz (2013), p. 1980.

[367] *See* only Schwartz (2013), p. 1968, Schwartz and Pfeifer (2017).

[368] *See* only Andrews (1999). *See* further Working Party on the Protection of Individuals (1999), para. 1 states: "[...] the Working Party takes the view that the current patchwork of narrowly-focussed sectoral laws and voluntary self-regulation cannot at present be relied upon to provide adequate protection in all cases for personal data transferred from the European Union."

[369] Chander and Schwartz (2023), pp. 100–105; Schwartz (2013), pp. 1980–1985.

Participating US companies had to declare their compliance with the Safe Harbor Privacy Principles issued by the U.S. Department of Commerce. After registering on a list with the Department of Commerce, they benefited from the adequacy decision adopted for these principles along with a list of FAQs, in accordance with Article 25 Sec. 2 DPD, adopted on 26 July 2000.[370] The adequacy decision under the Safe Harbor agreement was long criticised by data protection activists and finally invalidated by the ECJ in 2015.[371] In response to that decision, the Privacy Shield Agreement was concluded in 2016, which hastily addressed some of the points criticised by the Court, only to be declared invalid by the ECJ as well.[372] The fact that the Safe Harbor agreement was able to remain in force for 15 years and that a new Privacy Shield agreement was concluded only one year after it was declared invalid by the ECJ, soon to be declared invalid by the Court as well, indicates that the commercial relevance of transatlantic data flows were an influential factor in the decision-making process. Thus, the adequacy decisions both for Safe Harbor as well as Privacy Shield can also be contextually understood in light of the economic negotiating leverage of the US.[373] In fact, *Paul Schwartz* points out that transatlantic data flows, particularly following the adoption of the DPD, have been the subject to "*ad hoc policy efforts between the United States and EU that have created numerous paths to satisfy the EU's requirement of "adequacy"*" in a "*collaborative effort marked by accommodation and compromise*".[374] *Schwartz* further illustrates a "*market oriented approach within the EU*" underlying the dialectic of the EU data protection framework against the backdrop of the nexus of data privacy and digital trade: "*In light of the Directive's strong assertion of EU authority over information flows, and in particular, in light of its grant to the EU's data protection commissioners of data embargo power, why did the EU engage in these multi-party negotiations? Why make concessions rather than uphold its requirements without compromise and rely on the market's Brussels Effect to export its rules? The answer, in short, is that the EU negotiated due to its own competing policy goals and because of the limits on its power in a global information economy.*".[375] This argumentation suggests a preponderance of the economic and strategic rationales in view of the EU's trade-off between digital trade and data privacy with regard to the US. A caveat to this argument is, of course, that neither the Safe Harbor nor the Privacy Shield agreement has withstood scrutiny by the ECJ. In fact, as *Svetlana Yakovleva* points out, the European Commission has introduced an economic reasoning by referring to

---

[370] Cf. Commission Decision of 26 July 2000 pursuant to Directive 95/46/EC of the European Parliament and of the Council on the adequacy of the protection provided by the Safe Harbour privacy principles and related frequently asked questions issued by the US Department of Commerce, 2000/520/EC, OJEC, 25 August 2000, L 215/7.

[371] ECJ, C-362/14, *Schrems I*, 6 October 2015, ECLI:EU:C:2015:650.

[372] ECJ, C-311/18, *Schrems II*, 16 July 2020, ECLI:EU:C:2020:55. See further European Commission (2016), pp. 7–12, para. 3.

[373] Gunasekara (2007), p. 165.

[374] Schwartz (2013), p. 1967.

[375] Schwartz (2013), pp. 1987–1989.

data protection as an important policy element for building *"trust"* in the online environment.[376] The ECJ, however, against the backdrop of the EU's constitutional principles under the EU Charter seems to emphasise fundamental rights protection of privacy and data protection with regard to cross-border data transfers. Under the ECJ's ruling in *Schrems II*, the Standard Contractual Clauses (SCCs) most commonly used in practice for data transfers were generally considered permissible. However, the ECJ ruled that such clauses may in some cases require the adoption of *"supplementary measures"* in order to achieve the level of protection required under EU law, insofar as they cannot provide guarantees beyond a contractual obligation.[377] In this context, many observers emphasised a loss of legal certainty and stressed the need for companies exporting data to the US to carefully review the lawfulness and practicability of data-intensive business relations with the US[378] However, despite recurring setbacks before the ECJ, the European Commission is determined to find a solution that, on the one hand, reflects the significance of digital trade between the EU and the US and, on the other hand, takes into account the discrepancies in data privacy standards. An EU-US *"Trade and Technology Council"*, established during the EU-US Summit on 15 June 2021 in Brussels, is mandated to serve as a forum to *"coordinate approaches to key global trade, economic, and technology issues and to deepen transatlantic trade and economic relations based on [...] shared values"*.[379] On 10 July 2023, the European Commission adopted an adequacy decision for the newly introduced EU-US Data Privacy Framework.[380] With the adequacy decision, all personal data can now be transferred from the EU to certified US companies without the requirement for further appropriate safeguards or additional measures. It remains to be seen how this third attempt to reconcile the transatlantic collision of data protection will play out in practice and how the ECJ will position itself on the EU-US data protection framework in the future.

4.4.2.2.2 United States of America

The US approach to the nexus of data privacy and digital trade is significantly divergent from the EU regime, as the US are notably unbound from constitutional constraints with regard to the governance of personal data (*see supra* Sect. 4.3.2.1).[381] Thus, in the currently suspended TTIP negotiations, for example, it

---

[376] Yakovleva (2018), p. 478.
[377] ECJ, C-311/18, *Schrems II*, 16 July 2020, ECLI:EU:C:2020:55, para. 133.
[378] Burri (2021), pp. 59–62. *See* further Congressional Research Service (2021).
[379] *See* further European Commission (2024).
[380] European Commission (2023).
[381] *See* with further explanations to the discrepancies in the discourse on digital trade policy between the US and the EU Aaronson (2015), pp. 685–694; Yakovleva (2020b), pp. 464–466. *See* for a decidedly US centric perspective Singelton (2002). *See* on the relationship of data protection to other objectives of EU data protection law and the resulting relationship between data subject and data processor Schwartz and Pfeifer (2017), pp. 129–132.

has become clear that the issue of data privacy poses a major stumbling block in EU-US trade relations, with the commitments on data flows and the ban on data localisation proving highly controversial.[382] The GDPR, as the epitome of the European model for managing the nexus between digital trade and data privacy, has fuelled political conflict with the US, which has traditionally advocated economic liberalisation of data flows and rejected government restrictions on the cross-border flow of personal data.[383] The media coverage on the so-called "*GDPR Day*" in May 2018 was dominated by worries about stifling regulation, horrendous fines for data privacy breaches, and the EU's supposed claim to lead the world in data regulation.[384] In an opinion piece for the Financial Times the then Secretary of Commerce *Wilbur Ross* wrote: "*As currently envisioned, GDPR's implementation could significantly interrupt transatlantic co-operation and create unnecessary barriers to trade, not only for the US, but for everyone outside the EU.*".[385] Although some estimates of the economic impact of the GDPR have been quite dramatic, its actual effect can only be discerned gradually, not least because of the complicated international enforcement environment and the fact that much depends on the actual implementation of the rules over time.[386] In addition to the dreaded elevation of barriers to transatlantic digital trade, US criticisms were also levelled against the GDPR being a vehicle to digital protectionism. With a view to this context, President *Barack Obama* has been quoted: "*We have owned the internet. Our companies have created it, expanded it, perfected it in ways that they can't compete. And oftentimes what is portrayed as high-minded positions on issues sometimes is just designed to carve out some of their commercial interests.*".[387] Such an assessment is prompted by stakeholders' concerns that the regulatory rationale of effectively protecting personal data in a world of international data transfer is in fact a covert attempt to advance a protectionist digital industrial policy that exerts governmental control over commercially valuable personal data.[388] Stakeholders in US trade policy have largely managed to frame an economic discourse on data privacy related restraints on personal data exchange by using the label of "*digital protectionism*".[389] While the EU is rather cautious about the nexus of data flows and trade for reasons of data privacy protection, the position of the US as the birthplace of the Internet and home to the world's largest Internet companies is traditionally geared toward a market-

---

[382] Yakovleva and Irion (2020), p. 214.

[383] *See* from a perspective of AI regulation Hervé (2021).

[384] *See* for example Gordon and Ram (2018). *See* with more references to media coverage Schwartz (2019), pp. 776–778.

[385] Ross (2018).

[386] *See* with further references Burri and Schär (2016), p. 502. *See* also Burgess (2022). *See* further European Commission (2020c).

[387] Farrell (2015).

[388] Mishra (2015), pp. 144–151.

[389] *See* for example Aaronson (2019), pp. 548–550; Yakovleva (2020b), pp. 473–482. *See* also *supra* Sect. 4.4.1.1.1.

based integration of cross-border data flows into the trade regime.[390] Indeed, the trade-off between the normative discourses around data privacy is straightforward, as essentially only the economic discourse prevails, which considers data privacy to be an interest of consumer protection. In fact, the self-regulatory and sectoral approach to data privacy in the US promotes the *"free flow"* of data and does not provide for any mandatory transfer requirements for personal data. In this approach of balancing data privacy and trade interests, the economic component of building consumer trust in the online market is the primary motivation for adopting data privacy laws. This market-oriented objective for the integration of data privacy and digital trade can be broken down into maximum freedom for data flows and the least trade-restrictive impact of data privacy on the processing and transmission of personal data.[391] Nevertheless, the market-oriented US approach recognizes privacy as a relevant driver of consumer trust and therefore seeks to distinguish a beneficial from a protectionist level of data privacy.[392] In this context, the US is increasingly advocating that the relationship between digital trade, open data flows, and legitimate interests related to data privacy be actively reconciled and brought to a transparent state of consensus.[393] The USMCA's requirements for national privacy instruments, for example, fit within this context (*see* further *infra* Sect. 5.3.2.1). The USMCA requires the adoption of a legal framework, explicitly references the APEC Privacy Framework and the OECD Guidelines as relevant international standards, and even identifies core principles for the protection of personal information. The further development of this externalised privacy policy is closely related to the US's renewed internal discussions about stronger privacy protections under a potential federal privacy law.[394] In this respect, in October 2023, the US withdrew its support for a number of proposals in the plurilateral Joint Statement on Electronic Commerce negotiations, particularly relating to cross-border data flows and source code (*see supra* Sect. 3.3.1.2). The reason cited for this decision was to create sufficient "policy space" for domestic policy considerations.[395]

4.4.2.2.3 People's Republic of China

China's approach to the nexus of digital trade and data privacy is evidence of a unique perspective on data governance and the regulation of cross-border data

---

[390] *See* with regard to US business interests in digital trade discourse Yakovleva (2020b), p. 482.

[391] *See* further Chander and Schwartz (2023), pp. 85–86.

[392] Yakovleva (2020b), p. 476.

[393] *See* for example WTO (2018), p. 1, para. 1.3: *"Meaningful trade rules can support the role of the digital economy in promoting global economic growth and development while also allowing governments to address the growing concerns of Internet users about the security and privacy of their personal data."*.

[394] Centre for Information Policy Leadership (2020). *See* also Congressional Research Service (2020), pp. 20–21. *See* further *supra* Sect. 4.3.2.1.

[395] Lawder (2023).

flows.³⁹⁶ As noted above, since the enactment of the CSL in 2017, China has been working diligently to establish an intricate data governance regime for personal data (*see supra* Sect. 4.3.2.3). Following the enactment of the CSL, the DSL, and the PIPL, CAC published draft rules for "*Security Assessment Measures for Outbound Data Transfers*" in October 2021, which were open for public comment until 28 November 2021. In fact, this is the third draft following two earlier drafts in 2017 and 2019 that did not take effect and has been released at a time when many of the pending elements of the data governance framework have been settled.³⁹⁷ Article 1 of Draft 2021 references these laws and aims to comprehensively implement their respective provisions on cross-border data transfers in order to "*standardize outbound data transfer activities, protect the rights and interests of personal data, safeguard national security and social public interest, and promote the safe and free flow of data across borders*".³⁹⁸ With respect to personal data, Article 38 of the PIPL allows for cross-border transfers under generally very stringent rules that assign extensive discretionary powers to the State Cybersecurity and Informatization Department. This portrays a government that is reluctant to relinquish government control of and access to (personal) data as a matter of regulatory sovereignty and data security.³⁹⁹ However, Article 38 PIPL also stipulates that: "*Where treaties or international agreements that the People's Republic of China has concluded or acceded to contain relevant provisions such as conditions on providing personal data outside the borders of the People's Republic of China, those provisions may be carried out.*". An economic discourse of data privacy seems to be evident in another provision of the PIPL. Article 43 PIPL states that: "*Where any country or region adopts discriminatory prohibitions, limitations or other similar measures against the People's Republic of China in the area of personal information protection, the People's Republic of China may adopt reciprocal measures against said country or region on the basis of actual circumstances.*". The location of this provision in the section on "*Rules on the Cross-Border Provision of Personal Information*" makes it clear that a reservation is made here to make economically relevant data accessible only in the event of reciprocal action. This was taken as an indication that the Chinese government is increasingly interested in international data transfer agreements.⁴⁰⁰ It is currently unclear how the implementation of this provision will manifest in the context of international trade relations. However, it is evident from recent experience that PTAs with Chinese participation may contain provisions that address the governance of cross-border data (*see supra* Sect. 3.4.2.2.3). It is therefore rightly pointed out that the entry into force of the PIPL is closely linked to China's announcement of its intention to join, among other agreements, the CPTPP,

---

³⁹⁶ *See* generally Erie and Streinz (2021).
³⁹⁷ Sacks et al. (2021).
³⁹⁸ *See* for a translation DigiChina (2021b).
³⁹⁹ *See* generally Gao (2021).
⁴⁰⁰ *See* further DigiChina (2021a).

which contains regulations for cross-border data flows.[401] As a result, the provisions included in the Regional Comprehensive Economic Partnership (RCEP), which took effect on 1 January 2022, have come under close scrutiny as the latest agreement on trade signed by China (*see* also *infra* Sect. 5.3.2.3). In general, however, there are significant doubts as to a favourable relationship between China's evolving data governance, particularly with respect to personal data, and its trade competitiveness, due to extensive security oversight and bureaucratic requirements.[402]

4.5 Conclusion

This chapter has analysed the key elements of the nexus between digital trade and data privacy. First, the fundamentals of data privacy regulation in the context of digital trade were mapped out, showing that there is a broad nexus between economic considerations and data privacy measures due to the hinging element of the multifaceted nature of personal data. As data privacy relates to the usage, storage, and transfer of personal data, it is of vital relevance to today's data-driven digital economy. In terms of an international context relevant to trade in the digital economy, it has been emphasised that the ambiguity of normative rationales for data privacy against the backdrop of national socio-cultural specificities in emphasising privacy has initially resulted in reduced consideration being given to the regulation of data flows in international public law.[403] In the absence of international consensus on data privacy standards and mechanisms, the underlying diversity of domestic data privacy rules has significant implications for cross-border data flows. Data privacy measures as a crucial element of domestic data governance touch upon the very foundation of digital trade: the flow of digital data across-borders. Domestic data protection regimes have been shown to have a wide range of ramifications for cross-border data flows, in particular to protect national approaches to data privacy from being circumvented and deprived of their protective effect in third countries. In this respect, the design and rigour of national systems for regulating data flows are in turn highly dependent on the respective national view of an appropriate standard of data protection. This makes data privacy regulation a vital and essential component of digital trade governance. The relativity of a high level of data privacy and the resulting discord over the inherent legitimacy of data privacy related constraints on economic activity is a source of political conflict in trade governance. From the perspective of digital trade, which relies on a sophisticated infrastructure of cross-border data flows, divergent domestic data privacy rules are likely to constitute non-tariff barriers. However, data privacy regulations are deeply embedded in a complex discourse that incorporates an economic dimension

---

[401] Sacks et al. (2021).
[402] World Economic Forum (2022).
[403] Kuner (2013), pp. 33–34.

as well as vital non-economic policy imperatives, such as the protection of fundamental rights to privacy and data protection. Indeed, determining precisely what constitutes a *"high"* standard of data privacy, for example, depends to a large extent on the individual domestic trade-off in the normative rationale of the underlying protection framework between economic and non-economic elements of data privacy.[404] With regard to the transnational data privacy environment, the question must therefore always be asked as to whose data privacy standards are at stake.[405]

Against this background, the ambiguous character of domestic data privacy regulation makes the nexus between digital trade and data privacy highly controversial. This chapter has illustrated that data privacy regulations are the centre of a trade policy collision between approaches that favour economic liberalisation of personal data and others that advocate domestic regulatory leverage for non-economic considerations. This *"data privacy collision"* touches on a whole range of normative discourses around data privacy in the context of trade. There has emerged a trade policy discourse on data privacy that involves distinct elements of economics, morality, and sovereignty. With regard to an individual trade-off between those discourses, *Svetlana Yakovleva* has underscored *"The discourse and value structures coming with it will ultimately predetermine where the line will be drawn between legitimate privacy and personal data protection and illegitimate protectionism."*.[406] In fact, most of current approaches to the nexus of digital trade and data privacy referred to in this chapter (notably US's, the EU's) subscribe to the objective of dismantling *"digital protectionism"*, with each seemingly framing its own approach towards this notion.[407] Given that the governance of data flows has been increasingly subjected to the rationale of International Economic Law, WTO law and PTAs are the venues of this conflict between data privacy and digital trade. The most seminal example of this data privacy collision to date concerns transatlantic relations between the US and the EU.[408]

Nevertheless, in a dynamic, data-driven global environment, existing approaches to the nexus of data privacy and digital trade are evolving and maturing, with new players entering the scene. The ongoing process of adapting to the digital transformation will also mean that the current approaches are not set in stone but will instead mutually inspire and influence each other. However, given the deeply entrenched divergences in underlying approaches to data privacy governance, achieving global harmonisation of data privacy regimes is likely to be elusive. Any convergence and bridging of the divides in a trade context will involve a tedious and incremental negotiation process.[409] Despite rising stakes, for the time being it can arguably be assumed that digital trade is an international issue, while data privacy remains

---

[404] Yakovleva (2018), p. 478.

[405] Peng (2011), p. 765.

[406] Yakovleva (2020b), p. 515.

[407] Yakovleva (2020b), p. 517.

[408] *See* further Schwartz (2013).

[409] *See* for example with regard to the transatlantic EU-US relations Schwartz (2013).

essentially a local one.[410] The question therefore arises as to how the emerging conflicts from the nexus of local data privacy standards and inherently global trade issues can and should be mitigated by trade law.

Jurisprudence

ECJ, C-131/12, Google Spain and Google [Google-Spain], 13 May 2014, ECLI:EU:C:2014:317

ECJ, C-362/14, Maximillian Schrems v Data Protection Commissioner [Schrems I], 6 October 2015, ECLI:EU:C:2015:650

ECJ, Opinion 1/15, Accord PNR UE-Canada [Opinion 1/15], 26 July 2017, ECLI:EU:C:2016:656

ECJ, C-311/18, Data Protection Commissioner v Facebook Ireland Limited and Maximillian Schrems [Schrems II], 16 July 2020, ECLI:EU:C:2020:55

References

Aaronson SA (2015) Why trade agreements are not setting information free: the lost history and reinvigorated debate over cross-border data flows, human rights, and national security. World Trade Rev 14(04):671–700. https://doi.org/10.1017/S1474745615000014

Aaronson SA (2017) What might have been and could still be: the Trans-Pacific Partnership's potential to encourage an open internet and digital rights. J Cyber Policy 2(2):232–254. https://doi.org/10.1080/23738871.2017.1356859

Aaronson SA (2019) What are we talking about when we talk about digital protectionism? World Trade Rev 18(4):541–577. https://doi.org/10.1017/S1474745618000198

Aaronson SA, Leblond P (2018) Another digital divide: the rise of data realms and its implications for the WTO. J Int Econ Law 21(2):245–272. https://doi.org/10.1093/jiel/jgy019

Aaronson SA, Maxim R (2013) Trade and the internet: the challenge of the NSA revelations: policies in the US, EU and Canada. https://doi.org/10.2139/ssrn.2407270

Acquisti A (2010) The economics of personal data and the economics of privacy: background paper #3 joint WPISP-WPIE roundtable. The economics of personal data and privacy: 30 years after the OECD privacy guidelines

Acquisti A, Taylor C, Wagman L (2016) The economics of privacy. J Econ Lit 54(2):442–492. https://doi.org/10.1257/jel.54.2.442

Alhadeff J, van Alsenoy B, Dumortier J (2012) The accountability principle in data protection regulation: origin, development and future directions. In: Guagnin D et al (eds) Managing privacy through accountability. Palgrave Macmillan UK, London, pp 49–82

Andrews EL (1999) Europe and U.S. are still at odds over privacy. https://archive.nytimes.com/www.nytimes.com/library/tech/99/05/biztech/articles/27europe-us-privacy.html. Accessed 5 Apr 2024

APEC (2005) Privacy Framework. https://www.apec.org/publications/2005/12/apec-privacy-framework. Accessed 5 Apr 2024

---

[410] Yakovleva (2020a), p. 882.

APEC (2015) Privacy Framework. https://www.apec.org/Publications/2017/08/APEC-Privacy-Framework-(2015). Accessed 5 Apr 2024

Article 29 Data Protection Working Party (2010) Opinion 3/2010 on the principle of accountability. 00062/10/EN. Adopted on 13 July 2010

Article 29 Data Protection Working Party (2014) Joint work between experts from the Article 29 Working Party and from APEC Economies, on a referential for requirements for Binding Corporate Rules submitted to national Data Protection Authorities in the EU and Cross Border Privacy Rules submitted to APEC CBPR Accountability Agents. https://www.apec.org/docs/default-source/Groups/ECSG/20140307_Referential-BCR-CBPR-reqs.pdf. Accessed 5 Apr 2024

Bracy J (2024) New draft bipartisan US federal privacy bill unveiled. International Association of Privacy Professionals. https://iapp.org/news/a/new-draft-bipartisan-us-federal-privacy-bill-unveiled/. Accessed 7 Apr 2024

Bradford A (2020) The Brussels effect: how the European Union rules the world. Oxford University Press, New York

Burgess M (2022) How GDPR is failing: the world-leading data law changed how companies work. But four years on, there's a lag on cleaning up Big Tech. https://www.wired.com/story/gdpr-2022/. Accessed 5 Apr 2024

Burri M (2017) Current and emerging trends in disruptive technologies: implications for the present and future of EU's trade policy. EP/EXPO/B/INTA/2017/06. https://doi.org/10.2861/96860

Burri M (2021) Interfacing privacy and trade. Case West Res J Int Law 53:35–88

Burri M, Schär R (2016) The reform of the EU Data Protection Framework: outlining key changes and assessing their fitness for a data-driven economy. J Inf Policy 6:479–511. https://doi.org/10.5325/jinfopoli.6.2016.0479

Buttarelli G (2016) The EU GDPR as a clarion call for a new global digital gold standard. Int Data Privacy Law 6(2):77–78. https://doi.org/10.1093/idpl/ipw006

Bygrave LA (2014) Data privacy law: an international perspective. Oxford University Press

Casalini F, López González J (2019) Trade and cross-border data flows. OECD trade policy papers no. 220. OECD Publishing, Paris. https://doi.org/10.1787/b2023a47-en

Centre for Information Policy Leadership (2009) Data protection accountability: the essential elements. https://www.informationpolicycentre.com/uploads/5/7/1/0/57104281/data_protection_accountability-the_essential_elements__discussion_document_october_2009_.pdf. Accessed 5 Apr 2024

Centre for Information Policy Leadership (2018) The case for accountability: how it enables effective data protection and trust in the digital society. https://www.informationpolicycentre.com/uploads/5/7/1/0/57104281/cipl_accountability_paper_1_-_the_case_for_accountability_-_how_it_enables_effective_data_protection_and_trust_in_the_digital_society.pdf. Accessed 5 Apr 2024

Centre for Information Policy Leadership (2020) What does the USMCA mean for a US Federal Privacy Law. White paper

Chander A (2020) Is data localization a solution for Schrems II? J Int Econ Law 23(3):771–784. https://doi.org/10.1093/jiel/jgaa024

Chander A, Lê UP (2015) Data nationalism. Empory Law J 64:677–739

Chander A, Schwartz PM (2023) Privacy and/or trade. Univ Chic Law Rev 90:49–135

Chander A, Kaminski ME, McGeveran W (2021) Catalyzing privacy law. Minn Law Rev 105:1733–1802

Christakis T (2020) After Schrems II: uncertainties on the legal basis for data transfers and constitutional implications for Europe. https://europeanlawblog.eu/2020/07/21/after-schrems-ii-uncertainties-on-the-legal-basis-for-data-transfers-and-constitutional-implications-for-europe/#conclusion. Accessed 5 Apr 2024

Congressional Research Service (2020) Data flows, online privacy, and trade policy. R45584

Congressional Research Service (2021) EU data transfer requirements and U.S. intelligence laws: understanding Schrems II and its impact on the EU-U.S. privacy shield. R46724

Cory N, Dascoli L (2021) How barriers to cross-border data flows are spreading globally, what they cost, and how to address them. Information Technology & Innovation Foundation. https://itif.org/publications/2021/07/19/how-barriers-cross-border-data-flows-are-spreading-globally-what-they-cost/. Accessed 5 Apr 2024

Council of Europe (1949) Statute of the Council of Europe. https://rm.coe.int/1680306052. Accessed 5 Apr 2024

Council of Europe (1981) Explanatory report to the Convention for the Protection of Individuals with regard to Automatic Processing of Personal Data

Council of Europe (2018) The modernised Convention 108: novelties in a nutshell. https://rm.coe.int/16808accf8. Accessed 5 Apr 2024

Crompton M, Cowper C, Jefferis C (2009) The Australian Dodo Case: an insight for data protection regulation. World Data Prot Rep 9(1):3–9

Cukier K (2010) Data, data everywhere. https://www.economist.com/special-report/2010/02/27/data-data-everywhere. Accessed 5 Apr 2024

Davis Polk (2021) China's personal data law comes into force accompanied by draft rules on cross-border data transfers. https://www.davispolk.com/insights/client-update/chinas-personal-data-law-comes-force-accompanied-draft-rules-cross-border#_ftn2. Accessed 5 Apr 2024

de Hert P, Czerniawski M (2016) Expanding the European data protection scope beyond territory: Article 3 of the General Data Protection Regulation in its wider context. Int Data Privacy Law 6(3):230–243. https://doi.org/10.1093/idpl/ipw008

Diggelmann O, Cleis MN (2014) How the right to privacy became a human right. Hum Rights Law Rev 14(3):441–458. https://doi.org/10.1093/hrlr/ngu014

DigiChina (2018) Translation: cybersecurity law of the People's Republic of China - Effective June 1, 2017. https://digichina.stanford.edu/work/translation-cybersecurity-law-of-the-peoples-republic-of-china-effective-june-1-2017/. Accessed 5 Apr 2024

DigiChina (2021a) Seven major changes in China's finalized personal information protection law. https://digichina.stanford.edu/work/seven-major-changes-in-chinas-finalized-personal-information-protection-law/. Accessed 5 Apr 2024

DigiChina (2021b) Translation: outbound data transfer security assessment measures (draft for comment) - Oct. 2021 - DigiChina. https://digichina.stanford.edu/work/translation-outbound-data-transfer-security-assessment-measures-draft-for-comment-oct-2021/. Accessed 5 Apr 2024

DigiChina (2021c) Translation: personal information protection law of the People's Republic of China - Effective Nov. 1, 2021 - DigiChina. https://digichina.stanford.edu/work/translation-personal-information-protection-law-of-the-peoples-republic-of-china-effective-nov-1-2021/. Accessed 5 Apr 2024

DigiChina (2021d) Translation: data security law of the People's Republic of China - effective Sept. 1, 2021 - DigiChina. https://digichina.stanford.edu/work/translation-data-security-law-of-the-peoples-republic-of-china/#_ftn11. Accessed 5 Apr 2024

Drake WJ (2016) Background paper for the workshop on data localization and barriers to trans-border data flows. https://www3.weforum.org/docs/Background_Paper_Forum_workshop%2009.2016.pdf. Accessed 5 Apr 2024

Edelman G (2022) Don't look now, but Congress might pass an actually good privacy bill: a bill with bipartisan support might finally give the US a strong federal data protection law. Wired. https://www.wired.com/story/american-data-privacy-protection-act-adppa/. Accessed 5 Apr 2024

Erie MS, Streinz T (2021) The Beijing effect: China's digital silk road as transnational data governance. N Y Univ J Int Law Polit 54(1):1–92

European Commission (2010) Communication from the Commission: a comprehensive approach on personal data protection in the European Union. COM(2010) 609 final

European Commission (2016) Transatlantic data flows: restoring trust through strong safeguards. Communication from the Commission, COM/2016/0117 final

European Commission (2017) Communication from the Commission to the European Parliament and the Council Exchanging and Protecting Personal Data in a Globalised World. COM(2017) 7final

European Commission (2020a) Communication from the Commission: a European strategy for data. COM(2020) 66 final

European Commission (2020b) On artificial intelligence - a European approach to excellence and trust. White paper

European Commission (2020c) Communication from the Commission to the European Parliament and the Council: data protection as a pillar of citizens' empowerment and the EU's approach to the digital transition - two years of application of the General Data Protection Regulation. COM (2020) 264 final

European Commission (2023) Data protection: European Commission adopts new adequacy decision for safe and trusted EU-US data flows. Press release. https://ec.europa.eu/commission/presscorner/detail/en/ip_23_3721. Accessed 5 Apr 2024

European Commission (2024) EU-US Trade and Technology Council Factsheet. Factsheet: EU-US Trade and Technology Council (2021-2024) | Shaping Europe's digital future (europa.eu). Accessed 5 Apr 2024

European Union (2007) Explanations relating to the Charter of Fundamental Rights (2007/C303/02)

Fabbrini F, Celeste E (2021) EU data protection law between extraterritoriality and sovereignty. In: Fabbrini F, Celeste E, Quinn J (eds) Data protection beyond borders: transatlantic perspectives on extraterritoriality and sovereignty. Hart, Oxford

Farrell H (2015) Obama says that Europeans are using privacy rules to protect their firms against U.S. competition. Is he right? The Washington Post. https://www.washingtonpost.com/news/monkey-cage/wp/2015/02/17/obama-says-that-europeans-are-using-privacy-rules-to-protect-their-firms-against-u-s-competition-is-he-right/. Accessed 5 Apr 2024

Finck M, Pallas F (2020) They who must not be identified—distinguishing personal from non-personal data under the GDPR. Int Data Privacy Law 10(1):11–36. https://doi.org/10.1093/idpl/ipz026

Fischer JL (2021) The challenges and opportunities for a US Federal Privacy Law. In: Fabbrini F, Celeste E, Quinn J (eds) Data protection beyond borders: transatlantic perspectives on extraterritoriality and sovereignty. Hart, Oxford, pp 27–44

Fleming S (2021) What is digital sovereignty and why is Europe so interested in it? https://www.weforum.org/agenda/2021/03/europe-digital-sovereignty/. Accessed 5 Apr 2024

Gao HS (2021) Data regulation with Chinese characteristics. In: Burri M (ed) Big data and global trade law. Cambridge University Press, Cambridge, pp 245–267

Gasser U (2016) Recoding privacy law: reflections on the future relationship among law. Technol Privacy Harv Law Rev Forum 130(2):61–70

Gasser U (2021) Futuring digital privacy. In: Burri M (ed) Big data and global trade law. Cambridge University Press, Cambridge, pp 195–211

Gordon S, Ram A (2018) Information wars: how Europe became the world's data police. Financial Times. https://www.ft.com/content/1aa9b0fa-5786-11e8-bdb7-f6677d2e1ce8. Accessed 5 Apr 2024

Greenleaf G (2009) Five years of the APEC Privacy Framework: failure or promise? Comput Law Secur Rev 25(1):28–43. https://doi.org/10.1016/j.clsr.2008.12.002

Greenleaf G (2012) The influence of European data privacy standards outside Europe: implications for globalization of Convention 108. Int Data Privacy Law 2(2):68–92. https://doi.org/10.1093/idpl/ips006

Gunasekara G (2007) The "final" privacy frontier? Regulating trans-border data flows. Int J Law Inf Technol 17(2):147–179. https://doi.org/10.1093/ijlit/eam004

Hervé A (2021) Data protection and artificial intelligence. In: Peng S, Lin C-F, Streinz T (eds) Artificial intelligence and international economic law: disruption, regulation, and reconfiguration. Cambridge University Press, Cambridge, pp 193–214

Hill JF (2014) The growth of data localization post-Snowden: analysis and recommendations for U.S. policymakers and business leaders. The Hague Institute for Global Justice, Conference on the future of cyber governance. https://ssrn.com/abstract=2430275 or https://doi.org/10.2139/ssrn.2430275

Holvast J (2009) History of privacy. In: Matyáš V et al (eds) The future of identity in the information society: 4th IFIP WG 9.2, 9.6, 11.6, 11.7/FIDIS International Summer School, Brno, Czech Republic, September 1–7, 2008; revised selected papers, vol 298. Springer, Berlin, pp 13–42

Hon WK (ed) (2017) Data localization laws and policy: the EU data protection international transfers restriction through a cloud computing lens. Edward Elgar, Cheltenham

Hoofnagle CJ (2016) Federal trade commission privacy law and policy. Cambridge University Press, New York

Hufbauer GC, Zhiyao L (2019) Global E-commerce talks stumble on data issues, privacy, and more. Peterson Institute for International Economics policy brief 19-14. https://www.piie.com/publications/policy-briefs/global-e-commerce-talks-stumble-data-issues-privacy-and-more. Accessed 5 Apr 2024

Humerick M (2018) The tortoise and the hare of international data privacy law: can the United States catch up to rising global standards? Catholic Univ J Law Technol 27:1

Kokott J, Sobotta C (2013) The distinction between privacy and data protection in the jurisprudence of the CJEU and the ECtHR. Int Data Privacy Law 3(4):222–228. https://doi.org/10.1093/idpl/ipt017

Kuner C (2009a) An international legal framework for data protection: issues and prospects. Comput Law Secur Rev 25(4):307–317. https://doi.org/10.1016/j.clsr.2009.05.001

Kuner C (2009b) Global data transfers on the internet: lessons from the ancient world. SSRN Journal. https://doi.org/10.2139/ssrn.1445458

Kuner C (2010) Data protection law and international jurisdiction on the internet (part 1). Int J Law Inf Technol 18(2):176–193. https://doi.org/10.1093/ijlit/eaq002

Kuner C (2011) Regulation of transborder data flows under data protection and privacy law: past, present and future. OECD digital economy papers, no. 187. OECD Publishing, Paris. https://doi.org/10.1787/5kg0s2fk315f-en

Kuner C (2013) Transborder data flows and data privacy law. Oxford University Press, Oxford

Kuner C (2015) Extraterritoriality and regulation of international data transfers in EU data protection law. Int Data Privacy Law 5(4):235–245. https://doi.org/10.1093/idpl/ipv019

Kuner C (2017) Reality and illusion in EU data transfer regulation post Schrems. German Law J 18(4):881–918

Kuner C, Bygrave LA, Docksey C, Drechsler L (2020) The EU General Data Protection Regulation (GDPR): a commentary, 1st edn. Oxford University Press, Oxford

Lauf F (2021) Data sovereignty and data economy—two repulsive forces? Fraunhofer-Gesellschaft. https://publica.fraunhofer.de/entities/publication/9cf79aa5-de13-4b49-acc2-94f89dad405c/details. Accessed 5 Apr 2024

Lawder D (2023) US drops digital trade demands at WTO to allow room for stronger tech regulation. Reuters. https://www.reuters.com/world/us/us-drops-digital-trade-demands-wto-allow-room-stronger-tech-regulation-2023-10-25/. Accessed 5 Apr 2024

Li B, Xiong S, Zhou A (2023) China issues new guidelines for SCC mechanism for cross-border data transfer. ReedSmith. https://www.reedsmith.com/de/perspectives/2023/06/china-issues-new-guidelines-for-scc-mechanism-for-cross. Accessed 5 Apr 2024

Luo Y, Dan X (2024) China eases restrictions on cross-border data flows. Covington Inside Privacy. https://www.insideprivacy.com/uncategorized/china-eases-restrictions-on-cross-border-data-flows/. Accessed 5 Apr 2024

Madrid Resolution (2009) International standards on the protection of personal data and privacy. https://www.edps.europa.eu/sites/default/files/publication/09-11-05_madrid_int_standards_en.pdf. Accessed 5 Apr 2024

Manyika J, Chui M, Brown B, Bughin J, Dobbs R, Roxburgh C, Hung Byers A (2011) Big data: the next frontier for innovation, competition, and productivity. McKinsey Global Institute. https://www.mckinsey.com/capabilities/mckinsey-digital/our-insights/big-data-the-next-frontier-for-innovation. Accessed 5 Apr 2024

Manyika J, Lund S, Bughin J, Woetzel L, Stamenov K, Dhingra D (2016) Digital globalization: the new era of global flows. McKinsey Global Institute. https://www.mckinsey.com/capabilities/mckinsey-digital/our-insights/digital-globalization-the-new-era-of-global-flows. Accessed 5 Apr 2024

Mayer-Schönberger V, Cukier K (2014) Big data: a revolution that will transform how we live, work and think, 1. Mariner Books edition

Mishra N (2015) Data localization laws in a digital world: data protection or data protectionism? NUS Centre for International Law Research paper no. 19/05. The Public Sphere

Mishra N (2019) Privacy, cybersecurity, and GATS Article XIV: a new frontier for trade and internet regulation? World Trade Rev 19(3):1–24. https://doi.org/10.1017/S1474745619000120

Mitchell AD, Mishra N (2018) Data at the docks: modernizing international trade law for the digital economy. Vanderbilt J Entertain Technol Law 20:1073–1134

Mitchell AD, Mishra N (2019) Regulating cross-border data flows in a data-driven world: how WTO law can contribute. J Int Econ Law 22(3):389–416. https://doi.org/10.1093/jiel/jgz016

Mitchell AD, Samlidis T (2022) Cloud services and government digital sovereignty in Australia and beyond. Int J Law Inf Technol 29(4):364–394. https://doi.org/10.1093/ijlit/eaac003

Naef T (2023) Data protection without data protectionism, European yearbook of international economic law. Springer International Publishing, Cham

National Board of Trade (2014) No transfer, no trade: the importance of cross-border data transfers for companies based in Sweden

Nyst C, Falchetta T (2017) The right to privacy in the digital age. J Hum Rights Pract 9(1):104–118. https://doi.org/10.1093/jhuman/huw026

OECD (2002) OECD guidelines on the protection of privacy and transborder flows of personal data. OECD Publishing, Paris. https://doi.org/10.1787/9789264196391-en

OECD (2006) Report on the cross-border enforcement of privacy laws. OECD digital economy papers, no. 121. OECD Publishing, Paris. https://doi.org/10.1787/231304814207

OECD (2013a) Exploring the economics of personal data: a survey of methodologies for measuring monetary value. OECD digital economy papers no. 220. OECD Publishing, Paris. https://doi.org/10.1787/5k486qtxldmq-en

OECD (2013b) The OECD Privacy Framework. https://www.oecd.org/sti/ieconomy/oecd_privacy_framework.pdf. Accessed 5 Apr 2023

OECD (2015a) OECD Digital Economy Outlook 2015. OECD Publishing, Paris. https://doi.org/10.1787/9789264232440-en

OECD (2015b) The governance of globalized data flows - current trends and future challenges: working party on security and privacy in the digital economy. DSTI/ICCP/REG(2015)3

Ohm P (2010) Broken promises of privacy: responding to the surprising failure of anonymization. UCLA Law Rev 57:1701–1777

Pasadilla GO (2020) Next generation non-tariff measures: emerging data policies and barriers to digital trade. ARTNeT working paper series no. 187

Peng S (2011) Digitalization of services, the GATS and the protection of personal data. In: Sethe R, Heinemann A, Hilty RM (eds) Kommunikation: Festschrift für Rolf H. Weber zum 60. Geburtstag. Stämpfli, Bern, pp 753–769

Petkova B (2019) Privacy as Europe's first amendment. Eur Law J 25(2):140–154. https://doi.org/10.1111/eulj.12316

Poskauer (2015) A primer on Russia's new data localization law. https://privacylaw.proskauer.com/2015/08/articles/data-privacy-laws/a-primer-on-russias-new-data-localization-law/. Accessed 5 Apr 2024

Purtova N (2018) The law of everything. Broad concept of personal data and future of EU data protection law. Law Innov Technol 10(1):40–81. https://doi.org/10.1080/17579961.2018.1452176

Reidenberg JR (1995) The fundamental role of privacy and confidence in the network. Wake Forest Law Rev 30(105):105–125

Roessler B (2015) Should personal data be a tradable good? On the moral limits of markets in privacy. In: Roessler B, Mokrosinska D (eds) Social dimensions of privacy. Cambridge University Press, Cambridge, pp 141–161

Ross W (2018) EU data privacy laws are likely to create barriers to trade: GDPR creates serious, unclear legal obligations for both private and public entities. https://www.ft.com/content/9d261f44-6255-11e8-bdd1-cc0534df682c. Accessed 5 Apr 2024

Rotenberg J (2020) Privacy before trade: assessing the WTO-consistency of privacy-based cross-border data flow restrictions. Univ Miami Int Comp Law Rev 28(1):91–120

Rubinstein IS (2013) Big data: the end of privacy or a new beginning? Int Data Privacy Law 3(2):74–87. https://doi.org/10.1093/idpl/ips036

Sacks S, Shi M, Webster G, Triolo P (2021) Knowns and unknowns about China's new draft cross-border data rules: how far will China's cross-border data rules go in preventing transfers abroad? https://digichina.stanford.edu/work/knowns-and-unknowns-about-chinas-new-draft-cross-border-data-rules/. Accessed 5 Apr 2024

Schwartz PM (1999) Privacy and democracy in cyberspace. Vanderbilt Law Rev 52(6):1609–1702

Schwartz PM (2004) Property, privacy, and personal data. Harv Law Rev 117(7):2056–2128

Schwartz PM (2009) Preemption and privacy. Yale Law J 118(5):902–947

Schwartz PM (2013) The EU-U.S. privacy collision: a turn to institutions and procedures. Harv Law Rev 126:1966–2009

Schwartz PM (2019) Global data privacy: the EU way. N Y Univ Law Rev 94(4):772–818

Schwartz PM, Pfeifer K-N (2017) Transatlantic data privacy law. Georgetown Law J 106(1):117–179

Schwartz PM, Solove DJ (2011) The PII problem: privacy and a new concept of personally identifiable information. N Y Univ Law Rev 86:1814–1894

Sedgewick MB (2017) Transborder data privacy as trade. Calif Law Rev 105:1513–1542. https://doi.org/10.15779/Z382V2C94C

Sen N (2018) Understanding the role of the WTO in international data flows: taking the liberalization or the regulatory autonomy path? J Int Econ Law 21(2):323–348. https://doi.org/10.1093/jiel/jgy021

Singelton S (2002) Privacy as a trade issue: guidelines for U.S. trade negotiators. https://www.heritage.org/trade/report/privacy-trade-issue-guidelines-us-trade-negotiators. Accessed 5 Apr 2024

Skadden, Arps, Slate, Meagher & Flom LLP (2021) China's new data security and personal information protection laws: what they mean for multinational companies. https://www.skadden.com/Insights/Publications/2021/11/Chinas-New-Data-Security-and-Personal-Information-Protection-Laws. Accessed 5 Apr 2024

Solove DJ (2001) Privacy and power: computer databases and metaphors for information privacy. Stanf Law Rev 53:1393–1462

Solove DJ (2002) Conceptualizing privacy. Calif Law Rev 90(4):1087–1155

Solove DJ (2006) A taxonomy of privacy. Univ Pa Law Rev 154(3):477–560

Solove DJ, Schwartz PM (2018) Information privacy law, Aspen casebook series, 6th edn. Wolters Kluwer Law & Business, New York

Solove DJ, Schwartz PM (2019) ALI data privacy: overview and black letter text. SSRN Journal. https://doi.org/10.2139/ssrn.3457563

Svantesson DJB (2011) The regulation of cross-border data flows. Int Data Privacy Law 1(3):180–198. https://doi.org/10.1093/idpl/ipr012

Svantesson DJB (2015) Extraterritoriality and targeting in EU data privacy law: the weak spot undermining the regulation. Int Data Privacy Law 5(4):226–234. https://doi.org/10.1093/idpl/ipv024

Svantesson DJB (2020) Data localisation trends and challenges: considerations for the review of the privacy guidelines. OECD digital economy papers no. 301. OECD Publishing, Paris. https://doi.org/10.1787/7fbaed62-en

Swire PP, Litan RE (2010) None of your business: world data flows, electronic commerce, and the European privacy directive. Brookings Institution Press, Washington

The Economist (2012) Private data, public rules: the world's biggest internet markets are planning laws to protect personal data. But their approaches differ wildly. https://www.economist.com/international/2012/01/28/private-data-public-rules. Accessed 5 Apr 2024

U.S. Department of Commerce (2010) Guide to protecting the confidentiality of Personally Identifiable Information (PII): recommendations of the National Institute of Standards and Technology. Special publication 800-122

UN (1990), Guidelines for the regulation of computerised personal data files, E/CN.4/1990/72, 14 December 1990

UN (2013) General Assembly, Human Rights Council, Resolution 68/167 The Right to Privacy in the Digital Age, 13. December 2013, A/RES/68/167

UN (2014a) General Assembly, Human Rights Council, Resolution 69/166 The Right to Privacy in the Digital Age, 18 December 2014, A/RES/69/166

UN (2014b) Report of the High Commissioner for Human Rights, The Right to Privacy in the Digital Age, 30 June 2014, A/HRC/27/37

UN (2015) UN General Assembly, Human Rights Council, Resolution 28/16 The right to privacy in the digital age, 1 April 2015, A/HRC/RES/28/16

UNCTAD (2016) Data protection regulations and international data flows: implications for trade and development. https://unctad.org/publication/data-protection-regulations-and-international-data-flows-implications-trade-and. Accessed 5 Apr 2024

UNCTAD (2024) Global cyberlaw tracker. https://unctad.org/page/data-protection-and-privacy-legislation-worldwide. Accessed 5 April 2025

van der Marel E, Bauer M, Lee-Makiyama H (2014) A friendly fire on economic recovery: a methodology to estimate the costs of data regulations. ECIPE working paper, no. 02/2014, Brussels. https://ecipe.org/publications/dataloc-methodology/. Accessed 5 Apr 2024

Voskamp F, Kipker D-K, Yamato R (2013) Grenzüberschreitende Datenschutzregulierung im Pazifik-Raum. Datenschutz und Datensicherheit - DuD 37(7):452–456. https://doi.org/10.1007/s11623-013-0177-z

Wagner J (2018) The transfer of personal data to third countries under the GDPR: when does a recipient country provide an adequate level of protection? Int Data Privacy Law 8(4):318–337. https://doi.org/10.1093/idpl/ipy008

Wall A (2017) GDPR matchup: the APEC Privacy Framework and cross-border privacy rules. https://iapp.org/news/a/gdpr-matchup-the-apec-privacy-framework-and-cross-border-privacy-rules/. Accessed 5 Apr 2024

Warren SD, Brandeis LD (1890) The right to privacy. Harv Law Rev 4(5):193–220

Weber RH (2013) Transborder data transfers: concepts, regulatory approaches and new legislative initiatives. Int Data Privacy Law 3(2):117–130. https://doi.org/10.1093/idpl/ipt001

Whitman JQ (2004) The two western cultures of privacy: dignity versus liberty. Yale Law J 113(6):1151–1221

Willemyns I (2020) Agreement forthcoming? A comparison of EU, US, and Chinese RTAs in times of plurilateral E-commerce negotiations. J Int Econ Law 23(1):221–244. https://doi.org/10.1093/jiel/jgz048

Working Party on the Protection of Individuals (1999) Opinion 1/99 concerning the level of data protection in the United States and the ongoing discussions between the European Commission and the United States Government. 5092/98/EN/final WP15

World Economic Forum (2011) Personal data: the emergence of a new asset class. https://www.weforum.org/publications/personal-data-emergence-new-asset-class/. Accessed 5 Apr 2024

World Economic Forum (2022) What do China's data export regulations mean for its trade competitiveness? https://www.weforum.org/agenda/2022/11/china-data-export-regulations-threaten-trade-competitiveness/. Accessed 5 Apr 2024

WTO (2018) Joint Statement on Electronic Commerce Initiative, Communication from the United States, JOB/GC/178, 12 April 2018

Yakovleva S (2018) Should fundamental rights to privacy and data protection be a part of the EU's international trade 'deals'? World Trade Rev 17(03):477–508. https://doi.org/10.1017/S1474745617000453

Yakovleva S (2020a) Personal data transfers in international trade and EU law: a tale of two 'necessities'. J World Invest Trade 21(6):881–919. https://doi.org/10.1163/22119000-12340189

Yakovleva S (2020b) Privacy protection(ism): the latest wave of trade constraints on regulatory autonomy. Univ Miami Law Rev 74:416–519

Yakovleva S, Irion K (2020) Pitching trade against privacy: reconciling EU governance of personal data flows with external trade. Int Data Privacy Law 10(3):201–221. https://doi.org/10.1093/idpl/ipaa003

Zuboff S (2016) The secrets of surveillance capitalism. Frankfurter Allgemeine Zeitung. https://www.faz.net/aktuell/feuilleton/debatten/the-digital-debate/shoshana-zuboff-secrets-of-surveillance-capitalism-14103616.html. Accessed 5 Apr 2024

Zuboff S (2019) The age of surveillance capitalism: the fight for a human future at the new frontier of power, 1st edn. PublicAffairs, New York

Chapter 5
Mitigating the Data Privacy Collision in Digital Trade

5.1 Introduction

Considering the intangible nature of services and their consequential readiness to be digitalised, cross-border data flows are an important driving force for a number of cross-border service activities that were previously considered to be non-tradable (*see* further *supra* Sect. 2.3.1.2). The multilateral regulation of trade in services was conceived to reflect the peculiarities of such trade, which involves that trade in services is particularly subject to non-tariff barriers arising from the internal regulations of WTO members.[1] The GATS therefore had to address the need to ensure that domestic measures inconsistent with multilateral trade rules are implemented to pursue legitimate policy objectives to the exclusion of protectionist interests, on the one hand, and to mitigate unintended trade-restrictive consequences resulting from divergent domestic regulatory standards and the manner in which they are administered, on the other.[2] In view of the interaction of WTO law with "*behind the border*" regulation, rulemaking on cross-border trade in services necessarily required careful consideration of a balance between WTO members' domestic regulatory autonomy and multilateral trade law.[3] Therefore, WTO Members' concerns regarding the preservation of their regulatory autonomy under the impact of WTO law were a key consideration during the Uruguay Round negotiations.[4] Against this background, the preamble of the GATS underscores a dual objective of the agreement as it emphasises the WTO Members "*desire*" of an "*achievement of progressively higher levels of liberalization of trade in services through successive rounds of multilateral negotiations aimed at promoting the interests of all*

---

[1] Cf. Weiß (2020b), pp. 29–31. *See* generally Lowenfeld (2009), pp. 120–125.
[2] Lim and de Meester (2014), pp. 8–10.
[3] Lim and de Meester (2014), pp. 1–3.
[4] Adlung (2014), p. 373.

participants on a mutually advantageous basis" while "*recognizing the right of Members to regulate, and to introduce new regulations, on the supply of services within their territories in order to meet national policy objectives*". WTO Members have agreed in the Council for Trade in Services that, also with regard to digital trade, it is vital to seek to balance a Members' "*right to regulate*" with the economic imperative to ensure that internal regulatory measures do not impose undue barriers to trade.[5] In this context, this chapter analyses the role of trade law with respect to the nexus of digital trade and data privacy against the background of the relationship between international cooperation in times of digital globalisation and national regulatory autonomy in matters of data privacy. To this end an in-depth analysis of the constraints that international trade commitments impose on domestic regulatory autonomy with regard to data privacy measures will be conducted. At the core of this chapter lies the question of whether WTO law and current PTAs are positioned to mitigate the data privacy collision of unilateral data governance in data privacy matters that has been identified in the previous chapter. An initial section will analyse the relationship between multilateral trade law and domestic data privacy rules (Sect. 5.2). In a further section, current trade agreements are examined to determine the role and overall relevancy of domestic data privacy as well as room for manoeuvre for domestic measures in these treaties (Sect. 5.3).

5.2 WTO Law and Domestic Data Privacy Regulations

With the advent of digital trade, issues of compatibility of domestic data privacy measures with commitments under international trade law have increasingly come into focus in the academic literature.[6] Domestic data privacy measures as an articulation of national regulatory autonomy to address socio-cultural preferences in an individual trade-off between economic and non-economic elements could, in this sense, result in conflicts with trade law. However, WTO law is not insensitive to national specificities and domestic regulatory interests—quite the contrary.[7] A key provision addressing the balance between the multilateral trade commitments and national data privacy measures relates to Article XIV GATS, which provides for general exceptions to obligations under trade law.[8] Article XIV GATS preserves the

---

[5] *See* for example WTO (1999), pp. 2–3, para. 11.

[6] *See* generally Aaronson (2015); Kuner (2013), p. 52; MacDonald and Streatfeild (2014); Mishra (2019); Pérez Asinari (2002); Rotenberg (2020); Weber (2012). *See* particularly with regard to the European regime of data protection Irion et al. (2016); Mattoo and Meltzer (2019), pp. 779–782; Naef (2023), pp. 290–324; Reyes (2011); Ruotolo (2018); Shapiro (2003); Swire and Litan (2010), pp. 188–196.

[7] *See* further on the WTO's objective and purpose in this regard Weiß (2020b), pp. 98–101.

[8] This book will not examine other provisions that could serve as justification for interfering with trade law obligations by means of data privacy measures in detail. Among these are Article V GATS on economic integration, Article XIV bis regarding security exceptions or the confidentiality

right of WTO Members to adopt regulations in connection with matters of national interest, such as those relating to public morals or the maintenance of public order, the protection of human, animal or plant life, or health.[9] In this context, Article XIV (c)(ii) GATS provides for a general exception allowing specifically for measures that are *"necessary to secure compliance with laws or regulations which are not inconsistent with the provisions of this Agreement including those relating to the protection of the privacy of individuals in relation to the processing and dissemination of personal data and the protection of confidentiality of individual records and accounts"*. In addition, Article XIV(a) GATS authorizes measures *"necessary to protect public morals or maintain public order"*. which may pertain to social and moral elements involved in domestic data privacy measures. However, apart from general exceptions, WTO Members' room for manoeuvre in regulating data privacy also depends on the interpretation of their non-discrimination commitments relating to the MFN principle and NT under GATS, for example. Moreover, Article VI GATS specifically addresses the delicate relationship between WTO members' right to regulate and multilateral regulation of trade in services. Certainly, it is important to recall the specific provisions relating to data privacy that may limit certain commitments under the GATS, particularly with respect to telecommunication and financial services. This is the case with respect to Article 5(d) of the GATS Annex on Telecommunication and Article B.8 of the Understanding on Commitments in Financial Services. However, these provisions have only a very narrow scope of application and partly reflect the requirements of the general exceptions.[10] Against this background, the regulation of trade in services under the GATS is particularly well suited to a review of how WTO law relates to the nexus of digital trade and data privacy. However, since there has been no WTO dispute relating to domestic measures of data privacy and Article XIV(c)(ii) has never been invoked before the WTO dispute settlement bodies, any assessment of the interplay between digital trade and domestic data privacy legislation under WTO law is a theoretical exercise in nature.

5.2.1 *GATS Commitments and Domestic Data Privacy Regulation*

The following section examines the requirements that domestic data privacy measures must meet in order to be consistent with commitments under the GATS. It is important to note that this analysis is predicated on two distinctive factors. First, the regulatory structure under the positive list approach of the GATS must be taken into

---

exception pursuant to 5(d) of the Annex on Telecommunications. *See* with further references in this regard Naef (2023), pp. 325–331.
[9] *See* generally Cottier et al. (2008).
[10] *See* Yakovleva (2018), pp. 489–499. *See* also *supra* Sect. 3.3.2.6.4.

account, which means that specific commitments to liberalisation may be customised according to national schedules (*see* further *supra* Sect. 3.3.2.6.1). Thus, if there is no specific commitment to liberalize a particular trade in services activity in the national schedules, there is in principle no conflict to be expected between trade law and national data privacy rules in this regard. Second, the above analysis has illustrated a heterogeneous regulatory environment for data privacy. A comprehensive analysis of the GATS compliance of each potential data privacy measure is beyond the scope of this book, as there are a large number of different regulations governing national data privacy that may conflict with trade commitments. Against this background, the following analysis focuses primarily on the typical approaches to regulating the flow of personal data outlined above, as these are particularly relevant to cross-border trade (*see supra* Sect. 4.3.3).

5.2.1.1 Article II GATS (Most-Favoured-Nation Treatment)

The Most-Favoured-Nation rule in Article II GATS is a fundamental component of the multilateral regulation of trade in services as it seeks to ensure equality of opportunity and prohibits discrimination between like services and service suppliers from different countries.[11] MFN treatment under GATS seeks to ban both *de jure* and *de facto* discrimination of like services among WTO Members.[12] In the GATS context, MFN treatment is considered a general obligation and, as such, is not dependent on any specific obligation set forth in a particular case, subject to the exception in Article II:2 GATS (*see supra* Sect. 3.3.2.6.1). Article II:1 GATS stipulates that: *"With respect to any measure covered by this Agreement, each Member shall accord immediately and unconditionally to services and service suppliers of any other member treatment no less favourable than that it accords to like services and service suppliers of any other country."* The Appellate Body held that *"[t]he text of Article II:1 requires, in essence, that treatment by one Member of 'services and services suppliers' of any other Member be compared with treatment of 'like' services and service suppliers of 'any other country'."*.[13] Hence, for the purpose of determining a violation of MFN treatment under GATS, it is necessary to inquire, first, whether the measure falls within the scope of Article II:1 GATS; second, to establish whether there are in fact *"like"* services or service suppliers concerned; and third, whether such like services or service suppliers are accorded *"treatment no less favourable"*.[14]

---

[11] van den Bossche and Zdouc (2022), p. 360.

[12] Appellate Body Report, *EC-Bananas III*, WT/DS27/AB/R, 9 September 1997, paras. 233–234.

[13] Appellate Body Report, *Canada-Autos*, WT/DS139/AB/R, WT/DS142/AB/R, 31 May 2000, para. 171.

[14] van den Bossche and Zdouc (2022), p. 361.

5.2 WTO Law and Domestic Data Privacy Regulations

5.2.1.1.1 Measures by Members Affecting Trade in Services

With regard to the first criterion, it is to be identified whether data privacy measures of WTO Members can be considered to be covered by the scope of the Article II:1 GATS. Hence, there must be made a threshold determination whether a domestic data privacy measure is covered by the scope of application of the GATS. Pursuant to Article I:1 GATS, the agreement "*applies to measures by Members affecting trade in services*". With regard to the terminology used, Article XXVIII:a GATS clarifies that the term "*measure*" means "*measure by a Member, whether in the form of a law, regulation, rule, procedure, decision, administrative action, or any other form*". In turn, "*measures by Members*" are defined in Article I:3 (a) i) GATS as "*measures taken by central, regional or local governments and authorities*". Subsequently, such a measure must then be found to be "*affecting trade in services*". While "*trade in services*" is defined as the "*supply of a service*" in Article I:2 GATS (divided into four modes of supply pursuant to Article I:2 (a)-(d)), supply of a service refers to the "*production, distribution, marketing, sale and delivery of a service*" pursuant to Article XXVIII:b GATS. Furthermore, Article I:3 (b) of the GATS states that services include "*any service in any sector, except services supplied in the exercise of governmental authority*".[15] Further, it must then be established as to whether a domestic data privacy measure may "*affect*" such "*trade in services*". WTO jurisprudence considers that the use of the term "*affect*" indicates a broad reach for GATS.[16] It is stated in the *EC-Bananas III* case: "*consistently with their general approach, the drafters consciously adopted the terms "affecting" and "supply of a service" to ensure that the disciplines of the GATS would cover any measure bearing upon conditions of competition in supply of a service, regardless of whether the measure directly governs or indirectly affects the supply of the service.*".[17] With regard to the preliminary examination of whether data privacy measures by WTO Members touch upon "*trade in services*" pursuant to Article I:2 GATS, reference can be made to the relevant sections above, where the applicability of the GATS to digital services supplied on the basis of cross-border data flows is discussed (*see further supra* Sect. 3.3.2.6.2).

---

[15] The term "*measures by members affecting trade in services*" is exemplified in Article XXVIII:c. (i)-(iii) GATS to include the purchase, payment or use of a service; the access to and use of, in connection with the supply of a service, services which are required by those Members to be offered to the public generally; the presence, including commercial presence, of persons of a Member for the supply of a service in the territory of another Member.

[16] Cf. Appellate Body Report, *Canada—Autos*, WT/DS139/AB/R, WT/DS142/AB/R, 31 May 2000, para. 158 referring to Appellate Body Report, *EC-Bananas III*, WT/DS27/AB/R, 9 September 1997, para. 220 stating: "*The ordinary meaning of the word "affecting" implies a measure that has "an effect on", which indicates a broad scope of application. This interpretation is further reinforced by the conclusions of previous panels that the term "affecting" in the context of Article III of the GATT is wider in scope than such terms as "regulating" or "governing.".*"

[17] Panel Report, *EC-Bananas III*, WT/DS27/R/ECU, 22 May 1997, para. 7.281.

The broad conception of the provision of Article II:1 GATS means that a large number of national regulations are covered by it.[18] One must assume that data privacy regulations adopted by WTO Members through a parliamentary process will generally constitute "*measures*" according to the broad definition of Article XXVIII:a GATS in conjunction with Article I:3 (a) i) GATS. In fact, such data privacy instruments will often take the form of a "*law, regulation [or] rule*" by a "*central, regional or local government [...]*". However, the definition also includes measures such as decisions, procedures or administrative actions that are taken by authorities of a WTO Member on the grounds of data privacy laws. The situation is less clear, in turn, in the case of self-regulatory data privacy initiatives by private companies. These are unlikely to be covered by the scope of GATS if a participation of a governmental authority of a WTO Member can be ruled out. However, if the measure is the result of the execution of delegated authority, it is considered to be the measure of a Member.[19] Furthermore, trade in (digital) services is also particularly likely to be "*affected*" by data privacy measures of WTO Members.[20] From an abstract point of view, this can be affirmed, first of all, with regard to transnational elements of data privacy regulations, which may impede cross-border flows of personal data thereby developing a "*bearing upon conditions of competition*" in a digital economy. In similar vein, data privacy regulations generally involve considerable costs of compliance which can have "*an effect on*" cross-border trade (*see supra* Sect. 4.4.1.1.1). To give a concrete example from the (W/120) Services Sectoral Classification List employed by Members to schedule their commitments under GATS, data privacy measures in particular may impact the category of the so-called "*data processing services*" or the "*data base services*" as subsectors of the "*computer and related services*" sector according to I. B. c. and d.[21]

5.2.1.1.2 Like Services and Service Suppliers

The non-discrimination rule, which arises from the MFN treatment according to Article II:1 GATS, only applies between "*like services*" or "*like service suppliers*". Thus, if the services or service suppliers in question are not "*like*", discrimination under the MFN principle can be ruled out from the outset. The key issue for the application of Article II:1 GATS is therefore what is actually implied by the use of the term "*like*" under the GATS as this forms a basis for the subsequent analysis of the requirement of "*treatment no less favourable*". In this context, it is generally assumed that the interpretation of these terms will be parallel to that of the respective

---

[18] Wolfrum (2008), p. 81.
[19] Van den Bossche and Zdouc (2022), p. 362.
[20] *See* also Reyes (2011), p. 9.
[21] *See* also Crosby (2016), pp. 5–6; Reyes (2011), pp. 7–9.

terms in the context of NT obligations in Article XVII:1 GATS.[22] In this regard, the WTO Panel in *China-Electronic Payment Services* has stated that the determinations of *"like services"*, and *"like service suppliers"*, should be made on a case-by-case basis.[23] Further the Panel underscored that the determination *"must be made on the basis of the evidence as a whole"* and concluded: *"If it is determined that the services in question in a particular case are essentially or generally the same in competitive terms, those services would, in our view, be "like" for purposes of Article XVII."*.[24] Accordingly, the determination of *"likeness"* in the context of Article II:1 GATS is likewise determined by reference to a *"competitive relationship"* against the background of a market-based analysis.[25] Regarding the reference to both *"service"* and *"service supplier"* the Appellate Body in *Argentina—Measures Relating to Trade in Goods and Services* held: *"[...] in a holistic analysis of "likeness", considerations relating to both the service and the service supplier will be relevant, albeit to varying degrees, depending on the circumstances of each case"*.[26]

Furthermore, the Appellate Body found that the criteria for assessing *"likeness"* traditionally used as analytical tools in the context of trade in goods, are also relevant for assessing competitive relationships between services and service providers.[27] Among other considerations specifically relating to the competitive relationships between services and service suppliers, differentiating criteria adapted to trade in services could include criteria such as *"nature and characteristics,"* the *"classification and description of services under, for instance, the UN Central Product Classification (CPC)"*, as well as adaptions of the criteria *"properties, nature and quality,"* *"end use,"* and *"consumer preferences."*[28] Further, the analysis of the *"likeness"* of services and service suppliers may require the additional consideration

---

[22] Panel Report, *Argentina—Financial Services*, WT/DS453/R, 30 September 2015, para. 7.161: "the likeness analysis under Article II of the GATS does not differ from the likeness analysis under Article XVII of the GATS in the sense that it requires an approach based on the competitive relationship.". See also Appellate Body Report, *Argentina—Financial Services*, WT/DS453/AB/R, 14 April 2016, para. 6.34: "While the criteria for analysing "likeness" must be adapted to the particular context of Articles II:1 and XVII:1 of the GATS in accordance with the above considerations, this does not change the fundamental purpose of the comparison to be undertaken in order to determine "likeness" in the context of trade in services, namely, to assess whether and to what extent the services and service suppliers at issue are in a competitive relationship.".

[23] Panel Report, *China—Electronic Payment Services*, WT/DS413/R, 16 July 2012, para. 7.701.

[24] Panel Report, *China—Electronic Payment Services*, WT/DS413/R, 16 July 2012, para. 7.702.

[25] Appellate Body Report, *Argentina—Financial Services*, WT/DS453/AB/R, 14 April 2016, paras. 6.25–6.26.

[26] Appellate Body Report, *Argentina—Financial Services*, WT/DS453/AB/R, 14 April 2016, para. 6.29.

[27] Appellate Body Report, *Argentina—Financial Services*, WT/DS453/AB/R, 14 April 2016, paras. 6.30–6.34.

[28] Appellate Body Report, *Argentina—Financial Services*, WT/DS453/AB/R, 14 April 2016, para. 6.32.

of whether or how this analysis is influenced by the mode(s) of service delivery.[29] In addition, the Appellate Body found, under the so-called *"presumption approach"*, that, following the principles of a presumed likeness with regard to the context of trade in goods: *"where a measure provides for a distinction based <u>exclusively</u> on origin, there will or can be services and service suppliers that are the same in all respects except for origin and, accordingly, "likeness" can be presumed and the complainant is not required to establish "likeness" on the basis of the relevant criteria set out above"*.[30] Yet, the Appellate Body held that the scope of such a presumption is more limited due to the specific complexities involved in trade in services.[31] Moreover, in keeping with the general rule that the burden of proof rests upon the party that asserts the affirmative of a particular claim, the complainant bears the burden of making a prima facie case that a measure draws a distinction between services and service suppliers based exclusively on origin.[32] The prima facie case may be rebutted by demonstrating that origin is not the exclusive basis for the distinction made by the measure between the services and service providers at issue, or by presenting evidence relating to the criteria for determining *"likeness"* adapted to trade in services, thereby demonstrating that a certain factor affects the relevant criteria and that it has an impact on the competitive relationship between the services and service suppliers.[33]

With regard to the assessment of the likeness of services and service suppliers in the context of a data privacy measure, it must be recalled first of all that the business models of the digital economy that will typically be affected by such a measure are generally of considerable complexity. Due to the sophistication of the integration of sectors and subsectors of the (W/120) Sectoral Classification List in the context of digital services and the degree of customisation of services, the determination of likeness in a given instance is unlikely to be a straightforward task. This makes the application of the presumption approach somewhat improbable from the outset, as it cannot be assumed that it will necessarily be possible to establish a *prima facie* case that a data privacy measure is based exclusively on origin. Admittedly, a distinction could be found, particularly with regard to differing treatment of WTO members in

---

[29] Appellate Body Report, *Argentina—Financial Services*, WT/DS453/AB/R, 14 April 2016, para. 6.33.

[30] Appellate Body Report, *Argentina—Financial Services*, WT/DS453/AB/R, 14 April 2016, paras. 6.35–6.45. [emphasis by the author].

[31] Appellate Body Report, *Argentina—Financial Services*, WT/DS453/AB/R, 14 April 2016, paras. 6.38–6.45. See Appellate Body Report, *Argentina—Financial Services*, WT/DS453/AB/R, 14 April 2016, para. 6.41: *"Whether and to what extent such complexities have an impact on the determination of whether a distinction is based exclusively on origin in a particular case will depend on the nature, configuration, and operation of the measure at issue and the particular claims raised."*

[32] Appellate Body Report, *Argentina—Financial Services*, WT/DS453/AB/R, 14 April 2016, para. 6.42.

[33] Appellate Body Report, *Argentina—Financial Services*, WT/DS453/AB/R, 14 April 2016, paras. 6.44–6.45.

the context of data privacy measures that are designed to regulate cross-border data flows. Considering the regulatory approach of adequacy, distinguishing between countries in which adequacy is present and cross-border data flows are permitted without further conditions and those in which this is not the case, a measure could provide for a distinction based exclusively on origin. However, this distinction is generally not made on the basis of the origin of the services and service suppliers (and certainly not exclusively), but with a view to a holistic assessment of the underlying data privacy framework of the WTO Member in question.[34]

With respect to data privacy measures, it is therefore required to determine the likeness of services and service suppliers on a case-by-case basis, taking into account the relevant criteria pertaining to the competitive relationship between services and service suppliers. In this context, the data privacy practices underlying the service or of the service supplier may be relevant to this assessment.[35] Although recourse to the classification and description of services according to the Central Product Classification (CPC), as referenced by the Appellate Body in the Argentina—Financial Services case, may be hindered by the intermingling of service sectors in sophisticated digital business models,[36] as outlined above, adaptations of the criteria such as "*properties, nature and quality,*" "*end use,*" and "*consumer preferences.*" can be relevant in the determination of likeness. Hence, it can be argued that robust data privacy standards have a direct impact on the properties, nature and quality of services and services suppliers. For example, meeting high data privacy standards will typically affect the internal set-up of the service supplier (think of appointing a Data Protection Officer and the allocation of financial resources to ensure compliance with rules on storage, transfer and erasure of data records). Additionally, it is certainly reasonable to expect that consumer preferences will depend on which service and service supplier provides the higher level of data privacy protection, as this translates into confidence in the absence of data misuse—or the effective remediation of personal data breaches. However, careful attention must be paid to whether data privacy standards actually affect the competitive relationship or whether this remains theoretical in reality. Considering business-to-consumer constellations, some commentators argue that the results of the likeness assessment are not affected by such considerations, since consumers often act irrationally, especially in online environment.[37] Nevertheless, it is possible that a WTO Panel will consider the data privacy standard involved in the supply of a service as a distinguishing criterion as digital services become ever more sophisticated and consumer choices with regard to data privacy are becoming increasingly significant. In particular, this is not precluded by the fact that data privacy could be seen as a non-product related process and production method (PPM), which does not affect the objective quality of the service. In view of the wording of Article XVII GATS, in

---

[34] *See* also Irion et al. (2016), p. 29.
[35] *See* in this direction further Irion et al. (2016), pp. 28–31; Yakovleva (2018), pp. 491–492.
[36] *See* however Reyes (2011), p. 15.
[37] Cf. Irion et al. (2016), p. 30.

which the likeness of the service supplier is also relevant, there is no room for a discussion as to the legality of the differentiations in treatment in such cases, as is undertaken with regard to trade in goods.[38]

5.2.1.1.3 Treatment No Less Favourable

The third element of the tripartite test of the application of Article II:1 GATS concerns the determination of a *"treatment no less favourable"*. While Article II:1 GATS does not provide any guidance for the interpretation of this term, reference can be made here again to the use of the term in the context of Article XVII GATS, as *"both provisions share the essential nature of anti-discrimination provisions, and cover both de jure and de facto discrimination"*.[39] The Appellate Body in *Argentina—Financial Services* held that "[...] *on substance, the concept of 'treatment no less favourable' under both the most-favoured-nation and national treatment provisions of the GATS is focused on a measure's modification of the conditions of competition.*" and in particular underscored that: *"This legal standard does not contemplate a separate and additional inquiry into the regulatory objective of, or the regulatory concerns underlying, the contested* measure.", thereby rejecting the Panel's proposition that *"regulatory aspects"* could be used in the process of assessing the quality of a treatment.[40] In fact, the rationale behind a measure forming part of a WTO Member's right to regulate under GATS does not influence the determination of a *"treatment no less favourable"*.[41]

When examining whether a data privacy measure modifies the conditions of competition, it should first be noted that data privacy regulations generally do not differentiate de jure between foreign services and service suppliers. In individual cases, however, even with formal equal treatment, it cannot be ruled out that a given data privacy legislation may have different impacts on the competitive relationship towards different services or service suppliers. In particular, the various compliance obligations involved in data privacy regimes offer an opening for requirements which could de facto favour some foreign services or service providers over others. In addition to the substantial regulations for the protection of individuals in the

---

[38] Weiß (2020b), pp. 185–196. *See* in particular with respect to AI Chander (2021), pp. 121–122.

[39] *See* with further references Appellate Body Report, *Argentina—Financial Services*, WT/DS453/AB/R, 14 April 2016, para. 6.105.

[40] Appellate Body Report, *Argentina—Financial Services*, WT/DS453/AB/R, 14 April 2016, para. 6.106.

[41] Appellate Body Report, *Argentina—Financial Services*, WT/DS453/AB/R, 14 April 2016, para. 6.106—6.127. *See* also Irion et al. (2016), p. 30; Yakovleva (2018), pp. 489–490. With respect to the practice of some Panels in interpreting the NT provision of Article III GATT, the Appellate Body in *EC Bananas III* has underlined that there is *"no specific authority either in Article II or in Article XVII of the GATS for the proposition that the "aims and effects" of a measure are in any way relevant in determining whether that measure is inconsistent with those provisions"*, cf. Appellate Body Report, *EC-Bananas III*, WT/DS27/AB/R, 9 September 1997, para. 241.

5.2 WTO Law and Domestic Data Privacy Regulations

processing of personal data, measures that aim to govern the cross-border flow of personal data in particular play a key role when assessing the competitive relationship between *"like"* services and service suppliers of third countries. In fact, the adequacy approach to cross-border data flow regulation is particularly likely to conflict with MFN treatment pursuant to Article II:1 GATS. These concerns have been raised and discussed in scholarly literature, particularly against the backdrop of the EU's data protection framework.[42] In general, data privacy frameworks that adopt the adequacy approach subject the transfer of personal data to an evaluation of a third country's level of data privacy protection (*see* generally *supra* Sect. 4.3.3.3). In essence, an adequacy decision is a threshold determination for the unconditional exchange of personal data and, consequently, for facilitating cross-border services trade that involves the exchange of personal data. To be sure, an adequacy decision will typically not be the exclusive mechanism for legalising cross-border data transfers.[43] Otherwise, an adequacy decision would potentially have to be made on a country-by-country basis before any exchange of personal data could take place. However, in practice, there will typically be significant additional compliance burdens for services and service providers that operate without the benefit of an adequacy determination.[44] For example, these services and service suppliers have to comply with the requirements stipulated for additional safeguards and derogations for cross-border data transfers such as with regard to contractual elements like Standard Contractual Clauses (SCCs) or Binding Corporate Rules (BCRs). Foreign services and service providers which do not benefit from an adequacy decision are therefore treated less favourably than services and service suppliers which benefit from an adequacy decision.[45] In addition, there is a risk of discrimination if special arrangements are made with some WTO Members that are generally not eligible for adequacy decisions, while no benefits are given to other Members. This is a frequently raised issue with respect to the EU's data protection framework in the context of the sectoral schemes under the Safe Harbour and Privacy Shield agreements, for example.[46] In this context, it is irrelevant for the assessment of a less favourable treatment whether WTO Members adopt the adequacy approach for reasons of protection of fundamental rights to privacy (and data protection), as they cannot claim the underlying purpose when considering the

---

[42] Cf. Irion et al. (2016). pp. 26–39; Mitchell and Hepburn (2018), p. 199; Naef (2023), pp. 290–323; Reyes (2011), pp. 14–17; Sen (2018), pp. 335–338; Yakovleva (2020a), p. 893; Yakovleva and Irion (2016), pp. 19–26.

[43] *See supra* for example with regard to the EU's GDPR Sect. 4.3.2.2.

[44] *See* in particular the controversy in transatlantic relations between the EU and the US over the benefits of an adequacy decision, on the one hand, and the continued effectiveness of SCCs, on the other, in the aftermath of ECJ, C-362/14, *Schrems I*, 6 October 2015, ECLI:EU:C:2015:650 and ECJ, C-311/18, *Schrems II*, 16 July 2020, ECLI:EU:C:2020:55, *supra* Sect. 4.4.2.2.

[45] *See* also Naef (2023), p. 291.

[46] *See* for example Irion et al. (2016), pp. 30–31; Naef (2023), pp. 332–338; Reyes (2011), p. 16; Yakovleva and Irion (2016), p. 20.

non-discrimination requirement of Article II:1 GATS, but are instead required to invoke relevant exception clauses of Article XIV GATS (*see infra* Sect. 5.2.2).[47]

5.2.1.2 Article VI GATS (Domestic Regulation)

Article VI GATS aims to address the trade-restrictive effects of WTO Members' non-discriminatory regulations, which in itself prompts a source of conflict with respect to WTO Members' regulatory sovereignty.[48] WTO Members have agreed in principle that Article VI also applies to electronic commerce, but disagree on the exact form of application.[49] Regarding the structure of Article VI GATS, it can be generalised that sections VI:1-3 and VI:6 address procedural standards as they concern the application and administration as well as the respective review of measures, while sections VI:4 and VI:5 deal with the substantive content of domestic regulation.[50] Article VI:4 GATS in particular contains a negotiating mandate for the Council for Trade in Services to devise disciplines on domestic regulation, to ensure that measures relating to qualification requirements and procedures, technical standards and licensing requirements do not constitute unnecessary barriers to trade, while Article VI:5 GATS concerns the provisional application of the criteria of Article VI:4 GATS.[51] The question that arises with regard to the nexus of digital trade and data privacy as to whether Article VI:4 GATS provides a possibility for negotiating disciplines related to domestic data privacy regulations will be taken up elsewhere, as no such disciplines have been created to date (*see infra Sect.* 6.4). With regard to the procedural requirements for domestic regulations, the most relevant stipulation in the present context regarding the GATS compatibility of domestic rules on data privacy can be found in Article VI:1 GATS.[52] Article VI:1 GATS stipulates that: *"In sectors where specific commitments are undertaken, each Member shall ensure that all measures of general application affecting trade in services are administered in a reasonable, objective and impartial manner."*.

In addition to the above-mentioned criteria concerning a *"measure affecting trade in services"*, which has been generally affirmed with regard to domestic data privacy measures, Article VI:1 GATS stipulates the precondition that the measure must be of *"general application"*. The WTO Panel has opined on the meaning of *"general measures"* within the meaning of GATT Article X:3(a) GATT in conjunction with Article X:1 GATT, defining it as covering *"a range of situations or cases, rather*

---

[47] *See* also Yakovleva (2018), pp. 489- 490.

[48] *See* generally Delimatsis (2007a); Wouters and Coppens (2008), pp. 216–217. *See* with regard to negotiating history and *ratio legis* of Article VI GATS Delimatsis (2007b), pp. 93–96.

[49] Wunsch-Vincent and Hold (2012), pp. 184–185. *See* further WTO, Council for Trade in Services, Note by the Secretariat, 16 November 1998, S/C/W/68, para. 16.

[50] Krajewski (2008), pp. 167–168.

[51] Krajewski (2008), p. 178.

[52] *See* further with regard to Article VI:2a, 3, 4 and 5 GATS Naef (2023), pp. 304–307.

than being limited in their scope of application".[53] In most jurisdictions, this includes general laws and regulations, but not administrative decisions and decisions of courts or tribunals.[54] This requirement will therefore generally be met by omnibus data privacy regimes, which have a broad scope of application in both private and public contexts.[55] However, sectoral data privacy laws, for example, are also likely to be covered, as their scope of application typically is broad enough to cover a range of situations with regard to a certain context. In a similar vein, data privacy measures that aim to govern the cross-border flow of data will generally cover sectoral domains or jurisdictions, which is likely to be sufficiently extensive to qualify as measures of *"general application affecting trade in services"* within the meaning of Article VI:1 GATS.[56]

It follows from this that data privacy measures in the sectors for which there are scheduled specific commitments under the GATS must be *"administered in a reasonable, objective and impartial manner"*. With regard to the meaning of *"administer"* the WTO Panel has stated that it *"relates to the application of laws and regulations, including administrative processes and their results"*.[57] Notably, therefore, Article VI:1 GATS refers to the *application* of domestic measures, thereby embodying a fundamental standard of the rule of law and good governance.[58] Hence, Article VI:1 GATS cannot be employed to challenge a domestic data privacy measures substantive content.[59] Due to the lack of jurisprudence on Article VI GATS, the interpretation of the requirements for reasonable, objective and impartial administration is mainly informed by case law relating to the corresponding GATT provision Article X:3(a).[60] In the context of Article VI:1 GATS the administration of a measure is considered reasonable, if it is conform with *"accepted standards of rationality and of sound judgement"*, while it is objective if it *"disregards irrational, emotional or personal intentions"*, and impartial when it is taken *"without giving special consideration or privileges to one party or commercial interest concerned while not giving the same amount of consideration or privileges to other parties or interests which are equally affected by the decision"*.[61] In general, these criteria reflect the demand for a minimum standard of due process and require that WTO Members be both consistent and predictable in the administration of their domestic

---

[53] Cf. Panel Report, *EC—Selected Customs Matters*, WT/DS315/R, 16 June 2006, para. 7.116. See further Delimatsis (2007a), p. 20.

[54] Krajewski (2008), p. 169.

[55] Reyes (2011), pp. 18–19.

[56] See with regard to the EU's DPD Yakovleva and Irion (2016), p. 22.

[57] Panel Report, *EC—Selected Customs Matters*, WT/DS315/R, 16 June 2006, para. 7.113–7.119.

[58] Krajewski (2008), p. 168.

[59] Irion et al. (2016), p. 31.

[60] Mitchell and Voon (2014), p. 72. See also the detailed discussion of WTO jurisprudence on the scope of the parallel GATT provision of Article X:3(a) Delimatsis (2007a), pp. 19–31.

[61] See with further references to WTO jurisprudence Krajewski (2008), pp. 171–172.

measures.[62] Given that all three criteria are separate legal requirements, WTO Members may object to a generally applicable measure in a sector where specific commitments have been made if one of the three criteria is not met.[63]

With regard to the administration of domestic data privacy measures, the requirements of Article VI:1 GATS are particularly relevant for measures that govern the cross-border flow of personal data. In particular, the adequacy approach encounters a number of complexities in administering a transparent and comparable set of criteria for determining the adequacy of a third country's data privacy framework.[64] Indeed, it may be questionable whether the unilateral determination of the adequacy of a level of data privacy in a third country is carried out in a sufficiently reasonable, objective and impartial manner to meet the regulatory principles of consistency and predictability underlying Article VI:1 GATS. In this context, the EU's adequacy findings, in particular, have been subject to in-depth scrutiny and have been challenged in academic literature.[65] It has already been pointed out that the requirements for determining adequacy in Article 45 GDPR are somewhat vague (*see supra* Sect. 4.3.2.2) and that the determination procedure is prone to imprecision and bureaucracy (*see supra* Sect. 4.4.2.2.1). Furthermore, it may be questioned whether an adequacy decision is made solely by taking into account the level of data privacy in the third country or whether individual political and economic considerations also play a role as well which could constitute a breach of the standards of objectivity and impartiality.[66] From this, some analyses conclude with regard to the EU's administration of its data privacy measures governing cross-border data flows: "[...] *at the level of its application – it is impossible to conclude that there never was and never will be a violation of GATS Article VI.1*".[67] The principles of Article VI:1 GATS could also conflict with those data privacy measures that rely on a data localisation approach. There is a significant risk that the due process obligations will be infringed upon here, particularly if data localisation aligns with policy elements pertaining to data sovereignty (*see supra* Sect. 4.4.1.2.2). Ultimately, it is worth reiterating that the application of Article VI GATS depends to a large extent on the definition of the scope of the specific GATS commitments with regard to digital trade.[68]

---

[62] Delimatsis (2007a), p. 28; Mitchell and Voon (2014), pp. 74–77.

[63] Delimatsis (2007a), pp. 27–28; Krajewski (2008), p. 172.

[64] With regard to the EU's data protection regime, *Tobias Naef* identifies in particular the number of adequacy decisions, the selection of countries, the consistency and the procedures of the adequacy assessment Naef (2023), pp. 297–301.

[65] Naef (2023), pp. 297–301; Reyes (2011), pp. 19–20; Yakovleva and Irion (2016), p. 23. *Tobias Naef* further addresses the administration of the EU's SCCs and BCRs.

[66] *See* for example Reyes (2011), pp. 19–20; Yakovleva and Irion (2016), p. 23.

[67] Cf. Irion et al. (2016), p. 31. *See* also Reyes (2011), pp. 19–20. *See* for an argument that the EU's adequacy assessment does generally not interfere with the standards in Article VI:1 GATS Naef (2023), pp. 296–304.

[68] *See* further Tuthill and Roy (2012), p. 158.

5.2.1.3 Article XVI GATS (Market Access)

Article XVI:1 GATS binds WTO Members to accord services and service suppliers of any other Member treatment no less favourable than that provided for under the terms, limitations and conditions agreed and specified in their schedules. The flexible liberalisation of trade in services under the GATS therefore intricately links market access commitments to the policy preferences of individual WTO Members, as reflected in their respective national schedules. Article XVI:2 (a)-(f) GATS, in turn, list restrictions that WTO Members may maintain or introduce, most of which concern quantitative restrictions.

Against this backdrop, a breach of market access commitments resulting from a data privacy measure would first require a commitment to market access for the supply of services that involve data flows. In this context, reference can be made to the comments above, according to which the WTO dispute settlement bodies in *US-Gambling* have quite self-evidently subsumed the provision of services based on cross-border data flows under Mode 1 (cross-border supply) of Article I:2(a) GATS (*see supra* Sect. 3.3.2.6.2).[69] While it cannot be ruled out that other modes of supply may also involve cross-border data flows (particularly Mode 2 and 3), it is clear that the liberalisation of market access for digital services depends in particular on commitments in relation to cross-border supply under Mode 1 GATS. Therefore, if a WTO Member has scheduled a Mode 1 commitment for a specific service sector as *"unbound"*, it will generally be able to limit services or service suppliers relying on the processing of personal data from another WTO Member. Conversely, a WTO Member may have provided full market access by scheduling *"none"* and thereby committing not to maintain any of the types of measures listed in the six sub-paragraphs of Article XVI:2 GATS.[70] Secondly, the scheduled market access commitments would have to be affected by a data privacy measure. Given the quantitative nature of the market access restrictions in Article XVI:2 GATS, it is reasonable to take a closer look at data privacy measures that aim to regulate cross-border data flows. This is particularly relevant in light of WTO jurisprudence in *US-Gambling*, in which the WTO Appellate Body held that a total ban on online gambling services would amount to a *"zero quota"* and therefore would be relevant to Articles XVI:2(a) and (c) GATS (*see supra* Sect. 3.3.2.6.4).[71] Therefore, if a domestic data privacy measure results in the complete prohibition of cross-border data flows at the expense of foreign services and service suppliers such as in the case of data localisation measures, one could argue that this would constitute a *"zero quota"* and a violation of the market access obligation.[72] As a result, this is

---

[69] *See* also in this context Appellate Body Report, *China—Publications and Audiovisual Products*, WT/DS363/AB/R, 21 December 2009, paras. 396–397.

[70] Cf. Appellate Body Report, *US-Gambling*, WT/DS285/AB/R, 20 April 2005, para. 215.

[71] Appellate Body Report, *US-Gambling*, WT/DS285/AB/R, 20 April 2005, paras. 221–264.

[72] Mattoo and Meltzer (2019), p. 780; Mitchell and Hepburn (2018), pp. 200–201; Weber (2012), pp. 32–33; Yakovleva and Irion (2016), p. 22.

particularly relevant when data privacy regulations entail rules on data localisation.[73] For example, a given data privacy law may prohibit the processing of consumers' financial or health data abroad, which would make cross-border activities of a health care or a financial services provider utilising foreign data centres unfeasible.[74] One might also think of data privacy measures that implement adequacy schemes, which require an adequacy decision for the unconditional transfer of personal data, notably the EU's data protection regulation.[75] However, as explained above, these privacy regimes typically involve a combination of approaches to regulating the flow of data, so as not to be compelled to require an assessment of every possible destination of the transfer of personal data (*see supra* Sect. 4.3.3.5). Therefore, in addition to the adequacy decision, further safeguards such as with regard to as Standard Contractual Clauses (SCCs) or Binding Corporate Rules (BCRs) are provided for, which enable data transfer in the absence of an adequacy decision. Adequacy systems will therefore generally not infringe upon the respective market access commitments of a WTO Member.[76] However, this could be decided differently if there is no adequacy determination in place and the use of additional safeguards is called into question, resulting in *de facto* data localisation (*see supra* Sect. 4.3.3.4).[77] Data privacy regimes that are based on the accountability of the data exporter generally do not impose quantitative restrictions on the cross-border transfer of personal data and are therefore typically not relevant in terms of a breach of market access obligations.

5.2.1.4 Article XVII GATS (National Treatment)

Article XVII GATS aims to prevent discrimination of foreign services or service suppliers in favour of domestic ones. According to Article XVII:1 GATS each Member "*shall accord to services and service suppliers of any other Member treatment no less favourable than that it accords to its own like services and service suppliers*" under the precondition of respective sectors inscribed in its schedule, and subject to any conditions and qualifications set out therein. Here again, there is a clear reference to the political preferences of WTO Members as manifested in the national schedules. According to Article XVII:2 GATS both formally identical treatment or formally different treatment is covered by the provision, which Article XVII:3 GATS stipulates "*shall be considered to be less favourable if it modifies the conditions of competition in favour of services or service suppliers of the Member compared to like services or service suppliers of any other Member*".

---

[73] Crosby (2016), p. 7; Naef (2023), pp. 308–310.

[74] *See* for a concrete example against the background of the KORUS Agreement MacDonald and Streatfeild (2014), pp. 629–633.

[75] Irion et al. (2016), p. 32; Reyes (2011), pp. 20–22.

[76] *See* with regard to the EU's data protection framework Yakovleva and Irion (2016), p. 22.

[77] *See* with regard to the EU's data protection framework Mattoo and Meltzer (2019), p. 780; Naef (2023), pp. 310–311; Yakovleva (2020a), pp. 893–894.

The analysis with respect to Article XVII GATS proceeds analogously to the testing of the MFN clause of Article II:1 GATS (*see supra* Sect. 5.2.1.1).

Hence, assuming that there is likeness between foreign and domestic services and service providers,[78] it can generally be said that less favourable treatment by substantive data privacy measures will be rarely caused by formally different treatment. Rather, data privacy regulations generally apply to domestic and foreign services in the same way, resulting in formally identical treatment. Nevertheless, it is possible that certain requirements of a given data privacy law may be considered easier to fulfil by domestic operators, so that *de facto* discrimination may exist in such a situation. At the same time, it is evident that particular attention must again be paid to the regulation of cross-border data flows by means of data privacy measures. Depending on its design, implementation and concrete application, the adequacy approach, for example, may affect the conditions of competition and bias them in favour of domestic services or service suppliers. Imposing additional requirements on foreign services and service providers with respect to cross-border transfers of personal data (e.g. in the absence of an adequacy decision) generally results in less favourable treatment.[79] Moreover, data privacy regimes that impose either *de facto* or *de jure* data localisation generally alter the conditions of competition in favour of the WTO Member's domestic services or service suppliers by preventing foreign services and service suppliers from providing Mode 1 services across borders and mandating local representation.[80] Again, data flow regulation that is solely based on principles of accountability generally would not alter the conditions of competition in favour of a member's services or service providers as compared to like services or service providers of another member.

5.2.2 Article XIV GATS (General Exceptions)

Article XIV GATS provides for general exceptions that allow WTO Members to maintain measures that are otherwise inconsistent with the general and specific obligations under the GATS. WTO Members' commitments to non-discrimination, market access, and a competitive level playing field in services may, in some

---

[78] *See* for a discussion of the role of high privacy standards in evaluating the likeness of services and service suppliers *supra* Sect. 5.2.1.1.

[79] This is exemplified by the EU's data flow regulation under the GDPR, cf. Naef (2023), pp. 318–320. Moreover, the GDPR, which not only obliges foreign services and service providers to comply with the rules for the transfer of personal data to third countries, but may also be applicable to the cross-border provision of foreign services simultaneously in terms of substance due to its extensive scope of application, creates overlapping requirements for foreign services and service providers, thus altering the conditions of competition in favour of a domestic service or service provider. *See* in this regard with further references Naef (2023), p. 320; Yakovleva and Irion (2016), pp. 20–21.

[80] Mattoo and Meltzer (2019), p. 780.

instances, constrain the pursuit of legitimate non-economic policy objectives and public interests.[81] In this context, Article XIV GATS prioritizes the safeguarding of specified societal values and interests over trade liberalisation.[82] In this sense, Article XIV GATS seeks to strike a balance between a national "*right to regulate*" and international trade law, while ensuring that the pursuit of domestic policy objectives is not used as a pretext for the installation of disguised restrictions on trade. Therefore, Article XIV (a)-(e) GATS authorize a number of exceptions for domestic policy measures provided that such measures are "*[. . .] not applied in a manner which would constitute a means of arbitrary or unjustifiable discrimination between countries where like conditions prevail, or a disguised restriction on trade in services [. . .]*".

Article XIV GATS provides a framework for reconciling international law and domestic values and regulatory preferences, notably also with regard to the governance of data and data flows.[83] In the following, first, the legal systematic of Article XIV GATS will be presented in more detail. Subsequently, Article XIV GATS will be examined to determine whether domestic data privacy measures that conflict with trade law obligations according to the above findings can be brought into conformity with WTO law by means of this provision. Notably, the exception provisions of Article XIV(c)(ii) GATS and XIV(a) GATS will be subject to in-depth review. Finally, it is important to consider the "*necessity*" of a regulatory measure as well as the requirements of the chapeau of Article XIV GATS.

5.2.2.1 Legal Systematic of Article XIV GATS

Multilateral regulation of trade in services under the GATS is still comparatively recent, and, as shown, the GATS provides WTO Members with considerable leeway to adapt their commitments to accommodate domestic policies (*see supra* Sect. 3.3. 2.6.1). Given the conceptual similarity of the general exceptions, notably with regard to "*necessity*" and the requirements of the chapeau, WTO dispute settlement bodies have determined that prior decisions under Article XX of the GATT are relevant to the analysis of Article XIV of the GATS.[84] Hence, as with the general exceptions to trade in goods under Article XX GATT, Article XIV GATS provides for a "*two-tier analysis*" of a measure that a Member seeks to justify.[85] The WTO Panel in *Argentina—Financial Services* has provided a concise description of this test: "*Article XIV of the GATS provides for an analysis in two stages: (i) first, the*

---

[81] Cottier et al. (2008), p. 290.

[82] Van den Bossche and Zdouc (2022), p. 592.

[83] *See* generally Burri (2017), pp. 88–93; Mishra (2019), pp. 9–20; Mishra (2021); Mitchell and Hepburn (2018), pp. 201–205; Mitchell and Mishra (2018), pp. 1094–1096.

[84] *See* for example Appellate Body Report, *US-Gambling*, WT/DS285/AB/R, 20 April 2005, para. 291.

[85] Appellate Body Report, *US-Gambling*, WT/DS285/AB/R, 20 April 2005, para. 292.

5.2 WTO Law and Domestic Data Privacy Regulations

Panel must determine whether the measure falls within the scope of one of the subparagraphs of Article XIV of the GATS; and (ii) after having found that the measure at issue is justified under one of the subparagraphs of Article XIV of the GATS, the Panel must examine whether this measure satisfies the requirements laid down in the introductory clause or chapeau of Article XIV of the GATS.".[86] Accordingly, the first tier of analysis considers whether the domestic measure is addressed to the particular interest of the paragraph of Article XIV GATS in question and whether there is a sufficient nexus between that measure and the protected interest.[87] The Appellate Body in *US-Gambling* has underscored that the required *"degree of connection"* between the measure and the interest is specified in the text of the relevant paragraphs themselves, through the use of terms such as *"in relation to"* and *"necessary to"*.[88] However, in view of the fact that Article XIV GATS provides only one degree of connection in terms of justifications for derogating from all multilateral commitments under Article XIV GATS lit (a)—(c)—namely *"necessity"*—academic literature suggests to directly refer to a *"necessity test"*.[89] The assessment of *"necessity"* as a determinant of the relationship between a particular domestic measure and the policy it pursues provides the most important reference for distinguishing between legitimate exercise of domestic regulatory autonomy and undue restriction of international trade.[90] Once a measure is provisionally justified under one of the paragraphs of Article XIV GATS, in the second tier, the so-called *"chapeau"* of Article XIV GATS *"imposes additional disciplines"* on said measures as it requires that the measure in question is *"applied in a manner"* that does not constitute *"arbitrary or unjustifiable discrimination between countries where like conditions prevail"*, or a *"disguised restriction on trade in services"*.[91]

Against the backdrop of still nascent WTO case law with regard to Article XIV GATS, scholars have pointed out the lack of predictability in the application of the general exception of Article XIV GATS by the WTO dispute settlement bodies.[92] In particular, WTO dispute settlement bodies have so far omitted to develop abstract and generally applicable standards of analysis for the examination of Article XIV GATS, arguably to be able to flexibly respond in a measure-specific manner.[93] Cases in which the general exceptions of Article XIV GATS have been invoked in the context of trade disputes between WTO Member States are rare. Moreover, the

---

[86] Panel Report, *Argentina—Financial Services*, WT/DS453/R, 30 September 2015, para. 7.586. *See* also for a more comprehensive description of the two-tier test, Appellate Body Report, *US-Gambling*, WT/DS285/AB/R, 20 April 2005, para. 292.

[87] Appellate Body Report, *US-Gambling*, WT/DS285/AB/R, 20 April 2005, para. 292.

[88] *See* with further references Appellate Body Report, *US-Gambling*, WT/DS285/AB/R, 20 April 2005, para. 292.

[89] Cottier et al. (2008), p. 295. *See* also Marceau and Trachtman (2009), p. 215.

[90] *See* further Weiß (2020b), pp. 246–265.

[91] *See* further Appellate Body Report, *EC Seal Products*, WT/DS400/AB/R, WT/DS401/AB/R, 22 May 2014, para. 5.296.

[92] *See* for example Yakovleva and Irion (2020a), p. 211.

[93] Cottier et al. (2008), p. 322.

success rate in invoking general exceptions under Article XIV GATS is rather low.[94]

5.2.2.2 Exception for Data Privacy Pursuant to Article XIV(c)(ii)

Article XIV(c)(ii) GATS refers to the adoption or enforcement of domestic measures which are *"necessary to secure compliance with laws or regulations which are not inconsistent with the provisions of this Agreement"* relating to *"the protection of the privacy of individuals in relation to the processing and dissemination of personal data"* and has never been invoked in a case before the WTO dispute settlement bodies.[95] Nevertheless, given the previous practice of applying the general exception provisions of Article XX GATT and Article XIV GATS by the WTO dispute settlement bodies it is possible to develop a general understanding of how a WTO Panel would proceed in balancing trade and data privacy. In this context, the WTO Appellate Body in *US-Gambling* held, based on a similar wording, that for the interpretation of Article XIV(c), the case law on Article XX(d) GATT can be drawn upon.[96] This means according to the WTO Panel in *Argentina—Financial Services* that: *"[i]n order to justify its measures successfully under subparagraph (c) of Article XIV, [a WTO Member] should first demonstrate that measures [. . .] are designed to secure compliance with the relevant [. . .] laws and regulations that are not in themselves inconsistent with the GATS; and secondly, that these measures are "necessary" to secure such compliance"*.[97] The WTO Panel has opined that in order to determine whether a measure is designed to secure compliance within the meaning of Article XIV(c) GATS: *"the Member invoking such a defence must (i) identify the laws and regulations with which the challenged measure is intended to secure compliance, and prove that (ii) those laws and regulations are not in themselves inconsistent with WTO law; and (iii) that the measure challenged is designed to secure compliance with those laws or regulations"*.[98] In a first step, therefore, it is necessary to designate the concrete law or regulation that is underlying the data privacy measure in question. With respect to the first prong of the test, the Appellate Body noted that *"laws and regulations"* refers to domestic laws and

---

[94] *See* with further references Weiß (2020b), p. 229.

[95] *See* in this context, however, the discussions following the adoption of China's CSL in the Council for Trade in Services (CTS), cf. Greenleaf (2018).

[96] Panel Report, *US-Gambling*, WT/DS285/R, 10 November 2004, para. 6.537 states „*We note that, textually, Article XIV(c) is very similar to Article XX(d) of the GATT 1994. Accordingly, on the basis of the comments made by the Appellate Body to which we have referred above regarding the applicability of jurisprudence under the GATT 1994 to the GATS, we will refer to and rely upon such jurisprudence to the extent to which it is applicable and relevant in our interpretation of Article XIV(c).*". *See* also Panel Report, *Argentina—Financial Services*, WT/DS453/R, 30 September 2015, paras. 7.592–7.593.

[97] Panel Report, *Argentina—Financial Services*, WT/DS453/R, 30 September 2015, para. 7.593.

[98] Panel Report, *Argentina—Financial Services*, WT/DS453/R, 30 September 2015, para. 7.595.

regulations and not to international, unless incorporated into domestic law.[99] Regarding the second requirement, the Panel in *US-Gambling* held that *"Article XIV(c) provides a non-exhaustive list of laws or regulations 'which are not inconsistent with the provisions of this Agreement'*".[100] Moreover, *"the legislation of a defending Member shall be considered WTO-consistent until proven otherwise."*.[101] Given that Article XIV(c)(ii) GATS explicitly refers to the *"protection of the privacy of individuals in relation to the processing and dissemination of personal data [...]"* it should be rather straightforward to demonstrate GATS consistency of a given data privacy law or regulation (if such consistency is challenged).[102] However, it may very well be that in determining whether a domestic data privacy measure secures compliance with data privacy laws and regulations, issues may arise regarding the interpretation of concepts that are undefined in WTO law. The above analysis of international and regional data privacy frameworks has shown that data privacy rules have been refined and adapted to meet the increased privacy requirements in a digitally globalised world (*see supra* Sect. 4.3). It has therefore been argued that an evolutionary interpretation of the terms in Article XIV(c)(ii) GATS should be adopted to address and cover all relevant dimensions of data privacy in a data-driven economy and society.[103] Discord may occur, in particular, but not exclusively, in the context of the definition of *"protection of privacy"*, and very crucially with regard to the definition of *"personal data"*.[104] As illustrated above, on a global level, concepts of personal data vary in scope (*see supra* Sect. 4.2.3.1). In individual cases, therefore, there may be disagreement among WTO members as to whether a particular set of data may be classified as *"personal data"* thereby questioning consistency of a data privacy law or regulation with GATS. For example, given the emerging developments in digital technology related to AI, there may be significant disagreement about when data can be classified as personal data, once it can be de-anonymised (*see also supra* Sect. 4.2.3.2). Therefore, a WTO Panel deciding on the application of Article XIV(c)(ii) GATS could be confronted at this early juncture with the inconsistent approaches to data privacy at the international level, even if only in individual cases. With regard to the third prong of the test, the WTO Appellate Body has stated that *"a measure can be said 'to secure compliance' with laws or regulations when its design reveals that it secures compliance with specific rules, obligations, or requirements under such laws or regulations, even if*

---

[99] Appellate Body Report, *Mexico—Taxes on Soft Drinks*, WT/DS308/AB/R, 3 March 2006, paras. 69–79.

[100] Panel Report, *US-Gambling*, WT/DS285/R, 10 November 2004, para. 6.540.

[101] Panel Report, *Argentina—Financial Services*, WT/DS453/R, 30 September 2015, para. 7.620.

[102] *See* also regarding the strategic relevance of what laws or regulations are identified Irion et al. (2016), p. 36.

[103] Mishra (2019), pp. 11–12.

[104] *See* also MacDonald and Streatfeild (2014), p. 644.

the measure cannot be guaranteed to achieve such result with absolute certainty."[105] Furthermore, the measures must "*enforce obligations*" contained in the laws and regulations rather than only ensure attainment of the objectives of those laws and regulations.[106] In this context, academic literature has pointed out that with respect to the specific measure granting "*adequacy*" to a data privacy standard of a given third country, it can be argued that such a measure aims at ensuring compliance with the underlying data privacy law, as it is intended to prevent circumvention of the data privacy principles of the applicable legal framework.[107] It is likely that a data localisation measure will also be found to secure compliance with an underlying data privacy law, as such a measure is adopted to enforce domestic rules, even if it is not entirely certain that the objective will be achieved.

5.2.2.3 Exceptions for Public Morals or Public Order Pursuant to Article XIV(a)

With respect to national data privacy measures that are inconsistent with a WTO Member's trade law obligations, Article XIV(a) GATS may also be relevant. In academic literature, this potential justification for national data governance measures in relation to data privacy is still relatively unexplored, however.[108] Nevertheless, in addition to defending a national data privacy measure pursuant to Article XIV(c)(ii) GATS as a measure necessary to ensure compliance with laws or regulations protecting the privacy of natural persons in connection with the processing and dissemination of personal data, a WTO Member might argue that the measure in question is "*necessary*" for the protection of public morals or the maintenance of public order. Indeed, this may prove to be strategically advisable, as WTO jurisprudence has consistently granted WTO members considerable discretion to unilaterally determine the substance of public morality and public order.[109] WTO dispute settlement bodies have repeatedly applied a non-intrusive public morals standard and granted a rather high degree of deference to national authorities, as a substantive assessment of a national measure raises thorny issues about the regulatory autonomy

---

[105] Appellate Body Report, *Argentina—Financial Services*, WT/DS453/AB/R, 14 April 2016, para. 6.203 further explains: "*[. . .] the phrase 'to secure compliance' circumscribes the scope of Article XIV(c) of the GATS, as it speaks to the function of the measures that a Member can seek to justify under this provision. This phrase calls for an initial examination of the relationship between the inconsistent measure and the relevant laws or regulations and, for this purpose, directs panels assessing whether a measure secures compliance with laws or regulations to scrutinize the design of the measures sought to be justified.*".

[106] With further references Panel Report, *US-Gambling*, WT/DS285/R, 10 November 2004, para. 6.538. *See* also Cottier et al. (2008), pp. 307–308.

[107] Reyes (2011), p. 29.

[108] *See* however Mishra (2021), pp. 266–267. *See* generally with regard to human rights Breining-Kaufmann (2005), pp. 107–108.

[109] Cottier et al. (2008), pp. 301–302.

5.2 WTO Law and Domestic Data Privacy Regulations

of member states and the democratic legitimacy of the WTO dispute settlement system.[110] In *US-Gambling*, the WTO Panel outlined the requirements of Article XIV(a) GATS in more detail, underscoring *"inherent difficulties and sensitivities associated with interpretation of the terms "public morals" and "public order""* and acknowledging that the *"content of these concepts for Members can vary in time and space, depending upon a range of factors, including prevailing social, cultural, ethical and religious values"*.[111] The Panel further notes that, in the context of Article XX GATT, the Appellate Body has repeatedly held that Members have the right to determine the level of protection they deem appropriate in applying similar social concepts.[112] Consequently, with regard to Article XIV GATS, the Panel stated: *"Members should be given some scope to define and apply for themselves the concepts of "public morals" and "public order" in their respective territories, according to their own systems and scales of values."*.[113] The Appellate Body in *US-Gambling* summarised the findings of the Panel as follows: *"the Panel held that, the term 'public morals' denotes standards of right and wrong conduct maintained by or on behalf of a community or nation.' The Panel further found that the definition of the term 'order', read in conjunction with footnote 5 of the GATS, 'suggests that 'public order' refers to the preservation of the fundamental interests of a society, as reflected in public policy and law.'."*[114] In this latter context, the scope of public order is narrowed by footnote 5, which states that the public order exception *"may be invoked only where a genuine and sufficiently serious threat is posed to one of the fundamental interests of society"*. In this respect, the Panel had stated that such fundamental interests *"can relate, inter alia, to standards of law, security and morality"* and underscored that to the extent that both concepts seek to protect largely similar values, some overlap may exist.[115] However, WTO panels are not required to make a separate, explicit finding that the standard in footnote 5 is met.[116] In other GATS Article XIV(a) dispute settlement cases, such as the *China—Publications and Audiovisual Products* case, the dispute settlement bodies have also

---

[110] With further references Delimatsis (2011), p. 278; Nuzzo (2017), p. 275. *See* with regard to the legitimacy of the WTO judiciary Weiß (2020b), pp. 262–265.

[111] Panel Report, *US-Gambling*, WT/DS285/R, 10 November 2004, para. 6.461. *See* also more recently Panel Report, *Colombia-Textiles*, WT/DS461/R, 15 January 2014, para. 7.338.

[112] Panel Report, *US-Gambling*, WT/DS285/R, 10 November 2004, para. 6.461. In this context, the Panel references further WTO jurisprudence, *see* Appellate Body Report, *Korea –Various Measures on Beef*, WT/DS161/AB/R, WT/DS169/AB/R, 11 December 2000, para. 176 and Appellate Body Report, *EC—Asbestos*, WT/DS135/AB/R, 12 March 2001, para. 168. *See* in this context also Appellate Body Report, *EC-Seal Products*, WT/DS400/AB/R, WT/DS401/AB/R, 22 May 2014, paras. 5.194–5.203.

[113] Panel Report, *US-Gambling*, WT/DS285/R, 10 November 2004, para. 6.461.

[114] Appellate Body Report, *US-Gambling*, WT/DS285/AB/R, 20 April 2005, para. 296. *See* also Panel Report, *China—Publications and Audiovisual Products*, WT/DS363/R, 12 August 2009, para. 7.759.

[115] Panel Report, *US-Gambling*, WT/DS285/R, 10 November 2004, paras. 6.467–6.468.

[116] Cf. Appellate Body Report, *US-Gambling*, WT/DS285/AB/R, 20 April 2005, para. 298.

interpreted the exception clause rather expansively and in a flexible manner, thus allowing room for an evolutionary interpretation.[117]

Considering this extensive margin of appreciation for WTO Members and the absence of references to additional requirements relating to compliance with laws or regulations that are not inconsistent with the provisions of the GATS, Article XIV (a) GATS appears somewhat easier to comply with in its basic requirements than Article XIV(c)(ii) GATS.[118] The sheer breadth of the phrasing "*standards of right and wrong*" in the dispute settlement bodies' interpretation of public morals in *US-Gambling*, combined with the wide latitude of WTO Members to define and apply the concepts of public morals and public order in their respective territories according to their own systems and value systems, means that a wide range of social regulations fall within the scope of Article XIV(a) GATS.[119]

Against this background, it is reasonable to assume that the treatment of individuals so as to preserve their dignity can be perceived as a moral requirement relevant to Article XIV(a) GATS.[120] Hence, the invocation of Article XIV(a) GATS is particularly meaningful with respect to WTO Members whose measures for the protection of individuals in the processing of their personal data are essentially informed by the safeguarding of fundamental rights to privacy and data protection, rooted in human dignity and self-determination. In this context, a WTO Member should be able to demonstrate that a national data privacy measure is designed to protect public morals.[121] The assessment of the nexus between trade law and domestic data privacy rules in this respect is reminiscent of the controversial relationship between trade and human rights more generally.[122] Moreover, the exception for public order, which is exclusive to the general exception in Article XIV(a) GATS, could also prove to allow for a rather extensive interpretation in the sense of a "*catch-all term*" thus expanding the regulatory autonomy of WTO members in regard to fundamental interests of society.[123] This pertains notably to the consideration of societal elements of the data privacy discourse outlined above, such as with regard to the safeguarding of democratic participation, but also with respect to data sovereignty (*see supra* Sect. 4.4.1.2). Against this backdrop, for example, in light of the EU constitutional mandate to data protection under Article 8 of the EU Charter, the case for including data protection measures to be covered by

---

[117] *See* with further references to the WTO case law Mishra (2021), pp. 266–267. *See* also Delimatsis (2011).

[118] Mitchell and Hepburn (2018), pp. 201–202.

[119] Nadakavukaren Schefer (2010), p. 239. The author underscores „*If the focus is on a society's own value system, rather than on an international value system, Members will be much freer to form their social trade regulations at a level which protects humans the environment, or culture more strongly than other societies would.*".

[120] Nadakavukaren Schefer (2010), p. 239.

[121] *See* also Mattoo and Meltzer (2019), p. 781; Mishra (2021), pp. 267–268.

[122] *See* in this context Aaronson (2015); Yakovleva (2020b), pp. 499–506. *See* generally Aaronson (2007).

[123] Delimatsis (2011), p. 277; Weber and Burri (2014), p. 132.

both public morals and public order is compelling.[124] In a similar context, *Christopher Kuner* assesses: *"The origins of data protection law in consumer protection and human rights law also indicate that courts and data protection authorities may regard some of its rules as ordre publique which will be applied regardless of the applicable law."*.[125] It is this reference to individual societal, cultural and moral values that distinguishes Article XIV(a) GATS in relation to Article XIV(c) (ii) GATS and makes it relevant for a number of underlying rationales and national idiosyncrasies with regard to data privacy regulation. Certainly, it can be argued that, besides Article XIV(c)(ii) GATS as a *lex specialis* for domestic measures undertaken in the context of the protection of the privacy of individuals in relation to the processing and dissemination of personal data, there is not much room for the application of Article XIV(a) GATS.[126] However, the normative ambiguity of data privacy that exists between elements of an economic and non-economic nature results in the conclusion that Article XIV(a) GATS must be recognised as having a scope of application with respect to data privacy.

Certainly the measure for which justification is claimed under the subparagraph of Article XIV(a) GATS must nevertheless be *"necessary"*.[127] In addition, the requirements of the chapeau must be met. The broad scope of interpretation of national authorities for *"public morals"* is susceptible to be narrowed and limited in the further steps of the review of general exceptions.[128]

5.2.2.4 "Necessary" Within the Meaning of Article XIV of the GATS

While jurisprudence with respect to Article XX GATT originally referred to *"necessity"* as the demonstration that no other WTO-compatible or less restrictive alternative was reasonably available to pursue the policy objective, requiring that the domestic measure be the least trade-restrictive of all measures reasonably expected to employ, this interpretation has evolved.[129] A *"weighing and balancing"* test has been set forth with respect to the evaluation of *"necessity"* pursuant to Article XX (d) GATT by the Appellate Body in *Korea—Various Measures on Beef* and has been further developed in *EC—Asbestos*.[130] This *"weighing and balancing"* test

---

[124] *See* with regard to the relationship between public morals and public order Cottier et al. (2008), p. 299.

[125] Kuner (2010), p. 182.

[126] *See* for example Mishra (2019), p. 13. *See* however Mishra (2021), p. 266.

[127] Panel Report, *US-Gambling*, WT/DS285/R, 10 November 2004, para. 6.455.

[128] Nuzzo (2017), p. 278.

[129] Kapterian (2010), pp. 101–106; Marceau and Trachtman (2009), pp. 216–217.

[130] Appellate Body Report, *Korea—Various Measures on Beef*, WT/DS161/AB/R, WT/DS169/AB/R, 11 December 2000, para. 164–185; Appellate Body Report, *EC—Asbestos*, WT/DS135/AB/R, 12 March 2001, para. 172. Note, however, that the relationship between the Least Restrictive Measure test and the weighing and balancing test is not entirely clear, *see* Kapterian (2010), p. 106; Marceau and Trachtman (2009), pp. 216–217.

developed by WTO jurisprudence with respect to trade in goods under GATT is applicable to trade in services under GATS as held by the Appellate Body in *US-Gambling* and has so far been applied consistently, regardless of the underlying paragraph of Article XIV GATS.[131] Overall, the Appellate Body has emphasised that this process is *"a holistic operation that involves putting all the variables of the equation together and evaluating them in relation to each other after having examined them individually, in order to reach an overall judgment [...]"*[132] and has underscored that *"necessity"* is an *"objective standard"*, meaning that *"a panel must, on the basis of the evidence in the record, independently and objectively assess the 'necessity' of the measure before it"*.[133] By this it is to be determined whether there is a WTO-compliant alternative measure which the WTO Member can *"reasonably be expected to employ"* or a less WTO-inconsistent measure that is *"reasonably available"*.[134] However, the elements of balancing and, in particular, the procedure for doing so remain ambiguous in WTO jurisprudence. Notwithstanding their refinement in the course of evolutionary cycles of WTO jurisprudence—particularly against the backdrop of increasing sensitivity to conflicts between trade interests and social objectives—there is ample room for divergent interpretative approaches towards *"necessity"* that are directly relevant to domestic regulatory authority with respect to data privacy.[135]

5.2.2.4.1 The Elements of Weighing and Balancing

In *US-Gambling*, the Appellate Body has provided a comprehensive description of the weighing and balancing exercise that conveys a sense of what this process entails: *"The process begins with an assessment of the "relative importance" of the interests or values furthered by the challenged measure. Having ascertained the importance of the particular interests at stake, a panel should then turn to the other factors that are to be "weighed and balanced". The Appellate Body has pointed to two factors that, in most cases, will be relevant to a panel's determination of the "necessity" of a measure, although not necessarily exhaustive of factors that might be considered. One factor is the contribution of the measure to the realization of the*

---

[131] Cf. Appellate Body Report, *US-Gambling*, WT/DS285/AB/R, 20 April 2005, para. 305 referring to Appellate Body Report, *Korea–Various Measures on Beef*, WT/DS161/AB/R, WT/DS169/AB/R, 11 December 2000, para. 166 and Appellate Body Report, *EC–Asbestos*, WT/DS135/AB/R, 12 March 2001, para. 172. See further Appellate Body Report, *Argentina—Financial Services*, WT/DS453/AB/R, 14 April 2016, para. 6.182.

[132] Appellate Body Report, *Brazil-Retreaded Tyres*, WT/DS332/AB/R, 3 December 2007, para. 182.

[133] Appellate Body Report, *US-Gambling*, WT/DS285/AB/R, 20 April 2005, para. 304.

[134] Cf. Appellate Body Report, *US-Gambling*, WT/DS285/AB/R, 20 April 2005, para. 304 referring to Appellate Body Report, *Korea—Various Measures on Beef*, WT/DS161/AB/R;WT/DS169/AB/R, 11 December 2000, para. 166.

[135] *See* further Kapterian (2010); Weiß (2020b), pp. 250–265; Yakovleva (2020a), pp. 899–900.

ends pursued by it; the other factor is the restrictive impact of the measure on international commerce.".[136] The Appellate Body underscored further: "*A comparison between the challenged measure and possible alternatives should then be undertaken, and the results of such comparison should be considered in the light of the importance of the interests at issue. It is on the basis of this "weighing and balancing" and comparison of measures, taking into account the interests or values at stake, that a panel determines whether a measure is "necessary" or, alternatively, whether another, WTO-consistent measure is "reasonably available".*".[137] With regard to the latter, the Appellate Body held: "*An alternative measure may be found not to be "reasonably available", however, where it is merely theoretical in nature, for instance, where the responding Member is not capable of taking it, or where the measure imposes an undue burden on that Member, such as prohibitive costs or substantial technical difficulties. Moreover, a "reasonably available" alternative measure must be a measure that would preserve for the responding Member its right to achieve its desired level of protection with respect to the objective pursued [. . .].*".[138]

With respect to the burden of proof, the Appellate Body held: "*It is well-established that a responding party invoking an affirmative defence bears the burden of demonstrating that its measure, found to be WTO-inconsistent, satisfies the requirements of the invoked defence [. . .]*", while it is not, however, "*the responding party's burden to show, in the first instance, that there are no reasonably available alternatives to achieve its objectives*".[139] A responding party must "*make a prima facie case that its measure is 'necessary' by putting forward evidence and arguments that enable a panel to assess the challenged measure in the light of the relevant factors to be 'weighed and balanced' in a given case.*".[140] The Appellate Body emphasised: "*if the panel concludes that the respondent has made a prima facie case that the challenged measure is 'necessary'—that is, 'significantly closer to the pole of 'indispensable' than to the opposite pole of simply 'making a contribution to''—then a panel should find that challenged measure 'necessary' within the terms of Article XIV(a) of the GATS.*".[141] However, if the complaining party "*raises a WTO-consistent alternative measure [. . .] the responding party will be required to demonstrate why its challenged measure nevertheless remains 'necessary' in the light of that alternative or, in other words, why the proposed alternative is not, in fact, "reasonably available". If a responding party*

---

[136] Appellate Body Report, *US-Gambling*, WT/DS285/AB/R, 20 April 2005, para. 306. *See* further on the respective weight of these factors in relation to each other as evidenced in WTO case law, Delimatsis (2014), p. 98.

[137] Cf. Appellate Body Report, *US-Gambling*, WT/DS285/AB/R, 20 April 2005, para. 307; Appellate Body Report, *Argentina—Financial Services*, WT/DS453/AB/R, 14 April 2016, para. 6.182.

[138] Appellate Body Report, *US-Gambling*, WT/DS285/AB/R, 20 April 2005, para. 308.

[139] Appellate Body Report, *US-Gambling*, WT/DS285/AB/R, 20 April 2005, para. 309.

[140] Appellate Body Report, *US-Gambling*, WT/DS285/AB/R, 20 April 2005, para. 310.

[141] Appellate Body Report, *US-Gambling*, WT/DS285/AB/R, 20 April 2005, para. 310.

demonstrates that the alternative is not "reasonably available", in the light of the interests or values being pursued and the party's desired level of protection, it follows that the challenged measure must be "necessary" [...]".[142] In this context, the allocation of the burden of proof is of great importance for the regulatory discretion of WTO Members, since in practice a large number of cases are decided on the grounds of evidentiary issues, making it an important element in determining whether a regulatory measure will withstand scrutiny of the WTO dispute settlement bodies.[143]

These principles of the *"necessity"* test under Article XIV GATS must be further explored in the context of data privacy measures. Firstly, when assessing the relative importance of the objective pursued, domestic data privacy measures can claim the acknowledgement of the privacy of individuals and the protection of their personal data in Article XIV(c)(ii) GATS. Furthermore, privacy is universally recognised as a human right at the international level (*see supra* Sect. 4.4.1.2.1). Global recognition of the increasing relevance of the protection of individuals in the processing of their personal data is underscored by the recent proliferation of data privacy legislation and the corresponding renewal and updating of existing international frameworks. Moreover, the respective policy debates at the global level are characterised by the distinct approach of the EU, which recognizes *"data protection"* as a fundamental right *sui generis* (*see supra* Sect. 4.3.2.2). In addition, a robust data privacy framework is also a crucial building block for developing trust in Internet-based business models (*see supra* Sect. 4.4.1.1.2). Against this background, measures adopted on the grounds of data privacy laws and regulations can generally demonstrate a rather high importance of the underlying objectives.[144]

Secondly, with regard to a measure's contribution to the objective, the Appellate Body underscored that it is a *"panel's duty [...] to assess, in a qualitative or quantitative manner, the extent of the measure's contribution to the end pursued, rather than merely ascertaining whether or not the measure makes any contribution"*[145] The likelihood that a measure will be deemed necessary increases proportionally to the extent to which a measure contributes to achieving the legitimate policy objective. The Appellate Body has held: *"The greater the contribution, the*

---

[142] Appellate Body Report, *US-Gambling*, WT/DS285/AB/R, 20 April 2005, para. 311.

[143] Weiß (2020b), p. 268.

[144] *See* also Mishra (2019), p. 14. In *US-Gambling*, the WTO Panel held that *"On the basis of the foregoing, it is clear to us that the interests and values protected by the Wire Act, the Travel Act (when read together with the relevant state laws) and the Illegal Gambling Business Act (when read together with the relevant state laws) serve very important societal interests that can be characterized as "vital and important in the highest degree" in a similar way to the characterization of the protection of human life and health against a life-threatening health risk by the Appellate Body in EC—Asbestos."*, cf. Panel Report, *US-Gambling*, WT/DS285/R, 10 November 2004, para. 6.492. This assessment should therefore also apply to the rules on the protection of the privacy of individuals with regard to the processing and dissemination of personal data, in particular because of the widely recognized fundamental rights nature of privacy.

[145] Appellate Body Report, *Argentina—Financial Services*, WT/DS453/AB/R, 14 April 2016, para. 6.234.

more easily a measure might be considered to be 'necessary'.".[146] Therefore, the focus must be on the exact regulatory measure and the concrete way in which this measure contributes to the objective of securing compliance with data privacy laws or regulations which are not inconsistent with the provisions of the GATS or to protect public morals or to maintain public order. An abstract assessment of this requirement is made difficult by the vague notion of privacy and the resulting nuance of underlying laws and regulations and the diversification of corresponding measures. Evaluating whether a measure contributes to the ends provided by Article XIV (a) GATS and Article XIV(c)(ii) GATS involves a variety of considerations, including technical as well as socio-economic and socio-cultural factors. In this context, the question could be raised, to what extent WTO panels can address the extraordinarily complex technological features of a networked world.[147] As far as the technological requirements for the protection of personal data in a cross-border context are concerned, it is not evident which data privacy measures are technologically viable in a globally networked reality.[148] In fact, the efficacy of the adequacy approach and the resulting regulation of cross-border data flows in achieving a high standard of data privacy is widely debated.[149] Certainly, it is argued that a denial of adequacy can be an effective contribution to the objective of safeguarding data privacy, as it requires conditional safeguards to the transfer of personal data or even translates into the retainment of personal data inside a given jurisdiction.[150] However, given the inherently global structure of the Internet, there are also compelling counterarguments to the effectiveness of measures designed to associate personal data transfers with a territorial element. The contribution of *de facto* or *de jure* data localisation to compliance with a data privacy regulation, for example, is highly controversial, as, arguably, a decentralised cross-border distribution of data would allow to avoid a "*jackpot scenario*" for hackers and cybercriminals.[151] Depending on how they are designed and implemented, data localisation measures, for example, may contribute to the protection of personal data to some degree, while

---

[146] Appellate Body Report, *Korea –Various Measures on Beef*, WT/DS161/AB/R, WT/DS169/AB/R, 11 December 2000, para. 163.

[147] *See* generally Weiß (2020b), p. 262. In this context, the establishment of an expert group under Article 13 Sec. 2 DSU could be explored to assess the intricate technological interrelations between the inherent global architecture of the Internet and the concrete impact of a data privacy measure, and to assess the contribution of a given measure in achieving compliance with a data privacy regulation, *see* also Chen (2015), p. 220.

[148] Mishra (2021), pp. 268–269.

[149] *See* in particular with regard to the EU's data protection regime Kuner (2017), pp. 918–919: "*Regulation of international data transfers in EU law must move beyond formalistic measures and legal fictions to implement actual protection in practice. It must also discard illusions, such as the idea that DPAs and national courts can perform large-scale assessments of the adequacy of non-EU data protection systems. Data protection law cannot by itself resolve issues relating to surveillance for national security or intelligence-gathering purposes, which will require further reform and transparency regarding intelligence-gathering practices.*".

[150] *See* for example Naef (2023), p. 334.

[151] With further references Chander and Lê (2015), pp. 718–721.

in other instances they may subvert individual privacy.[152] Arguably, the location of data is less important than system design, data encryption, and additional security measures such as logical access controls and incident detection and response procedures, for example.[153] With this in mind, some commenters believe it is a "*misguided*" privacy policy to base the assessment of a data privacy standard on the geographic location where the information is stored, rather than the measures taken to store the data securely.[154] Therefore, when analysing whether the effectiveness of a data localisation measure is sufficiently proven with respect to the compliance with data privacy regulations, one will encounter a highly complex regulatory environment and indeed a number of technical counter-arguments.[155] With regard to the exception in Article XIV(c)(ii) GATS, in particular, this increases the pressure on the initial identification of the laws and regulations with which a regulatory measure is intended to achieve compliance.[156] When in doubt, the identification should rather be placed on a broad footing with regard to such laws or regulations.

Thirdly, with regard to the trade restrictiveness of a measure in question, the WTO dispute settlement bodies will have to assess the degree of a measure's trade-restrictiveness, rather than ascertaining whether or not the measure involves some restriction on trade.[157] Again, the individual data privacy measure and its specific impact on cross-border trade must be examined, as the degree of trade restrictiveness must be understood in the light of the importance of the ends pursued.[158] At this point, reference can be drawn to the difficult determination of the economic effects of data privacy measures (*see supra* Sect. 4.4.1.1). Moreover, in this context, the heterogeneity of data privacy instruments at the global level must be emphasised, as they may have widely different effects on cross-border trade. This is evident with regard to, for example, the different approaches to the regulation of data flows under data privacy law (*see supra* Sect. 4.3.3). It is important to keep in mind that the trade restriction imposed by a data flow regulation, such as data localisation, cannot be unambiguously determined a priori and depends, among other things, on the technical design and specifications.[159]

Fourthly, with regard to alternative measures, it is a WTO Panel's task to conduct to a "*[...] comparison between the challenged measure and possible alternatives [...] and the results of such comparison should be considered in the light of the*

---

[152] Svantesson (2020), p. 27.

[153] *See* further Hon (2017), pp. 315–316.

[154] Cory and Dascoli (2021), p. 5.

[155] *See* further Hon (2017), p. 261; Mishra (2019), pp. 14–15. *See* on the role of technical codes of conduct for data privacy Reidenberg (1999), pp. 1956–1957.

[156] Irion et al. (2016), p. 36.

[157] Appellate Body Report, *Argentina—Financial Services*, WT/DS453/AB/R, 14 April 2016, para. 6.234.

[158] Cottier et al. (2008), p. 318.

[159] Mishra (2019), p. 16.

importance of the interests at issue."[160] With respect to data privacy regulation, of particular importance in this context are the differing levels of interference with the movement of data that result from different approaches to cross-border data regulation. As the above analysis has shown, the data localisation and adequacy approaches generally have the greatest potential for trade-restrictive impact on cross-border data flows, while accountability mechanisms and, in particular, self-regulatory measures generally have less or even no impact (*see supra* Sect. 4.3.3). These alternative approaches to data privacy regulation of cross-border data flows could therefore be seen as preferable means to mitigate the data privacy collision in trade.[161] Notably, however, a responding party may invoke that an alternative measure does not preserve *"its right to achieve its desired level of protection with respect to the objective pursued under [. . .] Article XIV"*.[162] WTO Members *"have the right to determine for themselves the level of enforcement of their WTO-consistent laws and regulations."*[163] And indeed, the level of protection for data privacy under accountability and self-regulatory mechanisms is arguably not as high as it is afforded under the adequacy approach (*see* further *supra* Sect. 4.3.3.5). A practical problem, besides the WTO tribunal's uncertain capacity to evaluate the conception and design of a data privacy measure against the complex backdrop of a networked world, relates to the allocation of the burden of proof as it might be challenging for the complaining party to raise an alternative regulatory measure the responding party can be reasonably expected to employ. The Appellate Body has held that not only must the proposed measure be less trade-restrictive in order to qualify as a *"genuine alternative"*, but it must also secure for the responding Member the right to achieve the level of protection it desires in relation to the objective it seeks to achieve.[164] This may explain, why a data privacy measure has not yet been brought before the WTO dispute settlement bodies.[165]

---

[160] Cf. Appellate Body Report, *US-Gambling*, WT/DS285/AB/R, 20 April 2005, para. 307; Appellate Body Report, *Argentina—Financial Services*, WT/DS453/AB/R, 14 April 2016, para. 6.182.

[161] *See* further Mishra (2019), pp. 17–18.

[162] Appellate Body Report, *US-Gambling*, WT/DS285/AB/R, 20 April 2005, para. 308.

[163] Appellate Body Report, *Korea–Various Measures on Beef*, WT/DS161/AB/R, WT/DS169/AB/R, 11 December 2000, para. 176.

[164] Appellate Body Report, *EC Seal Products*, WT/DS400/AB/R, WT/DS401/AB/R, 22 May 2014, para. 5.261; Appellate Body Report, *Brazil-Retreaded Tyres*, WT/DS332/AB/R, 3 December 2007, para. 156. *See* with further references to WTO Jurisprudence in Appellate Body Reports *EC-Asbestos* and *Korea Various Measures on Beef* Appellate Body Report, *US-Gambling*, WT/DS285/R, 20 April 2005, para. 308.

[165] With respect to the Chinese model of Internet control, for example, *Tim Wu* has questioned: *"How much control is legitimate domestic regulation, and how much is a barrier to trade and a breach of promises made to other members of the WTO? Over the next decade, the WTO and its major members will face a choice that can be framed as a decision on burden of proof."*, cf. Wu (2006), p. 287.

5.2.2.4.2 The Ambiguous Procedure of Weighing and Balancing

From what has already been discussed above it is clear that the WTO dispute settlement bodies weighing and balancing of the *"necessity"* of a given data privacy measure will be a delicate endeavour, particularly if a data privacy measure is designed to take into account elements beyond the economic discourse thus referencing primarily the safeguarding of moral standards and societal values. This concerns, on the one hand, a general lack of predictability and consistency in the weighing and balancing exercise and, on the other hand, an additional element of precariousness with respect to high-profile policy objectives such as fundamental rights. In this context, the conception and consecutive application of the weighing and balancing procedure by the Appellate Body was found to be rather indetermined and even inconsistent with respect to its very requirements.[166] Assessing the relative importance of an objective and weighing it against its trade-restrictive effect can lead to an examination of the proportionality of a social policy against its trade costs in the sense of a rigorous cost-benefit analysis, which would involve a review of the level of protection sought for domestically—a practice that should not occur under the weighing and balancing concept, in which a Member may choose its respective level of protection.[167] It is therefore uncertain whether the discretion given to a WTO Member in the conception of the necessity test to determine the desired level of protection and the measure that best contributes to achieving that objective is actually respected. Indeed, the *"necessity"* test can be construed in terms of a proportionality analysis, which allows a WTO panel to second guess the domestic policy imperative when determining the objective to be pursued and the level of protection to be achieved, and even to substitute its own assessment in lieu of domestic policy perceptions.[168] This unpredictability of WTO jurisprudence with regard to the deference to domestic regulatory autonomy has led to a variety of opinions with regard to the evaluation of the weighing and balancing exercise. In this context, some scholars have argued that the *"necessity"* test after the Uruguay Round has moved in the direction of greater flexibility for domestic regulations, whereby, depending on the circumstances of the individual case, the second-best solution can now also be considered *"necessary"*.[169] Thus, international trade law would fundamentally provide domestic policy space for exploring data privacy regulation in a shifting and dynamic environment. On the other hand, it has been argued that the risk of reverting to a purely economic analysis of the *"necessity"* of a data privacy measure designed to safeguard fundamental human rights to privacy and data

---

[166] Weiß (2020b), pp. 255–259.
[167] Regan (2007); Weiß (2020b), pp. 255–265; Yakovleva (2020a), pp. 899–907.
[168] Weiß (2020b), pp. 259–265; Yakovleva (2020a), pp. 903–907.
[169] Cottier et al. (2008), p. 327. *See* with further references Weiß (2020b), p. 250, who underscores: *"[...] the interpretive development of the term "necessary" is not a straightforward success story for the benefit of domestic regulatory autonomy"*, noting that there are *"still contrarotating tendencies in the WTO case law"*.

5.2 WTO Law and Domestic Data Privacy Regulations

protection may be detrimental to the exercise of those rights. In this sense, *Svetlana Yakovleva* claims that the *"international trade law's accommodation of privacy and personal data regulation undermines the autonomy of states to pursue a fundamental rights approach."*.[170] The argument has been made that an instrumental approach to human rights in the context of an economization of human rights would result in the application of those rights only to the extent that they serve, or at least do not unduly hinder, the economic aims of the WTO agreements.[171] While the human rights discourse is highly relevant to the debate on the balancing of data privacy and trade, data privacy so far has had little bearing on the debates on non-economic interests in WTO law.[172] In the absence of precedent before a WTO Panel it is not possible to predict with confidence how the dispute settlement system would rule on the *"necessity"* of a given data privacy measure. In principle, however, *"necessity"* is a flexible concept which, depending on its application, may promote rather than restrict national regulatory diversity.[173] A particular reference point for the *"necessity"* test in relation to national data privacy measures arises from the nature of privacy as a human right. A defending party of a regulatory measure that is adopted in relation to privacy or data protection will generally be able to claim a high degree of relative importance in terms of the objective pursued as it can invoke the protection of fundamental rights. WTO jurisprudence has applied different standards for assessing importance in its case law and, with respect to highest priority objectives such as human health and life, has downgraded the weighing and balancing test to a less restrictive means test, giving rise to the theory of a double standard of the balancing test.[174] Against this background, it can be argued that the interpretation of *"necessity"* can and should be broad so as to offer WTO Members a wide margin of appreciation in designing and enforcing data privacy measures to accommodate national specificities of data privacy regulation. This applies in particular with regard to regulation intended to safeguard fundamental rights to privacy and data protection in the sense of a human rights perspective of the GATS.[175] This is likely to be particularly, but certainly not exclusively, relevant to the exception under Article XIV(a) GATS with respect to the protection of public morals or maintaining public order in connection with a data privacy measure. Here the WTO dispute settlement bodies provide a responding party with a particular degree of leeway when determining a provisional justification (*see supra* Sect. 5.2.2.3). Narrowing the margin of appreciation of a WTO Member by means of a rather

---

[170] Yakovleva (2018), p. 478.

[171] Breining-Kaufmann (2005), pp. 102–104. The author emphasizes that this also depends on the interpretation of the objective of the WTO. *See* further regarding the „*finality*"of the WTO, Weiß (2020b), pp. 81–89.

[172] Burri (2021), p. 36.

[173] Cottier et al. (2008), p. 316.

[174] *See* with further references Weiß (2020b), pp. 259–262.

[175] *See* with regard to a universal human rights understanding as an external guideline for GATS interpretation Krajewski (2003), pp. 60–61; Delimatsis (2011), p. 287.

restrictive "*necessity*" test in the sense of a pure cost-benefit analysis runs counter to such efforts and seems to not do justice to a balance of economic and non-economic values by means of the general exceptions of the GATS. In this sense, for example, a rather trade restrictive localisation of personal data could be deemed necessary, when adopted with regard to data transfers to countries whose governments have a proven record of structural violations of data privacy principles.[176] Given the unsettled background of data privacy in an international context and the wide discretionary authority of WTO dispute settlement bodies in the weighing and balancing of the relevant facts, however, it is not possible to predict the outcome of the "*necessity*" test in an abstract manner.[177]

5.2.2.5 Chapeau of Article XIV GATS

The chapeau of Article XIV GATS demands that a measure be applied in a manner that does not constitute "*arbitrary or unjustifiable discrimination*" between countries where like conditions prevail or a "*disguised restriction*" on trade in services. Hence, the chapeau pertains to the *application* of a measure adopted or enforced that is inconsistent with one of the commitments under the GATS but is considered provisionally justified under Article XIV(c)(ii) GATS or Article XIV(a) GATS. Given that disputes under Article XX GATT have often dealt with the first two types of situations (i.e., arbitrary or unjustifiable discrimination) collectively, as the presence of either of these situations sufficient to conclude that a measure cannot be justified, the same approach applies to Article XIV GATS.[178] The Appellate Body in *US—Shrimp* underscored that: "*The task of interpreting and applying the chapeau is, hence, essentially the delicate one of locating and marking out a line of equilibrium between the right of a Member to invoke an exception [. . .] and the rights of the other Members under varying substantive provisions [. . .], so that neither of the competing rights will cancel out the other and thereby distort and nullify or impair the balance of rights and obligations constructed by the Members themselves in that Agreement.*".[179] Hence, the analysis is focused on the determination of the good faith of a WTO Member in applying or enforcing the measure at issue in a manner consistent with the GATS.[180] The chapeau "*serves to ensure that Members' rights to avail themselves of exceptions are exercised reasonably, so as not to frustrate the*

---

[176] Mishra (2019), p. 15; Mitchell and Mishra (2019), p. 394.

[177] Mishra (2019), pp. 18–19.

[178] Panel Report, *Argentina—Financial Services*, WT/DS453/R, 30 September 2015, para. 7.745.

[179] Appellate Body Report, *US-Shrimp*, WT/DS58/AB/R, 12 October 1998, para. 159. The Appellate Body further held "*The location of the line of equilibrium, as expressed in the chapeau, is not fixed and unchanging; the line moves as the kind and the shape of the measures at stake vary and as the facts making up specific cases differ.*", see Appellate Body Report, *US-Shrimp*, WT/DS58/AB/R, 12 October 1998, para. 159.

[180] Appellate Body Report, *US-Shrimp*, WT/DS58/AB/R, 12 October 1998, para. 158. *See also* Cottier et al. (2008), p. 321.

rights accorded other Members by the substantive rules of the GATS."[181] This way, the chapeau is the final determinant of whether a data privacy measure is WTO-compliant, and its interpretation should be harmonised with the interpretative approach toward necessity so that the requirements cannot be played off against each other.[182] Given that WTO dispute settlement bodies have not established general rules and standards for examining the chapeau, its application is mainly case- and fact-specific.[183] Nevertheless, WTO jurisprudence has identified a number of elements that deter arbitrary or unjustifiable discrimination, including flexibility and willingness to negotiate, but a key element in interpreting the chapeau is the consistency in the application of a particular measure as it manifests its rationality.[184] The Appellate Body has stressed that one of the most important factors in the assessment of arbitrary or unjustifiable discrimination pertains to whether the discrimination "*can be reconciled with, or is rationally related to, the policy objective with respect to which the measure has been provisionally justified[...]*".[185] In this sense, WTO jurisprudence applies the chapeau in a manner that requires almost absolute uniformity of application, which means that inconsistent application risks precluding justification under Article XIV GATS.[186]

As for data privacy measures, at first glance they do not appear to be discriminatory, as they address both domestic and foreign services and service providers. With respect to neutral measures, WTO case law has previously held in *US-Gambling* that these must be placed in a proper context and that, to this end, evidence may be presented on the overall number of suppliers and enforcement patterns, as well as on the reasons for specific instances of non-enforcement.[187] Therefore, with regard to the denial of the adequacy status, for example, particular attention must be paid to the decision-making practice. Since legal, political and strategic elements are interwoven in the element of adequacy, this decision-making practice is particularly susceptible to discriminatory effects. Therefore, academic literature points out that inconsistent enforcement of data flow regulation under the adequacy approach is susceptible to challenges under the chapeau of Article XIV GATS.[188] Moreover, with respect to the negotiation of sectoral data flow regimes such as the EU-US Safe Harbor agreement it has been argued, that the rejection of a

---

[181] Appellate Body Report, *US-Gambling*, WT/DS285/R, 20 April 2005, para. 339.

[182] Weiß (2020b), p. 272.

[183] Cottier et al. (2008), p. 322.

[184] Lydgate (2017), p. 564; Weiß (2020b), p. 275.

[185] Appellate Body Report, *EC Seal Products*, WT/DS400/AB/R, WT/DS401/AB/R, 22 May 2014, para. 5.306.

[186] *See* with further references Chander and Schwartz (2023), pp. 58–59; Yakovleva and Irion (2020a), p. 211.

[187] Appellate Body Report, *US-Gambling*, WT/DS285/R, 20 April 2005, para. 356.

[188] Cf. for example Chander and Schwartz (2023), p. 58–59; Perez Asinari (2003); Shapiro (2003). *See* also Kuner (2017), p. 901.

third country's request to negotiate such an agreement constitutes a discrimination and consequently activates the chapeau of Article XIV GATS.[189]

5.3 Data Privacy Rules in Preferential Trade Agreements

PTAs are currently providing *"laboratories"* for the development of a transnational data governance, as they increasingly include specific provisions to enable and facilitate digital trade.[190] In this context, the above analysis has shown that PTAs have recently been designed to include specific digital trade provisions, involving, for example, the regulation of data flows and data localisation (*see supra* Sect. 3.4.2). Furthermore, it has been illustrated that a number of stakeholders are beginning to close the existing gaps in multilateral trade governance in line with national visions and priorities for a global digital economy, which results in a regionalisation of templates for digital trade (*see supra* Sect. 3.4.2.2). As data privacy is a key policy issue in the governance of digital trade, provisions to balance privacy and trade considerations have also increasingly been integrated into PTAs. As the nexus between privacy and trade is gaining in significance, this development is being addressed by a growing number of scholarly contributions.[191] In the following, the incorporation of data privacy provisions in trade agreements is discussed in analogy to the above analysis of the proliferation of provisions for the regulation of cross-border data flows.

5.3.1 Quantitative Considerations

In order to take a brief look at the status quo of the proliferation of data privacy provisions in trade agreements, data from the TAPED dataset will be referred to, as before (*see supra* Sect. 3.4.2).[192] Currently there are 91 PTAs that include provisions on data privacy, often in relation to the notion of *"data protection"*.[193] Regulations concerning data privacy belong to a set of deep digital trade rules.[194] Therefore, such

---

[189] Cf. with further references Irion et al. (2016), p. 38; Mattoo and Meltzer (2019), p. 782. *See* in detail Naef (2023), pp. 340–342.

[190] Herman (2010), p. 6; Wunsch-Vincent and Hold (2012), pp. 192–193. *See* also *supra* Sect. 3.4.2.

[191] Berka (2017); Burri (2021), pp. 67–82; Greenleaf (2017); Mattoo and Meltzer (2019); UNCTAD (2016), pp. 36–38; Wolfe (2018).

[192] Burri and Polanco (2020).

[193] Burri (2021), p. 74.

[194] Wunsch-Vincent and Hold (2012), p. 206.

rules are increasingly included in the specific digital trade chapters of trade agreements.[195]

5.3.2 Qualitative Considerations

Given that data privacy regimes are a key element of domestic data governance frameworks, provisions on data privacy are also a critical factor for the digital trade governance that is evolving in current PTAs. In this context, the different domestic approaches to a trade-off between economic and non-economic aspects of data privacy are reflected in a wide range of regulatory approaches to the nexus of digital trade and data privacy in PTAs, both binding and non-binding.[196] In the following, the distinctive policies of the US, the EU, and China with respect to their contemporary digital trade templates are exemplified in order to provide a frame of reference for the overall development of a digital trade policy as outlined above (*see supra* Sect. 3.4). A consideration of the patterns in the trade policies of these major trade actors will allow for a comparative perspective on the scope for data privacy measures.

5.3.2.1 United States of America

As has been illustrated above, recent PTAs negotiated under US auspices, notably the CPTPP and the USMCA, contain robust rules to ensure the flow of data between the parties (*see supra* Sect. 3.4.2.2.1). The comprehensive commitments regarding data flows including personal information as well as the ban on the localisation on computing facilities under Article 14.11 Sec. 2 CPTPP and Article 14.13 Sec. 2 CPTPP are subject to an exception for *"legitimate public policy objectives"* under Article 14.11 Sec. 3 CPTPP and Article 14.13 Sec. 3 CPTPP. The CPTPP provides for exceptions to the respective commitments, if measures are not applied in a manner that would constitute *"a means of arbitrary or unjustifiable discrimination or a disguised restriction on trade"*, and the measure at issue does not impose *"restrictions greater than are required to achieve the objective"*. The USMCA repeats and further specifies these requirements in Article 19.11 Sec. 2 USMCA, but notably only with regard to the *"Cross-Border Transfer of Information by Electronic Means"*.[197] Article 19.12 USMCA, which addresses the localisation of

---

[195] Here again, as *supra* Sect. 3.4.2., the following refers primarily to the umbrella term *"digital trade"* to identify rules that relate to various aspects of e-commerce on the one hand but also to specific data-related issues on the other, if not otherwise indicated.

[196] Burri (2021), pp. 74–82.

[197] The USMCAs foresees in fn. 5 to Article 19.11. Sec. 2 (b): *"A measure does not meet the conditions of this paragraph if it accords different treatment to data transfers solely on the basis*

computing facilities, notably does not provide for exceptions regarding public policy objectives. Nevertheless, the treaty language of the CPTPP and USMCA with regard to cross-border data flows echoes the exemption requirements of Article XIV GATS and Article XX GATT, as it provides for an element of *"necessity"* of the measures and in particular reiterates the requirements of the chapeaux. However, it was evidently intended to avoid the terminology of *"necessity"* and thereby directly invoke WTO case law including the allocation of the burden of proof under the necessity test.[198] The wording that no restrictions may be imposed that are *"greater than are required"* to achieve the objective can be interpreted as putting more emphasis on a least trade restrictive measure than on the latitude of national regulators to determine their individual level of data privacy protection. For example, there are concerns that this will lead to *"regulatory chill"* that will prevent governments from enforcing data privacy policies with restrictions on data transfer.[199] This analysis is also consistent with the fact that, unlike with the CPTPP, under the USMCA, the provision for an exemption from locating computing facilities was removed entirely. Moreover, both the CPTPP and USMCA attempt to reconcile economic objectives with domestic interests without establishing an explicit list of public policy objectives, but by stipulating that they must be of a *"legitimate"* nature. On the one hand, of course, this leaves the parties a great deal of leeway in determining the scope of the exemptions, potentially widening its application, but on the other hand it leads to a lack of transparency and ultimately to legal uncertainty.[200]

It can be assumed that data privacy concerns are generally among these legitimate public policy objectives, since data privacy has come to enjoy a well-established status under human rights treaties and, moreover, Article XIV(c)(ii) GATS explicitly provides for an exception in this context. Moreover, both the CPTPP (Article 14.8) and the USMCA (Article 19.8) contain independent provisions on *"personal information protection"*, in contrast to previous treaties concluded under US auspices.[201] Both treaties commit the signatories to endeavour to adopt non-discriminatory practices that protect the users of digital trade from personal information violations (Article 14.8 Sec. 3 CPTPP, Article 19.8 Sec.4 USMCA), and that the parties shall publish information about the personal information protections they provide to digital trade users (Article 14.8 Sec. 4 CPTPP, Article 19.8 Sec. 5 USMCA) . Finally, in recognition of the existing heterogeneity of approaches to data privacy, the parties also *"encourage"* the development of mechanisms to promote interoperability among these different regimes, and further *"The Parties shall endeavor to exchange information on the mechanisms applied in their jurisdictions and explore*

---

that they are cross-border in a manner that modifies the conditions of competition to the detriment of service suppliers of another Party.".

[198] *See* also Yakovleva and Irion (2020a), p. 213.

[199] Cf. Greenleaf (2018), p. 4.

[200] Burri (2021), p. 71; Yakovleva and Irion (2020a), p. 213.

[201] Yakovleva (2020b), pp. 490–492.

5.3 Data Privacy Rules in Preferential Trade Agreements

ways to extend these or other suitable arrangements to promote compatibility between them" (Article 14.8 Sec. 5 CPTPP, Article 19.8. Sec. 6 USMCA).[202] Both agreements require the parties to "*adopt or maintain a legal framework that provides for the protection of the personal information of the users of digital trade*" taking into account "*principles and guidelines of relevant international bodies*" (Article 14.8 Sec. 2 CPTPP, Article 19.8 Sec. 2 USMCA). These provisions for the protection of personal information have been further specified in the USMCA compared to the CPTPP, suggesting that it is an up-to-date blueprint for other US agreements.[203] The USMCA specifies that principles and guidelines of relevant international bodies notably include those of the APEC Privacy Framework or the OECD Privacy Guidelines. Both frameworks are widely recognised as being rather favourable to economic interests, suggesting a particular outlook on the nexus of trade and privacy.[204] Beyond these requirements, the USMCA provides for key privacy principles such as collection limitation; choice; data quality; purpose; use limitation; security safeguards; transparency; individual participation; and accountability (cf. Article 19.8. Sec. 3 USMCA). Interestingly, the same paragraph reiterates that restrictions on the cross-border flow of personal data must be necessary and proportionate to the risks involved, thereby arguably prioritising an economic discourse on data privacy.[205] Moreover, the USMCA explicitly recognizes that the APEC Cross-Border Privacy Rules system as a valid mechanism to facilitate cross-border information transfers while protecting personal information (cf. Article 19.8 Sec. 6 USMCA).[206] Hence, the USMCA structurally relates data privacy to consumer protection, following the US model of linking privacy and trade (*see* also *supra* Sect. 4.4.2.2.2).[207]

5.3.2.2 European Union

The rather hesitant introduction of data flow provisions in EU trade agreements is largely due to the high priority accorded to data protection as a fundamental right which is not to be undermined by binding trade commitments (*see* further *supra* Sect. 4.4.2.2.1). In fact, the European Commission has repeatedly made clear that European data protection standards are not the subject of negotiations in trade

---

[202] *See* with regard to a policy background for interoperability efforts dating back to the Obama administration's 2012 report on "*Consumer Data Privacy in a Networked World*" Chander and Schwartz (2023), pp. 88–89.

[203] Chander and Schwartz (2023), pp. 87–89. The negotiating template contained in the USMCA was also included in the U.S.-Japan Digital Trade Agreement, for example, which stipulates in its Article 3 that paragraphs (a) through (c) of Article XIV of the GATS are incorporated into and made part of the agreement, *mutatis mutandis*.

[204] *See* also Yakovleva and Irion (2020a), p. 213.

[205] Burri (2021), p. 77.

[206] *See* further Harris (2018).

[207] Chander and Schwartz (2023), pp. 85–89.

agreements or affected by the conclusion of such arrangements.[208] Therefore, as has been illustrated above, the EU's dialogues on data protection and its trade negotiations with third countries *"have to follow separate tracks"*.[209] The difficult negotiations on data flows under the EU-Japan Economic Partnership Agreement, which entered into force in February 2019, clearly demonstrate the reciprocal relationships between data protection and digital trade. Under the double track approach, the agreement does not include explicit regulation of data flows, while the separate adequacy decision of 23 January 2019 has created the *"world's largest area of safe data flows"*.[210] The absence of explicit data flow regulation, however, *"seemingly does not remove personal data from the emergent trade law institutions"*.[211] In this context, in a resolution titled *"Towards a digital trade strategy"* the European Parliament (EP) emphasised: *"that nothing in trade agreements shall prevent the EU and its Member States from maintaining, improving and applying its data protection rules"*.[212] Furthermore the EP urged: *"the Commission to draw up rules for cross-border data transfers as soon as possible which fully comply with the EU's existing and future data protection and privacy rules"* and called *"on the Commission, furthermore, to incorporate into the EU's trade agreements a horizontal provision, which fully maintains the right of a party to protect personal data and privacy, provided that such a right is not unjustifiably used to circumvent rules for cross-border data transfers for reasons other than the protection of personal data"*.[213] As has been illustrated above, the Commission drafted a negotiating template in 2018 aimed at mitigating the tension between the EU's digital trade policy and its constitutional commitment to respect the right to privacy and the protection of personal data as fundamental rights (*see supra* Sect. 3.4.2.2.2).[214] In addition to commitments aimed to ensure the cross-border data flow and to alleviate barriers to digital trade in the form of localisation requirements, the horizontal obligations provide that: *"Each Party recognizes that the protection of personal data and privacy is a fundamental right [. . .]"*, and further stipulate that *"Each Party*

---

[208] Cf. for example European Commission (2017), p. 6, para. 3.1; European Commission (2015), p. 12, p. 2.1.2.

[209] European Commission (2017), p. 9, para. 3.1.

[210] European Commission (2019).

[211] Bartl and Irion (2017), p. 13. And further with regard to missing safeguards for data protection *"There are very few institutional safeguards preventing biting on data protection laws from the side, through regulatory cooperation—either by directly challenging certain provisions in the regulatory cooperation institutions, or through interpretation of provisions in chapters on electronic commerce, financial services, or telecommunications."*

[212] The EP further called *"[. . .] on the Commission to strictly prohibit unjustified data localisation requirements in free trade agreements (FTAs)"*, considered *"that the removal of such requirements should be a top priority"*, emphasised *"that the relevant data protection legislation should be adhered to"*; and regretted *"attempts to use such requirements as a form of non-tariff barrier to trade and as a form of digital protectionism"*, cf. European Parliament (2017), paras. 8–13.

[213] European Parliament (2017), para. 11.

[214] Velli (2019).

may adopt and maintain the safeguards it deems appropriate to ensure the protection of personal data and privacy, including through the adoption and application of rules for the cross-border transfer of personal data.".[215] Data privacy is accorded a high priority, so much so that it is also stipulated: *"Nothing in this agreement shall affect the protection of personal data and privacy afforded by the Parties' respective safeguards."*. These horizontal commitments provide a very wide policy space based on a subjective assessment of the data privacy measures that are *"deemed appropriate"*, which in particular transcends the conditions set out in Article XIV GATS. In this respect, *Svetlana Yakovleva* and *Kristina Irion* point out that the wording of the exception for data protection is similar to that of the national security exception in Article XIV*bis* GATS, which guarantees broader regulatory autonomy.[216] These horizontal obligations were used as a basis for a number of trade negotiations, *inter alia*, with Australia, New Zealand as well as the WTO Joint Statement Initiative.[217] It should not be neglected, however, that the EU is flexible in the application of these provisions and that it is possible for an individual adjustment to be made to account for the particular partner of a PTA.[218] One of the most recent implementations of this template concerns the TCA concluded between the EU and the UK where it is emphasised in a separate chapter on data flows and personal data protection that: *"Nothing in this Agreement shall prevent a Party from adopting or maintaining measures on the protection of personal data and privacy, including with respect to cross-border data transfers, provided that the law of the Party provides for instruments enabling transfers under conditions of general application for the protection of the data transferred."* (Article 202 Sec. 2 TCA). It is clear that this exemption for personal data protection measures relates in particular to the EU's data protection regime under the GDPR. Particularly interesting is, however, that Article 202 Sec. 1 TCA has dropped the reference to fundamental rights protection as it merely stipulates: *"Each Party recognises that individuals have a right to the protection of personal data and privacy."*. On the other hand, the EU's agreement with Vietnam, which entered into force in 2020 merely contains a Chapter on *"Liberalisation of Investment, Trade in Services and Electronic Commerce"* without explicit reference to data flows and data protection.[219] In addition, it is noteworthy that several EU trade agreements contain specific provisions on regulatory cooperation.[220] This is in line with the EU's general objective of exploring stronger frameworks for cooperation on trade-related digital issues with like-minded partners

---

[215] European Commission (2018).

[216] Yakovleva and Irion (2020b), pp. 13–14. *See* with regard to the application essential security exceptions in WTO law Weiß (2020a).

[217] WTO, Joint Statement on Electronic Commerce Initiative, Communication from the EU, 26 April 2019, INF/ECOM/22, paras. 2.3, 2.6, 2.7.

[218] Burri (2021), p. 81.

[219] *See* also Burri (2021), p. 81 and further EU-Viet Nam Free Trade Agreement between the EU and the Socialist republic of Vietnam, Chapter 8.

[220] Burri (2021), pp. 78–79; Willemyns (2020), p. 232.

as part of an open and assertive trade policy.[221] However, against the backdrop of the EU's approach to data privacy in trade agreements, it is doubtful that the EU will negotiate on regulatory cooperation in the area of data privacy in PTAs.[222] In this context, the EU emphasizes the right to regulate to achieve legitimate policy goals, such as privacy and data protection, and often provides for an obligation to evaluate the functioning of data flow rules within a three-year period.[223]

5.3.2.3 People's Republic of China

With respect to data privacy, China has long lacked a clear stance in trade agreements, as domestic data regulation is still nascent and has only recently taken on clearer shape (*see supra* Sect. 4.4.2.2).[224] China has long been reluctant to regulate digital trade in trade agreements, which has been echoed in the absence of data privacy provisions.[225] The RCEP is particularly well suited for analysis in this regard because it builds in part on the CPTPP due to its overlapping base of participants. In this context, the RCEP in its institutional design gives rather broad regulatory discretion to its participating members.[226] This is also reflected in the provisions relating to *"Cross-Border Transfer of Information by Electronic Means"* (Article 12.15 RCEP) and *"Location of Computing Facilities"* (Article 12.14 RCEP). While there is a clear obligation in Article 12.15. Sec. 2 RCEP stating that cross-border data flows shall not be prevented if such activity is for the conduct of the business of a covered person, and that no party shall require a covered person to use or locate computing facilities in that Party's territory as a condition for conducting business in that party's territory, these obligations are counterbalanced with broad exception in Article 12.15 Sec. 3 RCEP and Article 12.14. Sec.3 RCEP. To be sure, Article 12.15 Sec. 3(a) RCEP and Article 12.14. Sec. 3(a) RCEP reflect the language of Article XIV GATS by providing that a party may take any measure inconsistent with Sec. 2 that it considers *"necessary"* to achieve a legitimate public policy objective, provided that the measure is not applied in a manner that would constitute a means of arbitrary or unjustifiable discrimination or a disguised restriction on trade. However, the RCEP deviates from the substantive guidelines of Article XIV GATS in that footnotes to the respective commitments state: *"For the purposes of this subparagraph, the Parties affirm that the necessity behind the implementation of*

---

[221] European Commission (2021), pp. 14–15, para. 3.2.3.
[222] *See* generally Mancini (2020), pp. 198–204. Notably, the EU has excluded the use of a clause for cooperation on digital trade issues for safeguards for the protection of personal data and privacy in its horizontal rules for cross-border data flows and for the protection of personal data, *see* European Commission (2018).
[223] *See* further Burri (2021), p. 80.
[224] Huang (2017), pp. 321–323.
[225] Willemyns (2020), p. 240.
[226] *See* generally Wang (2022), p. 679.

5.3 Data Privacy Rules in Preferential Trade Agreements

such legitimate public policy shall be decided by the implementing Party.". This self-judgment mechanism subjects cross-border data flow restrictions and data localisation measures largely to participating parties' own assessments.[227] Although this means that the measures adopted by the parties must at least be drafted in a non-discriminatory manner, one has to note that the provisions of Chapter 12 are not subject to the dispute settlement provisions of RCEP (cf. Article 12.17 Sec. 3 RCEP).[228] In addition, Article 12.15. Sec. 3 (b) and Article 12.14. Sec. 3 (b) provide broad reservations for measures that the parties consider necessary to protect their essential security interests which other Parties shall not dispute. Additionally, RCEP contains a dedicated Article on *"Online Personal Information Protection"*, which requires the participants to the agreement to *"adopt or maintain a legal framework which ensures the protection of personal information of the users of electronic commerce"* (Article 12.8. Sec. 1 RCEP). The additional explanations in footnote 8 offer a wide range of regulatory measures as compliant, while Article 12.8 Sec. 2 RCEP refers to unspecified international standards, principles, guidelines, and criteria for the development of a data privacy framework in accordance with Sec. 1. Furthermore, certain transparency criteria are to be met by each party by publishing information on the protection of personal data that it provides, and juridical persons are to be *"encouraged"* to disclose, including on the Internet, their policies and procedures relating to the protection of personal data (cf. Article 12.8 Sec. 3 RCEP). Finally, Article 12.8 Sec. 5 RCEP contains the rudimentary obligation to cooperate *"to the extent possible, for the protection of personal information transferred from a Party."*.

5.3.3 Evaluation

The current digital trade templates in relation to data privacy are in some ways a continuation of the data privacy collision identified above. The reason for this is that the data privacy collision is the result of a divergent domestic approach to the nexus of digital trade and data privacy. Naturally the PTAs of the respective countries will attempt to externalize domestic rules and approaches. Hence, US treaties that have traditionally focused on achieving the free movement of data involve public interest exemption clauses designed in the spirit of Article XIV GATS. In some cases, arguably, the agreements go even further by removing exemption clauses and using terminology that is absent from the GATS general exceptions and therefore are ambiguous as to what exactly is implied. The US approach has been criticised for tending to limit domestic leeway in implementing data privacy safeguards including data flow restrictions, or at least subjecting them to firm guidelines.[229] In particular,

---

[227] Burri (2021), p. 82; Wang (2022), p. 679.
[228] *See* also Leblond (2020).
[229] *See* only Greenleaf (2018), pp. 3–5.

the strong prohibition of data localisation in US agreements is believed to severely limit the national regulatory leeway for innovative and experimental domestic data regulation.[230] Concerns about a *"one-size-fits-all"* approach to digital development prompt *Thomas Streinz*, for example, to conclude that there is a danger of prematurely adopting what he calls the *"Silicon Valley"* consensus and enshrining it in international trade law.[231] Nevertheless, novel provisions in these treaties in relation to personal information protection suggest that the US is increasingly valuing the role of data privacy in the context of digital trade. In particular, the USMCA complements the treaty's commitment to create domestic privacy laws guided by international standards, such as the APEC Privacy Framework or the OECD Guidelines, with a concrete set of key principles that arguably surpasses to some extent domestic regulations in the US.[232] The provisions of the USMCA are not geared to deny the *raison d'être* of data privacy standards with regard to cross-border trade. Yet, as *Svetlana Yakovleva* has put it *"[...] privacy and personal data protection become normalized—or redefined – as tools of international trade and are viewed as trade values"*.[233]

Meanwhile, it can be observed that a number of countries negotiate a greater degree of regulatory autonomy and flexibility in the area of data privacy than is arguably provided for in the GATS.[234] A particular salient example of this approach is the EU, which is increasingly carving out policy space for data privacy in PTAs and leaving behind the multilateral model of Article XIV GATS.[235] Unlike the US-led PTAs, the EU's negotiating position based on horizontal provisions, as set forth in the TCA, for example, is not a comprehensive and open data flow regime enforcement, but provides for specific prohibitions on localisation requirements to ensure cross-border data flows.[236] Notably, however, the EU template provides wide regulatory latitude for data protection exceptions that the EU subjectively may *"deem appropriate"*.[237] Consistent with the EU's domestic position, the articulation of data protection as a fundamental right in trade agreements ensures the domestic room for manoeuvre necessary to accommodate non-economic interests in privacy and data protection. While the EU's horizontal provisions underscore that: *"Each Party recognizes that the protection of personal data and privacy is a fundamental right and that high standards in this regard contribute to confidence in the digital economy and the development of trade."* the protection of personal information under Article 19.8 USMCA merely requires that: *"The Parties recognize the economic and social benefits of protecting the personal information of users of digital*

---

[230] Streinz (2019), p. 341.
[231] Streinz (2019), p. 341.
[232] Burri (2021), p. 78.
[233] Yakovleva (2020b), p. 492.
[234] Peng (2011), pp. 765–766.
[235] Naef (2023), pp. 410–411; Velli (2019).
[236] Yakovleva (2020b), pp. 494–495.
[237] Burri (2021), pp. 80–81; Yakovleva (2020b), p. 496.

5.3 Data Privacy Rules in Preferential Trade Agreements

trade and the contribution that this makes to enhancing consumer confidence in digital trade.".[238] In this sense, the agreements concluded by the US and the EU reflect the described divergences in the normative rationale for data privacy that is resulting in the current data privacy collision (*see supra* Sect. 4.4). A look at China's approach, as reflected in the RCEP, reveals widespread reservations about imposing onerous trade obligations with respect to the regulation of data flows and the localisation of computer facilities. The respective self-judgment clauses here are the most far-reaching departure from the pattern of reviewing public policy exceptions familiar from multilateral law. Overall, however, it must be emphasised that a number of current agreements substantively move beyond WTO law with regard to the nexus of digital trade and data privacy. Examples include the obligation to adopt a minimum standard of domestic data privacy regulation and even to have such regulation based on international standards such as the OECD Privacy Guidelines or the APEC Privacy Framework. More generally, given the heterogeneous nature of normative rationales underlying data privacy and the larger political economy of digital trade, positions adopted at the nexus of digital trade and data privacy between data protection and data protectionism seem to evolve. The rise of a digital economy outlined above (*see supra* Sect. 2.2.2) has led to an evolutionary contextualisation of the regulation of data flows against the background of a rising economic relevance of personal data in a global data sphere.[239] As has been pointed out above, the OECD Guidelines and the Council of Europe's Data Protection Instrument in particular have been overhauled in the light of recent technological developments.[240] The same applies to EU legislation, which was updated in 2018 by the GDPR. Likewise, China has now adopted a comprehensive data governance regime that addresses personal information, and the US is currently engaged in its most promising attempt at a federal data privacy law in years. Such evolutionary developments have been reflected in the area of digital trade, with China and the EU recently increasing their integration of data flows into trade agreements and the US implementing comprehensive provisions on personal information protection. Therefore, perspectives on the divergent approaches such as *"privacy first"* (EU), *"economy first"* (US), *"security first"* (China) certainly reflect cornerstones of national trade policy positions regarding the nexus of digital trade and data privacy, yet cannot be considered to be absolute against the dynamic backdrop of the digital transformation of trade.[241]

---

[238] As a result, the role of Canada, which is a party to both the CETA with the EU and the CPTPP agreement negotiated with the participation of the US, is particularly interesting, *see* further Wolfe (2018), p. 3.

[239] Cf. only the foreword to OECD (2013).

[240] *See supra* Sect. 4.3.1.

[241] *See* for example Congressional Research Service (2020), pp. 10–15.

5.4 Conclusion

This chapter has elaborated on the complexity of trade governance in a digital economy by examining the interaction between trade law and the data privacy collision analysed above (*see supra* Sect. 4.4). It has been shown that against the backdrop the highly heterogenous policy environment of data privacy, a WTO Panel mandated to resolve a trade dispute in relation to domestic data privacy measures would face a convoluted challenge. Both the ambiguous normative rationale underlying data privacy regulation and the complex technological realities of the global networked environment make it difficult for WTO dispute settlement bodies to balance trade interests with domestic data privacy policies. In particular, the examination of whether a national data privacy measure can be considered *"necessary"* within the meaning of Article XIV(c)(ii) GATS or Article XIV(a) GATS is uncertain against the backdrop of existing WTO jurisprudence. This chapter has examined the requirements of the *"necessity"* test under Article XIV GATS with respect to domestic data privacy measures, finding that the weighing and balancing exercise may provide WTO dispute settlement bodies with an intrusive tool to examine domestic regulatory measures and assessments, particularly with respect to the desired level of (data) protection. It is possible that some of the measures taken today by data privacy regulators to enforce a *"high"* standard of data privacy, notably with regard to protecting fundamental rights to privacy and data protection, would prove not to be WTO-compliant, as there are interferences with market access and NT obligations under GATS, for example. In these cases, it is highly debatable, whether WTO Members might successfully invoke Article XIV GATS with regard to domestic data privacy measures. At issue here is primarily whether WTO dispute settlement bodies will leave it to domestic regulators to determine the desired level of data privacy and to choose a measure they deem appropriate to achieve that level, or whether they will intervene to second-guess national decisions on data privacy. Notably, different interpretations of the term *"necessity"* in Article XIV GATS allow for both.[242] Indeed, it is doubtful whether a WTO Panel is able to strike the delicate balance between economic elements and societal and moral elements of the data privacy discourse, and whether such a balancing exercise before a WTO Panel is even desirable.[243] In this context, the fundamental question can be raised as to whether trade law should be entrusted with the task of resolving the data privacy collision, given the sensitive challenge of determining the *"right"* level of data privacy.[244] This question arises especially in light of the considerable uncertainty inherent in a highly dynamic digital economy, in which national regulatory approaches must be allowed room for experimentation and governance must accommodate and coordinate this national regulatory innovation rather than limit it—in the

---

[242] Weiß (2020b), p. 264.

[243] Mattoo and Meltzer (2019), p. 782; Mishra (2019), pp. 20–23; Peng (2011), p. 769; Swire and Litan (2010), p. 194.

[244] *See* Kaminski (2015). *See* with further references Yakovleva and Irion (2020a), p. 203.

interest of overall systemic resilience.[245] The lack of relevant jurisprudence on the data privacy exemption may be due to the common perception that the WTO in general and the balancing exercise between economic and non-economic interests under Article XIV GATS in particular are in fact incapable of mitigating the data privacy collision in a meaningful way. Moreover, given the stalemate of the multilateral system and the contemporary disregard towards the WTO dispute settlement system, reflected in the paralysis of the Appellate Body, the WTO is currently deprived of its capacity to settle arguments between its Members. Nonetheless, the stakes are high as elements of data governance, and in particular the regulation of cross-border data flows, are introduced into the trade domain, and the WTO dispute settlement system may increasingly face the task of balancing national data governance against international trade commitments. In this context, some scholars have reached the conclusion that digital trade disputes are different from traditional trade disputes and that additional dispute settlement procedures therefore need to be developed in the context of a digital trade agreement.[246] However, a key issue in the adaptation of WTO law to the digital trade and data privacy nexus lies with choosing an approach to the interpretation of trade law and the consequential use of judicial instruments in the context of the general exception of Article XIV GATS, given that other venues of further developing WTO law (notably treaty making) seem difficult to achieve (*see* also *supra* Sect. 3.3.1.2).[247] It is clear that the normative basis of data privacy measures in human rights, the complex technological context, and the societal significance of data privacy in a digitally globalised world for human dignity and the democratic process must be reflected in a carefully weighed standard of review by WTO dispute settlement bodies with respect to national data privacy measures.[248]

The approaches to addressing the digital trade and data privacy nexus reflected in recent PTAs highlight the challenging position that WTO law finds itself with regard to the data privacy collision in trade. Modern trade agreements under US influence such as the USMCA and the CPTPP provide for comprehensive and binding regulations on the liberalisation of data flows along the lines of the goal of a *"free flow"* with exception clauses largely reproducing the requirements of Article XIV GATS. While the EU has given up its hesitation to include data flow commitments in trade agreements, it nevertheless claims considerable carve-outs for data privacy. Indeed, as scholars have noted, this carve out is similar to a national security clause.[249] China on the other hand is even more prudent to commit to any influence of trade law on domestic data governance measures. A WTO Panel will thus find

---

[245] Shaffer (2021), pp. 52–53. *See* further *infra* Sect. 6.3.

[246] *See* for example Fukunaga (2021).

[247] *See* in this sense Weiß (2020b), p. 16.

[248] *See* with regard to *"data ethics"*-related measures Mishra (2021), pp. 271–273. *See* further with regard to the relationship between the standard of review in WTO law and domestic regulatory autonomy Weiß (2020b), pp. 379–382.

[249] Yakovleva and Irion (2020b), pp. 13–14.

itself in the argumentative arena of the data privacy collision with distinct national approaches arguing over which measure best contributes to "*data privacy*" and, notably, which perspective on the relative importance of data privacy between data protection and data protectionism should be weighed (*see* further *supra* Sect. 4.4). While PTAs address new treaty realities for balancing trade interests and data privacy concerns against the backdrop of a transforming nexus between digital trade and data privacy, WTO law seems permanently geared towards an (evolutionary) interpretation of existing rules. As the digital transformation progresses, this will not only result in legal uncertainty, but will also increasingly compromise the legitimacy of WTO law in the digital economy due to the widening discrepancy to with economic reality.

Jurisprudence

Panel Report, European Communities—Regime for the Importation, Sale and Distribution of Bananas [EC-Bananas III], WT/DS27/R/ECU, adopted 22 May 1997

Panel Report, Argentina—Measures Relating to Trade in Goods and Services [Argentina—Financial Services], WT/DS453/R, adopted 30 September 2015

Panel Report, China—Certain Measures Affecting Electronic Payment Services [China — Electronic Payment Services], WT/DS413/R, adopted 16 July 2012

Panel Report, European Communities—Selected Customs Matters [EC — Selected Customs Matters], WT/DS315/R, adopted 16 June 2006

Panel Report, United States—Measures Affecting Cross-Border Supply of Gambling and Betting Services [US-Gambling], WT/DS285/R, adopted 10 November 2004

Panel Report, Colombia—Measures Relating to the Importation of Textiles Apparel and Footwear Panel Report [Colombia-Textiles], WT/DS461/R, adopted 15 January 2014

Panel Report, China — Measures Affecting Trading Rights and Distribution Services for Certain Publications and Audiovisual Entertainment Products [China—Publications and Audiovisual Products], WT/DS363/R, adopted 12 August 2009

Appellate Body Report, European Communities—Regime for the Importation, Sale and Distribution of Bananas [EC-Bananas III], WT/DS27/AB/R, 9 September 1997

Appellate Body Report, Certain Measures Affecting the Automotive Industry [-Canada—Autos], WT/DS139/AB/R, WT/DS142/AB/R, 31 May 2000

Appellate Body Report, Argentina—Measures Relating to Trade in Goods and Services [Argentina—Financial Services], WT/DS453/AB/R, adopted 14 April 2016

Appellate Body Report, United States—Measures Affecting Cross-Border Supply of Gambling and Betting Services [US-Gambling], WT/DS285/AB/R, adopted 20 April 2005.

Appellate Body Report, Mexico—Tax Measures on Soft Drinks and Other Beverages [Mexico—Taxes on Soft Drinks], WT/DS308/AB/R, adopted 3 March 2006.

Appellate Body Report, Korea—Measures Affecting Imports of Fresh, Chilled and Frozen Beef [Korea—Various Measures on Beef], WT/DS161/AB/R, WT/DS169/AB/R, adopted 11 December 2000

Appellate Body Report, European Communities — Measures Affecting Asbestos and Products Containing Asbestos [EC—Asbestos], WT/DS135/AB/R, adopted 12 March 2001

Appellate Body Report, Measures Prohibiting the Importation and Marketing of Seal Products [EC Seal Products], WT/DS400/AB/R, WT/DS401/AB/R, adopted 22 May 2014

Appellate Body Report, China — Measures Affecting Trading Rights and Distribution Services for Certain Publications and Audiovisual Entertainment Products [China—Publications and Audiovisual Products], WT/DS363/AB/R, adopted 21 December 2009

Appellate Body Report, Brazil—Measures Affecting Imports of Retreaded Tyres [Brazil—Retreaded Tyres], WT/DS332/AB/R, 3 December 2007

Appellate Body Report, United States—Import Prohibition of Certain Shrimp and Shrimp Products [US-Shrimp], WT/DS58/AB/R, 12 October 1998

ECJ, C-362/14, Maximillian Schrems v Data Protection Commissioner [Schrems I], 6 October 2015, ECLI:EU:C:2015:650

ECJ, C-311/18, Data Protection Commissioner v Facebook Ireland Limited and Maximillian Schrems [Schrems II], 16 July 2020, ECLI:EU:C:2020:55

References

Aaronson SA (2007) Seeping in slowly: how human rights concerns are penetrating the WTO. World Trade Rev 6(3):413–449. https://doi.org/10.1017/S147474560700345X

Aaronson SA (2015) Why trade agreements are not setting information free: the lost history and reinvigorated debate over cross-border data flows, human rights, and National Security. World Trade Rev 14(04):671–700. https://doi.org/10.1017/S1474745615000014

Adlung R (2014) Trade in services in the WTO: from Marrakesh (1994), To Doha (2001), to... (?). In: Narlikar A, Daunton MJ, Stern RM (eds) The Oxford handbook on the World Trade Organization. Oxford University Press, Oxford, pp 370–391

Bartl M, Irion K (2017) The Japan EU economic partnership agreement: flows of personal data to the land of the rising Sun. Report for European Parliament (GUE-NGL)

Berka W (2017) CETA, TTIP, TiSA, and data protection. In: Griller S, Obwexer W, Vranes E (eds) Mega-regional trade agreements: CETA, TTIP, and TiSA: new orientations for EU external economic relations, vol 1, 1st edn. Oxford University Press, Oxford, pp 175–186

Breining-Kaufmann C (2005) The legal matrix of human rights and trade law: state obligations versus private rights and obligations. In: Cottier T (ed) Human rights and international trade, 1. Publ. International economic law series. Oxford University Press, Oxford, pp 95–136

Burri M (2017) The governance of data and data flows in trade agreements: the pitfalls of legal adaptation. UC Davis Law Rev 51:65–132

Burri M (2021) Interfacing privacy and trade. Case Western Reserve J Int Law 53:35–88

Burri M, Polanco R (2020) Digital trade provisions in preferential trade agreements: introducing a new dataset. J Int Econ Law 23(1):187–220. https://doi.org/10.1093/jiel/jgz044

Chander A (2021) Artificial intelligence and trade. In: Burri M (ed) Big data and global trade law. Cambridge University Press, Cambridge, pp 115–127

Chander A, Lê UP (2015) Data nationalism. Empory Law J 64:677–739

Chander A, Schwartz PM (2023) Privacy and/or trade. Univ Chic Law Rev 90:49–135

Chen Y-H (2015) The EU data protection law reform: challenges for service trade liberalization and possible approaches for harmonizing privacy standards into the context of GATS. Spanish Yearb Int Law 19:211–220

Congressional Research Service (2020) Data flows, online privacy, and trade policy. R45584

Cory N, Dascoli L (2021) How barriers to cross-border data flows are spreading globally, what they cost, and how to address them. Information Technology & Innovation Foundation, Washington, D.C. https://itif.org/publications/2021/07/19/how-barriers-cross-border-data-flows-are-spreading-globally-what-they-cost/. Accessed 5 Apr 2024

Cottier T, Delimatsis P, Diebold NF (2008) Art. XIV GATS general exceptions. In: Wolfrum R, Stoll P-T, Feinäugle C (eds) WTO - trade in services: trade in services, Max Planck commentaries on world trade law Ser, vol 6, 1st edn. BRILL, Leiden, pp 287–328

Crosby D (2016) Analysis of data localization measures under WTO services trade rules and commitments. The E15 Initative Policy Brief

Delimatsis P (2007a) Due process and 'good' regulation embedded in the GATS - disciplining regulatory behaviour in services through article VI of the GATS. J Int Econ Law 10(1):13–50. https://doi.org/10.1093/jiel/jgl035

Delimatsis P (2007b) International trade in services and domestic regulations. Oxford University Press, Oxford

Delimatsis P (2011) Protecting public morals in a digital age: revisiting the WTO rulings on US - gambling and China - publications and audiovisual products. J Int Econ Law 14(2):257–293. https://doi.org/10.1093/jiel/jgr012

Delimatsis P (2014) Who's affraid of necessity? And why it matters? In: Lim AH, de Meester B (eds) WTO domestic regulation and services trade: putting principles into practice. Cambridge University Press, Cambridge, pp 95–109

European Commission (2015) Trade for all: towards a more responsible trade and investment policy. European Commission, Luxembourg. https://doi.org/10.2781/472505

European Commission (2017) Communication from the Commission to the European Parliament and the Council Exchanging and Protecting Personal Data in a Globalised World. COM(2017)7

European Commission (2018) Horizontal provisions for cross-border data flows and for personal data protection. https://ec.europa.eu/newsroom/just/items/627665. Accessed 5 Apr 2024

European Commission (2019) European Commission adopts adequacy decision on Japan, creating the world's largest area of safe data flows, Press Release, https://ec.europa.eu/commission/presscorner/detail/en/IP_19_421. Accessed 5 Apr 2024

European Commission (2021) Communication from the European Commission: trade policy review - an open, sustainable and assertive trade policy. COM(2021) 66 final

European Parliament (2017) Towards a digital trade strategy. 2017/2065(INI)

Fukunaga Y (2021) Are digital trade disputes "Trade Disputes"? In: Peng S, Lin C-F, Streinz T (eds) Artificial intelligence and international economic law: disruption, regulation, and reconfiguration, first published. Cambridge University Press, Cambridge, pp 155–172

Greenleaf G (2017) Free trade agreements and data privacy: future perils of Faustian bargains. In: Svantesson DJB, Kloza D (eds) Trans-Atlantic data privacy relations as a challenge for democracy, European integration and democracy series, vol 4. Intersentia, Cambridge, pp 181–210

Greenleaf G (2018) Looming free trade agreements pose threats to privacy. UNSW Law Research Paper No. 18–38

Harris J (2018) Why CBPR recognition in the USMCA is a significant development for privacy. https://iapp.org/news/a/why-cbpr-recognition-in-the-usmca-is-a-significant-development-for-privacy/. Accessed 5 Apr 2024

Herman L (2010) Multilateralising regionalism: the case of E-Commerce. OECD Trade Policy Papers No. 99, Paris. https://one.oecd.org/document/TAD/TC/WP(2009)42/FINAL/en/pdf. Accessed 5 Apr 2024

Hon WK (ed) (2017) Data localization laws and policy: the EU data protection international transfers restriction through a cloud computing lens. Edward Elgar Publishing, Cheltenham

Huang J (2017) Comparison of E-commerce regulations in Chinese and American FTAs: converging approaches, diverging contents, and polycentric directions? NLR 64(2):309–337. https://doi.org/10.1007/s40802-017-0094-1

Irion K, Yakovleva S, Bartl M (2016) Trade and privacy complicated bedfellows: how to achieve data protection-proof free trade agreements. Independent study commissioned by BEUC et al. Institute for Information Law (IViR), Amsterdam

Kaminski ME (2015) Why trade is not the place for the EU to negotiate privacy. https://policyreview.info/articles/news/why-trade-not-place-eu-negotiate-privacy/354. Accessed 5 Apr 2024

Kapterian G (2010) A critique of the WTO jurisprudence on 'necessity'. The Int Comp Law Q 59(1):89–127

Krajewski M (2003) National Regulation and trade liberalization in services: the legal impact of the general agreement on trade in services (GATS) on National Regulatory Autonomy. Wolters Kluwer Law International, Alphen aan den Rijn

Krajewski M (2008) Art. VI GATS. In: Wolfrum R, Stoll P-T, Feinäugle C (eds) WTO - trade in services: trade in services, Max Planck commentaries on world trade law Ser, vol 6, 1st edn. BRILL, Leiden, pp 167–196

Kuner C (2010) Data protection law and international jurisdiction on the internet (part 1). Int J Law Information Technol 18(2):176–193. https://doi.org/10.1093/ijlit/eaq002

Kuner C (2013) Transborder data flows and data privacy law. Oxford University Press, Oxford

Kuner C (2017) Reality and illusion in EU data transfer regulation post Schrems. German Law J 18(4):881–918

Leblond P (2020) Digital Trade: Is RCEP the WTO's Future? https://www.cigionline.org/articles/digital-trade-rcep-wtos-future/. Accessed 5 Apr 2024

Lim AH, de Meester B (2014) An introduction to domestic regulation and GATS. In: Lim AH, de Meester B (eds) WTO domestic regulation and services trade: putting principles into practice. Cambridge University Press, Cambridge, pp 1–22

Lowenfeld AF (2009) International economic law, Repr. International economic law series, 2nd edn. Oxford University Press, Oxford

Lydgate E (2017) Is it rational and consistent? The WTO's surprising role in shaping domestic public policy. J Int Econ Law 20(3):561–582. https://doi.org/10.1093/jiel/jgx030

MacDonald DA, Streatfield CM (2014) Personal data privacy and the WTO. Houston J Int Law 36(3):625–653

Mancini I (2020) Deepening trade and fundamental rights? Harnessing data protection rights in the regulatory cooperation chapters of EU trade agreements. In: Weiß W, Furculita C (eds) Global politics and EU trade policy. European yearbook of international economic law. Springer International Publishing, Cham, pp 185–207

Marceau G, Trachtman JP (2009) Responding to national concerns. In: Bethlehem DL (ed) The Oxford handbook of international trade law. Oxford University Press, Oxford, pp 209–236

Mattoo A, Meltzer JP (2019) International data flows and privacy: the conflict and its resolution. J Int Econ Law 21(4):769–789. https://doi.org/10.1093/jiel/jgy044

Mishra N (2019) Privacy, Cybersecurity, and GATS article XIV: a new frontier for trade and internet regulation? World Trade Rev 19(3):1–24. https://doi.org/10.1017/S1474745619000120

Mishra N (2021) International trade law and data ethics. In: Peng S, Lin C-F, Streinz T (eds) Artificial intelligence and international economic law: disruption, regulation, and reconfiguration, first published. Cambridge University Press, Cambridge, pp 255–273

Mitchell AD, Hepburn J (2018) Don't fence me in: reforming trade and investment law to better facilitate cross-border data transfer. Yale J Law Technol 19(1):182–237

Mitchell AD, Mishra N (2018) Data at the docks: modernizing international trade law for the digital economy. Va J Entertain Technol Law 20:1073–1134

Mitchell AD, Mishra N (2019) Regulating cross-border data flows in a data-driven world: how WTO law can contribute. J Int Econ Law 22(3):389–416. https://doi.org/10.1093/jiel/jgz016

Mitchell AD, Voon T (2014) Reasonableness, impartiality and objectivity. In: Lim AH, de Meester B (eds) WTO domestic regulation and services trade: putting principles into practice. Cambridge University Press, Cambridge, pp 65–78

Nadakavukaren Schefer K (2010) Social regulation in the WTO: trade policy and international legal development. Edward Elgar, Cheltenham

Naef T (2023) Data protection without data protectionism. European yearbook of international economic law. Springer International Publishing, Cham

Nuzzo S (2017) Tackling diversity inside WTO: the GATT moral clause after Colombia—textiles. Eur J Legal Studies 10(1):267–293

OECD (2013) The OECD privacy framework. https://www.oecd.org/sti/ieconomy/oecd_privacy_framework.pdf. Accessed 5 Apr 2024

Peng S (2011) Digitalization of services, the GATS and the protection of personal data. In: Sethe R, Heinemann A, Hilty RM (eds) Kommunikation: Festschrift für Rolf H. Weber zum 60. Geburtstag. Stämpfli, Bern, pp 753–769

Pérez Asinari MV (2002) Is there any room for privacy and data protection within the WTO rules? Electronic Law Rev 9(4):249–280

Perez Asinari MV (2003) The WTO and the protection of personal data. Do EU measures fall within GATS exception? Which future for data protection within the WTO e-commerce Context? 18th BILETA Conference: Controlling Information in the Online Environment. https://www.bileta.org.uk/wp-content/uploads/The-WTO-and-the-Protection-of-Personal-Data.-Do-EU-Measures-Fall-within-GATS-Exception.pdf. Accessed 5 Apr 2024

Regan D (2007) The meaning of 'necessary' in GATT article XX and GATS article XIV: the myth of cost–benefit balancing. World Trade Rev 6(3):347–369. https://doi.org/10.1017/S1474745607003424

Reidenberg JR (1999) Resolving conflicting international data privacy rules in cyberspace. Stanford Law Rev 52:1315–1371

Reyes CL (2011) WTO-compliant protection of fundamental rights: lessons from the EU privacy directive. Melb J Int Law 12(1):1–36

Rotenberg J (2020) Privacy before trade: assessing the WTO-consistency of privacy-based cross-border data flow restrictions. Univ Miami Int Comp Law Rev 28(1):91–120

Ruotolo GM (2018) The EU data protection regime and the multilateral trading system: where dream and day unite. Questions Int Law:5–29

Sen N (2018) Understanding the role of the WTO in international data flows: taking the liberalization or the regulatory autonomy path? J Int Econ Law 21(2):323–348. https://doi.org/10.1093/jiel/jgy021

Shaffer G (2021) Trade law in a data-driven economy. In: Peng S, Lin C-F, Streinz T (eds) Artificial intelligence and international economic law: disruption, regulation, and reconfiguration, first published. Cambridge University Press, Cambridge, pp 29–53

Shapiro E (2003) All is not fair in the privacy trade: the Safe Harbor agreement and the World Trade Organization. Fordham Law Rev 71:2781–2821

Streinz T (2019) Digital Megaregulation uncontested? TPP's model for the global digital economy. In: Kingsbury B et al (eds) Megaregulation contested. Oxford University Press, pp 312–342

Svantesson DJB (2020) Data localisation trends and challenges: considerations for the review of the PrivacyGuidelines. OECD digital economy papers no. 301. OECD Publishing, Paris. https://doi.org/10.1787/7fbaed62-en

Swire PP, Litan RE (2010) None of your business: world data flows, electronic commerce, and the European privacy directive. Brookings Institution Press, Washington

Tuthill L, Roy M (2012) GATS classification issues for information and communication technology services. In: Burri M, Cottier T (eds) Trade governance in the digital age. Cambridge University Press, Cambridge, pp 157–178

UNCTAD (2016) Data protection regulations and international data flows: implications for trade and development. https://unctad.org/publication/data-protection-regulations-and-international-data-flows-implications-trade-and. Accessed 5 Apr 2024

van den Bossche P, Zdouc W (2022) The law and policy of the World Trade Organization: text, cases, and materials, 5th edn. Cambridge University Press, Cambridge

Velli F (2019) The issue of data protection in EU Trade commitments: cross-border data transfers in GATS and bilateral free Trade Agreements

Wang X (2022) Online personal data protection and data flows under the RCEP: a nostalgic new start? TRAD 56(4):657–692. https://doi.org/10.54648/TRAD2022027

Weber RH (2012) Regulatory autonomy and privacy standards under the GATS. Asian J WTO Int Health Law Policy 7(1):25–48

Weber RH, Burri M (2014) Classification of Services in the Digital Economy, Aufl. 2013. Springer, Berlin

Weiß W (2020a) Interpreting essential security exceptions in WTO law in view of economic security interests. In: Weiß W, Furculita C (eds) Global politics and EU trade policy. European yearbook of international economic law. Springer International Publishing, Cham, pp 214–236

Weiß W (2020b) WTO law and domestic regulation: exploring the determinants for the impact of the WTO on domestic regulatory autonomy. Beck International. Beck; Hart; Nomos, München, Oxford, Baden-Baden

Willemyns I (2020) Agreement forthcoming? A comparison of EU, US, and Chinese RTAs in times of Plurilateral E-commerce negotiations. J Int Econ Law 23(1):221–244. https://doi.org/10.1093/jiel/jgz048

Wolfe R (2018) Learning about digital trade: privacy and E-Commerce in CETA and TPP. EUI Working Paper RSCAS 2018/27. https://hdl.handle.net/1814/55144. Accessed 5 Apr 2024

Wolfrum R (2008) Art. II GATS Most-Favoured-nation treatment. In: Wolfrum R, Stoll P-T, Feinäugle C (eds) WTO - trade in services: trade in services, vol 6, 1st edn Max Planck Commentaries on World Trade Law Ser. BRILL, Leiden, pp 71–91

Wouters J, Coppens D (2008) GATS and domestic regulation: balancing the right to regulate and trade liberalization. In: Alexander K, Andenas M (eds) The World Trade Organization and trade in services. Nijhoff eBook titles. Martinus Nijhoff Publishers, Leiden, pp 207–264

WTO (1999) Council for Trade in Services, Progress Report to the General Council, S/L/74, 27 July 1999

Wu T (2006) The world trade law of censorship and internet filtering. Chic J Int Law 7(1):263–287

Wunsch-Vincent S, Hold A (2012) Towards coherent rules for digital trade. In: Burri M, Cottier T (eds) Trade governance in the digital age. Cambridge University Press, Cambridge, pp 179–221

Yakovleva S (2018) Should fundamental rights to privacy and data protection be a part of the EU's international trade 'deals'? World Trade Rev 17(03):477–508. https://doi.org/10.1017/S1474745617000453

Yakovleva S (2020a) Personal data transfers in international trade and EU law: a tale of two 'necessities'. J World Invest Trade 21(6):881–919. https://doi.org/10.1163/22119000-12340189

Yakovleva S (2020b) Privacy protection(ism): the latest wave of trade constraints on regulatory autonomy. Univ Miami Law Rev 74:416–519

Yakovleva S, Irion K (2016) The best of both worlds? Free trade in services and EU law on privacy and data protection. Institute for Information Law Research Paper No. 2016-05

Yakovleva S, Irion K (2020a) Pitching trade against privacy: reconciling EU governance of personal data flows with external trade. Int Data Privacy Law 10(3):201–221. https://doi.org/10.1093/idpl/ipaa003

Yakovleva S, Irion K (2020b) Toward compatibility of the EU trade policy with the general data protection regulation. AJIL Unbound 114:10–14. https://doi.org/10.1017/aju.2019.81

Chapter 6
Towards Reconciling Digital Trade and Data Privacy

6.1 Introduction

While there is something to be said for considering the contemporary collision of data privacy regimes in a trade context as a variant of the *"classic"* debate between different approaches to achieving a policy objective and the ensuing contentiousness of the appropriate level of regulation—strong, light, or none—there is more involved when it comes to the nexus of digital trade and data privacy.[1] Against the backdrop of converging regulatory spaces for domestic and international law, the issue of data privacy in the Internet era is not merely a matter of individual trade-offs relating to the degree of regulation enforceable within a given legal system. Data privacy in a trade context involves a number of externalised effects of a domestic balancing of economic interests, fundamental rights to privacy and data protection, considerations of (data) sovereignty as well as the controversy over the value of data privacy in a highly dynamic environment of digital transformation. Beyond that, the patterns of reciprocal influence between evolving technologies and data privacy laws are shifting, which suggests that the notion of privacy itself is in flux and will inevitably need to be reviewed and refined.[2] In this context, the nexus of digital trade and data privacy introduces a new dimension to the debate on the convergence or divergence of regulations at the international level in general and the implications of trade liberalisation for the autonomy of states to pursue regulatory objectives in particular, as it opens a genuinely digital context for trade governance.

Today, the prevailing perception of the nexus between digital trade and data privacy considers them to be engaged in a *"mortal contest"*.[3] Arguably, maximising benefits for digital trade through the liberalisation of cross-border flows of personal

---

[1] *See* Peng (2011), p. 769.
[2] Gasser (2021).
[3] *See* further Chander and Schwartz (2023), p. 50; Yakovleva and Irion (2020), pp. 204–208.

data would come at the expense of domestic regulatory autonomy for data privacy, thereby threatening to subordinate fundamental rights to privacy and data protection to economic interests. An overly rigorous domestic data privacy standard, in turn, will most likely have a negative spill-over effect on the promotion of cross-border digital trade. In this sense, both trade lobbyists as well as privacy activists might be inclined (and have been) to argue that data privacy and trade should be kept separate so as not to create a trade-off that would bind the parties in a dynamic environment and likely compromise the underlying values of both fields.[4] What is particularly intriguing regarding this conundrum, however, is the still little-explored realisation that in a digitally networked reality, only an integrated approach will prove to be sustainable and to be able to fully realize the respective rationales of digital trade and data privacy. Achieving a thriving environment for both digital trade and data privacy is inextricably intertwined by the digital transformation, as effective data privacy in an inherently global digital economy requires a transboundary perspective, and cross-border digital trade relations are considerably implicated by domestic regimes of data governance. The incitement of conflict between the fields of trade and privacy fails to consider that further disconnection between the domains is not conducive to either one or the other, and to the fundamental values that inform them. In this sense, the possibility of a "*win-win*" between data privacy and cross-border data flows is under-explored in a "*bipolar*" landscape that frames data privacy rules as trade barriers, some authors argue.[5]

The policy debate on the nexus of digital trade and data privacy should aim to focus on points of convergence between the fields to create a new baseline for a mutually beneficial relationship. From the trade perspective, data privacy regulation should not exist merely as a beneficial factor in promoting trade nor be misconstrued as inevitably inducing inward-looking governance and insulation from innovation. The data privacy perspective, in turn, while honouring its objective to ensure the safeguarding of fundamental rights to privacy and data protection, should try to consider a trade perspective, especially with regard to its cross-border dimensions. The data privacy collision between divergent national approaches cannot be mitigated by operating both fields in isolation from one another or by vainly attempting to subsume one under the other. In this sense, mitigating the data privacy collision in trade would certainly also promote the right to privacy and data protection in a digitally globalised environment. Therefore, the nexus between trade and data privacy needs to be conceptually broadened in order to achieve a better overall harmony by means of an integrated approach. Considering common relevant normative principles is one way to accomplish this. *Anumpam Chander* and *Paul Schwartz*, for example, argue that there is a "*shared commitment to opportunity and democratic self-rule*" in both privacy and trade and underscore that "*Privacy*

---

[4] *See* with further references Chander and Schwartz (2023), p. 52; Kaminski (2015); Swire and Litan (2010), pp. 194–196.
[5] Yakovleva and Irion (2020), pp. 205–208.

and trade need not to be in opposition to each other".[6] While this analysis undoubtedly has considerable merit, from today's perspective, overcoming the dichotomy between trade and privacy is certainly easier said than done, as data privacy law and trade law still have little appreciation for each other, and the conflict touches on highly delicate matters such as domestic regulatory authority, the relationship between trade and human rights, as well as a strategic outlook on the digital economy and novel forms of protectionism in an emerging digital trade environment. While trade in the digital economy will require an integrated approach to digital trade and data privacy to help mitigate the data privacy collision, today's regulators and academic researchers are at a stage of acquiring the necessary expertise and, overall, are in the midst of a learning process.[7] This is reflected in the precarious state of data on digital trade, which will have to be addressed through international collaboration and progressive efforts to conceptualize trade in the digital economy (Sect. 6.2). This concluding chapter draws on the findings of the previous analysis of the digital trade and data privacy nexus to develop approaches for moving forward. Scholarly literature that has examined the response of trade law to the challenges of the digital economy often identifies an intermediate step, which is concerned with the adaptation of contemporary trade rules to digital trade, and a more visionary perspective, which is engaged in the design of new rules and regulatory frameworks.[8] In a similar way, the following sections will examine the adaptation and further development of existing multilateral regulation on trade in services (Sect. 6.4) and evaluate the prospects for new regulation addressing the nexus of digital trade and data privacy (Sect. 6.5). Prior to this, however, it is necessary to consider in more detail the role that trade law can play in terms of an integrated approach to digital trade and data privacy (Sect. 6.3).

6.2 Fostering International Initiatives for Measuring and Conceptualising Digital Trade

Regulatory governance for the digital trade and data privacy nexus will require a robust understanding of cross-border economic activity in a global digital economy, which is significantly enabled and facilitated by cross-border data flows. In this context, substantial gaps have been identified in the analytical mapping and regulatory conceptualisation of the digital transformation of trade. Therefore, the underlying components and vectors for trade in the digital economy need to be comprehensively measured and categorised. This involves, in particular, the development of measurement methodologies as well as a typology for cross-border data

---

[6]Chander and Schwartz (2023), p. 105, p. 113.
[7]Wolfe (2018), p. 13.
[8]*See* for example Burri (2016); Meltzer (2016), pp. 18–24; Mitchell and Mishra (2018), pp. 1126–1132; Wunsch-Vincent and Hold (2012), pp. 216–219.

flows. The above analysis of the relevance of cross-border data flows, particularly for digital trade, has shown that while their impact on today's trade flows is generally considered to be very significant, both the quantity and the economic relevance of data flows in international trade are often assessed in an anecdotal manner, and are *de facto* still very much in obscurity. While this is a reflection of the broader challenge of measuring and conceptualising economic activity in a digital economy, it is clear that the lack of a standard methodology and terminology for digital trade is a serious obstacle to its governance at the international level.[9] In this context, an ongoing challenge is that the development of metrics, and even more so the resulting conception of digital trade in regulatory terms, will remain a source of controversy at the international level. This is because the definition of what is and is not considered digital trade, and which international forum is best positioned to address it, will inevitably lead to disagreements regarding the resulting constraints on unilateral action and influence by individual countries. This means that the conceptualisation of digital trade itself provides an initial set of parameters for addressing the critical implications of a digital global economy for national regulatory sovereignty. The difficulty of resolving such conflicts and, at the same time, the supposed advantages of such a vacuum for unilateral gains can be illustrated by the example of the ongoing argument concerning the integration of digital trade into the silo structure of current WTO law and the arrangements that are individually made in PTAs for this purpose. Given the cross-cutting nature of digital trade, it is debatable whether cross-border data flows should be understood as falling within the traditional trade framework, especially in relation to trade in services, or whether "*data trade*" needs to be categorised separately.[10] The cross-cutting nature of digital trade does not mandate a definition for digital trade as a standalone sector, but rather a holistic perspective on trade in the digital economy, thereby challenging pre-existing trade paradigms. Moreover, the hinging effect of data flows implicates a wide range of national data policies in regulating digital trade and raises the issue of different perspectives and particularities in the interplay between the digital economy and domestic affairs. This becomes particularly clear when addressing the issue of data privacy, as this book has revealed. While certain terminology such as "*digital protectionism*" has gained ground in policy discussions, the underlying discourses are often substantially divergent owing to different values and perspectives on data privacy.[11]

More empirical evidence is needed on how trade rules affect digital flows as well as how domestic policies affect the building blocks of trade in the digital economy. In the absence of a common measurement for digital trade at the international level, there is little agreement today on which specific policies actually are "*trade-restrictive*". Without a consolidated and shared body of data, there is plenty of leeway for discriminatory digital trade policy initiatives geared to the socio-economic interests

---

[9] *See* in particular with regard to an "*AI economy*" Peng et al. (2021).
[10] *See* Burri (2017), p. 414; Mitchell and Mishra (2019), p. 390.
[11] *See* Yakovleva (2020), p. 517.

of individual countries. With a view to persistent conceptual disagreement, it seems that some countries actively assume a role in shaping conceptual approaches to digital trade measurement unilaterally. The US in particular has conducted comprehensive studies and introduced its own framework for a taxonomy of data flows.[12] The EU has also announced its intention to integrate EU trade policy more closely with the bloc's economic priorities, as reflected in the European Digital Strategy, and has announced to establish an analytical framework for measuring data flows.[13] However, isolated approaches may include elements of individual socio-cultural perspectives on digital trade that could bias the resulting measurement methodology, e.g., in terms of emphasising or minimising attention to personal data. Recent years have seen an increase in the number of initiatives concerned with the development of measurement methodologies and taxonomies for digital trade. As has been pointed out, the OECD plays a leading role in the field of digital trade measurement and is involved in various collaborative projects, including the development of a Handbook on Measuring Digital Trade in collaboration with the WTO, UNCTAD and the IMF.[14] Moreover, the G20 Initiative of Data Free Flow with Trust (DFFT) has set out to map a *"multi-dimensional architecture of data flow."*.[15] Although there are increasingly joint undertakings by international organisations, further progress in this area is needed as agreement on measurement issues is only effective if achieved by the broadest possible initiative. This requires additional cross-organisational integration of efforts so that results achieved in one forum cannot be contested in another and political opportunities between different fora are eliminated.

6.3 An Integrated Approach to the Digital Trade and Data Privacy Nexus: What Role for Trade Law?

Since the finalisation of the Uruguay Round, the political economy of trade, the geopolitical structure of the WTO membership as well as the realities of cross-border economic activity have changed considerably. The digital transformation has driven a convergence of regulatory realms and exacerbated difficulties in coordination among WTO Members pertaining to domestic regulatory authority, the safeguarding of fundamental rights as well as strategic interests in an emergent digital economy.[16] The inherently global digital economy places a heavy burden on multilateral trade governance, which has institutionalised the political economy of a hegemony of

---

[12] U.S. Department of Commerce (2016).
[13] European Commission (2021).
[14] IMF et al. (2023).
[15] World Economic Forum (2020).
[16] *See* further for the complex political economy of digital trade Mitchell and Mishra (2018), pp. 1081–1088. For the emergence of *"data realms"*, *see* Aaronson and Leblond (2018). *See* for an account of the current challenges facing the WTO and trade law Weiß et al. (2022), pp. 1–7.

sovereign nations of the twentieth century.[17] This pertains in particular to the integration of data and cross-border data flows, which are of fundamental importance for trade and at the same time involve a wide range of non-economic issues. This fosters a convergence between economic and non-economic interests and the legal frameworks and institutions developed to promote them—with trade law increasingly playing a central role through government practice rather than original regulatory purpose. Clearly, elements of digital trade governance are scattered across a variety of fora, both private and public, including those related to, for example, fundamental rights, economic welfare and development, leading to overlaps and parallels.[18] Both (relatively) new fora, such as the Internet Governance Forum (IGF) or the World Wide Web Consortium (W3C), and legacy fora, such as the International Telecommunication Union (ITU), the OECD, and the G20, may contribute to a multilateral governance framework for data flows.[19] At the same time, a number of commentators argue in favour of entirely new governance regimes for cross-border flows of digital data.[20] Thus, the regulation of cross-border data flows is characterised by a convergence between the mandates of different international bodies and stakeholders, ranging from the private sector to non-governmental organisations to national and local governments. In particular, governments pursue *"different, or even multiple and complementary, approaches"* with instruments pertaining to unilateral mechanisms, plurilateral arrangements, trade agreements as well as standards and technology-driven initiatives.[21] For example, at the 2020 G20 meeting in Osaka, the Data Free Flow With Trust (DFFT) initiative was presented as part of the *"Osaka Track"*.[22] The initiative draws on a broad governance architecture outlining the status of global digital governance efforts as follows: *"The Osaka Track and global data governance do not rely on a single forum for cooperation but depend on international trade, laws and regulation, technology and other areas of governance, involving binding and non-binding rules applicable to governments, businesses or users on multilateral, regional, plurilateral or bilateral levels."*.[23]

---

[17] *See* for an account of the birth of the WTO and in particular US influence VanGrasstek (2013), pp. 62–64. *See* also with regard to a changed environment for trade Cho and Kelly (2013).

[18] Mitchell and Mishra (2018), pp. 1076–1077.

[19] *See* for an account of the actors of a *"Global Information Law"* Tietje (2012), pp. 49–52. *See* further with regard to Internet regulation in particular Mishra (2019b), pp. 20–23. *See* also Zeno-Zencovich (2021), pp. 186–188.

[20] Aaronson (2018). In fact, instruments of international law have rarely been used effectively in the field of the regulation of data flows and the Internet as the relevant infrastructure, *see* Streinz (2019), pp. 328–329.

[21] Casalini et al. (2021), pp. 30–31.

[22] *See* further World Economic Forum (2020), which has introduced *"the Osaka Track – a collective term for global governance processes needed to realize the DFFT vision and unleash the benefits from cross-border data flows"*, p. 6. Cf. also the very first point of the preamble of G20 Osaka Leaders' Declaration: "[...] *We will work together to foster global economic growth, while harnessing the power of technological innovation, in particular digitalization, and its application for the benefit of all.*" G20 (2019), p. 1, para. 1.

[23] World Economic Forum (2020), p. 6.

6.3 An Integrated Approach to the Digital Trade and Data Privacy Nexus:...

Given that cross-border data flows and economic activity are inextricably linked in a digital economy, international fora of economic cooperation and in particular trade agreements, increasingly assume a vital role for transnational data governance.[24] On the back of a well-established and successful system of rules-based economic liberalisation, many countries have recognised the incumbent world trade system under the WTO as an appropriate forum for the regulation of trade in the digital economy.[25] This significantly expanded trade governance environment extends the reach of trade law to encompass aspects of governing the nexus between digital trade and data privacy. However, it is arguable what role trade law can assume in developing an integrated approach to digital trade and data privacy.

At the outset, the underlying premise is that increasing regulatory convergence[26] through substantive harmonisation of data privacy regimes will facilitate the cross-border exchange of personal data and provide a consistent level of data privacy, thereby fostering cross-border digital trade.[27] Indeed, some commentators have argued that the WTO would be positioned for the development of substantive data privacy standards and thus function as a forum for regulatory harmonization or even single rules on data privacy.[28] *Joel Reidenberg's* seminal argument has been that *"[. . .] data protection needs an intergovernmental "General Agreement on Information Privacy" (GAIP) that includes a large number and wide range of signatory countries. GAIP should focus on establishing an institutional process of norm development designed to facilitate in the near term the coexistence of differing regimes, and over time promote harmonization of governing standards for information privacy.".*[29] Due to its proven institutional setting and development processes, Reidenberg came to the conclusion: *"Beyond a mere model, the World Trade Organization (WTO), successor to the GATT, offers a useful launching point for the GAIP.".*[30] However, the most salient argument (among a number of counterarguments) for not utilising the WTO's multilateral forum for substantive data privacy negotiations is the inherent tendency in trade rules toward market-oriented liberalisation and the economic perspective underlying associated negotiations.[31]

---

[24] Mitchell and Mishra (2018), p. 1077; Sen (2018), pp. 323–324. This is particularly the case with regard to the failure of regulatory initiatives in other multilateral fora such as the International Telecommunication Union (ITU), see World Bank Group (2016), p. 295.

[25] Mitchell (2001), pp. 687–688. *See* also with regard to the Joint Statement Initiative on Electronic Commerce *supra* Sect. 3.3.1.2.

[26] Regulatory convergence is used here as an overarching term for various mechanisms to reduce unnecessary regulatory incompatibilities, *see* with further references to definition and nomenclature Polanco and Sauvé (2018), pp. 578–579; Weiß (2020), pp. 286–287.

[27] *See* with further references Burri (2021a), p. 85.

[28] *See* further Swire and Litan (2010), p. 194. *See* with a more nuanced approach Chander and Schwartz (2023), pp. 117–125.

[29] Reidenberg (1999), p. 1360.

[30] Reidenberg (1999), p. 1361.

[31] Reidenberg argues that: *"[. . .] the incorporation of GAIP within the WTO along with other noneconomic values will transplant socialprotection norms to the trade arena. In effect, this*

The economic character of WTO law is likely to be a strong counterargument, especially for stakeholders that view data privacy as intrinsically tied to fundamental rights.[32] In this context, tensions over the alleged scrutiny of national data privacy provisions by means of WTO law have become so severe that the WTO felt compelled to underscore that: *"the WTO has had nothing whatever to do with Internet privacy. Moreover, a safeguard for individual privacy is built into the framework of the GATS itself."*.[33] Certainly, WTO law after all forms integral part of International *Economic* Law and must not be overburdened with the sociocultural intricacies of data privacy. While trade in the digital economy will require the WTO to more closely consider non-economic social values underlying domestic data policies, the WTO is not a forum to develop substantive data privacy standards.[34] *Sacha Wunsch-Vincent* and *Arno Hold* have underscored, that establishing standards where no standards are existent, would deviate from the principle of *"policed decentralisation"* via regulatory disciplines which hold a balance between harmonisation and heterogeneity.[35] Moreover, it is the deeply rooted national idiosyncrasies regarding an individual emphasis on data privacy that make harmonisation on a global level highly unlikely against a backdrop of political differences and even deliberate regulatory arbitrage by some stakeholders—no less by negotiations in a dedicated forum for cross-border trade.[36] The heterogeneity of the design of data privacy regulation rooted in the underlying divergent motivations of a historical and cultural nature point to deeply entrenched divergence which is echoed in divergent schemes for the regulation of data flows. In this vein, *Christopher Kuner* notes that cross-border data flow regulation is best understood as a form of legal pluralism, as there is no hierarchical legal structure that could provide an

---

transplantation will promote convergence of governance norms.", and further: *"Noneconomic values will bring non-market based governance norms to WTO. This is likely to happen with or without GAIP negotiations in a WTO context. Indeed, in the context of information flows, this transformation has already begun."*, referring to Article XIV (c)(ii) GATS, *see* Reidenberg (1999), p. 1362. *Swire* and *Litan* underscore: *"We are inclined to be cautious about expanding the reach of WTO treaties into complex issues such as privacy protection that are only modestly related to free trade and protectionism. WTO treaties are difficult to update quickly, and binding WTO privacy rules might soon become out of synch with technological and marketplace realities."*, Swire and Litan (2010), p. 196.

[32] *See* only Yakovleva (2018), p. 478.

[33] Cf. WTO (2001). The statement reads in full: *"No decision or action on the protection of Internet privacy has ever been taken in the WTO. Far from "forcing governments to forego sovereign privacy protections" (which it would have no power to do in any case), the WTO has had nothing whatever to do with Internet privacy. Moreover, a safeguard for individual privacy is built into the framework of the GATS itself."*.

[34] *See* also Chander and Schwartz (2023), p. 49; Mitchell and Mishra (2018), p. 1122; Perez Asinari (2003).

[35] Wunsch-Vincent and Hold (2012), p. 208 referring to a term coined by *Alan O. Sykes*.

[36] *See* in this sense with further references generally Mitchell and Mishra (2018), p. 1123; Yakovleva (2020), pp. 517–518. *See* for a dedicated perspective of data privacy law Kuner (2009).

overarching, authoritative governance framework.[37] The general exception for data privacy under Article XIV(c)(ii) GATS reflects a reluctance to address the intricate implications of the digital trade and data privacy nexus by merely recognising in principle the importance of data privacy to trade. This half-baked solution to the digital trade and data privacy nexus stemming from the 1994 Uruguay Round is referred to by *Anupam Chander* and *Paul Schwartz* as the "*privacy bracket*" of the GATS. The authors are certain, that maintaining the current "*privacy bracket*" in trade and thus continuing "*muddling through*" with divergent and ever more diverging approaches will lead to a "*continuing splintering of the rules for trade and privacy*".[38] While this prediction is reasonably to derive from an extrapolation of the historical evidence, it raises the issue of an appropriate way to address the relationship between digital trade and data privacy in trade regulation. Against the backdrop of the existing heterogeneity of data privacy regulations stemming from deeply rooted socio-cultural specificities, the limited mandate of the WTO and its general reform backlog, especially with regard to the digital economy and a digital divide among its heterogenous membership, a proposal to achieve regulatory harmonisation through the development of substantive data privacy rules at the WTO level would have to be rejected.[39]

In contrast to reconceptualising the WTO as a multilateral institution for regulatory harmonisation with respect to a wide host of (non-)economic interests in the digital economy, such as data privacy, a *recontextualisation* of the WTO to provide a functional instrument for international cooperation against the backdrop of a converging regulatory environment between economic and non-economic spheres in a global digital economy seems preferable.[40] Certainly, global integration brought about by digital technologies and cross-border data flows requires further regulatory convergence to transcend barriers and even prevent a balkanization of cyberspace.[41] An efficient interplay of digital regulations and technical standards not only promotes a favourable environment for the digital economy but is also a vital precondition for effective enforcement and the prevention of regulatory arbitrage. However, since both international harmonisation and domestic regulatory action have their distinctive virtues when it comes to the governance of international trade, the role of trade law should be defined rather by a balancing act that values and permits domestic regulatory authority to exist within internationally agreed disciplines.[42] This must apply in particular to national data privacy regimes in an dynamically evolving digital environment, the further development of which is

---

[37] Kuner (2013), p. 160.
[38] Chander and Schwartz (2023), pp. 56–65, p. 114.
[39] *See* also Mitchell and Mishra (2018), p. 1123.
[40] *See* in this sense with regard to a "*reconfiguration*" of International Economic Law against the backdrop of the emergence of AI Peng et al. (2021), pp. 17–21.
[41] Burri (2021a), p. 87; Chander (2012), p. 39. *See* with regard to privacy frameworks, Casalini and López González (2019), p. 7.
[42] *See* further Weiß (2020), p. 46, pp. 98–101 *See* also Krajewski (2003), p. 56.

uncertain, so that national approaches to data governance should, in case of doubt, be given more rather than less margin of appreciation. In this sense, one could argue that a balancing of trade and data privacy interests under WTO law must take into account the contemporary circumstances of data privacy protection in the digital era.[43] Coincidentally, the argument can be made that the challenges of governing digital trade are too complex in nature to be addressed through a regime of substantive harmonisation and that the initiatives of domestic regulators in the formation of international regimes would help to limit some of the sovereignty concerns involved in regulating data privacy, consumer protection or cybersecurity regulation.[44] In a context of *"radical uncertainty"* and diverse preferences, allowing room for regulatory experimentation is valuable, and a diversity of regulatory approaches will enhance resilience to systemic risks incurred by the breakdown of single systems.[45]

Against this background, the focus of trade law should be on fostering legal interoperability between domestic regulatory approaches towards data governance (*see supra* Sect. 3.5.2.3). The interoperability approach recognizes that different jurisdictions have different legal and political systems informed by distinct societal values and traditions, and that there is no unifying body of law to address a particular data-related issue on a global scale—thus making it *"the most realistic goal for global data governance"*.[46] In this sense, there is a role for WTO law in promoting regulatory coordination through interoperability, transparency, as well as mutual recognition of data flow regulation mechanisms under data privacy law.[47] Even if the WTO does not provide a forum to develop substantive data privacy standards, it is conceivable for the WTO to function as a forum for dialogue and furtherance of increasing regulatory convergence by reducing unnecessary incompatibilities in trade-related aspects of data governance.[48] This is particularly the case as the reduction of domestic legal barriers to trade through increasing interoperability of data privacy frameworks and their associated transfer mechanisms can be perceived to be subject of the WTO's mandate. Instituting a process of diligently pursuing regulatory interoperability in the sense of *"preparatory work"* within the WTO may eventually encourage a higher level policy interoperability, which in turn fosters innovation in goods and services and stimulates trade.[49] The WTO could serve as the venue for fostering *"bottom-up"* regulatory convergence through the discussion and adoption of a set of regulatory practices, in contrast to providing a platform for a *"top-down"* harmonisation of rules.[50] In fact, achieving legal interoperability often is

---

[43] *See* further Weiß (2020), p. 104.

[44] Ahmed (2019), pp. 114–115. *See* further Schulhofer (2016).

[45] Shaffer (2021), p. 44.

[46] Cory and Dascoli (2021), p. 18. *See* also Ahmed (2019), p. 115.

[47] *See* in this context with regard to the *"new governance theory"* Shaffer (2021), pp. 43–45. *See* also Mitchell and Mishra (2019), pp. 403–404.

[48] *See* regarding this definition of regulatory convergence Polanco and Sauvé (2018), p. 579.

[49] Gasser and Palfrey (2012), p. 135, pp. 137–141.

[50] *See* further on this differentiation Polanco and Sauvé (2018), p. 579; Shaffer (2021), pp. 42–43.

6.3 An Integrated Approach to the Digital Trade and Data Privacy Nexus:... 297

a gradual process as evidenced by the EU's data protection framework which relies on the data privacy approaches developed in the OECD Privacy Guidelines and the CoE's Convention 108, for example.[51] At the same time, interoperability provides an open concept, the instruments of which are not clearly defined. Legal interoperability can be achieved through a variety of instruments such as mutual recognition agreements, model clauses and provisions but also harmonisation and standardisation efforts or even single rules in dedicated international treaties.[52] Instruments of a *"bottom-up"* approach to regulatory convergence have been identified to encompass means of coordination and review as well as the formulation of good regulatory practices involving transparency requirements and regulatory impact assessments.[53] This leaves sufficient flexibility for WTO Members to choose among these instruments according to their preferences for the degree of engagement or disengagement in any particular interoperability effort in the context of ongoing WTO consultations. In this sense, an initiative for legal interoperability of data flow regulations in particular could make full use of the WTO's institutional infrastructure, notably the WTO committees and the Trade Policy Review Mechanism.[54] In fact, the WTO's non-judicial governance in the form of committees, working groups and review processes constitutes a form of *"hidden"* governance that has been analysed to generate and disseminate information and facilitate regulatory learning.[55] Recognising that stakeholders have so far tended to ensure that their data privacy standards extend to data processing in other countries, the WTO can serve as a forum for increasingly framing cross-border data flow regulation as a matter of international relevance.[56] Such an initiative on interoperability of cross-border data regulation within the WTO will thus be one important element in developing a shared vision for digital technology governance, which is essential as a foundation for further regional and multilateral initiatives to reduce regulatory diversity.[57] Potential loss of domestic regulatory autonomy with regard to the regulation of data flows under data privacy law will be offset by the ability to influence the actions of regulators in other states in order to collectively make use of the possibilities of the digital era against a backdrop of technological convergence.[58]

Given that the regulation of cross-border data flows, as a central pillar of digital trade, takes place in a context that is both characterised by complex technological

---

[51] Gasser and Palfrey (2012), p. 135.

[52] *See* for an analysis of the WTO's influence on domestic regulatory autonomy in this respect Weiß (2020), pp. 285–376. *See* also with regard to the shortcomings of mutual recognition in a digital trade context Ahmed (2019), pp. 113–114.

[53] Polanco and Sauvé (2018), p. 595.

[54] *See* in this sense also Mitchell and Mishra (2019), p. 404.

[55] *See* further Lang and Scott (2009).

[56] Kuner (2013), p. 142.

[57] Chatham House (2022).

[58] *See* with further references on the positive effects of internationalisation of regulation in this regard Weiß (2020), p. 6.

infrastructures and the involvement of a multitude of stakeholders, it is, however, essential to update the mechanisms of international discourse and law making and to integrate a multidimensional philosophy into the WTO's processes.[59] With regard to data privacy in particular it has been stated that: *"effective solutions which are perceived as legitimate will require an expansion of political space, the emergence of a political community which transcends national borders."*.[60] In this sense, the WTO could serve as a forum for debate on what *Thomas Cottier* has called the *"framing of global public policies"*.[61] This forum function of the WTO is an essential process of learning about digital trade and its close connection to data privacy, which must precede any negotiation process.[62] The rapprochement of the WTO's governance framework with the multi-stakeholder environment of transnational data regulation—particularly with regard to the multistakeholder model of Internet governance (*see supra* Sect. 3.5.2.1)—is of essential importance in both guiding consultations and enabling informed decision-making.[63] Increasingly, standards and technology-driven initiatives developed by non-governmental and private sector organisations are becoming more important in addressing cross-border privacy issues.[64] Coordination with other international institutions and organisations must be expanded and strengthened, notably with the OECD, which has pioneered research into digital trade, but also with relevant stakeholders of digital regulation such as the IGF, ICANN, ISOC or W3C (*see supra* Sect. 3.5.2.1). Such cooperation mandates are not unfamiliar to WTO law[65] and can very well be combined with proposals for institutional reform of the WTO.[66] For example, the WTO Secretariat could assume a coordinating role vis-à-vis other international organisations and actors in a multistakeholder environment.[67]

The continuous development of digital trade rules in recent PTAs has shown that without an active and ambitious approach to digital trade, the WTO multilateral framework will forfeit its relevance in this area and abandon its proven and

---

[59] Usman Ahmed put this quite succinctly as approaching a mentality of regulatory cooperation and moving away from *"horse trading"* in traditional trade negotiations, see Ahmed (2019), p. 101. See also Burri (2021a), p. 86.

[60] Kobrin (2004), p. 131.

[61] Cottier (1996), p. 427.

[62] Wolfe (2018), p. 12.

[63] Mishra (2019a), pp. 507–508; Mitchell and Mishra (2019), p. 405; Weber (2021), p. 67.

[64] Casalini et al. (2021), pp. 29–30. See in similar vein with respect to AI regulation and its challenges to the WTO Peng et al. (2021), pp. 17–21.

[65] For example, Article III:5 WTO Agreement reads: *"With a view to achieving greater coherence in global economic policy-making, the WTO shall cooperate, as appropriate, with the International Monetary Fund and with the International Bank for Reconstruction and Development and its affiliated agencies."*. Moreover, there have been commitments to engage with multilateral environmental institutions, see with further references Mitchell and Mishra (2019), p. 405.

[66] *See* further Weiß et al. (2022), p. 443. *See* with regard to the integration of digital technologies to transform the functions and operations of the WTO Toohey (2021).

[67] *See* further Bohne (2010), pp. 165–201.

established regulatory basis for a governance trade in the digital economy. Increasingly, influential PTAs such as the CETA, but also the CPTTP, feature chapters that deal with regulatory convergence between the signatories.[68] It is not possible to predict how the practice of addressing digital governance in separate chapters in PTAs and now even in specific agreements on digital trade or the digital economy will unfold. This could lead to the emergence of stand-alone regulatory instruments that are structurally rooted in trade regulation but increasingly open to social regulation, building on the pathways of regulatory convergence. For multilateral trade law, however, the emerging trends suggest that it needs to be positioned firmly as a facilitator and mediator between different approaches towards data privacy governance.

6.4 Recontextualising the Multilateral Framework for Trade in Services

In light of its substantive remit and against the backdrop of WTO jurisprudence, notably in the *US-Gambling* and *China-Audiovisual Products* cases, the GATS is currently the most salient reference point for issues of digital governance in WTO law and thereby also for the nexus of digital trade and data privacy.[69] However, the above analysis has illustrated that digital governance under the current WTO framework is fraught with uncertainties due to the unresolved conceptual issues of digital trade on the one hand and the inadequacies of unchanged GATS rules dating back to 1994 on the other. This analysis has identified significant uncertainties relating to both the economic liberalisation of digital trade in services under national schedules as well as the scope of the general exceptions under Article XIV GATS for national data governance and particularly for domestic data privacy regimes. To move beyond the current status quo, the multilateral framework for trade in services should be progressively recontextualised in light of the emergence of digital trade, with particular attention to the trade-related aspects of national data governance:

- In an initial step, WTO Members may negotiate commitments not subject to scheduling under Articles XVI or XVII, including those regarding qualifications, standards or licensing matters pursuant to Article XVIII GATS. In *US-Gambling* the Panel stated that "*[...] the drafters seem to have realized that there may be other types of restrictions that would not be covered by the disciplines of Articles XVI and XVII.*" and further "*It seems, therefore, that it was considered best to simply provide a legal framework for Members to negotiate and schedule specific commitments that they would define, on a case-by-case basis, in relation to any*

---

[68] *See* in detail Mancini (2020); Polanco and Sauvé (2018).
[69] *See* for example Chander (2013), p. 156. The author argues: "*By subsuming an electronic version of the service within a services commitment and by interpreting treaty commitments in a dynamic form, the treaty can take account of changing technologies.*".

measures that do not fall within the scope of Article XVI or XVII.".[70] In this context, a *"Reference Paper on regulatory principles"* in basic telecommunications services was developed as part of the telecommunications negotiations that have resumed after the Uruguay Round.[71] Moreover, the need for further strengthening of services-trade on the one hand, and the political momentum for doing so on the other, is illustrated by the recently concluded negotiations under the Joint Initiative on Services Domestic Regulation. In recognition of the importance of good regulatory practice in facilitating trade in services the participants have negotiated a *"Reference Paper on Services Domestic Regulation"*, the disciplines of which will be incorporated as additional commitments into their GATS Schedules, thereby subject to the MFN principle.[72] Such scheduling of specific commitments in the context of digital trade would allow for increasing transparency and regulatory certainty for measures in digital governance.[73] In particular, the scheduling of additional commitments could foster issues of regulatory interoperability of standards on encryption or consumer protection as well as measures to combat spam and enhance transparency.[74] With regard to the digital trade and data privacy nexus in particular, it has been proposed that a further alignment of data privacy principles could be supported by a Reference Paper on Data Privacy.[75] Although there is little prospect of moving towards authoritative principles for the transnational regulation of data privacy within the framework of WTO law, the scope of Article XVIII GATS should be explored with a view to establishing best practices for the regulation of data flows under data privacy law and achieving interoperability of different domestic regimes. A Reference Paper on Interoperability of Domestic Data Governance may identify pathways to enhance the facilitation and security of international transfers of personal data. Since a Reference Paper would only apply to those WTO Members that incorporate the paper into their specific commitments, a rather limited group of countries may form the nucleus for greater interoperability and transparency of domestic data flow regimes. In fact, just as within the telecommunications context, a Reference Paper could build on decades of experience, particularly in

---

[70] Panel Report, *US-Gambling*, WT/DS285/R, 10 November 2004, para. 6.311.

[71] *See* for an overview of the Reference Paper Roseman (2003), pp. 88–89.

[72] WTO (2021a). *See* further WTO (2021b). However, the scope of the Reference Paper steers clear of extending to *"any terms, limitations, conditions, or qualifications set out in a Member's Schedule pursuant to Articles XVI or XVII of the Agreement"* and rather applies *"to measures by Members relating to licensing requirements and procedures, qualification requirements and procedures, and technical standards affecting trade in services"*, WTO (2021b), p. 6.

[73] Burri (2016), p. 345; Mattoo and Meltzer (2019), p. 787; Mitchell and Mishra (2018), p. 1127. In this context, the EU has proposed that *"WTO Members engage in exploratory work towards possible improvements of the provisions contained in the Reference Paper, as well as in discussions on a complementary set of provisions pertaining to telecommunications services that are relevant for today's electronic commerce landscape."*, WTO (2018).

[74] *See* also Tuthill (2017), p. 102.

[75] Mattoo and Meltzer (2019), p. 787.

6.4 Recontextualising the Multilateral Framework for Trade in Services

industrialised countries, and thus be instrumental in a *"transfer of know how"* allowing developing countries to *"the opportunity to avoid years of trial and error"* in cross-border data flow regulation.[76] A focus on aspects of *"interoperability"* and *"data governance"* rather than on the substantive principles of data privacy would be instrumental in depoliticising the debate. This could entice both countries concerned about interference with national data privacy standards and developing countries, that feel deprived of development opportunities by multilateral data governance agreements, to join negotiations.

- A further policy option relates to the integration of dedicated rules on data flows and data localisation into the GATS by means of an Annex to the GATS. Although the GATS is intrinsically relevant to domestic data governance, it has been pointed out that its current framework lacks robust commitments regarding cross-border data flows and a ban on data localisation. In light of the development of such provisions in recent PTAs, scholarly literature suggests that a horizontal commitment on cross-border data flows and an explicit prohibition of data localisation measures could be included in the GATS.[77] While this might seem feasible in principle given the recent consensus in digital trade templates in PTAs, the issue of integrating such provisions at the multilateral level is likely to depend heavily on the issue of the binding nature of such provisions and even more so on the scope of exceptions to them. The integration of commitments on data flows and data localisation into the GATS would require an assessment of exceptions and derogations to these commitments, particularly for data privacy reasons, but also for other motives such as cybersecurity, consumer protection, or development issues. However, this is a delicate and thorny issue among the WTO Membership for which the time has realistically not yet come to reach a viable multilateral solution. Although data privacy and digital trade are inextricably intertwined, the nexus of digital trade and data privacy is only insufficiently reflected by the regulatory framework of the GATS. In particular, the GATS does not ensure that all members adopt a minimum standard of data privacy, let alone commit to mutually compatible and interoperable frameworks.[78] The reluctance to address the manifold controversies over cross-border data flows as a hinging element between economic and non-economic objectives in a digital economy has been described as the *"privacy bracket"* of GATS.[79] To be sure, the data privacy exception of Article XIV(c)(ii) GATS, which was negotiated at the beginning of the commercialisation of the Internet, has since has taken on an expanded role and greater relevance in a digital economy.[80] This has not made a

---

[76] Roseman (2003), p. 90.

[77] *See* for example Mitchell and Mishra (2019), pp. 406–407.

[78] Chander and Schwartz (2023), p. 8; Mitchell and Mishra (2019), p. 399.

[79] Chander and Schwartz (2023), pp. 56–96. The authors argue that *"GATS neither establishes global minimum standards for privacy, nor provides an international process for creating such standards. It simply allows signatory nations to protect privacy so long as this action can be said to be "necessary"*. Chander and Schwartz (2023), p. 53.

[80] This is evident when looking at the evolution of the OECD Guidelines and other international frameworks that needed to be updated as the digital era progressed, *see supra* Sect. 4.3.1.3.

multilateral solution to data-related issues, of which the nexus of digital trade and data privacy is an essential part, any more likely. The paused negotiations under the Joint Statement Initiative on this issue are evidence of this (*see supra* Sect. 3. 3.1.2). In similar vein, a proactive clarification of the scope of Article XIV(c) (ii) GATS and Article XIV(a) GATS as well as with respect to the interpretation of the necessity test in relation to domestic data privacy measures would be desirable but does not appear to be achievable at this time. At present, a sustainable amendment of the GATS in a multilateral process seems rather unlikely. This means that the sword of Damocles is hanging over digital trade relations, as a challenge of domestic data privacy measures could trigger the escalation of the data privacy collision in trade law (assuming that the currently paralyzed WTO Dispute Settlement System were to be revived). However, the uncertain state of the GATS regime on data related issues also seems to make the outcome of such a challenge largely unpredictable and therefore generally unattractive. Realistically, trade law will be employed as a political bargaining chip on such data issues, but the key determinations are not going to be made in the multilateral trade framework.

- A third policy option is concerned with the dilemma that arises in the context of the classification of digital services under the 1994 GATS. It has been argued that an indeterminate classification of digital services under the Services Sectoral Classifications List (W/120) means that there is currently considerable regulatory uncertainty as to a significant part of trade in the digital economy. This also affects the nexus between digital trade and data privacy, as it is unclear to what extent domestic data privacy measures might conflict with commitments under international trade law. Even if the WTO dispute settlement bodies consider having broad authority in the interpretation of the existing schedules, clarifications are likely to be achieved only selectively and only if disputes arise. Potential remedies to the classification conundrum could be either to update the GATS classification list or to encourage WTO members to clarify their existing liberalisation commitments—neither option of which is readily achievable. Although the underlying UN provisional Central Product Classification has been revised in the meantime, attempts to include these revisions or additional classification schemes during the Doha Round negotiations did not yield substantive results.[81] In fact, a revision of the (W/120) classification list would be a great challenge procedurally, yet even more so politically.[82] In turn, while it is important to create transparency and clarity about WTO Members' commitments particularly with regard to Mode 1 cross-border supply of services, it will be difficult to update the specific commitments under GATS to reflect this.[83] The

---

[81] Adlung (2014), p. 377; Kelsey (2018), p. 287; Sen (2018), pp. 341–342. Therefore, academic literature also discusses approaches to extend existing categories of services Weber (2010), pp. 10–13.
[82] Tuthill and Roy (2012), p. 176; Zhang (2015), pp. 31–33.
[83] Burri (2016), p. 346.

6.4 Recontextualising the Multilateral Framework for Trade in Services

process of scheduling modifications or withdrawal of existing commitments pursuant to Article XXI GATS will typically involve negotiations on *"compensatory adjustments"* which have to be made on a MFN basis (Article XXI:2b GATS). In addition, there is no certainty outside the WTO's dispute settlement bodies case law as to the implications of such modifications for the commitments in relation to a digital service economy. Therefore, with respect to digital trade and data privacy nexus, scheduling horizontal reservations for the benefit of data privacy policies involves a host of risks and uncertainties that currently render a cost-benefit analysis of such an initiative negative.[84]

- A fourth policy option involves the consistent and stringent application of Article III GATS which could help to reduce legal uncertainties pertaining to national data governance frameworks and make the implementation of data privacy regimes in relation to cross-border data flows more transparent.[85] Indeed, the application of Article III GATS was determined to extend *"to all laws and regulations affecting the supply of a service through electronic means"*.[86]

- A fifth policy option concerns the facilitation of the cross-border interplay of data privacy regimes and, in particular, of mechanisms for regulating data flows under data privacy law. With regard to digital services, mutual recognition of data privacy schemes could be approached through Article VII:1 GATS relating to *"standards or education, criteria for the authorization, licensing or certification of services suppliers"*.[87] Article VII:5 GATS underscores that *"recognition should be based on multilaterally agreed criteria"* and further that *"Members shall work in cooperation with relevant intergovernmental and non-governmental organizations towards the establishment and adoption of common international standards and criteria for recognition and common international standards for the practice of relevant services trades and professions."*. Against this backdrop, Article VII GATS allows for mutual recognition agreements but does not bind WTO Members to positively address foreign standards.[88]

- A sixth policy option relates to the need to address the trade inhibitive effect of non-discriminatory data privacy regulations against the backdrop of a heterogeneous data privacy environment. Scholarly literature suggests to invoke Article VI:4 GATS in order to negotiate disciplines for the application of

---

[84] *See* also Naef (2023), pp. 316–317.

[85] Mattoo and Meltzer (2019), p. 788. *See* also regarding the effective use of Trade Policy Review Mechanisms and WTO committee meetings in this respect Mitchell and Mishra (2019), p. 404.

[86] *See* WTO (1999), p. 2, para. 9.

[87] With further references, *see* Chander (2012), p. 39; Mattoo and Meltzer (2019), p. 788; Mitchell and Mishra (2019), pp. 403–404. who also refer to the incentivisation of mutual recognition through the development of new disciplines on *"qualification requirements and procedures, technical standards and licensing requirements"* under Article VI:5 GATS with regard to data flows. *See* for the latter also Tuthill (2017), p. 108; Wunsch-Vincent (2004), pp. 88–91.

[88] Given the difficult conditions for mutual recognition in the context of services at the multilateral level, the GATS remains a step behind the relevant provisions of the TBT and SPS, Wouters and Coppens (2008), p. 244.

domestic data privacy regimes.[89] Article VI:4 GATS is reflective of the recognition that domestic regulations may hinder trade even if they do not discriminate between foreign and domestic suppliers.[90] In this context, the TBT and SPS Agreements attest to elements within WTO law that address the minimisation of trade barriers arising from the substantive content of domestic regulations, an effort that is also reflected in Article VI:4 GATS.[91] That being said, the possibility of activating Article VI:4 GATS for the development of future disciplines limiting the discretion of WTO Members in adopting data privacy measures is doubtful in view of the scope of the provision.[92] The provision clearly limits the mandate for negotiation of disciplines to measures relating to qualification requirements and procedures, technical standards and licensing requirements. Art VI:4 GATS provides that disciplines shall aim to ensure that such requirements are, *inter alia*: (a) based on objective and transparent criteria, such as competence and the ability to supply the service; (b) not more burdensome than necessary to ensure the quality of the service; (c) in the case of licensing procedures, not in themselves a restriction on the supply of the service. Against this background, a number of reasons can be identified that preclude or at least make it very challenging to invoke Article VI:4 GATS with respect to data privacy measures.

First, with regard to the scope of future disciplines, there is a consensus in the Working Party on Domestic Regulation (WPDR), which was tasked by the Council on Trade in Services (CTS) with elaborating the necessary disciplines, that an extension beyond these items is not within the scope of consensus among WTO Members.[93] In view of the GATS negotiations, it must be pointed out that the negotiating mandate of Article VI GATS was not intended to include all types of service regulations, standards or qualifications.[94] Therefore, it is unclear whether voluntary standards or standards from entities that do not have regulatory authority delegated by governments should be included in future disciplines.[95] Hence, some scholars are sceptical with regard to the application of Article VI:4 GATS in the context of data privacy regulations as they are not pertaining to neither authorisation or qualification or licensing requirements, nor are to be considered a technical standard.[96] Others, however, argue that data privacy

---

[89] *See* for example Chen (2015), p. 219; Mitchell and Mishra (2019), p. 404.

[90] Krajewski (2008), p. 179.

[91] *See* Krajewski (2008), p. 179. *See* generally Weiß (2020), pp. 285–288.

[92] *See* further with regard to future disciplines under Article VI:4 GATS Wouters and Coppens (2008), pp. 225–257.

[93] Krajewski (2003), p. 135. *See* however with regard to the scope of regulatory convergence mechanisms in PTAs Polanco and Sauvé (2018), pp. 581–582.

[94] Delimatsis (2007), p. 37.

[95] Weber (2012), pp. 35–36.

[96] Irion et al. (2016), p. 31; Weber (2012), pp. 35–36. *See* with regard to the EU's system for data transfers Naef (2023), p. 307.

measures could be perceived as technical standards, thus establishing Article VI:4 GATS as a relevant provision for domestic data privacy measures.[97] The WPDR has defined technical standards as measures that lay down the characteristics of a services or the manner in which it is supplied and also including the procedures relating to the enforcement of such standards.[98] Against the background of this definition, the scope and objective of Article VI:4 GATS do not seem to be easily applicable to data privacy measures. Indeed, it is questionable whether data privacy standards have an impact on the *"characteristics"* of a given service or the *"manner"* in which it is supplied.[99] Nevertheless. data privacy generally involves a technological component, which, if Article VI:4 GATS were to be interpreted in a (very) broad sense, could lead to the conclusion that it is a form of a technical standard.

Secondly, however, even if Article VI:4 GATS would be applicable, it seems to be unlikely to reach agreement among WTO Members on when and how data privacy measures are *"no more burdensome than necessary to ensure the quality of the service"* pursuant to Article VI:4(b) GATS. In particular, the reference to service quality can easily be interpreted in the spirit of favouring the economic elements of the data privacy discourse, according to which data privacy is generally considered an element of domestic regulation that hinders the exploitation of personal data for economic efficiency and innovation. The social and moral aspects of data privacy are less easily translated in terms of the quality of a service.[100] In any case, it can be assumed that WTO Members that base domestic data privacy measures in a context of fundamental rights protection, such as the EU, will not submit to the *"trade-setting"* of Article VI GATS to agree on data privacy disciplines.

Against the background of an overall rather reluctant activation of Article VI GATS so far and combined with the lack of agreement on the understanding of data privacy rules as technical standards and the sensitivities surrounding the *"necessity"* of data privacy measures, Article VI GATS will not be a suitable instrument to contribute to an integrated approach to digital trade and data privacy.

---

[97] Peng (2011), p. 764.
[98] *See* with further references Krajewski (2008), p. 185.
[99] *See supra* with regard to the issue whether a high standard of data privacy may affect the assessment of likeness of services and service suppliers Sect. 5.2.1.1.2.
[100] *See* generally Mattoo and Sauvé (2003), p. 226.

6.5 Negotiating a Digital Trade and Data Privacy Agreement

Against the backdrop of the scale of the upheaval brought about by the digital transformation of trade, scholars have proposed the drafting of specific agreements that take into account the emergence of digital trade[101] and, in particular, address the reconciliation of digital trade and data privacy.[102] In this context, the EU has committed in its most recent trade policy review to the goal of seeking *"the rapid conclusion of an ambitious and comprehensive WTO agreement on digital trade"*.[103] However, both the current negotiations under the Joint Statement Initiative on Electronic Commerce and the lengthy debates in the WTO's 1998 Work Programme on Electronic Commerce have made clear that negotiating a comprehensive agreement on digital trade within the WTO is fraught with significant obstacles. The opposition of some key developing countries to new rules on digital trade has already been expressed in the WTO Work Programme and has recently sparked a heated discussion with respect to the WTO Moratorium on Customs Duties on Electronic Transmissions (*see supra* Sect. 3.3.1.1).[104] Indeed, bridging the *"digital divide"* with the so-called developing countries is a key factor for the success of the multilateral platform in digital trade governance.[105] At present, a plurilateralisation of the digital trade negotiations under the Joint Statement Initiative seems to be the most promising route to substantive rules for digital trade. It has, however, been noted, that the progress of the plurilateral discussions, the issue of the role of the WTO Secretariat as well as their relation to the 1998 Work Programme touch upon fundamental elements of the WTO constitution.[106] Moreover, with regard to the entrenched controversies surrounding digital trade, notably with respect to data-related issues, it is still questionable whether the Joint Statement Initiative can deliver tangible results against the backdrop of the deeply rooted divergences among leading participants.[107] A regionalisation of rules for digital trade in a burgeoning landscape of PTAs and even dedicated Digital Economy/Trade Agreements can only serve to a limited extent as a laboratory for multilateral solutions, given that in the absence of binding WTO requirements, national idiosyncrasies in

---

[101] *See* for example Burri (2016), p. 355; Burri (2021b); Meltzer (2016), p. 21.

[102] *See* for example Chander and Schwartz (2023), pp. 117–125; Swire and Litan (2010), pp. 194–196. The former authors argue for a Global Agreement on Privacy (GAP) to be incorporated by reference into the WTO framework, drawing in part on the initiative for a General Agreement on Information Privacy (GAIP) by Reidenberg (1999), pp. 1359–1362. *See* also *supra* Sect. 6.3.

[103] European Commission (2021), pp. 14–15, para. 3.2.3.

[104] *See* also Lamp (2021).

[105] Kelsey (2018); Mitchell and Mishra (2018), pp. 1124–1126.

[106] Kelsey (2018), p. 284. *See* further with regard to the legal architecture of a WTO Electronic Commerce Agreement Burri (2021c), p. 34.

[107] *See* for example Abendin and Duan (2021), pp. 720–721; Hufbauer and Zhiyao (2019), p. 9.

6.5 Negotiating a Digital Trade and Data Privacy Agreement

the design of rules for digital trade arguably tend to be entrenched rather than bridged. Further decoupling of digital trade templates could prove detrimental to the development of a global legal framework for digital trade, which is essential in preventing the unilateral exercise of power in bilateral and plurilateral fora, potentially bypassing the interests of developing countries.[108]

The diversity of regulatory approaches in PTAs that address the intersection of digital trade and data privacy is an indication that negotiating multilateral rules involving the governance of data and cross-border data flows will require significant effort. As has been shown, there is a strong connection between multilateral digital trade liberalisation and domestic data privacy considerations as a reflection of national regulatory autonomy, which means that it is unlikely that they can be disentangled in a WTO-level agreement. A comprehensive digital trade agreement would be required to address key barriers to digital trade, such as divergent governance of data flows and data localisation requirements, thus extending to sensitive trade-related aspects of domestic data governance with respect to cybersecurity, consumer protection and data privacy. With respect to digital trade, this pertains primarily to non-tariff barriers arising from divergent domestic rules on data privacy, which can be effective impediments to trade. Against the backdrop of a heterogeneity of data privacy standards on a global level, existing regulatory instruments such as the TBT and SPS Agreements, incentivising the use of international standards and introducing a *"necessity"* test for domestic measures, come to mind.[109] The TBT Agreement, for example, provides that technical regulations ought not to be *"more trade-restrictive than necessary to fulfil a legitimate objective"* (cf. Article 2.2 TBT).[110] As discussed above, however, there is little consensus on international data privacy standards, at least not anywhere near enough to provide a basis for a multilateral consensus of these standards. Given the sensitivity of the issues involved in data privacy, it seems hardly possible to apply a *"necessity"* element to data privacy in a trade context, as this could be interpreted as subordinating domestic regulatory authority on data privacy to trade policy considerations.[111] On the contrary, against the aforementioned complex regulatory environment it can reasonably argued whether issues of a transnational data governance such as those related to data privacy should be subject to WTO rule-making in the first place.[112] Moreover, one can debate as to whether the nature of the decentralised Internet and the ensuing challenges of its governance are reconcilable with the fundamental nature of the WTO as a quintessential twentieth-century international organisation, designed to orchestrate trade between territorial nation-states.[113] Nonetheless, the need for a sustainable approach to the nexus of digital trade and data privacy for trade law was

---

[108] Mitchell and Mishra (2018), p. 1132.
[109] Aaronson (2019), p. 548; Aaronson and Leblond (2018), p. 271.
[110] *See* further on the conception of *"necessary"* in Article 2.2 TBT Weiß (2020), p. 247.
[111] Mattoo and Sauvé (2003), p. 226.
[112] *See* for example Yakovleva (2020), p. 515; Zeno-Zencovich (2021).
[113] Peng et al. (2021), pp. 8–10.

recognised early on and has only strengthened. In this context, with regard to *"electronic commerce"* a 1998 WTO study referred to the *"major challenge"* of securing a *"legal framework for trade liberalization without infringing on the freedom of governments to pursue legitimate domestic objectives"* and especially underscored that the handling of *"ensuring privacy of information"* will determine how much of the *"growth potential in electronic commerce will actually materialize."*.[114] Furthermore, progress on this and other matters has at times been blocked in other relevant fora such as the UN or the TU by those who have argued for a specific version of rules in the WTO.[115] The question of whether the WTO is the most appropriate forum for data governance issues may therefore be secondary to the fact that, in practice, it is an eminently capable international organisation for multilateral governance by virtue of its broad membership, its regulatory tradition, and the enforceability and transparency of its rules. The complexity of the task of orchestrating the learning process and eventually facilitating consensus on transnational issues of the digital trade and data privacy nexus can also be cited as a reason why the WTO as a proven organisation for global governance should be called upon. Progress in this regard, however, will be incremental, and it is foreseeable that it can and will only be achieved at the WTO level with regard to high-level principles.[116]

- There seems to be a certain degree of consensus in modern PTAs that, the complete absence of data privacy rules results in barriers to digital trade. Against this background, a WTO-level digital trade agreement could include a similar commitment to adopt a minimum set of data privacy standards at the national level.[117] The adoption of basic principles of data privacy regulation would not only reduce uncertainty and encourage trade, but, more importantly, provide a more robust basis for international interoperability efforts.[118] In this context, it must be reiterated that despite significant disparities between international, regional and national data privacy instruments at a granular level, there is some congruence of data privacy principles at the highest level.[119] For example, over a period of several decades, a series of privacy frameworks, reports, and guidelines from both governmental and nongovernmental organisations have led to what are known as the Fair Information Practice Principles (FIPPs).[120] These principles have influenced the development of data privacy around the world and, in particular, have informed the OECD Privacy Guidelines, which are themselves

---

[114] Bacchetta et al. (1998), pp. 64–65, p. 69.

[115] *See* Kelsey (2018), p. 283 fn. 66 with further references.

[116] Burri (2016), p. 349.

[117] *See* also Mitchell and Mishra (2019), pp. 409–412.

[118] UNCTAD (2016), p. 65.

[119] OECD (2015), p. 15; Reidenberg (1999), pp. 1325–1329; Schwartz (2013), pp. 1975–1976.

[120] The FIPPs are initially based on a report of the U.S. Department of Housing, Education, and Welfare (HEW) in 1973. The five principles are (1) notice/awareness; (2) choice/consent; (3) access/participation; (4) integrity/security; (5) enforcement/redress. *See* further Solove and Schwartz (2018), pp. 663–665.

structured around eight concepts.[121] To this day these concepts are highly influential: (1) Collection Limitation, (2) Data Quality, (3) Purpose Specification, (4) Use Limitation, (5) Security Safeguards, (6) Openness, (7) Individual Participation, and (8) Accountability. While generally not included as such in national laws, they form the basis for the compliance practices of many organisations in the private sector and are reflected in many data privacy laws such as, for example, the GDPR[122] or the CCPA.[123] However, the concrete balancing and implementation of these principles is highly controversial and should therefore not be determined by a trade treaty, as this would constitute a significant encroachment on national regulatory sovereignty.[124] In this context, *Anupam Chander* and *Paul Schwartz* argue for a Global Agreement on Privacy (GAP), which should be concluded within the context of the WTO, but which would include joint data privacy principles developed in a forum outside the WTO.[125] The GAP would then provide for an adequacy seal and the option of scheduling negotiated exclusions and, in particular, would benefit from enforcement through the WTO dispute settlement system.[126] However, this would require the successful development of a set of shared data privacy standards among the leading stakeholders in the data privacy collision, including the EU and the US. Such an international consensus is widely considered illusive in the medium term, as can be vividly illustrated by recent history relating to the Safe Harbour Agreement and the Privacy Shield, which both were annulled by the ECJ.[127] Although the progressive development of a federal US data privacy law and joint initiatives such as the EU-US Trade and Technology Council and the EU-US Data Privacy Framework are beginning to bring about some rapprochement, these initiatives are still a long way from achieving a shared set of data privacy standards. Nevertheless, some recent trade agreements stipulate the adoption of a domestic regulatory frameworks for data privacy by referring to *"international standards"* or even directly to the APEC Privacy Framework or the OECD Privacy Guidelines as exemplary frameworks. With regard to an agreement at the WTO level, however, such a determination would have to be examined cautiously in order to

---

[121] Rotenberg (2001), pp. 15–16.

[122] Article 5 GDPR sets out principles relating to the processing of personal data, the data controller is responsible for and must be able to demonstrate compliance with under the accountability concept (Article 5 Sec. 2 GDPR). These include pursuant to Article 5 Sec. 1 GDPR: lawfulness, fairness and transparency; purpose limitation; data minimization; accuracy; storage limitation; integrity and confidentiality.

[123] *See* further Sanuik-Heinig (2021).

[124] *See* for divergences in execution of the principles Gunasekara (2007), p. 153; Reidenberg (1999), p. 1330.

[125] Chander and Schwartz (2023), p. 117. *See* in this context also Shaffer (2021), pp. 45–46.

[126] Chander and Schwartz (2023), pp. 122–125.

[127] Cf. ECJ, C-362/14, *Schrems I*, 6 October 2015, ECLI:EU:C:2015:650 and ECJ, C-311/18, *Schrems II*, 16 July 2020, ECLI:EU:C:2020:55.

preserve deference to regulatory autonomy of WTO members with regard to the design and implementation of national data privacy rules.[128]
- A further element for an agreement at WTO level should include provisions on the transparency of domestic regulation relating to data governance. Transparency of data regulation around data privacy is a decisive factor in countering the heterogeneous data privacy environment and reducing the resulting trade barriers. Transparency is vital to a WTO governance model that encourages regulatory learning and dialogue, as it supports the exchange of information, scrutiny, and cross-checking of approaches.[129] With regard to the application of Article III GATS to laws and regulations relating to the provision of a service by electronic means, a transparency clause specifically designed for a data privacy context may contain more far-reaching obligations with regard to the particular circumstances in which cross-border transfers of personal data are permitted, for example. Such a transparency commitment must be closely aligned with the data flow methodology to be developed (*see supra* Sect. 6.2).
- The most important, yet most ambitious, element of a WTO agreement on digital trade and data privacy pertains to the establishment of a process to achieve increasing regulatory convergence regarding data privacy. While enhanced transparency obligations hardly interfere with domestic regulatory autonomy and thus represent an achievable negotiation goal, establishing a mechanism towards greater regulatory convergence must be approached with caution in order not to suggest that data privacy is being negotiated at the WTO level.[130] However, regulatory convergence can be envisaged in particular for the area of data transfer rules, in order to gradually align divergent standards and to promote interoperability. The focus of interoperability efforts for different national data privacy rules in the context of digital trade should be on facilitating the cross-border flow of personal data, as this generally holds the greatest potential for discriminatory trade barriers while respecting the primacy of domestic regulatory authority to determine a given standard of data privacy. In this sense, a WTO treaty should foster a balance between international harmonisation and national regulatory autonomy with regard to data privacy and meaningfully pursue reconciliation of the respective spheres.[131] A WTO-level agreement must provide for a decentralised model that incorporates regulatory flexibility to facilitate the interface and interoperability between different regulatory systems.[132] However, with regard to the highly sensitive issue of data privacy, it is debatable how this can be

---

[128] *See* for a proposal for a compromise provision Mitchell and Mishra (2019), pp. 410–411.

[129] Shaffer (2021), pp. 43–44.

[130] In its horizontal rules for cross-border data flows and for the protection of personal data, the EU has excluded the use of a clause for cooperation on digital trade issues for safeguards for the protection of personal data and privacy, including cross-border transfers of personal data, *see* European Commission (2018). *See* further Mancini (2020), pp. 198–204.

[131] *See* further Weiß (2020), p. 46.

[132] *See* Shaffer (2021), pp. 45–46. The author proposes to adopt the model of the 2017 WTO Trade Facilitation Agreement (TFA) in this regard. *See* on the TFA *supra* Sect. 3.3.2.4.

achieved in practice. In this context, it has been identified above, that a common element to the governance of data flows under data privacy law is the use of accountability mechanisms (*see supra* Sect. 4.3.3.2). Scholarly literature has considered the interoperability of regulatory measures and accountability assigned to organisations as elements of an inherently decentralised approach consistent with the principles of *"embedded liberalism"*, interfering with national regulatory authority only to the extent required to enable trade liberalisation.[133] Instruments based on accountability mechanisms, such as APEC's CBPR or the EU's SCCs and BCRs, have been identified as *"escape valves"* from the data privacy collision.[134] In addition, sectoral schemes based on mutual recognition such as Safe Harbour and Privacy Shield agreements, that build bridges between divergent data privacy regimes are a starting point for mitigating the data privacy collision.[135] These examples serve to illustrate a roadmap for bringing all parties involved in the data privacy collision together at the WTO.

Jurisprudence

Panel Report, United States – Measures Affecting Cross-Border Supply of Gambling and Betting Services [US-Gambling], WT/DS285/R, adopted 10 November 2004

ECJ, C-362/14, Maximillian Schrems v Data Protection Commissioner [Schrems I], 6 October 2015, ECLI:EU:C:2015:650

ECJ, C-311/18, Data Protection Commissioner v Facebook Ireland Limited and Maximillian Schrems [Schrems II], 16 July 2020, ECLI:EU:C:2020:55

References

Aaronson SA (2018) Data is different: why the world needs a new approach to governing cross-border data flows. Centre for International Governance Innovation Papers No. 197. https://www.cigionline.org/static/documents/documents/paper%20no.197_0.pdf. Accessed 5 Apr 2024

Aaronson SA (2019) What are we talking about when we talk about digital protectionism? World Trade Rev 18(4):541–577. https://doi.org/10.1017/S1474745618000198

---

[133] Wolfe (2018), p. 11. The term *"embedded liberalism"* was coined by John G. Ruggie (1998), pp. 62–85.

[134] Chander and Schwartz (2023), pp. 95–105. With a view to a lack of international enforcement the authors propose a Global Privacy Enforcement Treaty (GPET) as part of the WTO, focused on strengthening accountability mechanisms for cross-border data flows, cf. at pp. 115–117. See also Mattoo and Meltzer (2019), p. 787.

[135] Chander and Schwartz (2023), p. 46; Mitchell and Mishra (2019), p. 411; Shaffer (2021), pp. 50–51.

Aaronson SA, Leblond P (2018) Another digital divide: the rise of data realms and its implications for the WTO. J Int Econ Law 21(2):245–272. https://doi.org/10.1093/jiel/jgy019

Abendin S, Duan P (2021) Global E-commerce talks at the WTO: positions on selected issues of the United States, European Union, China, and Japan. World Trade Rev 20(5):707–724. https://doi.org/10.1017/S1474745621000094

Adlung R (2014) Trade in services in the WTO: from Marrakesh (1994), to Doha (2001), to... (?). In: Narlikar A, Daunton MJ, Stern RM (eds) The Oxford handbook on the World Trade Organization. Oxford University Press, Oxford, pp 370–391

Ahmed U (2019) The importance of cross-border regulatory cooperation in an era of digital trade. World Trade Rev 18(1):99–120. https://doi.org/10.1017/S1474745618000514

Bacchetta M, Low P, Mattoo A, Schuknecht L, Wager H, Wehrens M (1998) Electronic commerce and the role of the WTO. Special studies / World Trade Organization, Geneva. https://hdl.handle.net/10419/107052. Accessed 5 Apr 2024

Bohne E (2010) The World Trade Organization: institutional development and reform. Governance and public management series. Palgrave Macmillan, Basingstoke, Hampshire

Burri M (2016) Designing future-oriented multilateral rules for digital trade. In: Sauvé P, Roy M (eds) Research handbook on trade in services. Research handbooks on the WTO series. Edward Elgar Publishing, Cheltenham, pp 331–356

Burri M (2017) The regulation of data flows through trade agreements. Georgetown J Int Law 48:407–448

Burri M (2021a) Interfacing privacy and trade. Case West Reserve J Int Law 53:35–88

Burri M (2021b) Towards a new treaty on digital trade. J World Trade 55(1):77–100. https://doi.org/10.54648/TRAD2021003

Burri M (2021c) A WTO agreement on electronic commerce: an enquiry into its legal substance and viability. Trade Law 4.0 Working Paper No 1. Available at SSRN: https://ssrn.com/abstract=3976133. Accessed 5 Apr 2024

Casalini F, López González J (2019) Trade and cross-border data flows. OECD Trade Policy Papers No. 220. OECD Publishing, Paris. https://doi.org/10.1787/b2023a47-en

Casalini F, González JL, Nemoto T (2021) Mapping commonalities in regulatory approaches to cross-border data transfers. OECD Trade Policy Papers No. 248

Chander A (2012) Principles for trade 2.0. In: Burri M, Cottier T (eds) Trade governance in the digital age. Cambridge University Press, Cambridge, pp 17–44

Chander A (2013) The electronic silk road: how the web binds the world in commerce. Yale University Press, New Haven

Chander A, Schwartz PM (2023) Privacy and/or trade. Univ Chic Law Rev 90:49–135

Chatham House (2022) Digital trade and digital technical standards: opportunities for strengthening US, EU and UK cooperation on digital technology governance. https://www.chathamhouse.org/sites/default/files/2022-01/2022-01-24-digital-trade-digital-technical-standards-bergsen-et-al.pdf. Accessed 5 Apr 2024

Chen Y-H (2015) The EU Data Protection Law Reform: challenges for service trade liberalization and possible approaches for harmonizing privacy standards into the context of GATS. Spanish Yearb Int Law 19:211–220

Cho S, Kelly CR (2013) Are world trading rules Passé? Va J Int Law 53:623–666

Cory N, Dascoli L (2021) How barriers to cross-border data flows are spreading globally, what they cost, and how to address them. Information Technology & Innovation Foundation. https://itif.org/publications/2021/07/19/how-barriers-cross-border-data-flows-are-spreading-globally-what-they-cost/. Accessed 5 Apr 2024

Cottier T (1996) The impact of new technologies on multilateral trade regulation and governance - the new global technology regime. Chic-Kent Law Rev 72:415–436

Delimatsis P (2007) Due process and 'good' regulation embedded in the GATS - disciplining regulatory behaviour in services through Article VI of the GATS. J Int Econ Law 10(1):13–50. https://doi.org/10.1093/jiel/jgl035

References

European Commission (2018) Horizontal provisions for cross-border data flows and for personal data protection. https://ec.europa.eu/newsroom/just/items/627665 Accessed 5 Apr 2024

European Commission (2021) Communication from the European Commission: Trade Policy Review - An Open, Sustainable and Assertive Trade Policy. COM(2021) 66 final

G20 (2019) Osaka Leaders' Declaration. https://www.consilium.europa.eu/media/40124/final_g20_osaka_leaders_declaration.pdf. Accessed 5 Apr 2024

Gasser U (2021) Futuring digital privacy. In: Burri M (ed) Big data and global trade law. Cambridge University Press, Cambridge, New York, pp 195–211

Gasser U, Palfrey J (2012) Fostering innovation and trade in the global information society. In: Burri M, Cottier T (eds) Trade governance in the digital age. Cambridge University Press, Cambridge, pp 123–154

Gunasekara G (2007) The "final" privacy frontier? Regulating trans-border data flows. Int J Law Inf Technol 17(2):147–179. https://doi.org/10.1093/ijlit/eam004

Hufbauer GC, Zhiyao L (2019) Global E-commerce talks stumble on data issues, privacy, and more. Policy Brief 19-14 Peterson Institute for International Economics Policy Brief 19-14. https://www.piie.com/publications/policy-briefs/global-e-commerce-talks-stumble-data-issues-privacy-and-more. Accessed 5 Apr 2024

IMF, WTO, UNCTAD, OECD (2023) Handbook on measuring digital trade, Second Edition. OECD Publishing, Paris/International Monetary Fund/UNCTAD, Geneva/WTO, Geneva, https://doi.org/10.1787/ac99e6d3-en

Irion K, Yakovleva S, Bartl M (2016) Trade and privacy complicated bedfellows: how to achieve data protection-proof free trade agreements. Independent study commissioned by BEUC et al., Amsterdam, Institute for Information Law (IViR)

Kaminski ME (2015) Why trade is not the place for the EU to negotiate privacy. https://policyreview.info/articles/news/why-trade-not-place-eu-negotiate-privacy/354. Accessed 5 Apr 2024

Kelsey J (2018) How a TPP-Style E-commerce outcome in the WTO would endanger the development dimension of the GATS Acquis (and potentially the WTO). J Int Econ Law 21(2):273–295. https://doi.org/10.1093/jiel/jgy024

Kobrin SJ (2004) Safe harbours are hard to find: the trans-Atlantic data privacy dispute, territorial jurisdiction and global governance. Rev Int Stud 30(1):111–131. https://doi.org/10.1017/S0260210504005856

Krajewski M (2003) National regulation and trade liberalization in services: the legal impact of the General Agreement on Trade in Services (GATS) on National Regulatory Autonomy. Wolters Kluwer Law International, Alphen aan den Rijn

Krajewski M (2008) Art. VI GATS. In: Wolfrum R, Stoll P-T, Feinäugle C (eds) WTO - trade in services: trade in services, 1st ed. Max Planck Commentaries on World Trade Law Ser, v.6. BRILL, Leiden, pp 167–196

Kuner C (2009) An international legal framework for data protection: issues and prospects. Comput Law Secur Rev 25(4):307–317. https://doi.org/10.1016/j.clsr.2009.05.001

Kuner C (2013) Transborder data flows and data privacy law. Oxford University Press, Oxford

Lamp N (2021) A historical perspective on India's and South Africa's threat to block the implementation of the joint statement initiatives in the WTO, and a potential way forward. https://ielp.worldtradelaw.net/2021/02/a-historical-perspective-on-indias-and-south-africas-threat-to-block-the-implementation-of-the-joint.html. Accessed 5 Apr 2024

Lang A, Scott J (2009) The hidden world of WTO governance. Eur J Int Law 20(3):575–614. https://doi.org/10.1093/ejil/chp041

Mancini I (2020) Deepening trade and fundamental rights? Harnessing data protection rights in the regulatory cooperation chapters of EU trade agreements. In: Weiß W, Furculita C (eds) Global politics and EU trade policy. European yearbook of international economic law. Springer International Publishing, Cham, pp 185–207

Mattoo A, Meltzer JP (2019) International data flows and privacy: the conflict and its resolution. J Int Econ Law 21(4):769–789. https://doi.org/10.1093/jiel/jgy044

Mattoo A, Sauvé P (2003) Domestic regulation and trade in services: looking ahead. In: Mattoo A, Sauvé P (eds) Domestic regulation and service trade liberalization. Trade and development. World Bank, Washington, DC, pp 221–230

Meltzer JP (2016) Maximizing the opportunities of the internet for international trade. Policy Options Paper. ICTSD and World Economic Forum. Available at SSRN: https://ssrn.com/abstract=2841913

Mishra N (2019a) Building bridges: international trade law, internet governance, and the regulation of data flows. Vanderbilt J Transnatl Law 52(2):463–509

Mishra N (2019b) Privacy, cybersecurity, and GATS Article XIV: a new frontier for trade and internet regulation? World Trade Rev 19(3):1–24. https://doi.org/10.1017/S1474745619000120

Mitchell AD (2001) Towards compatibility: the future of electronic commerce within the global trading system. J Int Econ Law 4(4):683–723. https://doi.org/10.1093/jiel/4.4.683

Mitchell AD, Mishra N (2018) Data at the docks: modernizing international trade law for the digital economy. Vanderbilt J Entertain Technol Law 20:1073–1134

Mitchell AD, Mishra N (2019) Regulating cross-border data flows in a data-driven world: how WTO law can contribute. J Int Econ Law 22(3):389–416. https://doi.org/10.1093/jiel/jgz016

Naef T (2023) Data protection without data protectionism. European yearbook of international economic law. Springer International Publishing, Cham

OECD (2015) The governance of globalized data flows - current trends and future challenges: working party on security and privacy in the digital economy. DSTI/ICCP/REG(2015)3

Peng S (2011) Digitalization of services, the GATS and the protection of personal data. In: Sethe R, Heinemann A, Hilty RM (eds) Kommunikation: Festschrift für Rolf H. Weber zum 60. Geburtstag. Stämpfli, Bern, pp 753–769

Peng S, Lin C-F, Streinz T (2021) Artificial intelligence and international economic law: a research and policy agenda. In: Peng S, Lin C-F, Streinz T (eds) Artificial intelligence and international economic law: disruption, regulation, and reconfiguration, First published. Cambridge University Press, Cambridge, New York, Port Melbourne, New Delhi, Singapore, pp 1–26

Perez Asinari MV (2003) The WTO and the protection of personal data. Do EU measures fall within GATS exception? Which future for data protection within the WTO e-commerce context? 18th BILETA Conference: Controlling Information in the Online Environment. https://www.bileta.org.uk/wp-content/uploads/The-WTO-and-the-Protection-of-Personal-Data.-Do-EU-Measures-Fall-within-GATS-Exception.pdf. Accessed 5 Apr 2024

Polanco R, Sauvé P (2018) The treatment of regulatory convergence in preferential trade agreements. World Trade Rev 17(4):575–607. https://doi.org/10.1017/S1474745617000519

Reidenberg JR (1999) Resolving conflicting international data privacy rules in cyberspace. Stanford Law Rev 52:1315–1371

Roseman D (2003) Domestic regulation and trade in telecommunications services: experience and prospects under the GATS. In: Mattoo A, Sauve P (eds) Domestic regulation and service trade liberalization. Trade and development. World Bank, Washington, DC, pp 83–107

Rotenberg M (2001) Fair information practices and the architecture of privacy (what Larry doesn't get). Stan Tech Law Rev:1–34

Ruggie JG (1998) Constructing the world polity: essays on international institutionalization. The new international relations. Routledge, London

Sanuik-Heinig C (2021) 50 years and still kicking: an examination of FIPPs in modern regulation. https://iapp.org/news/a/50-years-and-still-kicking-an-examination-of-fipps-in-modern-regulation/. Accessed 5 Apr 2024

Schulhofer SJ (2016) An international right to privacy? Be careful what you wish for. IJCLAW 14(1):238–261. https://doi.org/10.1093/icon/mow013

Schwartz PM (2013) The EU-U.S. privacy collision: a turn to institutions and procedures. Harv Law Rev 126:1966–2009

Sen N (2018) Understanding the role of the WTO in international data flows: taking the liberalization or the regulatory autonomy path? J Int Econ Law 21(2):323–348. https://doi.org/10.1093/jiel/jgy021

References

Shaffer G (2021) Trade law in a data-driven economy. In: Peng S, Lin C-F, Streinz T (eds) Artificial intelligence and international economic law: disruption, regulation, and reconfiguration, First published. Cambridge University Press, Cambridge, New York, Port Melbourne, New Delhi, Singapore, pp 29–53

Solove DJ, Schwartz PM (2018) Information privacy law, Sixth edition. Aspen casebook series. Wolters Kluwer Law & Business, New York

Streinz T (2019) Digital megaregulation uncontested? TPP's model for the global digital economy. In: Kingsbury B et al (eds) Megaregulation contested. Oxford University Press, pp 312–342

Swire PP, Litan RE (2010) None of your business: world data flows, electronic commerce, and the European Privacy Directive. Brookings Institution Press, Washington

Tietje C (2012) Global information law. In: Burri M, Cottier T (eds) Trade governance in the digital age. Cambridge University Press, Cambridge, pp 45–62

Toohey L (2021) Trade law architecture after the Fourth Industrial Revolution. In: Peng S, Lin C-F, Streinz T (eds) Artificial intelligence and international economic law: disruption, regulation, and reconfiguration. Cambridge University Press, Cambridge, New York, Port Melbourne, New Delhi, Singapore, pp 337–352

Tuthill LL (2017) Implications of the GATS for digital trade and digital trade barriers in services. Digiworld Econ J 107:95–115

Tuthill L, Roy M (2012) GATS classification issues for information and communication technology services. In: Burri M, Cottier T (eds) Trade governance in the digital age. Cambridge University Press, Cambridge, pp 157–178

U.S. Department of Commerce (2016) Measuring the value of cross-border data flows. Economics and Statistics Administration and the National Telecommunications and Information Administration. https://www.ntia.doc.gov/files/ntia/publications/measuring_cross_border_data_flows.pdf. Accessed 5 Apr 2024

UNCTAD (2016) Data protection regulations and international data flows: implications for trade and development. https://unctad.org/publication/data-protection-regulations-and-international-data-flows-implications-trade-and. Accessed 5 Apr 2024

VanGrasstek C (2013) The history and future of the World Trade Organization. World Trade Organization, Geneva, Switzerland

Weber RH (2010) Digital trade in WTO-law - taking stock and looking ahead. Asian J WTO Int Health Law Policy 5(1):1–24

Weber RH (2012) Regulatory autonomy and privacy standards under the GATS. Asian J WTO Int Health Law Policy 7(1):25–48

Weber RH (2021) Global law in the face of datafication and artificial intelligence. In: Peng S, Lin C-F, Streinz T (eds) Artificial intelligence and international economic law: disruption, regulation, and reconfiguration. Cambridge University Press, Cambridge, New York, Port Melbourne, New Delhi, Singapore, pp 54–69

Weiß W (2020) WTO law and domestic regulation: exploring the determinants for the impact of the WTO on domestic regulatory autonomy. Beck International. Beck; Hart; Nomos, München, Oxford, Baden-Baden

Weiß W, Ohler C, Bungenberg M (2022) Welthandelsrecht, 3. Auflage. Studium und Praxis. C.H. Beck, München

Wolfe R (2018) Learning about digital trade: privacy and E-commerce in CETA and TPP. EUI Working Paper RSCAS 2018/27. https://hdl.handle.net/1814/55144. Accessed 5 Apr 2024

World Bank Group (2016) World Development Report 2016: Digital Dividends. https://www.worldbank.org/en/publication/wdr2016. Accessed 5 Apr 2024

World Economic Forum (2020) Data Free Flow with Trust (DFFT): paths towards free and trusted data flows. http://www3.weforum.org/docs/WEF_Paths_Towards_Free_and_Trusted_Data%20_Flows_2020.pdf. Accessed 5 Apr 2024

Wouters J, Coppens D (2008) Gats and domestic regulation: balancing the right to regulate and trade liberalization. In: Alexander K, Andenas M (eds) The World Trade Organization and trade in services. Nijhoff eBook titles. Martinus Nijhoff Publishers, Leiden, pp 207–263

WTO (1999) Council for Trade in Services, Progress Report to the General Council, S/L/74, 27 July 1999

WTO (2001) The WTO and Internet Privacy. https://www.wto.org/english/tratop_e/serv_e/gats_factfiction10_e.htm. Accessed 5 Apr 2024

WTO (2018) Joint Statement on Electronic Commerce, Communication from the European Union, JOB/GC/194, 12 July 2018

WTO (2021a) Joint Initiative on Services Domestic Regulation, Reference Paper on Services Domestic Regulation, INF/SDR/1, 27 September 2021

WTO (2021b) Joint Initiative on Services Domestic Regulation, Declaration of the Conclusion of Negotiations on Services Domestic Regulation, WT/L/1129, 2 December 2021

Wunsch-Vincent S (2004) WTO, E-commerce, and information technologies from the Uruguay Round through the Doha Development Agenda. UN ICT Task Force

Wunsch-Vincent S, Hold A (2012) Towards coherent rules for digital trade. In: Burri M, Cottier T (eds) Trade governance in the digital age. Cambridge University Press, Cambridge, pp 179–221

Yakovleva S (2018) Should fundamental rights to privacy and data protection be a part of the EU's international trade 'deals'? World Trade Rev 17(03):477–508. https://doi.org/10.1017/S1474745617000453

Yakovleva S (2020) Privacy protection(ism): the latest wave of trade constraints on regulatory autonomy. Univ Miami Law Rev 74:416–519

Yakovleva S, Irion K (2020) Pitching trade against privacy: reconciling EU governance of personal data flows with external trade. Int Data Priv Law 10(3):201–221. https://doi.org/10.1093/idpl/ipaa003

Zeno-Zencovich V (2021) Free-flow of data: is international trade law the appropriate answer? In: Fabbrini F, Celeste E, Quinn J (eds) Data protection beyond borders: transatlantic perspectives on extraterritoriality and sovereignty. Hart, Oxford, London, New York, New Delhi, Sydney, pp 173–188

Zhang R (2015) Covered or not covered: that is the question: services classification and its implications for specific commitments under the GATS. WTO Working Paper ERSD-2015-11

Printed by Printforce, the Netherlands